P9-CFW-750

WRITING FICTION

WRITING FICTION
A Guide to Narrative Craft

Ninth Edition

JANET BURROWAY

Florida State University

with

ELIZABETH STUCKEY-FRENCH

Florida State University

NED STUCKEY-FRENCH

Florida State University

PEARSON

Boston   Columbus   Indianapolis   New York   San Francisco   Upper Saddle River
Amsterdam   Cape Town   Dubai   London   Madrid   Milan   Munich   Paris   Montreal   Toronto
Delhi   Mexico City   São Paulo   Sydney   Hong Kong   Seoul   Singapore   Taipei   Tokyo

Vice President and Editor in Chief: Joseph Terry
Development Editor: Lai T. Moy
Head of Marketing: Roxanne McCarley
Senior Media Producer: Stefanie Snajder
Digital Editor: Sara Gordus
Media Project Manager: Jessica Kajkowski
Content Specialist: Erin Reilly
Project Manager: Donna Campion
Project Coordination, Text Design, and Electronic Page Makeup: Integra Software
  Services Pvt. Ltd.
Cover Designer/Manager: John Callahan
Cover Art: *Night* (1960), Frank di Gioia. Oil on canvas, 40 ¼ x 30 ⅜".
  © Albright-Knox Art Gallery/Corbis
Senior Manufacturing Buyer: Roy Pickering
Printer/Binder: Donnelley-Crawfordsville
Cover Printer: Donnelley-Crawfordsville

Credits and acknowledgments borrowed from other sources and reproduced, with
permission, in this textbook appear on the appropriate page within text.

Library of Congress Control Number: 2013957853

Copyright © 2015, 2011 by Janet Burroway, Elizabeth Stuckey-French, and
Ned Stuckey-French
Copyright © 2007 by Janet Burroway and Elizabeth Stuckey-French

All rights reserved. Manufactured in the United States of America. This publication
is protected by Copyright, and permission should be obtained from the publisher prior
to any prohibited reproduction, storage in a retrieval system, or transmission in any
form or by any means, electronic, mechanical, photocopying, recording, or likewise.
To obtain permission(s) to use material from this work, please submit a written request
to Pearson Education, Inc., Permissions Department, One Lake Street, Upper Saddle
River, New Jersey 07458, or you may fax your request to 201-236-3290.

10 9 8 7 6—DOC—19 18 17 16

Student ISBN 10:   0-321-92316-2
Student ISBN 13: 978-0-321-92316-5
Exam copy ISBN 10:   0-321-95404-1
Exam copy ISBN 13: 978-0-321-95404-6

In loving memory of David Daiches, mentor and friend

CONTENTS

PREFACE

The ninth edition of *Writing Fiction*, like its previous manifestations, attempts to guide the student writer from first impulse to final revision, employing concepts of fiction's elements familiar from literature study, but shifting the perspective toward that of the practicing writer. My coauthors, Elizabeth and Ned Stuckey-French, and I wish to address students, however inexperienced, as fellow artists. Students' concerns often include fear, but also have to do with questions of understanding and development of technique.

As experienced instructors are aware, the idea of a text for writing fiction is itself problematic. Unlike such subjects as math and history, where a certain mass of information needs to be organized and conveyed, the writing of fiction is more often a process of trial and error—the learning is perpetual and, paradoxically, the writer needs to know everything at once. If a text is too prescriptive, it's not true to the immense variety of possibilities; if it's too anecdotal, it may be cheering but is unlikely to be of use.

We're also aware that *Writing Fiction* is used by many instructors in both beginning and advanced writing courses and for students at very different levels of understanding. We have tried, therefore, to make it practical, comprehensive, and flexible, and to keep the focus on the student writer and the process of writing. Our means of doing this is to cover discrete elements in separate chapters, yet to build in each chapter on what has been covered earlier. Focus on the writing process and suggestions for getting started have seemed to us a logical place to begin the book, but we have tried to keep subsequent chapters sufficiently self-contained so that teachers may assign them in any order they prefer. Each chapter follows a similar structure, concluding with three short stories and a selection of writing exercises. Within each chapter, excerpts from other short stories are used in the text to offer quick illustrations of concepts. Boxed quotations from established authors—on topics such as writing from experience, story structure, openings and endings, and revision—offer students a quick and encouraging reminder of key chapter concepts.

New to the Ninth Edition

- **New Selections.** Almost half of the short stories included in the text are new to this edition, including works by established contemporary favorites such as Stacy Richter, Alice Walker, Karen Russell, George Saunders, Sandra Cisneros, and many others. These stories have been chosen primarily from contemporary American fiction, with attention to increased variety in form, mood, and content as well as emphasis on the multicultural representation of authors and experiences.

- **Integrated Coverage of Different Types of Fiction.** The former appendix on Kinds of Fiction has been expanded and integrated into Chapter 7 to acknowledge the growing interest in genre fiction, magic realism, and experimental fiction among new writers. The section emphasizes how the boundaries among these fiction types are blurring, and explains how the development of such elements as character, plot, setting, and theme differs from the development of these same elements in literary fiction.
- **Revision.** In the chapter on revision we have added an early draft of fiction writer Pia Z. Ehrhardt's story "Following the Notes," accompanied by an earlier version of the story and a process note to help students trace the evolution of the published piece.
- **New Appendix on Professionalism and Literary Citizenship.** This new guide outlines the steps you might take after graduating college and what you can do next to prepare for your life as a writer.

Above all, for the new edition Elizabeth, Ned, and I have kept the exigencies of the creative writing classroom in mind, intending to be catalytic rather than prescriptive, hoping to encourage both students and teachers to feel comfortable with themselves and the writing process.

ACKNOWLEDGMENTS

The ninth edition attempts to respond to teachers who use it in the classroom, those who write or e-mail spontaneously throughout the life of the edition, colleagues in universities and the Associated Writing Programs, and those asked by the publisher to engage in a formal process of review. There is really no appropriate term for these people. A "reviewer" usually makes a take-it-or-leave-it judgment, whereas the reviewers of a text are collaborators in an ongoing attempt to keep the book vital amid the changing needs of students, teachers, and the academic zeitgeist. Naturally, these teacher/writers tend to nudge the new edition in the direction of their own pedagogical needs and methods, and inevitably some advice conflicts with other. Nevertheless, reviewers are surprisingly often in agreement and as well as thorough, thoughtful, practical, and inspired.

Many people have helped with the ninth edition of *Writing Fiction*. Thanks go to our students and colleagues in the Writing Program at Florida State University.

We are also grateful to the following writers/teachers who have reviewed this edition: A. Papatya Bucak, Florida Atlantic University; Joe Cover, Missouri State University; Lori Joyce, Gloucester County College; Heather Peterson, University of Florida; Barbara Rodman, University of North Texas; Kami Westhoff, Western Washington University; Laura White, Maricopa Community College; Lowell Mick

White, Pittsburg State University; and Katherine Willis, Indiana University-Purdue University, Indianapolis.

We would like to acknowledge the writers Simone Poirier-Bures, Judith Slater, Anne Giles Rimbey, Gerald Shapiro, B.W. Jorgensen, Gordon Johnson, Tobey Kaplan, and Rachel Hall, whose exercises have been adapted from the Associated Writing Programs' publication titled *Pedagogy Papers*. We would also like to acknowledge the writers Robert Olen Butler, Doug Bauer, Lee Smith, Jill McCorkle, Ron Hansen, Tom Batt, Wally Lamb, and Allan Gurganus, whose insightful words from interviews published in the Associated Writing Programs' publication *The Writer's Chronicle* have been quoted in this text. *Glimmer Train's* "Writers Ask" newsletter has also been a wonderful resource for words of wisdom on all aspects of writing. Among the many writers and teachers who have shared exercises over the years, special thanks go to Nancy Huddleston Packer, John L'Heureux, Alice La Plante, Erin McGraw, Brad Owens, Rick Hillis, Bo Caldwell, Michelle Carter, and Leslee Becker. Some of the exercises were adapted from those appearing in *What If? Writing Exercises for Fiction Writers*, edited by Anne Bernays and Pamela Painter; *Writing Fiction Step by Step* by Josip Novakovich; and *Creating Fiction*, edited by Julie Checkoway.

—J.B., E.S-F, N.S-F

A Note from the Publisher

The following supplements can be value-packed at no additional cost or at a significant discount with *Writing Fiction*, Ninth Edition. Please contact your Pearson representative to arrange a value-pack.

- **A Workshop Guide for Creative Writing** (0-321-09539-1) is a laminated reference tool, including guidelines for criticism, workshop etiquette, and more. Available at no additional cost when packaged with *Writing Fiction*, Ninth Edition.
- **The Longman Journal for Creative Writing** (0-321-09540-5) helps students explore and discover their own writing habits and styles. Available at no additional cost when value-packed with *Writing Fiction*, Ninth Edition.
- **Merriam Websters Reader's Handbook: Your Complete Guide to Literary Terms** (0-321-10541-9) includes nearly 2,000 descriptions covering every major genre, style, and era of writing. Available at no additional cost when value-packed with *Writing Fiction*, Ninth Edition.

1

WHATEVER WORKS
The Writing Process

◆Get Started

◆Keep Going

◆A Word About Theme

◆Reading as Writers

◆About the Writing Workshop

You want to write. Why is it so hard?

There are a few lucky souls for whom the whole process of writing is easy, for whom the smell of fresh paper is better than air, who forget to eat, and who consider the world at large an intrusion on their good time at the keyboard. But you and I are not among them. We are in love with words except when we have to face them. We are caught in a guilty paradox in which we grumble over our lack of time, and when we have the time, we sharpen pencils, check e-mail, or clip the hedges.

Of course, there's also joy. We write for the satisfaction of having wrestled a sentence to the page, for the rush of discovering an image, for the excitement of seeing a character come alive. Even the most successful writers will sincerely say that these pleasures—not money, fame, or glamour—are the real rewards of writing. Fiction writer Alice Munro concedes:

It may not look like pleasure, because the difficulties can make me morose and distracted, but that's what it is—the pleasure of telling the story I mean to tell as wholly as I can tell it, of finding out in fact what the story is, by working around the different ways of telling it.

Nevertheless, writers may forget what such pleasure feels like when confronting a blank page, like the heroine of Anita Brookner's novel *Look at Me*:

> Sometimes it feels like a physical effort simply to sit down at the desk and pull out the notebook.... Sometimes the effort of putting pen to paper is so great that I literally feel a pain in my head....

It helps to know that most writers share the paradox of least wanting to do what we most want to do. It also helps to know some of the reasons for our reluctance. Fear of what could emerge on the page, and what it may reveal about our inner lives, can keep us from getting started.

There's another impediment to beginning, expressed by a writer character in Lawrence Durrell's *Alexandria Quartet*. Durrell's Pursewarden broods over the illusory significance of what he is about to write, unwilling to begin in case he spoils it. Many of us do this: The idea, whatever it is, seems so luminous, whole, and fragile, that to begin to write about that idea is to commit it to rubble. "The paradox of writing," says screenwriter Stephen Fischer, "is that you're trying to use words to express what words can't express." Knowing in advance that words will never exactly capture what we mean or intend, we must gingerly and gradually work ourselves into a state of accepting what words *can do* instead. No matter how many times we find out that what words can do is quite all right, we still shy again from the next beginning. Against this wasteful impulse I have a motto over my desk that reads: "Don't Dread; Do." It's a fine motto, and I contemplated it for several weeks before I began writing this chapter.

The mundane daily habits of writers are apparently fascinating. No author offers to answer questions at the end of a public reading without being asked: *Do you write in the morning or at night? Do you write every day? Do you compose longhand or on a computer?* Sometimes such questions show a reverent interest in the workings of genius. More often, I think, they are a plea for practical help: *Is there something I can do to make this job less horrific? Is there a trick that will unlock my words?*

Get Started

The variety of authors' habits suggests that there is no magic to be found in any particular one. Donald Hall will tell you that he spends a dozen hours a day at his desk, moving back and forth between as many projects. Philip Larkin said that he wrote a poem only every eighteen months or so and never tried to write one that was not a gift. Gail Godwin goes to her workroom every day "because what if the angel came and I wasn't there?" Julia Alvarez begins the day by reading first poetry, then prose, by her favorite writers "to remind me of the quality of writing I am aiming for." The late Andre Dubus recommended to students that they, like Hemingway, stop writing midsentence in order to begin the next day by completing the thought. Dickens could not deal with people when he was working: "The mere consciousness of an engagement will worry a whole day." Thomas Wolfe wrote standing up. Some writers can plop at the kitchen table without clearing the breakfast dishes; others need total seclusion, a beach, a cat, a string quartet.

There is something to be learned from all this, though. The question is not "How do you get it done?" but "How do *you* get it done?" Any discipline or indulgence that actually helps nudge you into position facing the page is acceptable and productive. If jogging after breakfast energizes your mind, then jog before you sit. If you have to pull an all-nighter on a coffee binge, do that. Some schedule, regularity, pattern in your writing day (or night) will always help, but only you can figure out what that pattern is for you.

JOURNAL KEEPING

There are, though, a number of tricks you can teach yourself in order to free the writing self, and the essence of these is to give yourself permission to fail. The best place for such permission is a private place, and for that reason a writer's journal is an essential, likely to be the source of originality, ideas, experimentation, and growth.

A journal is an intimate, a friend that will accept you as you are. Pick a notebook you like the look of, one you feel comfortable with, as you would pick a friend. I find a bound blank book too elegant to live up to, preferring instead a loose-leaf because I write my journal mainly at the computer and can stick anything in the binder at the flip of a three-hole punch. But you can glue scribbled napkins into a spiral too.

Keep the journal regularly, at least at first. It doesn't matter what you write, and it doesn't matter very much how much, but it does matter that you make a steady habit of the writing. Keeping a journal regularly will put you in the habit of observing in words. If you know at dawn that you are committed to writing so many words before dusk, you will half-consciously tell the story of your day to yourself as you live it, finding a phrase to catch whatever catches your eye. When that habit is established, you'll begin to find that whatever invites your attention or sympathy, your anger or curiosity, may be the beginning of invention. *Whoever* catches your attention may be the beginning of a character.

Don't worry about being thorough. Your journal might consist of brief notes and bits of description only you can make sense of. F. Scott Fitzgerald (*The Great Gatsby*) used his journals to keep, among other things, snatches of overheard conversation and potential titles for short stories and novels. Many fiction writers use journals to jot down specific details about people, places, and things they observe and find intriguing. (See exercise 2 at the end of this chapter.) Later, when you're writing fiction and attempting to bring to life a teenager or a city street or a tractor, it's useful to have a bank of striking details in your journal to draw on. Often one or two details about something will be enough to trigger a fuller memory about a place or a person or a situation.

But before the journal-keeping habit is developed, you may find that even a blank journal page has the awesome aspect of a void, and you may need some tricks of permission to let yourself start writing there. The playwright Maria Irene Fornes says that there are two of you: one who wants to write and one who doesn't. The one who wants to write had better keep tricking the one who doesn't. Or another way to think of this conflict is between right brain and left brain—the playful, detail-loving creator and the linear critic. The critic is an absolutely essential part of the writing process. The trick is to shut him or her up until there is something to criticize.

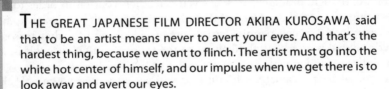

THE GREAT JAPANESE FILM DIRECTOR AKIRA KUROSAWA said that to be an artist means never to avert your eyes. And that's the hardest thing, because we want to flinch. The artist must go into the white hot center of himself, and our impulse when we get there is to look away and avert our eyes.

ROBERT OLEN BUTLER

FREEWRITING

Freewriting is a technique that allows you to take very literally the notion of getting something down on paper. It can be done whenever you want to write, or just to free up the writing self. The idea is to put

anything on paper and I mena anything, it doesn't matter as long as it's coming out of your head nad hte ends of your fingers, down ont the page I wonder if;m improving, if this process gets me going better now than it did all those— hoewever many years ago? I know my typing is geting worse, deteriorating even as we speak (are we speaking? to whom? IN what forM? I love it when i hit the caps button by mistake, it makes me wonder whether there isn;t something in the back or bottom of the brain that sez PAY ATTENTION now, which makes me think of a number of things, freud and his slip o tonuge, self-deception, the myriad way it operates in everybody's life, no not everybody's but in my own exp. Ilike Aunt Ch. mourniong for the dead cats whenevershe hasn't got her way and can't disconnect one kind of sadness from another, I wonder if we ever disconnect kinds of sadness, if the first homesickness doesn't oper-atfor everybody the same way it does for me, grandma's house the site of it, the grass out the window and the dog rolling a tin pie plate under the willow tree, great heavy hunger in the belly, the empty weight of loss, loss, loss

That's freewriting. Its point is to keep going, and that is the only point. When the critic intrudes and tells you that what you're doing is awful, tell the critic to take a dive, or acknowledge her/him (*typing is getting worse*) and keep writing. If you work on a computer, try dimming the screen so you can't see what you're doing. At times, you might find it liberating to freewrite to music, random or selected. If you freewrite often, pretty soon you'll be bored with writing about how you don't feel like writing (though that is as good a subject as any; the subject is of no importance and neither is the quality of the writing) and you will find your mind and your phrases running to things that interest you. Fine. Freewriting is the literary equivalent of scales at the piano or a short gym workout. All that matters is that you do it. The verbal muscles will develop of their own accord.

Though freewriting is mere technique, it can affect the freedom of the content. Many writers feel themselves to be *an instrument through which*, rather than a *creator of*, and whether you think of this possibility as humble or holy, it is worth finding out what you say when you aren't monitoring yourself. Fiction is written not so much to inform as to find out, and if you force yourself into a mode of informing when you haven't yet found out, you're likely to end up pontificating or lying some other way.

In *Becoming a Writer*, a book that only half-facetiously claims to do what teachers of writing claim cannot be done—to teach genius—Dorothea Brande suggests that the way to begin is not with an idea or a form at all, but with an unlocking of your thoughts on paper. She advises that you rise each day and go directly to your desk (if you have to have coffee, put it in a thermos the night before) and begin writing whatever comes to mind, before you are quite awake, before you have read anything or talked to anyone, before reason has begun to take over from the dream-functioning of your brain. Write for twenty or thirty minutes and then put away what you have written without reading it over. After a week or two of this, pick an additional time during the day when you can salvage a half hour or so to write, and when that time arrives, write, even if you "must climb out over the heads of your friends" to do it. It doesn't matter what you write. What does matter is that you develop the habit of beginning to write the moment you sit down to do so.

EXERCISES

The American Dairy Association used to use the tagline "You never outgrow your need for milk." If you're a writer, the same might be said of exercises. Exercises, or prompts as they are sometimes called, can be helpful for all writers. They help you get started, and they can give you focus—whether you are writing in your journal, doing those early morning pages Brande suggests, sneaking in a bit of freewriting during the day, or trying to get to that next scene in a story.

Exercises are a way to tap your unconscious. The process of writing does not proceed clearly and obviously from point A to point B, but if you've been thinking about your story—sleeping on it, puzzling over it, mulling about it, working on a draft—you may well have a solution waiting for you in your unconscious. Stories do not begin with ideas or themes or outlines so much as with images and obsessions, and they continue to be built by exploring those images and obsessions. Seemingly unrelated prompts can help you break loose that next page. Need to find out what should happen next with Sebastian and Nelly? Here's an exercise: Write two pages about the two of them trying to decide what television show to watch. Pretty soon Sebastian and Nelly are fighting about the remote control, but more than that they're fighting about how Sebastian is remote and always wants control. Nelly is telling him that their relationship has got to change, and he's acting like he doesn't have a clue. And you are off and running.

Exercises can be shared. Early in their careers, two young writers, JoAnn Beard and Mary Allen, were splitting a job editing a physics journal at the University of Iowa. One worked one day, one the next. They shared a desk but were never there at the same time. They decided to start leaving each other a daily writing exercise in the top drawer. "For tomorrow, write a scene that takes place in a car." Or, "Write a scene in which one character is lying." The exercises kept them going, broke the isolation of writing, tapped them into the material they would have written about anyway, and before too terribly long they each had a first book—Allen's *Rooms of Heaven* and Beard's *The Boys of My Youth*.

Gymnasts practice. Pianists practice. Artists sketch. Why shouldn't writers practice? Exercises are a way to exercise your skills, develop them, hone them, make them stronger. The novelist Stanley Elkin talked about sharing an office at the University of Illinois with his friend and fellow writer William H. Gass and being surprised to see Gass practicing sentences on the other side of the room.

Each chapter of *Writing Fiction* will end with some exercises designed to help you get started and move further into the issues discussed along the way. But don't stop there. Go to a bookstore or library and look through exercise collections such as *What If? Writing Exercises for Fiction Writers* by Anne Bernays and Pamela Painter. Collect exercises as you might collect possible names for characters or words you like the sound of. Develop your own exercises. Ask writing friends what has worked for them. Note the ones that work for you, and vary them and return to them again and again. Exercise. Exercise daily.

THE COMPUTER

I think it's important for a writer to try a pencil from time to time so as not to lose the knack of writing by hand, of jotting at the park or the beach without any source of energy but your own hand and mind.

But for most writers, a computer is a great aid to spontaneity. Freewriting flows more freely on a computer. The knowledge that you can so easily delete makes it easier to quiet the internal critic and put down whatever comes. Turn down the screen or ignore it, stare out the window into middle space. You can follow the thread of your thought without a pause.

However, when you're rereading what you've written, you might want to step away from the screen. Scrolling through your work on a computer screen is not the same as reading it on a printed page—it's too easy to overlook problems. Most writers print out hard copies of their drafts and go over them with pen in hand, taking notes and making changes. This allows them to read more carefully, to jump back and skip ahead easily, to get a better sense of the story's pacing, to notice clunky sentences and weak word choices. Many writers will also read their drafts aloud, either to themselves or to a helpful critic, a process that will make the story's weaknesses even clearer. These revision strategies— and more—will be further discussed in Chapter 9.

Computers are a wonderful tool, but they can't do everything.

THE CRITIC: A CAUTION

The cautionary note that needs to be sounded regarding all the techniques and technology that free you to write is that the critic is absolutely essential afterward. The revising process is continuous and begins as soon as you choose to let your critic in. Freedrafting allows you to create before you criticize, to do the essential play before the essential work. Don't forget the essential work. The computer lets you write a lot because you can so easily cut. Don't forget to do so.

I WANT HARD STORIES, I DEMAND THEM from myself. Hard stories are worth the difficulty. It seems to me the only way I have forgiven anything, understood anything, is through that process of opening up to my own terror and pain and reexamining it, re-creating it in the story, and making it something different, making it meaningful—even if the meaning is only in the act of the telling.

DOROTHY ALLISON

CHOOSING A SUBJECT

Some writers are lucky enough never to be faced with the problem of choosing a subject. The world presents itself to them in terms of conflict, crisis, and resolution. Ideas for stories pop into their heads day after day; their only difficulty is choosing among them. In fact, the habit of mind that produces stories is a habit that can be cultivated, so that the more and the longer you write, the less likely you are to run out of ideas.

But sooner or later you may find yourself faced with the desire (or the deadline necessity) to write a story when your mind is a blank. The sour and untrue impulse crosses your thoughts: Nothing has ever happened to me. The task you face then is to recognize among all the paraphernalia of your mind a situation, idea, perception, or character that you can turn into a story.

Some teachers and critics advise beginning writers to write only from their personal experience, but I feel that this is a misleading and demeaning rule. If your imagination never gets beyond your age group or off campus, never tackles issues larger than dormitory life, then you are severely underestimating the range of your imagination. It is certainly true that you must draw on your own experience (including your experience of the shape of sentences). But the trick is to identify what is interesting, unique, and original in that experience that will therefore surprise and attract the reader.

The kind of "writing what you know" that is *least* likely to produce good fiction is trying to tell just exactly what happened to you at such and such a time. Probably all good fiction is "autobiographical" in some way, but the awful or hilarious or tragic thing you went through may offer as many problems as possibilities when you start to turn it into fiction. To the extent you want to capture "what really happened," you remove your focus from what will work as narrative. Young writers, offended by being told that a piece is unconvincing, often defend themselves by declaring that *it really happened*. But credibility in words has almost nothing to do with fact. Aristotle went so far as to say that a "probable impossibility" made a better story than an "improbable possibility," meaning that a skillful author can sell us glass mountains, UFOs, and hobbits, whereas a less skilled writer may not be able to convince us that Mary Lou has a crush on Sam.

A SHORT STORY IS A WRITER'S WAY OF THINKING through experience.... Journalism aims at accuracy, but fiction's aim is truth. The writer distorts reality in the interest of a larger truth.

JOHN L'HEUREUX

The first step toward using autobiography in fiction is to accept this: Words are not experience. Even the most factual account of a personal experience involves choices and interpretations—your sister's recollection of the same event might be entirely different. If you are writing a memoir or personal essay, then it is important to maintain a basis in fact because, as Annie Dillard says, "that is the convention and the covenant between the nonfiction writer and his reader." But between fiction writer and reader it is the revelation of meaning through the creation of character, the vividness of scene, the effect of action that take priority over ordinary veracity. The test of this other truth is at once spiritual and visceral; its validity has nothing to do with whether such things did, or could, occur. Lorrie Moore says:

> ...[T]he proper relationship of a writer to his or her own life is similar to a cook with a cupboard. What the cook makes from the cupboard is not the same thing as what's in the cupboard....

Dorothy Allison strives to tell "the emotional truth of people's lives, not necessarily the historical truth."

Good. Now: What was it about this experience that made it matter to you? Try writing a *very* brief summary of what happened—no more than a hundred words. What kind of story might this be? Can the raw material of incident, accident, and choice be reshaped, plumped up, pared to the bone, refleshed, differently spiced? You experienced whatever it was chronologically—but is that the best way to bring its meaning out? Perhaps you experienced it over a period of months or years; what are the *fewest* scenes in the *least* amount of time that could contain the action? If "you" are at the center of the action, then "you" must be thoroughly characterized, and that may be difficult. Can you augment some revealing aspect of yourself, change yourself in some fundamental way, even make someone else altogether the central character? Use some of the suggestions in this chapter. Try freewriting moments from your memory in no particular order. Or freewrite the last scene first. Describe a place and exaggerate the description: If it's cold, make it murderously cold; if messy, then a disastrous mess. Describe the central character and be at least partly unflattering. All of these are devices to put some distance between you and raw experience so you can begin to shape the different thing that fiction is.

Writer Eudora Welty has suggested writing what you *don't* know about what you know—that is, exploring aspects of experience that remain puzzling or painful. In *Making Shapely Fiction*, Jerome Stern urges a broad interpretation of "writing what you know," recognizing that "the idea of *you* is complex in itself...your self is made of many selves...not only persons you once were, but also persons you have tried to be, persons you have avoided being, and persons you fear you might be." John Gardner, in *The Art of Fiction*, argues that "nothing can be more limiting to the imagination" than the advice that you write about what you know. He suggests instead that you "write the kind of story you know and like best."

This is a useful idea, because the kind of story you know and like best has also taught you something about the way such stories are told; how they are shaped; what kind of surprise, conflict, and change they involve. Many beginning writers who are not yet avid readers have learned from television more than they realize about structure, the way characters behave and talk, how a joke is arranged, how a lie is revealed, and so forth. The trouble is that if you learn fiction from television, or if the kind of story you know and like best is genre fiction—science fiction, fantasy, romance, mystery—you may have learned about technique without having learned anything about the unique contribution you can make to such a story. The result is that you end up writing imitation soap opera or space odyssey, second-rate somebody else instead of first-rate you.

The essential thing is that you write about something you really care about, and the first step is to find out what that is. Playwright Claudia Johnson advises her students to identify their real concerns by making a "menu" of them. Pick the big emotions and make lists in your journal: *What makes you angry? What are you afraid of? What do you want? What hurts?* Or consider the crucial turning points of your life: *What really changed you? Who really changed you?* Those will be the areas to look to for stories, whether or not those stories are autobiographical. Novelist Ron Carlson says, "I always write from my own experiences, whether I've had them or not."

Another journal idea is to jot down the facts of the first seven years of your life under several categories: *Events, People, My Self, Inner Life, Characteristic Things.* What from those first seven years still occupies your mind? Underline or highlight the items on your page(s) that you aren't done with yet. Those items are clues to your concerns and a possible source of storytelling.

A related device for your journal might be borrowed from *The Pillow Book of Sei Shonagun.* A courtesan in tenth-century Japan, she kept a diary of the goings-on at court and concealed it in her wooden pillow—hence *pillow book.* Sei Shonagun made lists under various categories of specific, often quirky *Things.* This device is capable of endless variety and can reveal yourself to you as you find out what sort of things you want to list: *Things I wish had never been said. Red things. Things more embarrassing than nudity. Things to put off as long as possible. Things to die for. Acid things. Things that last only a day.*

Such devices may be necessary, because identifying what we care about is not always easy. We are surrounded by a constant barrage of information, drama, ideas, and judgments offered to us live, printed, and electronically. It is so much easier to know what we ought to think and feel than what we actually do. Worthy authorities constantly exhort us to care about worthy causes, only a few of which really touch us, whereas what we care about at any given moment may seem trivial, self-conscious, or self-serving.

This, I think, is in large part the value of Brande's first exercise, which forces you to write in the intuitively honest period of first light, when the half-sleeping brain is still dealing with its real concerns. Often what seems unworthy is precisely the thing that contains a universal truth, and by catching it honestly, then stepping back from it, you may achieve the authorial distance that is an essential part of significance. (All you really care about this morning is how you'll look at the dance tonight? This is a trivial obsession that can hit anyone, at any age, anywhere. Write about it as honestly as you can. Now who else might have felt this way? Someone you hate? Someone remote in time from you? Look out: You're on your way to a story.)

FORGET *INSPIRATION*. HABIT IS MORE DEPENDABLE. Habit will sustain you whether you're inspired or not. Habit will help you finish and polish your stories. Inspiration won't. Habit is persistence in practice.

OCTAVIA BUTLER

Eventually you will learn what sort of experience sparks ideas for your sort of story—and you may be astonished at how such experiences accumulate, as if your life were arranging itself to produce material for you. In the meantime, here are a half dozen suggestions for the kind of idea that may be fruitful.

The Dilemma, or Catch-22.   You find yourself facing—or know someone who is facing—a situation that offers no solution. Any action taken would be painful and costly. You have no chance of solving this dilemma in real life, but you're a writer, and it costs nothing to explore it with imaginary people in an imaginary setting, even if the outcome is a tragic one. Some writers use newspaper stories to generate this sort of idea. The situation is there in the bland black and white of this morning's news. But who are these people, and how did they come to be in such a mess? Make it up, think it through.

The Incongruity.   Something comes to your attention that is interesting precisely because you can't figure it out. It doesn't seem to make sense. Someone is breeding pigs in the backyard of a mansion. Who is it? Why is she doing it? Your inventing mind can find the motives and the meanings. An example from my own experience: Once when my phone was out of order, I went out very late at night to make a call from a public phone at a supermarket plaza. At something like two in the morning all the stores were closed but the plaza was not empty. There were three women there, one of them with a baby in a stroller. What were they doing there? It was several years before I figured out a possible answer, and that answer was a short story.

The Connection.   You notice a striking similarity in two events, people, places, or periods that are fundamentally unlike. The more you explore the similarity, the more striking it becomes. My novel *The Buzzards* came from such a connection: The daughter of a famous politician was murdered, and I found myself in the position of comforting the dead girl's fiancé. At the same time I was writing lectures on the Agamemnon of Aeschylus. Two politicians, two murdered daughters—one in ancient Greece and one in contemporary America. The connection would not let go of me until I had thought it through and set it down.

The Memory.   Certain people, places, and events stand out in your memory with an intensity beyond logic. There's no earthly reason you should remember the smell of Aunt K's rouge. It makes no sense that you still flush with shame at the thought of that ball you "borrowed" when you were in fourth grade. But for some reason these things are still vivid in your mind. That vividness can be explored, embellished, given form. Stephen Minot wisely advises in *Three Genres*, though, that if you are going to write from a memory, *it should be a memory more than a year old*. Otherwise you are likely to be unable to distinguish between what happened and what must happen in the story or between what is in your mind and what you have conveyed on the page.

The Transplant.   You find yourself having to deal with a feeling that is either startlingly new to you or else obsessively old. You feel incapable of dealing with it. As a way of distancing yourself from that feeling and gaining some mastery over it, you write about the feeling as precisely as you can, but giving it to an imaginary someone in an imaginary situation. What situation other than your own would produce such a feeling? Who would be caught in that situation? Think it through.

The Revenge.   An injustice has been done, and you are powerless to do anything about it. But you're not really, because you're a writer. Reproduce the situation with another set of characters, in other circumstances or another setting. Cast the outcome to suit yourself. Punish whomever you choose. Even if the story ends in a similar injustice, you have righted the wrong by enlisting your reader's sympathy on the side of right. (Dante was particularly good at this: He put his enemies in the inferno and his friends in paradise.) Remember too that as human beings we are intensely, sometimes obsessively, interested in our boredom, and you can take revenge against the things that bore you by making them absurd or funny on paper.

Keep Going

A story idea may come from any source at any time. You may not know you have an idea until you spot it in the random jottings of your journal. Once you've identified the idea, the process of thinking it through begins and doesn't end until you finish (or abandon) the story. Most writing is done between the mind and the hand, not between the hand and the page. It may take a fairly competent typist about three hours to type a twelve-page story. It may take days or months to write it. It follows that even when you are writing well, most of the time spent writing is not spent putting words on the page. If the story idea grabs hard hold of you, the process of thinking through may be involuntary, a gift. If not, you need to find the inner stillness that will allow you to develop your characters, get to know them, follow their actions in your mind—and it may take an effort of the will to find such stillness.

The metamorphosis of an idea into a story has many aspects, some deliberate and some mysterious. "Inspiration" is a real thing, a gift from the subconscious to the conscious mind. Still, perhaps influenced by the philosophy—although it was not always the practice—of the Beat authors, some new writers may feel that "forcing" words is aesthetically false; and yet few readers can tell which story "flowed" from the writer's pen and which was set down one hard-won word at a time. Toni Morrison has said that she will frequently rewrite a passage eight times, simply to create the impression of an unbroken, inspired flow; Cynthia Ozick often begins with "simple forcing" until the breakthrough comes, and so bears with the "fear and terror until I've pushed through to joy."

Over and over again, successful writers attest that unless they prepare the conscious mind with the habit of work, the gift does not come. Writing is mind-farming. You have to plow, plant, weed, and hope for growing weather. Why a seed turns into a plant is something you are never going to understand, and the only relevant response to it is gratitude. You may be proud, however, of having plowed.

Many writers besides Dorothea Brande have observed that it is ideal, having turned your story over in your mind, to write the first draft at one sitting, pushing on through the action to the conclusion, no matter how dissatisfied you are with this paragraph, that character, this phrasing, or that incident. There are two advantages to doing this. The first is that you are more likely to produce a coherent draft when you come to the desk in a single frame of mind, with a single vision of the whole, than when you write piecemeal, having altered ideas and moods. The second is that fast writing tends to make for fast pace in the story. It is always easier, later, to add and develop than it is to sharpen the pace. If you are the sort of writer who stays on page one for days, shoving commas around and combing the thesaurus for a word with slightly better connotations, then you should probably force yourself to try this method (more than once). A note of caution, though: If you write a draft at one sitting, it will not be the draft you want to show anyone, so schedule the sitting well in advance of whatever deadline you may have.

It may happen that as you write, the story will take off in some direction totally other than you intended. You thought you knew where you were going and now you don't. You may find that although you are doing precisely what you had in mind, it doesn't work—Brian Moore calls this "the place where the story gets sick," and often found he had to retrace his steps from an unlikely plot turn or unnatural character action. At such times, the story needs more imaginative mulching before it will bear fruit. Or you may find, simply, that your stamina gives out, and that though you have practiced every writerly virtue known, you're stuck. You have writer's block.

"Writer's block" is not so popular a term as it was a few years ago— sometimes writers can be sensitive even to their own clichés. But it may also be that writers began to understand and accept their difficulties. Sometimes the process seems to require working yourself into a muddle and past the muddle to despair. When you're writing, this feels terrible. You sit spinning your wheels, digging deeper and deeper into the mental muck. You decide you are going to trash the whole thing and walk away from it—only you can't, and you keep going back to it like a tongue to an aching tooth. Or you decide you are going to sit there until you bludgeon it into shape—and as long as you sit there it remains recalcitrant. W. H. Auden observed that the hardest part of writing is not knowing whether you are procrastinating or must wait for the words to come.

"What's called writer's block," claims novelist Tom Wolfe, "is almost always ordinary fear." Indeed, whenever I ask a group of writers what they find most difficult, a significant number answer that they feel they aren't good enough, that the empty page intimidates them, that they are in some way afraid. Many complain of their own laziness; but laziness, like money, doesn't really exist except to represent something else—in this case fear, severe self-judgment, or what Natalie Goldberg calls "the cycle of guilt, avoidance, and pressure."

I know a newspaper editor who says that writer's block always represents a lack of information. I thought this inapplicable to fiction until I noticed that I was mainly frustrated when I didn't know enough about my characters, the scene, or the action—when I had not gone to the imaginative depth where information lies.

Encouragement comes from the poet William Stafford, who advised his students always to write to their lowest standard. Somebody always corrected him: "You mean your highest standard." No, he meant your lowest standard. Jean Cocteau's editor gave him the same advice. "The thought of having to produce a masterpiece is giving you writer's cramp. You're paralysed at the sight of a blank sheet of paper. So begin any old way. Write: 'One winter evening...'" In *On Writer's Block: A New Approach to Creativity*, Victoria Nelson points out that "there is an almost mathematical ratio between soaring, grandiose ambition...and severe creative block." More writers prostitute themselves "up" than "down"; more are false in the determination to write great literature than to throw off a romance.

A rough draft is rough; that's its nature. Let it be rough. Think of it as making clay. The molding and the gloss come later.

And remember: Writing is easy. Not writing is hard.

A Word About Theme

The process of discovering, choosing, and revealing the theme of your story begins as early as a first freewrite and continues, probably, beyond publication. The theme is what your story is about and what you think about it, its core and the spin you put on it. John Gardner points out that theme "is not imposed on the story but evoked from within it—initially an intuitive but finally an intellectual act on the part of the writer."

What your story has to say will gradually reveal itself to you and to your reader through every choice you as a writer make—the actions, characters, setting, dialogue, objects, pace, metaphors and symbols, viewpoint, atmosphere, style, even syntax and punctuation, and even in some cases typography.

Because of the comprehensive nature of theme, I have placed the discussion of it in Chapter 9 ("Play It Again, Sam: Revision"), after the individual story elements have been addressed. But this is not entirely satisfactory, since each of those elements contributes to the theme as it unfolds. You may want to skip ahead and take a look at that chapter, or you may want to anticipate the issue by asking at every stage of your manuscript: What really interests me about this? How does this (image, character, dialogue, place,...) reveal what I care about? What connections do I see between one image and another? How can I strengthen those connections? Am I saying what I really mean, telling my truth about it?

Reading as Writers

Learning to read as a writer involves focusing on craft, the choices and the techniques of the author. In *On Becoming a Novelist*, John Gardner urges young writers to read "the way a young architect looks at a building, or a medical student watches an operation, both devotedly, hoping to learn from a master, and critically alert for any possible mistake." "Bad poets imitate; good poets steal," was T. S. Eliot's advice.

Ask yourself as you read: What is memorable, effective, moving? Reread, if possible, watching for the techniques that produced those reactions in you. *Why did the author choose to begin at this point? Why did s/he make this choice of imagery, setting, ending? What gives this scene its tension; what makes me feel sympathetic?* You can also learn from stories that don't personally move you—how would you have handled the same material, and what would have changed with that approach? Be greedy from your own viewpoint as an author: *What from this story can I learn/imitate/steal?*

About the Writing Workshop

At some point in the process of writing your story, you may find it useful to submit your story to a writing workshop to be critiqued, and if you are enrolled in a fiction-writing class, workshopping your stories may be required. These days nearly every higher learning institution in America offers some form of workshop-based creative writing course or program. The writer's workshop is so commonplace now that it has given rise to a new verb—"to workshop."

To workshop is much more than to discuss. It implies a commitment on the part of everyone concerned to give close attention to work that is embryonic. The atmosphere of such a group is intense and personal in a way that other college classes are not, since the major texts of the course are the raw efforts of its participants. At the same time, unlike the classic model of the artist's atelier or the music conservatory, the instruction is assumed to come largely from the group rather than from a single master of technical expertise. Thus, the workshop represents a democratization of both the material for study and its teaching.

Although workshops inevitably vary, a basic pattern has evolved in which twelve to twenty students are led by an instructor who is also a published writer. The students take turns writing and distributing stories, which the others read and critique. What is sought in such a group is mutual goodwill—the desire to make the story under scrutiny the best that it can be—together with an agreed-to toughness on the part of writer and readers.

This sounds simple enough, but as with all democratization, the perceived danger is that the process will flatten out the story's edge and originality, and that the result will be a homogenized "revision by committee." The danger is partly real and deserves attention. Partly, such fear masks protectiveness toward the image—solitary, remote, romantic—of the writer's life.

But those who have taken part in the process tend to champion it. John Gardner asserted that not only could writing be taught, but that "writing ability is mainly a product of good teaching supported by a deep-down love of writing." John Irving says of his instructors, "They clearly saved me valuable time...[and] time is precious for a young writer." Isabel Allende says, "The process is lonely, but the response connects you with the world."

There are, I think, three questions about the workshop endeavor that have to be asked: Is it good for the most startlingly talented, those who will go on to "become" published professional writers? Is it good for the majority who will not publish but will instead become (as some of my most gifted students have) restaurateurs, photographers, technical writers, high school teachers? And is it good for literature and literacy generally to have students of all fields struggle toward this play and this craft? My answer must in all cases be a vigorous yes. The workshop aids both the vocation and the avocation. Writing is a solitary struggle, and from the beginning writers have sought relief in the company and understanding of other writers. At its best the workshop provides an intellectual, emotional, and social (and some argue a spiritual) discipline. For the potential professionals there is the important focus on craft; course credit is a form of early pay for writing; deadlines help you find the time and discipline to do what you really want to; and, above all, the workshop offers attention in an area where attention is hard to command. For those who will not be professional writers, a course in writing fiction can be a valuable part of a liberal arts education, making for better readers, better letters home, better company reports, and better private memoirs. For everyone, the workshop can help develop critical thinking, a respect for craft, and important social skills. You may not know yet whether you want to become a professional writer, but in order to help you consider the possibility, I have included a discussion of professionalism as an appendix to this book.

There are also some pitfalls in the process: that students will develop unrealistic expectations of their chances in a chancy profession; that they will dull or provincialize their talents by trying to please the teacher or the group; that they will be buoyed into self-satisfaction by too-lavish praise or crushed by too-harsh criticism. On the other hand, workshop peers recognize and revere originality, vividness, and truth at least as often as professional critics. Hard work counts for more than anyone but writers realize, and facility with the language can be learned out of obsessive attention to it. The driven desire is no guarantee of talent, but it is an annealing force. And amazing transformations can and do occur in the creative writing class. Sometimes young writers who exhibit only a propensity for cliché and the most hackneyed initial efforts make sudden, breathtaking progress. Sometimes the leap of imaginative capacity is inexplicable, like a sport of nature.

The appropriate atmosphere in which to foster this metamorphosis is a balance constructed of right-brain creative play and left-brain crafted language, and of obligations among readers, writers, and teachers. Of these obligations, a few seem to me worth noting.

HOW WORKSHOPS WORK

The most basic expectation is that the manuscript itself should be professionally presented—that is, double-spaced, with generous margins, proofread for grammar, spelling, and punctuation. In most workshops the content is left entirely to the writer, with no censorship of subject. The reader's obligation is to read the story twice, once for its sense and story, a second time to make marginal comments, observations, suggestions. A summarizing end note is usual and helpful. This should be done with the understanding—on the part of both writer and reader—that the work at hand is by definition a work in progress. If it were finished, then there would be no reason to bring it into workshop. Workshop readers should school themselves to identify the successes that are in every story: the potential strength, the interesting subject matter, the pleasing shape, or the vivid detail.

It's my experience that the workshop itself proceeds most usefully to the writer if each discussion begins with a critically neutral description and interpretation of the story. This is important because workshopping can descend into a litany of *I like/I don't like,* and it's the responsibility of the first speaker to provide a coherent reading as a basis for discussion. It's often a good idea to begin with a detailed summary of the narrative action—useful because if class members understand the events of the story differently, or are unclear about what happens, this is important information for the author, a signal that she has not revealed what, or all, she meant. The interpretation might then address such questions as: *What kind of story is this? What defining choices do the characters face? What is its conflict-crisis-resolution structure? What is it about? What does it say about what it is about? How sympathetic should the reader feel with the main character? How does its imagery relate to its theme?*

Only after some such questions are addressed should the critique begin to deal with whether the story is successful in its effects. The first speaker should try to close with two or three questions that, in his/her opinion, the story raises and invite the class to consider these. Most of the questions will be technical: *Is the point of view consistent, are the characters fully drawn, is the imagery vivid and specific?* But now and again it is well to pause and return to more substantive matters: *What's the spirit of this story, what is it trying to say, what does it make me feel?*

THE WRITER'S ROLE

For the writer, the obligations are more emotionally strenuous, but the rewards are great. The hardest part of being a writer in a workshop is to learn this: Be still, be greedy for suggestions, take everything in, and don't defend.

This is difficult because the story under discussion is still new and may feel highly personal. The author has a strong impulse to explain and plead. If the criticism is "This isn't clear," it's hard not to feel "You didn't read it right"— even if you understand that it is not up to the workshop to "get it" but up to the author to be clear. If the reader's complaint is "This isn't credible," it's very hard not to respond "But it really happened!"—even though you know perfectly well that credibility is a different sort of fish than fact, and that autobiography is irrelevant. There is also a self-preservative impulse to keep from changing the core of what you've done: "Don't they realize how much time and effort I've already put in?"

But only the author's attempt at complete receptivity will make the workshop work. Chances are that your first draft really does not say the most meaningful thing inherent in the story; that most meaningful thing may announce itself sideways, in a detail, within parentheses, an afterthought, a slip. Somebody else may see the design before you do. Sometimes the best advice comes from the most surprising source. The thing you resist the hardest may be exactly what you need.

After the workshop, the writer's obligation alters slightly. It's important to take the written critiques and take them seriously, let them sink in with as good a will as you brought to the workshop. But part of the obligation is also not to let them sink in too far. Reject without regret whatever seems on reflection wrongheaded, dull, destructive, or irrelevant to your vision. It's just as important to be able to discriminate between helpful and unhelpful criticism as it is to be able to write. More often than not, the most useful criticism will simply confirm what you already suspected yourself. So listen to everything and receive all criticism as if it were golden. Then listen to yourself and toss the dross.

(For further discussion of giving and receiving workshop feedback, please see Chapter 9.)

Writing Exercises

Keep a journal for two weeks. Decide on a comfortable amount to write daily, and then determine not to let a day slide. To get started, refer to the journal suggestions in this chapter—freewriting, pages 4–5; the Dorothea Brande exercise, page 5; a menu of concerns, page 10; a review of your first seven years, page 10; and a set of *Pillow Book* lists, page 10. At the end of the two weeks, assess your efforts and decide what habit of journal keeping you can develop and stick to. A page a day? A paragraph a day? Three pages a week? Then do it. Probably at least once a day you have a thought worth putting into words, and sometimes it's better to write one sentence a day than to let the habit slide. Like physical exercise and piano practice, a journal is most useful when it's kept up regularly and frequently. If you pick an hour during which you write each day, no matter how much or how little, you may find yourself looking forward to, and saving things up for, that time.

In addition to keeping a journal, you might try some of these story triggers:

1. Identify the kernel of a short story from your experience of one of the following:
   - an early memory
   - an unfounded fear
   - a scar
   - a bad haircut
   - yesterday
   - a sudden change in a relationship
   - the loss of a small object
   - conflict over a lesson you were taught or never taught
   - an experience you still do not fully understand

   Freedraft a passage about it; then write the first page of the story.

2. Take your notebook and go to a place where you can observe people—a library, restaurant, bus station, wherever. Choose a few people and describe them in detail in your notebook. What are they wearing? What are they doing and why do you think they're doing it? If they

are talking, can you overhear (or guess) what they're saying? What are they thinking?

Next, choose one character and invent a life for him or her. Write at least two pages. Where does s/he live? Work? What relationships does s/he have? Worries? Fears? Desires? Pleasures? Does this character have a secret? Do you find yourself beginning a story?

3. Have you ever worked as a carpenter, cabdriver, janitor, dentist, bar pianist, waiter, actor, film critic, drummer, teacher, coach, stockbroker, therapist, librarian, or mail carrier? Or maybe you have the inside scoop on a job that a close friend or family member has had. Make a list of jobs you've had or of which you have secondhand knowledge—no matter how odd or how mundane. Now list some incidents that happened at one or another of those jobs, then pick one incident and begin describing it. Don't limit yourself to what actually happened.

2

SEEING IS BELIEVING
Showing and Telling

◆ *Significant Detail*

◆ *Comparison*

◆ *The Active Voice*

◆ *Prose Rhythm*

◆ *Mechanics*

Literature offers us feelings for which we do not have to pay. It allows us to love, condemn, condone, hope, dread, and hate without any of the risks those feelings ordinarily involve. For even good feelings—intimacy, power, speed, drunkenness, passion—have consequences, and powerful feelings may risk powerful consequences. Fiction also must contain ideas, which give significance to characters and events. If the ideas are shallow or untrue, the fiction will be correspondingly shallow or untrue. But the ideas must be experienced through or with the characters; they must be felt or the fiction will fail also.

Much nonfiction writing, from editorials to advertising, also tries to persuade us to feel one way rather than another, but nonfiction works largely by means of logic and reasoning. Fiction tries to reproduce the emotional impact of experience. And this is a more difficult task, because unlike the images of film and drama, which directly strike the eye and ear, words are transmitted first to the mind, where they must be translated into images.

In order to move your reader, the standard advice runs, "Show, don't tell." This dictum can be confusing, considering that words are all a writer has to work with. What it means is that your job as a fiction writer is to focus attention not on the words, which are inert, nor on the thoughts these words produce, but through these to felt experience, where the vitality of understanding lies. There are techniques for accomplishing this—for making narrative vivid, moving, and resonant—which can be partly learned and always strengthened.

Significant Detail

In *The Elements of Style*, William Strunk, Jr., writes:

> If those who have studied the art of writing are in accord on any one point, it is on this: the surest way to arouse and hold the attention of the reader is by being specific, definite and concrete. The greatest writers...are effective largely because they deal in particulars and report the details that matter.

Specific, definite, concrete, particular details—these are the life of fiction. Details (as every good liar knows) are the stuff of persuasiveness. Mary is sure that Ed forgot to go pay the gas bill last Tuesday, but Ed says, "I know I went, because this old guy in a knit vest was in front of me in the line, and went on and on about his twin granddaughters"—and it is hard to refute a knit vest and twins even if the furnace doesn't work. John Gardner, in *The Art of Fiction*, speaks of details as "proofs," rather like those in a geometric theorem or a statistical argument. The novelist, he says, "gives us such details about the streets, stores, weather, politics, and concerns of Cleveland (or wherever the setting is) and such details about the looks, gestures, and experiences of his characters that we cannot help believing that the story he tells us is true."

A detail is "definite" and "concrete" when it appeals to the senses. It should be seen, heard, smelled, tasted, or touched. The most superficial survey of any bookshelf of published fiction will turn up dozens of examples of this principle. Here is a fairly obvious one.

> It was a narrow room, with a rather high ceiling, and crowded from floor to ceiling with goodies. There were rows and rows of hams and sausages of all shapes and colors—white, yellow, red and black; fat and lean and round and long—rows of canned preserves, cocoa and tea, bright translucent glass bottles of honey, marmalade and jam.
>
> I stood enchanted, straining my ears and breathing in the delightful atmosphere and the mixed fragrance of chocolate and smoked fish and earthy truffles. I spoke into the silence, saying: "Good day" in quite a loud voice; I can still remember how my strained, unnatural tones died away in the stillness. No one answered. And my mouth literally began to water like a spring. One quick, noiseless step and I was beside one of the laden tables.

I made one rapturous grab into the nearest glass urn, filled as it chanced with chocolate creams, slipped a fistful into my coat pocket, then reached the door, and in the next second was safely round the corner.

Thomas Mann, *Confessions of Felix Krull, Confidence Man*

The shape of this passage is a tour through the five senses. Mann lets us see: *narrow room, high ceiling, hams, sausages, preserves, cocoa, tea, glass bottles, honey, marmalade, jam.* He lets us smell: *fragrance of chocolate, smoked fish, earthy truffles.* He lets us hear: *"Good day," unnatural tones, stillness.* He lets us taste: *mouth, water like a spring.* He lets us touch: *grab, chocolate creams, slipped, fistful into my coat pocket.* The writing is alive because we do in fact live through our sense perceptions, and Mann takes us past words and through thought to let us perceive the scene in this way.

In this process, a number of ideas not stated reverberate off the sense images, so that we are also aware of a number of generalizations the author might have made but does not need to make; we will make them ourselves. Mann could have had his character "tell" us: *I was quite poor, and I was not used to seeing such a profusion of food, so that although I was very afraid there might be someone in the room and that I might be caught stealing, I couldn't resist taking the risk.*

Such a version would be very flat, and none of that telling is necessary, as all these points are "shown." The character's relative poverty is inherent in the tumble of images of sight and smell; if he were used to such displays, his eyes and nose would not dart about as they do. His fear is inherent in the "strained, unnatural tones" and their dying away in the stillness. His desire is in his watering mouth, his fear in the furtive speed of "quick" and "grab" and "slipped."

The points to be made here are two, and they are both important. The first is that the writer must deal in sense detail. The second is that these must be details "that matter." As a writer of fiction you are at constant pains not simply to say what you mean, but to mean more than you say. Much of what you mean will be an abstraction or a judgment—*love requires trust, children can be cruel.* But if you write in abstractions or judgments, you are writing an essay, whereas if you let us use our senses and form our own interpretations, we will be involved as participants in a real way. Much of the pleasure of reading comes from the egotistical sense that we are clever enough to understand. When the author explains to us or interprets for us, we suspect that he or she doesn't think us bright enough to do it for ourselves.

A detail can also matter because it suggests plot development. Chekhov famously said that if a pistol is placed on the mantle in the first act, it must go off in the third. Similarly, when a story offers a new kind of detail or level of specificity, it may suggest a change in character or a development of the plot. For example, in Stuart Dybek's story "We Didn't," which is reprinted at the end of this chapter, the narrator and his girlfriend have been making out on the beach but are suddenly caught short: "Headlights bounded toward us, spotlights crisscrossing, blue dome lights revolving as squad cars converged." The police cars and search lights change the scene completely, but more than that, they operate metaphorically and announce a turning point in the story, interrupting the lovers and throwing a spotlight on the young couple's differences and the problems that the story is about.

A detail is *concrete* if it appeals to one of the five senses; it is *significant* if it also conveys an idea or a judgment or both. *The windowsill was green* is concrete, because we can see it. *The windowsill was shedding flakes of fungus-green paint* is concrete and also significant because it conveys the idea that the paint is old and suggests the judgment that the color is ugly. The second version can also be seen more vividly. (For further discussion of selecting detail, see "How Fictional Elements Contribute to Theme," page 323, in Chapter 9.)

Here is a passage from a young writer that fails through lack of appeal to the senses.

> Debbie was a very stubborn and completely independent person and was always doing things her way despite her parents' efforts to get her to conform. Her father was an executive in a dress manufacturing company and was able to afford his family all the luxuries and comforts of life. But Debbie was completely indifferent to her family's affluence.

This passage contains a number of judgments we might or might not share with the author, and she has not convinced us that we do. What constitutes stubbornness? Independence? Indifference? Affluence? Further, since the judgments are supported by generalizations, we have no sense of the individuality of the characters, which alone would bring them to life on the page. What things was she always doing? What efforts did her parents make to get her to conform? What level of executive? What dress manufacturing company? What luxuries and comforts?

> Debbie would wear a tank top to a tea party if she pleased, with fluorescent earrings and ankle-strap sandals.
>
> "Oh, sweetheart," Mrs. Chiddister would stand in the doorway wringing her hands. "It's not *nice*."
>
> "Not who?" Debbie would say, and add a fringed belt.
>
> Mr. Chiddister was Artistic Director of the Boston branch of Cardin and had a high respect for what he called "elegant textures," which ranged from handwoven tweed to gold filigree, and which he willingly offered his daughter. Debbie preferred her laminated wrist bangles.

We have not passed a final judgment on the merits of these characters, but we know a good deal more about them, and we have drawn certain interim conclusions that are our own and not forced on us by the author. Debbie is independent of her parents' values, rather careless of their feelings, energetic, and possibly a tart. Mrs. Chiddister is quite ineffectual. Mr. Chiddister is a snob, though perhaps Debbie's taste is so bad we'll end up on his side.

But maybe that isn't at all what the author had in mind. Perhaps it was more like this version:

> One day Debbie brought home a copy of *Ulysses*. Mrs. Strum called it "filth" and threw it across the sunporch. Debbie knelt on the parquet and retrieved her bookmark, which she replaced. "No, it's not," she said.
>
> "You're not so old I can't take a strap to you!" Mr. Strum reminded her.
>
> Mr. Strum was controlling stockholder of Readywear Conglomerates and was proud of treating his family, not only on his salary, but also on his expense account. The summer before, he had justified their company on a trip to Belgium, where they toured the American Cemetery and the torture chambers of Ghent Castle. Entirely ungrateful, Debbie had spent the rest of the trip curled up in the hotel with a shabby copy of some poet.

Now we have a much clearer understanding of *stubbornness, independence, indifference,* and *affluence*—both their natures and the value we are to place on them. This time our judgment is heavily weighed in Debbie's favor, partly because people who read books have a sentimental sympathy with people who read books, but also because we hear hysteria in "filth" and "take a strap to you," whereas Debbie's resistance is quiet and strong. Mr. Strum's attitude toward his expense account suggests that he's corrupt, and his choice of "luxuries" is morbid. The passage does contain two overt judgments, the first being that Debbie was "entirely ungrateful." Notice that by the time we get to this, we're aware that the judgment is Mr. Strum's and that Debbie has little enough to be grateful for. We understand not only what the author says but also that she means the opposite of what she says, and we feel doubly clever to get it; that is the pleasure of irony. Likewise, the judgment that the poet's book is "shabby" shows Mr. Strum's crass materialism toward what we know to be the finer things. At the very end of the passage, we are denied a detail that we might very well be given: *What* poet did Debbie curl up with? Again, by this time we understand that we are being given Mr. Strum's view of the situation and that it's Mr. Strum (not Debbie, not the author, and certainly not us) who wouldn't notice the difference between John Keats and Stanley Kunitz.

One may object that both rewrites of the passage are longer than the original. Doesn't "adding" so much detail make for long writing? The answer is yes and no. No, because in the rewrites we know so much more about the values, activities, lifestyles, attitudes, and personalities of the characters that it would take many times the length of the original to "tell" it all in generalizations. Yes in the sense that detail requires words and that if you are to realize your characters through detail, then you must be careful to select the details that convey the characteristics essential to our understanding. You can't convey a whole person, or a whole action, or everything there is to be conveyed about a single moment of a single day. You must select the significant.

In fact, the greater significance of realistic details may emerge only as you continue to develop and revise your story, for, as Flannery O'Connor says, "the longer you look at one object, the more of the world you see in it." Certain details "tend to accumulate meaning from the action of the story itself," becoming "symbolic in the way they work," O'Connor notes. "While having their essential place in the literal level of the story, [details] operate in depth as well as on the surface, increasing the story in every direction."

No amount of concrete detail will move us, therefore, unless it also implicitly suggests meaning and value. Following is a passage that fails, not because it lacks detail, but because those details lack significance.

> Terry Landon, a handsome young man of twenty-two, was six foot four and broad-shouldered. He had medium-length thick blond hair and a natural tan, which set off the blue of his intense and friendly long-lashed eyes.

Here we have a good deal of generic sensory information, but we still know very little about Terry. There are so many broad-shouldered twenty-two-year-olds in the world, so many blonds, and so on. This sort of cataloging of characterics suggests an all-points bulletin: *male Caucasian, medium height, light hair, last seen wearing gray raincoat.* Such a description may help the police locate a suspect in a crowd, but the assumption is that the identity of the person is not known. As an author you want us to know the character individually and immediately.

The fact is that all our ideas and judgments are formed through our sense perceptions, and daily, moment by moment, we receive information that is not merely sensuous in this way. Four people at a cocktail party may *do* nothing but stand and nibble canapés and may *talk* nothing but politics and the latest films. But you feel perfectly certain that X is furious at Y, who is flirting with Z, who is wounding Q, who is trying to comfort X. You have only your senses to observe with. How do you reach these conclusions? By what gestures, glances, tones, touches, choices of words?

It may be that this constant emphasis on judgment makes the author, and the reader, seem opinionated or self-righteous. "I want to present my characters objectively/neutrally. I'm not making any value judgments. I want the reader to make up his or her own mind." Yet human beings are constantly judging: *How was the film? He seemed friendly. What a boring class! Do you like it here? She's very thin. That's fascinating. I'm so clumsy. You're gorgeous tonight. Life is crazy, isn't it?*

When we are not passing such judgments, it's because we are indifferent. Although you may not want to sanctify or damn your characters, you do want us to care about them, and if you refuse to direct our judgment, you may be inviting our indifference. Usually when you "don't want us to judge," you mean that you want our feelings to be mixed, paradoxical, complex. *She's horribly irritating, but it's not her fault. He's sexy, but there's something cold about it underneath.* If this is what you mean, then you must direct our judgment in both or several directions, not in no direction.

Even a character who doesn't exist except as a type or function will come to life if presented through significant detail, as in this portrait of an aunt in Dorothy Allison's story "Don't Tell Me You Don't Know." Like many of the female relatives the adult narrator mentions, the aunt embodies a powerful, nurturing force that nonetheless failed to protect the narrator from childhood abuse.

> My family runs to heavy women, gravy-fed working women, the kind usually seen in pictures taken at mining disasters. Big women, all of my aunts move under their own power and stalk around telling everybody else what to do. But Aunt Alma was the prototype, the one I had loved most, starting back when she had given us free meals in the roadhouse she'd run for awhile.... Once there, we'd be fed on chicken gravy and biscuits, and Mama would be fed from the well of her sister's love and outrage.

For a character who is a "prototype," we have a remarkably clear image of this woman. Notice how Allison moves us from generalization toward sharpness of image, gradually bringing the character into focus. First she has only a size and gender; then a certain abstract "power" and an appeal to our visual memory of the grieving, tough women seen in documentary photographs; then a distinct role as the one who "had given us free meals" when the family hit hard times. Once in focus as manager of a particular roadhouse, Alma's qualities again become generalized to the adult women of the family.

> The power in them, the strength and the heat!... How could my daddy, my uncles, ever stand up to them, dare to raise hand or voice to them? They were a power on the earth.

Finally, the focus narrows to the individual again, whose body has been formed by the starchy foods that poverty made a necessity and that at least kept hunger temporarily at bay: "My aunt always made biscuits. What else stretched so well? Now those starch meals shadowed her loose shoulders and dimpled her fat white elbows."

New details can lead the reader, or the narrator, to view a character differently. When someone who once seemed graceful and athletic begins suddenly and unaccountably to stumble or drop things, we begin to reevaluate that person and perhaps worry about his or her health. A stroke? Multiple sclerosis? In Stacey Richter's story "Goal 666," which appears at the end of this chapter, the narrator has joined a heavy metal band and is thrilled to be among its tough, macho members. So thrilled in fact that he later realizes he has overlooked some details—details he should have factored into his assessment of the band members, details that reveal a difference between performance and reality, details that tell us that we too need to be alert and may not be on the ride we thought we were on:

> After that night we had a masculine bond, so I was slow to notice details I might have caught earlier. Though Anders had mega-fierce tattoos, and Stefan, the small but muscular drummer, had huge, furry sideburns creeping across his cheeks, and Max had the extremely satanic name of Max—there was something not right about these men. There was an air of innocence to them. Despite the fiery badness of The Lords, and their lusty embrace of songs I had written, these guys were scrupulous about washing their hands after using the bathroom. They returned all their phone calls promptly and refrained from resting their forearms on the dinner table. Going for a meal with these guys was like going to a tea party: napkin in the lap, chewing with the mouth closed, salad fork, dessert spoon, and so on.

The point is not that an author must never express an idea, general quality, or judgment. But, in order to carry the felt weight of fiction, these abstractions must be realized through the senses: "I smelled chicken gravy and hot grease, the close thick scent of love and understanding." Through details these abstract qualities live.

GOOD WRITERS MAY "TELL" ABOUT ALMOST ANYTHING IN fiction except the characters' feelings. One may tell the reader that the character went to a private school... or one may tell the reader that the character hates spaghetti; but with rare exceptions the characters' feelings must be demonstrated: fear, love, excitement, doubt, embarrassment, despair become real only when they take the form of events—action (or gesture), dialogue, or physical reaction to setting. Detail is the lifeblood of fiction.

JOHN GARDNER

WRITING ABOUT EMOTION

Fiction offers feelings for which the reader doesn't pay—and yet to evoke those feelings, it is often necessary to portray sensory details that the reader may have experienced. Simply labeling a character's emotion as love or hatred will have little effect, for such abstraction operates solely on a vague, intellectual level; rather, emotion is the body's physical reaction to information the senses receive. The great Russian director Stanislavski, originator of realistic "Method" acting, urged his students to abandon the clichéd emotive postures of the nineteenth-century stage in favor of emotions evoked by the actor's recollection of sensory details connected with a personal past trauma. By recalling such details as the tingling of fingertips, the smell of singed hair, and the tensing of calf muscles, an emotion such as anger might naturally be induced within the actor's body.

> THE PAST IS BEAUTIFUL BECAUSE one never realizes an emotion at the time. It expands later, and thus we don't have complete emotions about the present,only about the past.... That is why we dwell on the past, I think.
>
> VIRGINIA WOOLF

Similarly, in written fiction, if the writer depicts the precise physical sensations experienced by the character, a particular emotion may be triggered by the reader's own sense memory. In his story "The Easy Way," author Tom Perrotta describes the moment in which a lottery winner learns of a jealous friend's death: "I stood perfectly still and let the news expand inside of me, like a bubble in my chest that wouldn't rise or pop. I waited for anger or grief to fill the space it opened, but all I felt just then was an unsteadiness in my legs, a faulty connection with the ground." By tracing the physical reaction and staying true to the shock of the moment, Perrotta conveys the initial impact of this loss.

"Get control of emotion by avoiding the *mention* of the emotion," urges John L'Heureux. "To avoid melodrama, aim for a restrained tone rather than an exaggerated one. A scene with hysteria needs more, not less control in the writing: keep the language deflated and rooted in action and sensory detail."

There are further reasons to avoid labeling emotion: Emotion is seldom pure, conflicting feelings often run together, we rarely stop to analyze our passions as we're caught up in them, and the reader may cease to participate when a label is simply given.

FILTERING

John Gardner, in *The Art of Fiction*, points out that in addition to the faults of insufficient detail and excessive use of abstraction, there's a third failure:

> ...the needless filtering of the image through some observing consciousness. The amateur writes: "Turning, she noticed two snakes fighting in among the rocks." Compare: "She turned. In among the rocks, two snakes were

fighting…" Generally speaking—though no laws are absolute in fiction—
vividness urges that almost every occurrence of such phrases as "she noticed"
and "she saw" be suppressed in favor of direct presentation of the thing seen.

The filter is a common fault and often difficult to recognize—although
once the principle is grasped, cutting away filters is an easy means to more
vivid writing. As a fiction writer you will often be working through "some observing consciousness." Yet when you step back and ask readers to observe the
observer—to look *at* rather than *through* the character—you start to tell-not-
show and rip us briefly out of the scene. Here, for example, is a student passage
quite competent except for the filtering:

> Mrs. Blair made her way to the chair by the window and sank gratefully
> into it. *She looked out the window and there*, across the street, *she saw* the
> ivory BMW parked in front of the fire plug once more. *It seemed to her*,
> *though*, that something was wrong with it. *She noticed* that it was listing
> slightly toward the back and side, and *then saw* that the back rim was rest-
> ing almost on the asphalt.

Remove the filters from this paragraph and we are allowed to stay in
Mrs. Blair's consciousness, watching with her eyes, sharing understanding as it
unfolds for her:

> Mrs. Blair made her way to the chair by the window and sank gratefully
> into it. Across the street the ivory BMW was parked in front of the fire
> plug again. Something was wrong with it, though. It was listing toward the
> back and side, the back rim resting almost on the asphalt.

A similar filtering occurs when the writer chooses to begin a flashback and
mistakenly supposes that the reader is not clever enough to follow this technique without a guiding transition:

> Mrs. Blair *thought back to* the time that she and Henry had owned an ivory
> car, though it had been a Chevy. *She remembered clearly* that it had a hood
> shaped like a sugar scoop, and chrome bumpers that stuck out a foot front
> and back. And there was that funny time, *she recalled*, when Henry had
> to change the flat tire on Alligator Alley, and she'd thought the alligators
> would come up out of the swamp.

Just as the present scene will be more present to the reader without a filter, so
we will be taken more thoroughly back to the time of the memory without a filter:

> She and Henry had owned an ivory car once, though it had been a Chevy,
> with a hood shaped like a sugar scoop and chrome bumpers that stuck out

a foot front and back. And there was that funny time Henry had to change the flat tire on Alligator Alley, and she'd thought the alligators would come up out of the swamp.

Observe that the pace of the reading is improved by the removal of the filters—at least partly, literally, because one or two lines of type have been removed.

Comparison

Every reader reading is a self-deceiver: We simultaneously "believe" a story and know that it is a fiction, a fabrication. Our belief in the reality of the story may be so strong that it produces physical reactions—tears, trembling, sighs, gasps, a headache. At the same time, as long as the fiction is working for us, we know that our submission is voluntary; we have, as Samuel Taylor Coleridge pointed out, suspended disbelief. "It's just a movie," says the exasperated father as he takes his shrieking six-year-old out to the lobby. For the father the fiction is working; for the child it is not.

Simultaneous belief and awareness of illusion are present in both the content and the craft of literature, and what is properly called artistic pleasure derives from the tension of this *is* and *is not*. The content of a plot, for instance, tells us that something happens that does not happen, that people who do not exist behave in such a way, and that the events of life—which we know to be random, unrelated, and unfinished—are necessary, are patterned, and come to closure. Pleasure in artistry comes precisely when the illusion rings true without destroying the knowledge that it is an illusion.

In the same way, the techniques of every art offer us the tension of things that are and are not alike. This is true of poetry, in which rhyme is interesting because *tend* sounds like *mend* but not exactly like; it is also true of music, whose interest lies in variations on a theme. And it is the fundamental nature of metaphor, from which literature derives.

Metaphor is the literary device by which we are told that something is or is like something that it clearly is not, or is not exactly, like. It is a way of showing, because it particularizes the essential nature of one thing by comparing it to another. What a good metaphor does is surprise us with the unlikeness of the two things compared while at the same time convincing us of the truth of the likeness. In the process it may also illuminate the meaning of the story and its theme. A bad metaphor fails to surprise or convince or both—and so fails to illuminate.

TYPES OF METAPHOR AND SIMILE

The simplest distinction between kinds of comparison—and usually the first one grasped by beginning students of literature—is between *metaphor* and *simile*. A simile makes a comparison with the use of *like* or *as*, a metaphor without. Though this distinction is technical, it is not entirely trivial, for a metaphor demands a more literal acceptance. If you say, "A woman is a rose," you ask for an extreme suspension of disbelief, whereas "A woman is like a rose" acknowledges the artifice in the statement.

In both metaphor and simile, the resonance of comparison is in the essential or abstract quality that the two objects share. When a writer speaks of "the eyes of the houses" or "the windows of the soul," the comparison of eyes to windows contains the idea of transmitting vision between the inner and the outer. When we speak of "the king of beasts," we don't mean that a lion wears a crown or sits on a throne (although in children's stories the lion often does precisely that, in order to suggest a primitive physical likeness); we mean that king and lion share abstract qualities of power, position, pride, and bearing.

In both metaphor and simile a physical similarity can yield up a characterizing abstraction. So if "a woman" is either "a rose" or "like a rose," the significance lies not in the physical similarity but in the essential qualities that such similarity implies: slenderness, suppleness, fragrance, beauty, color—and perhaps the hidden threat of thorns.

Every metaphor and simile I have used so far is either a cliché or a dead metaphor (a metaphor so familiar that it has lost its original meaning). Each of them may at one time have surprised with their aptness, but by now each has been used so often that the surprise is gone. I wished to use familiar examples in order to clarify that *resonance of comparison depends on the abstractions conveyed in the likeness of the things compared.* A good metaphor reverberates with the essential; this is the writer's principle of choice.

So Flannery O'Connor, in "A Good Man Is Hard to Find," describes the mother as having "a face as broad and innocent as a cabbage." A soccer ball is roughly the same size and shape as a cabbage; so is a schoolroom globe; so is a street lamp. But if the mother's face had been as broad and innocent as any of these things, she would be a different woman altogether. A cabbage is also rural, heavy, dense, and cheap, and so it conveys a whole complex of abstractions about the woman's class and mentality. There is, on the other hand, no innocence in the face of Shrike, in Nathanael West's *Miss Lonelyhearts,* who "buried his triangular face like a hatchet in her neck."

Sometimes the aptness of a comparison is achieved by taking it from an area of reference relevant to the thing compared. In *Dombey and Son,* Charles Dickens describes the ships' instrument maker, Solomon Gills, as having "eyes as red as if they had been small suns looking at you through a fog." The simile suggests a seascape, whereas in *One Flew Over the Cuckoo's Nest,* Ken Kesey's Ruckly, rendered inert by shock therapy, has eyes "all smoked up and gray and deserted inside like blown fuses." But the metaphor may range further from its original, in which case the abstraction conveyed must strike us as strongly and essentially appropriate. William Faulkner's Emily Grierson in "A Rose for Emily" has "haughty black eyes in a face the flesh of which was strained across the temple and about the eyesockets as you imagine a lighthouse-keeper's face ought to look." Miss Emily has no connection with the sea, but the metaphor reminds us not only of her sternness and self-sufficiency, but also that she has isolated herself in a locked house. The same character as an old woman has eyes that "looked like two pieces of coal pressed into a lump of dough," and the image domesticates her, robs her of her light.

Both metaphors and similes can be *extended,* meaning that the writer continues to present aspects of likeness in the things compared.

> There was a white fog... standing all around you like something solid.
> At eight or nine, perhaps, it lifted as a shutter lifts. We had a glimpse of
> the towering multitude of trees, of the immense matted jungle, with the
> blazing little ball of sun hanging over it—all perfectly still—and then the
> shutter came down again, smoothly, as if sliding in greased grooves.
>
> Joseph Conrad, *Heart of Darkness*

Notice that Conrad moves from a generalized image of "something solid" to the specific simile "as a shutter lifts"; reasserts the simile as a metaphor, "then the shutter came down again"; and becomes still more specific in the extension "as if sliding in greased grooves."

Also note that Conrad emphasizes the dumb solidity of the fog by comparing the larger natural image with the smaller manufactured object. This is a technique that contemporary writers have used to effects both comic and profound, as when Frederick Barthelme, in *The Brothers,* describes a young woman "with a life stretching out in front of her like so many unrented videos" or a man's head "bobbing like an enormous Q-Tip against the little black sky."

In a more usual metaphoric technique, the smaller or more ordinary image is compared with one more significant or intense, as in this example from Louise Erdrich's "Machimanito," where the narrator invokes the names of Anishinabe Indians dead of tuberculosis:

> Their names grew within us, swelled to the brink of our lips, forced our
> eyes open in the middle of the night. We were filled with the water of the
> drowned, cold and black—airless water that lapped against the seal of our
> tongues or leaked slowly from the corners of our eyes. Within us, like ice
> shards, their names bobbed and shifted.

A *conceit,* which can be either metaphor or simile, is a comparison of two things radically and startlingly unlike—in Samuel Johnson's words, "yoked by violence together." A conceit is as far removed as possible from the purely sensuous comparison of "the eyes of the potato." It compares two things that have very little or no immediately apprehensible similarity; and so it is the nature of the conceit to be long. The author must explain to us, sometimes at great length, why these things can be said to be alike. When John Donne compares a flea to the Holy Trinity, the two images have no areas of reference in common, and we don't understand. He must explain to us that the flea, having bitten both the poet and his lover, now has the blood of three souls in its body.

The conceit is more common to poetry than to prose because of the density of its imagery, but it can be used to good effect in fiction. In *The Day of the Locust*, Nathanael West uses a conceit in an insistent devaluation of love. The screenwriter Claude Estee says:

> Love is like a vending machine, eh? Not bad. You insert a coin and press home the lever. There's some mechanical activity inside the bowels of the device. You receive a small sweet, frown at yourself in the dirty mirror, adjust your hat, take a firm grip on your umbrella and walk away, trying to look as though nothing had happened.

"Love is like a vending machine" is a conceit; if the writer didn't explain to us in what way love is like a vending machine, we'd founder trying to figure it out. So he goes on to develop the vending machine in images that suggest not "love" but seamy sex. The last image—"trying to look as though nothing had happened"—has nothing to do with the vending machine; we accept it because by this time we've fused the two ideas in our minds.

Deborah Galyan employs conceit in "The Incredible Appearing Man," in a playfully self-conscious description of the overpowering effect of a new baby's presence.

> A baby transforms you, body and soul. The moment you give birth, your mind is instantaneously filled with Styrofoam peanuts. Your past is trash-compacted to make room for all the peanuts. As the baby grows, you add more peanuts, and the little tin can of your past gets more compressed. But it is still there, underneath all the peanuts. The smashed cans of your past never entirely disappear.

The comparison of a mind and a trash compactor is a conceit because physical or sensuous similarity is not the point. Rather, the similarity is in the abstract idea of material (metal cans or memories) that once loomed large being crushed and all but crowded out by the volume of daily experience.

METAPHORIC FAULTS TO AVOID

Comparison is not a frivolity. It is, on the contrary, the primary business of the brain. Some eighteenth-century philosophers spoke of the human mind as a *tabula rasa*, a blank slate on which sense impressions were recorded, compared, and grouped. Now we're more likely to speak of the mind as a "computer" "storing" and "processing" "data." What both metaphors acknowledge is that comparison is the basis of all learning and all reasoning. When a child burns his hand on the stove and hears his mother say, "It's hot," and then goes toward the radiator and again hears her say, "It's hot," the child learns not to burn his fingers. The implicit real-life comparison is meant to convey a fact, and it teaches a mode of behavior. By contrast, the goal of literary comparison is to convey not a fact but a perception, and thereby to enlarge our scope of understanding. When we speak of "the flames of torment," our impulse is comprehension and compassion.

Nevertheless, *metaphor* is a dirty word in some critical circles, because of the strain of the pursuit. Clichés, mixed metaphors, and similes that are inept, unapt, obscure, or done to death mar good prose and tax the patience of the most willing reader. If a metaphor is too familiar, it operates as an abstraction rather than a particularizing detail. If it is too far-fetched, it calls attention to the writer rather than to the meaning and produces a sort of hiccup in the reader's involvement.

There are more *don'ts* than *dos* to list for the writing of metaphor and simile, because every good comparison is its own justification by virtue of being apt and original.

To study good metaphor, read. In the meantime, avoid the following:

Cliché metaphors are metaphors so familiar that they have lost the force of their original meaning. They are inevitably apt comparisons; if they were not, they wouldn't have been repeated often enough to become clichés. But such images fail to surprise, and we blame the writer for this expenditure of energy without a payoff.

Or, to put it a worse way:

Clichés are *the last word* in bad writing, and *it's a crying shame* to see all you *bright young things* spoiling your *deathless prose* with phrases as *old as the hills*. You must *keep your nose to the grindstone*, because *the sweet smell of success* only comes to those who *march to the beat of a different drummer*.

It's a sad fact that at this stage of literary history, you may not say that eyes are like pools or stars, and you should be very wary of saying that they flood with tears. These have been so often repeated that they've become shorthand for emotions (attractions in the first and second instances, grief in the third) without the felt force of those emotions. Anytime you as writer record an emotion without convincing us to feel that emotion, you introduce a fatal distance between author and reader. Therefore, neither may your characters be hawk-eyed nor eagle-eyed; nor may they have ruby lips or pearly teeth or peaches-and-cream complexions or necks like swans or thighs like hams. Let them not shed single tears or freeze like deer caught in headlights. If you sense—and you may—that the moment calls for the special intensity of metaphor, you may have to sift through a whole stock of clichés that come readily to mind. Or it may be time for freewriting and giving the mind room to play. Sometimes your internal critic may reject as fantastic the comparison that, on second look, proves fresh and apt.

In any case, *pools* and *stars* have become clichés for *eyes* because they capture and manifest something essential about the nature of eyes. As long as eyes continue to contain liquid and light, there will be a new way of saying so.

Cliché can be useful as a device, however, for establishing authorial distance from a character or narrator. If the author tells us that Rome wasn't built in a day, we're likely to think the author has little to contribute to human insight; but if a character says so, in speech or thought, the judgment attaches to the character rather than to the author.

> The door closed and he turned to find the dumpy figure, surmounted by the atrocious hat, coming toward him. "Well," she said, *"you only live once* and paying a little more for it, I at least won't *meet myself coming and going."*
>
>   "Some day I'll start making money…"
>
>   "I think you're doing fine," she said, drawing on her gloves. "You've only been out of school a year. *Rome wasn't built in a day."*
>
> Flannery O'Connor, "Everything That Rises Must Converge"
> (italics added)

Far-fetched metaphors are the opposite of clichés: They surprise but are not apt. As the dead metaphor *far-fetched* suggests, the mind must travel too far to carry back the likeness, and too much is lost on the way. When such a comparison does work, we speak laudatorily of a "leap of the imagination." But when it does not, what we face is in effect a failed conceit: The explanation of what is alike about these two things does not convince. Very good writers, in the search for originality, sometimes fetch too far. Ernest Hemingway's talent was not for metaphor, and on the rare occasions that he used a metaphor, he was likely to strain. In this passage from *A Farewell to Arms*, the protagonist has escaped a firing squad and is fleeing the war.

> You had lost your cars and your men as a floorwalker loses the stock of his department in a fire. There was, however, no insurance. You were out of it now. You had no more obligation. If they shot floorwalkers after a fire in the department store because they spoke with an accent they had always had, then certainly the floorwalkers would not be expected to return when the store opened again for business. They might seek other employment; if there was any other employment and the police did not get them.

Well, this doesn't work. We may be willing to see the likeness between stock lost in a department store fire and men and cars lost in a military retreat; but "they" *don't* shoot floorwalkers as the Italian military shot defeated line officers. And although a foreign accent might be a disadvantage in a foreign war, it's hard to see how a floorwalker could be killed because of one, although it might make it hard for him to get hired in the first place, if...The mind twists trying to find any illuminating or essential logic in the comparison of a soldier to a floorwalker, and fails, so that the protagonist's situation is trivialized in the attempt.

Mixed metaphors are so called because they ask us to compare the original image with things from two or more different areas of reference: *As you walk the path of life, don't founder on the reefs of ignorance.* Life can be a path or a sea, but it cannot be both at the same time. The point of the metaphor is to fuse two images in a single tension. The mind is adamantly unwilling to fuse three.

Separate metaphors or similes too close together, especially if they come from areas of reference very different in value or tone, disturb in the same way the mixed metaphor does. The mind doesn't leap; it staggers.

> They fought like rats in a Brooklyn sewer. Nevertheless her presence was the axiom of his heart's geometry, and when she was away you would see him walking up and down the street dragging his cane along the picket fence like an idle boy's stick.

Any of these metaphors or similes might be acceptable by itself, but rats, axioms, and boys' sticks connote three different areas and tones, and two sentences cannot contain them all. Pointed in too many directions, a reader's attention follows none.

Obscure and *overdone metaphors* falter because the author has misjudged the difficulty of the comparison. The result is either confusion or an insult to the reader's intelligence. In the case of obscurity, a similarity in the author's mind isn't getting onto the page. One student described the spines on a prickly pear cactus as being "slender as a fat man's fingers." I was completely confused by this. Was it ironic, that the spines weren't slender at all? Ah no, he said. Hadn't I noticed how startling it was when someone with a fleshy body had bony fingers and toes? The trouble here was that the author knew what he meant but had left out the essential abstraction in the comparison, the startling quality of the contrast: "the spines of the fleshy prickly pear, like slender fingers on a fat man."

In this case, the simile was underexplained. It's probably a more common impulse—we're so anxious to make sure the reader gets it—to explain the obvious. In the novel *Raw Silk,* I had the narrator describe quarrels with her husband, "which I used to face with my dukes up in high confidence that we'd soon clear the air. The air can't be cleared now. We live in marital Los Angeles. This is the air—polluted, poisoned." A critic friend pointed out to me that anybody who didn't know about L.A. smog wouldn't get it anyway, and that all the last two words did was ram the comparison down the reader's throat. He was right. "The air can't be cleared now. We live in marital Los Angeles. This is the air." The rewrite is much stronger because it neither explains nor exaggerates; and the reader enjoys supplying the metaphoric link.

Metaphors using *topical references*, including brand names, esoteric objects, or celebrity names, can work as long as a sense of the connection is given; don't rely for effect on knowledge that the reader may not have. To write, "The sisters looked like the Dixie Chicks" is to make the trio do your job; and if the reader happens to be a Beethoven buff, or Hungarian, or reading your story twenty years from now, there may be no way of knowing what the reference refers to. "They had the blindingly blond, in-your-face exuberance of the Dixie Chicks" will convey the sense even for someone who doesn't watch country music cable. Likewise, "She was as beautiful as Theda Bara" may not mean much to you, whereas if I say, "She had the saucer eyes and satin hair of Theda Bara," the comparison will "show," and you'll get it, close enough.

The Active Voice

If your prose is to be vigorous as well as vivid, if your characters are to "come to life," you must make use of the active voice. The active voice occurs when the subject of a sentence performs the action described by the verb of that sentence: *She spilled the milk*. When the passive voice is used, the object of the active verb becomes the subject of the passive verb: *The milk was spilled by her*. The subject is acted upon rather than acting, and the effect is to weaken the prose and to distance the reader from the action.

The passive voice does have an important place in fiction, precisely because it expresses a sense that the character is being acted upon. If a prison guard is kicking the hero, then *I was slammed into the wall; I was struck blindingly from behind and forced to the floor* appropriately carries the sense of his helplessness.

In general, however, you should seek to use the active voice in all prose and to use the passive only when the actor is unknown or insignificant or when you want to achieve special stylistic effects like the one above.

But there is one other common grammatical construction that is *in effect* passive and can distance the reader from a sense of immediate experience. The verbs that we learn in school to call *linking verbs* are effectively passive because verbs with auxiliaries suggest an indefinite time and are never as sharply focused as active verbs. (Further editing his example cited earlier, Gardner contrasts the phrase "two snakes were fighting" with the improved "two snakes fought," which pinpoints a specific moment; he further suggests substitution of active verbs, as in "two snakes whipped and lashed, striking at each other.")

Linking verbs also invite complements that tend to be generalized or judgmental: *Her hair* looked *beautiful. He* was *very happy. The room* seemed *expensively furnished. They* became *morose.* Let her hair bounce, tumble, cascade, or swing; we'll see better. Let him laugh, leap, cry, or hug a tree; we'll experience his joy.

The following is a passage with very little action, nevertheless made vital by the use of active verbs:

At Mixt she neither drinks nor eats. Each of the sisters furtively stares at her as she tranquilly sits in post-Communion meditation with her hands immersed in her habit. *Lectio* has been halted for the morning, so there is only the Great Silence and the tinks of cutlery, but handsigns are being traded as the sisters lard their hunks of bread or fold and ring their dinner napkins. When the prioress stands, all rise up with her for the blessing, and then Sister Aimee gives Mariette the handsigns. *You, infirmary.*

Ron Hansen, *Mariette in Ecstasy*

Here, though the convent meal is silent and action is minimal, a number of the verbs suggest suppressed power: *stares, sits, lard, fold, ring, stands, rise, gives.*

Compare the first passage about Debbie on page 24 with the second of the rewrites on page 25. In the generalized original we have *was stubborn, was doing things, was executive, was able, was indifferent.* Apart from the compound verb *was doing,* all these are linking verbs. In the rewrite the characters *brought, called, threw, knelt, retrieved, replaced, said, reminded, justified, toured, spent,* and *curled up.* What energetic people! The rewrite contains two linking verbs: Mr. Strum *was stockholder* and *was proud;* these properly represent static states, a position and an attitude.

One beneficial side effect of active verbs is that they tend to call forth significant details. If you say "she was shocked," you are telling us; but if you are to show us that she was shocked through an action, you are likely to have to search for an image as well. "She clenched the arm of the chair so hard that her knuckles whitened." *Clenched* and *whitened* actively suggest shock, and at the same time we see her knuckles on the arm of the chair.

On Active Verbs

A general verb creates a general impression, but a precise, active verb conveys the exact picture in the reader's mind. For example:

General	Specific
walk	Does the waiter *scurry* or *amble*?
yell	Does the coach *demand* or *bellow*?
swim	Does the child *splash* or *glide*?
climb	Does the hiker *stumble up the hill* or *stride*?

To be is the most common of the linking verbs and also the most overused, but all the linking verbs invite generalization and distance. *To feel, to seem, to look, to appear, to experience, to express, to show, to demonstrate, to convey, to display*—all these suggest in fiction that the character is being acted upon or observed by someone rather than doing something. She felt *happy/sad/amused/ mortified* does not convince us. We want to see her and infer her emotion for ourselves. *He very clearly conveyed his displeasure*. It isn't clear to us. How did he convey it? To whom?

Linking verbs, like the passive voice, can appropriately convey a sense of passivity or helplessness when that is the desired effect. Notice that in the passage by Mann quoted earlier in this chapter, where Felix Krull is momentarily stunned by the sight of the food before him, linking verbs are used: *It was a narrow room, there were rows and rows*, while all the colors and shapes buffet his senses. Only as he gradually recovers can he *stand, breathe, speak*, and eventually *grab*.

I don't mean to suggest that as an author you should analyze your grammar as you go along. Most word choice is instinctive, and instinct is often the best guide. However, I do mean to suggest that you should be aware of the vigor and variety of available verbs, and that if a passage lacks energy, it may be because your instinct has let you down. How often *are* subjects portrayed in some condition or acted *upon*, when they could more forcefully *do*?

A note of caution about active verbs: Make sparing use of what John Ruskin called the "pathetic fallacy"—the attributing of human emotions to natural and man-made objects. Even a description of a static scene can be invigorated if the houses *stand*, the streets *wander*, and the trees *bend*. But if the houses *frown*, the streets *stagger drunkenly*, and the trees *weep*, we will feel more strain than energy in the writing.

Prose Rhythm

Novelists and short-story writers are not under the same obligation as poets to reinforce sense with sound. In prose, on the whole, the rhythm is all right if it isn't clearly wrong. But it can be wrong if, for example, the cadence contradicts the meaning; on the other hand, rhythm can greatly enhance the meaning if it is sensitively used.

> The river moved slowly. It seemed sluggish. The surface lay flat. Birds circled lazily overhead. Jon's boat slipped forward.

In this extreme example, the short, clipped sentences and their parallel structures—subject, verb, modifier—work against the sense of slow, flowing movement. The rhythm could be effective if the character whose eyes we're using is not appreciating or sharing the calm; otherwise it needs recasting.

> The surface lay flat on the sluggish, slow-moving river, and the birds circled lazily overhead as Jon's boat slipped forward.

There is nothing very striking about the rhythm of this version, but at least it moves forward without obstructing the flow of the river.

The first impression I had as I stopped in the doorway of the immense City Room was of extreme rush and bustle, with the reporters moving rapidly back and forth in the long aisles in order to shove their copy at each other or making frantic gestures as they shouted into their many telephones.

This long and leisurely sentence cannot possibly provide a sense of rush and bustle. The phrases need to move as fast as the reporters; the verbiage must be pared down because it slows them down.

I stopped in the doorway. The City Room was immense, reporters rushing down the aisles, shoving copy at each other, bustling back again, flinging gestures, shouting into telephones.

The poet Rolfe Humphries remarked that "*very* is the least very word in the language." It is frequently true that adverbs expressing emphasis or suddenness—*extremely, rapidly, suddenly, phenomenally, quickly, immediately, instantly, definitely, terribly, awfully*—slow the sentence down so as to dilute the force of the intended meaning. "'It's a very nice day,'" said Humphries, "is not as nice a day as 'It's a day!'" Likewise, "They stopped very abruptly" is not as abrupt as "They stopped."

Just as action and character can find an echo in prose rhythm, so it is possible to help us experience a character's emotions and attitudes through control of the starts and stops of prose tempo. In the following passage from *Persuasion*, Jane Austen combines generalization, passive verbs, and a staccato speech pattern to produce a kind of breathless blindness in the heroine.

…[A] thousand feelings rushed on Anne, of which this was the most consoling, that it would soon be over. And it was soon over. In two minutes after Charles's preparation, the others appeared; they were in the drawing room. Her eye half met Captain Wentworth's, a bow, a courtesy passed; she heard his voice; he talked to Mary, said all that was right, said something to the Miss Musgroves, enough to mark an easy footing; the room seemed full, full of persons and voices, but a few minutes ended it.

The opening paragraph of the Stuart Dybek story "We Didn't" (included at the end of this chapter) consists of several sentences, all of which open with the phrase "we didn't," followed by a prepositional phrase identifying a place where the young couple did not consummate their relationship. The repetition reveals the narrator's frustrations and introduces the complexities of the relationship described.

Often, an abrupt change in the prose rhythm will signal a discovery or change in mood; such a shift can also reinforce a contrast in characters, actions, and attitudes. In this passage from Frederick Busch's short story "Company," a woman whose movements are relatively confined watches her husband move, stop, and move again.

Every day did not start with Vince awake that early, dressing in the dark, moving with whispery sounds down the stairs and through the kitchen, out into the autumn morning while groundfog lay on the milkweed burst open and on the stumps of harvested corn. But enough of them did.

I went to the bedroom window to watch him hunt in a business suit.

He moved with his feet in the slowly stirring fog, moving slowly himself with the rifle held across his body and his shoulders stiff. Then he stopped in a frozen watch for woodchucks. His stillness made the fog look faster as it blew across our field behind the barn. Vince stood. He waited for something to shoot. I went back to bed and lay between our covers again. I heard the bolt click. I heard the unemphatic shot, and then the second one, and after a while his feet on the porch, and soon the rush of water, the rattle of the pots on top of the stove, and later his feet again, and the car starting up as he left for work an hour before he had to.

The long opening sentence is arranged in a series of short phrases to move Vince forward. By contrast, "But enough of them did" comes abruptly, its abruptness as well as the sense of the words suggesting the woman's alienation. When Vince starts off again more slowly, the repetition of "moved, slowly stirring, moving slowly," slows down the sentence to match his strides. "Vince stood" again stills him, but the author also needs to convey that Vince stands for a long time, waiting, so we have the repetitions "he stopped, his stillness, Vince stood, he waited." As his activity speeds up again, the tempo of the prose speeds up with another series of short phrases, of which only the last is drawn out with a dependent clause, "as he left for work an hour before he had to," so that we feel the retreat of the car in the distance. Notice that Busch chooses the phrase "the rush of water," not the flow or splash of water, and how the word *rush* also points to Vince's actions. Here, meaning reinforces a tempo that, in turn, reinforces meaning. (An added bonus is that variety in sentence lengths and rhythms helps to hold readers' attention.)

"The Things They Carried" by Tim O'Brien demonstrates a range of rhythms with a rich variation of effects. Here is one example:

The things they carried were largely determined by necessity. Among the necessities or near-necessities were P-38 can openers, pocket knives, heat tabs, wristwatches, dog tags, mosquito repellent, chewing gum, candy, cigarettes, salt tablets, packets of Kool-Aid, lighters, matches, sewing kits, Military Payment Certificates, C rations, and two or three canteens of water. Together, these items weighed between 15 and 20 pounds....

In this passage, the piling of items one on the other has the effect of loading the men down and at the same time increasingly suggests the rhythm of their marching as they "hump" their stuff. Similar lists through the story create a rhythmic thread, while variations and stoppages underlie shifts of emotion and sudden crises.

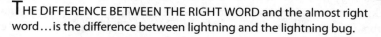

THE DIFFERENCE BETWEEN THE RIGHT WORD and the almost right word...is the difference between lightning and the lightning bug.

MARK TWAIN

Mechanics

Significant detail, the active voice, and prose rhythm are techniques for achieving the sensuous in fiction, means of helping the reader "sink into the dream" of the story, in John Gardner's phrase. Yet no technique is of much use if the reader's eye is wrenched back to the surface by misspellings or grammatical errors, for once the reader has been startled out of the story's "vivid and continuous dream," that reader may not return.

Spelling, grammar, paragraphing, and punctuation are a kind of magic; their purpose is to be invisible. If the sleight of hand works, we will not notice a comma or a quotation mark but will translate each instantly into a pause or an awareness of voice; we will not focus on the individual letters of a word but extract its sense whole. When the mechanics are incorrectly used, the trick is revealed and the magic fails; the reader's focus is shifted from the story to its surface. The reader is irritated at the author, and of all the emotions the reader is willing to experience, irritation at the author is not one.

There is no intrinsic virtue in standardized mechanics, and you can depart from them whenever you produce a result that adequately compensates for a distracting effect. But only then. Poor mechanics signal amateurism to an editor and suggest that the story itself may be flawed. Unlike the techniques of narrative, the rules of spelling, grammar, and punctuation can be coldly learned anywhere in the English-speaking world—and they should be learned by anyone who aspires to write.

We Didn't

STUART DYBEK

We did it in front of the mirror
And in the light. We did it in darkness,
In water, and in the high grass.

Yehuda Amichai, "We Did It"

We didn't in the light; we didn't in darkness. We didn't in the fresh-cut summer grass or in the mounds of autumn leaves or on the snow where moonlight threw down our shadows. We didn't in your room on the canopy bed you slept in, the bed you'd slept in as a child, or in the backseat of my father's rusted Rambler, which smelled of the smoked chubs and kielbasa he delivered on weekends from my uncle Vincent's meat market. We didn't in your mother's Buick Eight, where a rosary twined the rearview mirror like a beaded, black snake with silver, cruciform fangs.

At the dead end of our lovers' lane—a side street of abandoned factories—where I perfected the pinch that springs open a bra; behind the lilac bushes in Marquette Park, where you first touched me through my jeans and your nipples, swollen against transparent cotton, seemed the shade of lilacs; in the balcony of the now defunct Clark Theater, where I wiped popcorn salt from my palms and slid them up your thighs and you whispered, "I feel like Doris Day is watching us," we didn't.

How adept we were at fumbling, how perfectly mistimed our timing, how utterly we confused energy with ecstasy.

Remember that night becalmed by heat, and the two of us, fused by sweat, trembling as if a wind from outer space that only we could feel was gusting across Oak Street Beach? Entwined in your faded Navajo blanket, we lay soul-kissing until you wept with wanting.

We'd been kissing all day—all summer—kisses tasting of different shades of lip gloss and too many Cokes. The lake had turned hot pink, rose rapture, pearl amethyst with dusk, then washed in night black with a ruff of silver foam. Beyond a momentary horizon, silent bolts of heat lightning throbbed, perhaps setting barns on fire somewhere in Indiana. The beach that had been so crowded was deserted as if there was a curfew. Only the bodies of lovers remained, visible in lightning flashes, scattered like the fallen on a battlefield, a few of them moaning, waiting for the gulls to pick them clean.

On my fingers your slick scent mixed with the coconut musk of the suntan lotion we'd repeatedly smeared over each other's bodies. When your bikini top fell away, my hands caught your breasts, memorizing their delicate weight, my palms cupped as if bringing water to parched lips.

Along the Gold Coast, high-rises began to glow, window added to window, against the dark. In every lighted bedroom, couples home from work were stripping off their business suits, falling to the bed, and doing it. They did it before mirrors and pressed against the glass in streaming shower stalls; they did it against walls and on the furniture in ways that required previously unimagined gymnastics, which they invented on the spot. They did it in honor of man and woman, in honor of beast, in honor of God. They did it because they'd been released, because they were home free, alive, and private, because they couldn't wait any longer, couldn't wait for the appointed hour, for the right time or temperature, couldn't wait for the future, for Messiahs, for peace on earth and justice for all. They did it because of the Bomb, because of pollution, because of the Four Horsemen of the Apocalypse, because extinction might be just a blink away. They did it because it was Friday night. It was Friday night and somewhere delirious music was playing—flutter-tongued flutes, muted trumpets meowing like cats in heat, feverish plucking and twanging, tom-toms, congas, and gongs all pounding the same pulsebeat.

I stripped your bikini bottom down the skinny rails of your legs, and you tugged my swimsuit past my tan. Swimsuits at our ankles, we kicked like swimmers to free our legs, almost expecting a tide to wash over us the way the tide rushes in on Burt Lancaster and Deborah Kerr in *From Here to Eternity*—a love scene so famous that although neither of us had seen the movie, our bodies assumed the exact position of movie stars on the sand and you whispered to me softly, "I'm afraid of getting pregnant," and I whispered back, "Don't worry, I have protection," then, still kissing you, felt for my discarded cutoffs and the wallet in which for the last several months I had carried a Trojan as if it was a talisman. Still kissing, I tore its flattened, dried-out wrapper, and it sprang through my fingers like a spring from a clock and dropped to the sand between our legs. My hands were shaking. In a panic, I groped for it, found it, tried to dust it off, tried as Burt Lancaster never had to, to slip it on without breaking the mood, felt the grains of sand inside it, a throb of lightning, and the Great Lake behind us became, for all practical purposes, the Pacific, and your skin tasted of salt and to the insistent question that my hips were asking your body answered yes, your thighs opened like wings from my waist as we surfaced panting from a kiss that left you pleading *Oh, Christ yes, a yes* gasped sharply as a cry of pain so that for a moment I thought that we *were* already doing it and that somehow I had missed the instant when I entered you, entered you in the bloodless way in which a young man discards his own virginity, entered you as if passing through a gateway into the rest of my life, into a life as I wanted it to be lived *yes* but Oh then I realized that we were still floundering unconnected in the slick between us and there was sand in the Trojan as we slammed together still feeling for that perfect fit, still in the *Here* groping for an *Eternity* that was only a fine adjustment away, just a millimeter to the left or a fraction of an inch farther south though with all the adjusting the sandy Trojan was slipping off and then it was gone but *yes* you kept repeating although your head was shaking *no-not-quite-almost* and our hearts were going like mad and you said, *Yes. Yes wait…Stop!*

"What?" I asked, still futilely thrusting as if I hadn't quite heard you.

"Oh. God!" You gasped, pushing yourself up. "What's coming?"

"Gin, what's the matter?" I asked, confused, and then the beam of a spotlight swept over us and I glanced into its blinding eye.

All around us lights were coming, speeding across the sand. Blinking blindness away, I rolled from your body to my knees, feeling utterly defenseless in the way that only nakedness can leave one feeling. Headlights bounded toward us, spotlights crisscrossing, blue dome lights revolving as squad cars converged. I could see other lovers, caught in the beams, fleeing bare-assed through the litter of garbage that daytime hordes had left behind and that night had deceptively concealed. You were crying, clutching the Navajo blanket to your breasts with one hand and clawing for your bikini with the other, and I was trying to calm your terror with reassuring phrases such as "Holy shit! I don't fucking believe this!"

Swerving and fishtailing in the sand, police calls pouring from their radios, the squad cars were on us, and then they were by us while we struggled to pull on our clothes.

They braked at the water's edge, and cops slammed out, brandishing huge flashlights, their beams deflecting over the dark water. Beyond the darting of those beams, the far-off throbs of lightning seemed faint by comparison.

"Over there, goddamn it!" one of them hollered, and two cops sloshed out into the shallow water without even pausing to kick off their shoes, huffing aloud for breath, their leather cartridge belts creaking against their bellies.

"Grab the sonofabitch! It ain't gonna bite!" one of them yelled, then they came sloshing back to shore with a body slung between them.

It was a woman—young, naked, her body limp and bluish beneath the play of flashlight beams. They set her on the sand just past the ring of drying, washed-up alewives. Her face was almost totally concealed by her hair. Her hair was brown and tangled in a way that even wind or sleep can't tangle hair, tangled as if it had absorbed the ripples of water—thick strands, slimy looking like dead seaweed.

"She's been in there awhile, that's for sure," a cop with a beer belly said to a younger, crew-cut cop, who had knelt beside the body and removed his hat as if he might be considering the kiss of life.

The crew-cut officer brushed the hair away from her face, and the flashlight beams settled there. Her eyes were closed. A bruise or a birthmark stained the side of one eye. Her features appeared swollen, her lower lip protruding as if she was pouting.

An ambulance siren echoed across the sand, its revolving red light rapidly approaching.

"Might as well take their sweet-ass time," the beer-bellied cop said.

We had joined the circle of police surrounding the drowned woman almost without realizing that we had. You were back in your bikini, robed in the Navajo blanket, and I had slipped on my cutoffs, my underwear dangling out of a back pocket.

Their flashlight beams explored her body, causing its whiteness to gleam. Her breasts were floppy; her nipples looked shriveled. Her belly appeared inflated by gallons of water. For a moment, a beam focused on her mound of pubic hair, which was overlapped by the swell of her belly, and then moved almost shyly away down her legs, and the cops all glanced at us—at you, especially—above their lights, and you hugged your blanket closer as if they might confiscate it as evidence or to use as a shroud.

When the ambulance pulled up, one of the black attendants immediately put a stethoscope to the drowned woman's swollen belly and announced, "Drowned the baby, too."

Without saying anything, we turned from the group, as unconsciously as we'd joined them, and walked off across the sand, stopping only long enough at the spot where we had lain together like lovers, in order to stuff the rest of our gear into a beach bag, to gather our shoes, and for me to find my wallet and kick sand over the forlorn, deflated Trojan that you pretended not to notice. I was grateful for that.

Behind us, the police were snapping photos, flashbulbs throbbing like lightning flashes, and the lightning itself, still distant but moving in closer, rumbling audibly now, driving a lake wind before it so that gusts of sand tingled against the metal sides of the ambulance.

Squinting, we walked toward the lighted windows of the Gold Coast, while the shadows of gapers attracted by the whirling emergency lights hurried past us toward the shore.

"What happened? What's going on?" they asked without waiting for an answer, and we didn't offer one, just continued walking silently in the dark.

It was only later that we talked about it, and once we began talking about the drowned woman it seemed we couldn't stop.

"She was pregnant," you said. "I mean, I don't want to sound morbid, but I can't help thinking how the whole time we were, we almost—you know—there was this poor, dead woman and her unborn child washing in and out behind us."

"It's not like we could have done anything for her even if we had known she was there."

"But what if we *had* found her? What if after we had—you know," you said, your eyes glancing away from mine and your voice tailing into a whisper, "what if after we did it, we went for a night swim and found her in the water?"

"But, Gin, we didn't," I tried to reason, though it was no more a matter of reason than anything else between us had ever been.

It began to seem as if each time we went somewhere to make out—on the back porch of your half-deaf, whiskery Italian grandmother, who sat in the front of the apartment cackling at *I Love Lucy* reruns; or in your girlfriend Tina's basement rec room when her parents were away on bowling league nights and Tina was upstairs with her current crush, Brad; or way off in the burbs, at the Giant Twin Drive-In during the weekend they called Elvis Fest—the drowned woman was with us.

We would kiss, your mouth would open, and when your tongue flicked repeatedly after mine, I would unbutton the first button of your blouse, revealing the beauty spot at the base of your throat, which matched a smaller spot I loved above a corner of your lips, and then the second button, which opened on a delicate gold cross—which I had always tried to regard as merely a fashion statement—dangling above the cleft of your breasts. The third button exposed the lacy swell of your bra, and I would slide my hand over the patterned mesh, feeling for the firmness of your nipple rising to my fingertip, but you would pull slightly away, and behind your rapid breath your kiss would grow distant, and I would kiss harder, trying to lure you back from wherever you had gone, and finally, holding you as if only consoling a friend, I'd ask, "What are you thinking?" although of course I knew.

"I don't want to think about her but I can't help it. I mean, it seems like some kind of weird omen or something, you know?"

"No, I don't know," I said. "It was just a coincidence."

"Maybe if she'd been farther away down the beach, but she was so close to us. A good wave could have washed her up right beside us."

"Great, then we could have had a ménage à trois."

"Gross! I don't believe you just said that! Just because you said it in French doesn't make it less disgusting."

"You're driving me to it. Come on, Gin, I'm sorry," I said. "I was just making a dumb joke to get a little different perspective on things."

"What's so goddamn funny about a woman who drowned herself and her baby?"

"We don't even know for sure she did."

"Yeah, right, it was just an accident. Like she just happened to be going for a walk pregnant and naked, and she fell in."

"She could have been on a sailboat or something. Accidents happen; so do murders."

"Oh, like murder makes it less horrible? Don't think that hasn't occurred to me. Maybe the bastard who knocked her up killed her, huh?"

"How should I know? You're the one who says you don't want to talk about it and then gets obsessed with all kinds of theories and scenarios. Why are we arguing about a woman we don't even know, who doesn't have the slightest thing to do with us?"

"I *do* know about her," you said. "I dream about her."

"You dream about her?" I repeated, surprised. "Dreams you remember?"

"Sometimes they wake me up. In one I'm at my *nonna's* cottage in Michigan, swimming for a raft that keeps drifting farther away, until I'm too tired to turn back. Then I notice there's a naked person sunning on the raft and start yelling, 'Help!' and she looks up and offers me a hand, but I'm too afraid to take it even though I'm drowning because it's her."

"God! Gin, that's creepy."

"I dreamed you and I are at the beach and you bring us a couple hot dogs but forget the mustard, so you have to go all the way back to the stand for it."

"Hot dogs, no mustard—a little too Freudian, isn't it?"

"Honest to God, I dreamed it. You go back for mustard and I'm wondering why you're gone so long, then a woman screams that a kid has drowned and everyone stampedes for the water. I'm swept in by the mob and forced under, and I think, This is it, I'm going to drown, but I'm able to hold my breath longer than could ever be possible. It feels like a flying dream—flying under water—and then I see this baby down there flying, too, and realize it's the kid everyone thinks has drowned, but he's no more drowned than I am. He looks like Cupid or one of those baby angels that cluster around the face of God."

"Pretty weird. What do you think all the symbols mean?—hot dogs, water, drowning..."

"It means the baby who drowned inside her that night was a love child—a boy—and his soul was released there to wander through the water."

"You don't really believe that?"

We argued about the interpretation of dreams, about whether dreams are symbolic or psychic, prophetic or just plain nonsense, until you said, "Look, Dr. Freud, you can believe what you want about your dreams, but keep your nose out of mine, okay?"

We argued about the drowned woman, about whether her death was a suicide or a murder, about whether her appearance that night was an omen or a coincidence which, you argued, is what an omen is anyway: a coincidence that means something. By the end of summer, even if we were no longer arguing about the woman, we had acquired the habit of arguing about everything else. What was better: dogs or cats, rock or jazz, Cubs or Sox, tacos or egg rolls, right or left, night or day?—we could argue about anything.

It no longer required arguing or necking to summon the drowned woman; everywhere we went she surfaced by her own volition: at Rocky's Italian Beef, at Lindo Mexico, at the House of Dong, our favorite Chinese restaurant, a place we still frequented because when we'd first started seeing each other they had let us sit and talk until late over tiny cups of jasmine tea and broken fortune cookies. We would always kid about going there. "Are you in the mood for Dong tonight?" I'd whisper conspiratorially. It was a dopey joke, meant for you to roll your eyes at its repeated dopiness. Back then, in winter, if one of us ordered the garlic shrimp we would both be sure to eat them so that later our mouths tasted the same when we kissed.

Even when she wasn't mentioned, she was there with her drowned body—so dumpy next to yours—and her sad breasts, with their wrinkled nipples and sour milk—so saggy beside yours, which were still budding—with her swollen belly and her pubic bush colorless in the glare of electric light, with her tangled, slimy hair and her pouting, placid face—so lifeless beside yours—and her skin a pallid white, lightning-flash white, flash-bulb white, a whiteness that couldn't be duplicated in daylight—how I'd come to hate that pallor, so cold beside the flush of your skin.

There wasn't a particular night when we finally broke up, just as there wasn't a particular night when we began going together, but it was a night in fall when I guessed that it was over. We were parked in the Rambler at the dead end of the street of factories that had been our lovers' lane, listening to a drizzle of rain and dry leaves sprinkle the hood. As always, rain revitalized the smells of smoked fish and kielbasa in the upholstery. The radio was on too low to hear, the windshield wipers swished at intervals as if we were driving, and the windows were steamed as if we'd been making out. But we'd been arguing, as usual, this time about a woman poet who had committed suicide, whose work you were reading. We were sitting, no longer talking or touching, and I remember thinking that I didn't want to argue with you anymore. I didn't want to sit like this in hurt silence; I wanted to talk excitedly all night as we once had. I wanted to find some way that wasn't corny sounding to tell you how much fun I'd had in your company, how much knowing you had meant to me, and how I had suddenly realized that I'd been so intent on becoming lovers that I'd overlooked how close we'd been as friends. I wanted you to like me again.

"It's sad," I started to say, meaning that I was sorry we had reached the point of silence, but before I could continue you challenged the statement.

"What makes you so sure it's sad?"

"What do you mean, what makes me so sure?" I asked, confused by your question.

You looked at me as if what was sad was that I would never understand. "For all either one of us knows," you said, "death could have been her triumph!"

Maybe when it really ended was the night I felt we had just reached the beginning, that one time on the beach in the summer when our bodies rammed so desperately together that for a moment I thought we did it, and maybe in our hearts we did, although for me, then, doing it in one's heart didn't quite count. If it did, I supposed we'd all be Casanovas.

We rode home together on the El train that night, and I felt sick and defeated in a way I was embarrassed to mention. Our mute reflections emerged like negative exposures on the dark, greasy window of the train. Lightning branched over the city, and when the train entered the subway tunnel, the lights inside flickered as if the power was disrupted, though the train continued rocketing beneath the Loop.

When the train emerged again we were on the South Side of the city and it was pouring, a deluge as if the sky had opened to drown the innocent and guilty alike. We hurried from the El station to your house, holding the Navajo blanket over our heads until, soaked, it collapsed. In the dripping doorway of your apartment building, we said good night. You were shivering. Your bikini top showed through the thin blouse plastered to your skin. I swept the wet hair away from your face and kissed you lightly on the lips, then you turned and went inside. I stepped into the rain, and you came back out, calling after me.

"What?" I asked, feeling a surge of gladness to be summoned back into the doorway with you.

"Want an umbrella?"

I didn't. The downpour was letting up. It felt better to walk back to the station feeling the rain rinse the sand out of my hair, off my legs, until the only places where I could still feel its grit were in the crotch of my cutoffs and each squish of my shoes. A block down the street, I passed a pair of jockey shorts lying in a puddle and realized they were mine, dropped from my back pocket as we ran to your house. I left them behind, wondering if you'd see them and recognize them the next day.

By the time I had climbed the stairs back to the El platform, the rain had stopped. Your scent still hadn't washed from my fingers. The station—the entire city it seemed—dripped and steamed. The summer sound of crickets and nighthawks echoed from the drenched neighborhood. Alone, I could admit how sick I felt. For you, it was a night that would haunt your dreams. For me, it was another night when I waited, swollen and aching, for what I had secretly nicknamed the Blue Ball Express.

Literally lovesick, groaning inwardly with each lurch of the train and worried that I was damaged for good, I peered out at the passing yellow-lit stations, where lonely men stood posted before giant advertisements, pictures of glamorous models defaced by graffiti—the same old scrawled insults and pleas: fuck you, eat me. At this late hour the world seemed given over to men without women, men waiting in abject patience for something indeterminate, the way I waited for our next times. I avoided their eyes so that they wouldn't see the pity in mine, pity for them because I'd just been with you, your scent was still on my hands, and there seemed to be so much future ahead.

For me it was another night like that, and by the time I reached my stop I knew I would be feeling better, recovered enough to walk the dark street home making up poems of longing that I never wrote down. I was the D. H. Lawrence of not doing it, the voice of all the would-be lovers who ached and squirmed. From our contortions in doorways, on stairwells, and in the bucket seats of cars we could have composed a Kama Sutra of interrupted bliss. It must have been that night when I recalled all the other times of walking home after seeing you, so that it seemed as if I was falling into step behind a parade of my former selves—myself walking home on the night we first kissed, myself on the night when I unbuttoned your blouse and kissed your breasts, myself on the night when I lifted your skirt above your thighs and dropped to my knees— each succeeding self another step closer to that irrevocable moment for which our lives seemed poised.

But we didn't, not in the moonlight, or by the phosphorescent lanterns of lightning bugs in your back yard, not beneath the constellations we couldn't see, let alone decipher, or in the dark glow that replaced the real darkness of night, a darkness already stolen from us, not with the skyline rising behind us while a city gradually decayed, not in the heat of summer while a Cold War raged, despite the freedom of youth and the license of first love—because of fate, karma, luck, what does it matter?—we made not doing it a wonder, and yet we didn't, we didn't, we never did.

Goal 666

STACEY RICHTER

We must love nature, and we must rape nature for Satan! What would daylight be without the night? What would a clearing be without the woods? All your fairy dust, all your little white Christmas lights that twinkle, your Stardust Woman on the lite rock radio station—it would all be nothing without the dark and heavy elements of Doom/Black Metal music. When I'm onstage I feel aggression, power, rage—the everlasting lust for domination! The other side is the feminine side, the soft and pink parts that must also be cherished, as the moon is cherished, but we must remember this: we are not of the light. We are the harbingers. We are Lords of Sludge, the most revered Doom/Classical Goth Metal band in Washington State!

The Vikings did nothing but invade! Those furcovered Goths were crazy and ultimate, the baddest of ass. When a Viking died he went to Valhalla, an indoor heaven where dead warriors engaged in perpetual battle!

The northern tradition continues still, with hellish great Scandinavian metal bands like Dissection, Dark Tranquillity, Exhumation, and Wizards of Ooze playing some of the most malevolent tunes to which Lord Satan ever lifted a pointed ear! I have the deepest reverence for the Norderland tradition, which was why I was honored to join Lords of Sludge, a Swedish heavy metal band that lost their lead singer when he ran off to become a hermit. He's practicing asceticism in the deepest forest! Their loss, my gain—since I'd been perfecting my top-secret method of Satanic throat singing and was finally ready to be a part of a great Doom/Black Metal band like Lords of Sludge. I'd been known as a tenor in church choir, but by wedging a ping-pong ball behind my teeth I perfected a means of producing a low rumble in the back of my throat that was evil in the extreme. Black Metal is spirit and power!

The three Swedish lads came from the cold land town of Uppsala, and were covered with tattoos of screaming skulls and flaming crosses—pussying great! That was my first impression. Like their Viking ancestors they were ultrapale with fierce hanks of hair falling in dirty curtains around their faces. I thought, These are manly men! and after the audition we all slapped each other on the backs and had a hearty laugh over the throbbing music—punctuated by light, lilting passages of classical acoustic guitar—that we would produce for the Dark Lord, who was a die-hard metal fan as every die-hard metal fan knows. Those crazy Swedes! That first night they introduced me to the tradition of the sauna, which they'd built of stone and wood in the back of the house they'd rented and painted entirely black, inside and out. After we were sufficiently heated, Anders, the lead guitarist, a strapping Swedish man with mega-antisocial facial tattoos and a wide, hairless chest, led us naked and sweating into the lush, snowy woods beyond the house. We rolled our bare, hot bodies in the fresh winter snow—ah nature, we must love nature and rape it for Satan—we leapt around like satyrs scouring the woods for wayward virgins. Men! We were naked men, three Swedish and one American.

After that night we had a masculine bond, so I was slow to notice details I might have caught earlier. Though Anders had mega-fierce tattoos and Stefan, the small but muscular drummer, had huge, furry sideburns creeping across his cheeks, and Max had the extremely satanic name of Max—there was something not right about these men. There was an air of innocence to them. Despite the fiery badness of The Lords, and their lusty embrace of songs I had written, these guys were scrupulous about washing their hands after using the bathroom. They returned all their phone calls promptly and refrained from resting their forearms on the dinner table. Going for a meal with these guys was like going to a tea party: napkin on the lap, chewing with the mouth closed, salad fork, dessert spoon, and so on.

The contagion was severe. Before I knew it I was uttering phrases like, "Would you mind turning up the treble in my monitor just a smidgen?" Our leader, Anders, would bound into practice, right on time, his strong Nordic features aglow, so filled with vitality that the little spiral tattoo on his cheek seemed to twirl. Ten minutes later, the two of us were deep in a conversation (about literacy, Sweden has an amazing 99 percent rate). The other two maniacs were listening attentively, nodding and occasionally throwing in a pertinent fact (socialized day care). No one was even smoking and I had totally forgotten about Goal 666 (for our Mexican *hermanos*, Meta Numero Seis, Seis, Seis): Corrupt the World/Spread the Metal!!!

Maniacs, brothers, Vikings: lend me your hellishly buzzing ears. We must labor with guitar and anvil to spread the fire of pure heavy metal! They say entropy is inevitable but we must still toil to ensure the decay progresses! In my own life, only constant vigilance has been able to halt the creep of flowering vines up the balcony of my meager studio apartment. Only a daily regimen of Satanic throat-singing and a pentagram drawn with chicken blood on my doorstep has kept kittens from being born in the backseat of my Camaro, butterflies from deciding my workplace was a bitchin' stop on their migration route, and my neighbor Maria from constantly bringing me hot dishes covered with cloth napkins. My sister always tells me I am a sweetheart, but with effort I find I am not a sweetheart. If I didn't take care, my voice would slip back up to a clear, tenor register and I might find myself humming, on a warm spring day, snatches of show tunes. *I Feel Pretty!* Yet, I've been able to avert the light so that die-hard blacking metal still burns on in the many hatred thrashing parts of my soul! We must not allow beauty to exist without corruption. Listen all maniacs! We must not give up the fight!

Because here's what happened. One afternoon I strolled into practice (still wearing my smock from Speedy Pro, where I'm a reproduction technician) and there, beneath the flaming, Day-Glo painting of the Fallen Angel himself, stood a girl. She had short, bleached hair and a lot of bitchin' ink sticking out of her leather vest, which she wore without a shirt. Pussy is advantageous but should be ornamental in the extreme! This chick was not ornamental, was not our first groupie, because right away I noticed she was perched over a musical instrument. Hold on to your lunch. It was a synthesizer.

Of all the limp-dick instruments in the universe, the synthesizer is the most flaccid. Guys who wear lipstick play synthesizer music for horny little fairies to dance to—I don't need to tell you this. It's well known among bitchin' sons of Lucifer the foul friend and those Swedish men were well aware of this. Well aware. Anders entered the cement bunker where we practiced our art, his stringy hair swinging about his broad shoulders, and introduced me to the girl. Her name, he said, was Liv. She was from Amsterdam, where she had been a member of an experimental music collective dedicated to bringing microtonal compositions to shut-ins, the institutionalized, and old people. Liv grinned and came out from behind the synthesizer to shake my hand. She wore a short leather skirt and that tiny vest as I mentioned. Her body was tremendous, a fierce combination of soft and athletic, so stunningly proportioned that it could have popped out of a lingerie catalog, but I found her face scrunched and ugly, like a pug's. The overall effect was confusing and for a moment I found I couldn't say anything as Liv sprang behind the synthesizer and began to bang on the keys.

I don't know a lot about synthesizers, but the sounds Liv managed to hack out startled me. Instead of the floaty tones I expected, she produced muscular, ugly noises that reminded me of hooks piercing sheet metal in hell. Then, she flipped some switches and made some other sounds that were like live cats being skewered by white hot knives. Nonetheless I was repulsed, as the synthesizer itself is a sissy instrument and should never be included in a rain of dark riffs. Particularly if played by a female, whose place it is to be soft and pink and stay in her scented room, praying to the moon.

While Liv played she had a big grin plastered on her face; beside her Anders laughed and tapped his foot. They seemed to be having a wonderful time. Then, abruptly, she stopped. "Anders," she called, her odd little face bright with delight, "fetch me my valise!"

Anders obeyed, hustling across the room to grab a small satchel and dropping it at her feet.

"I have brought a gift for you," she announced. She pulled out a record and presented it to me. It was a copy of "Head Abortion," a rare single from Flayed Open, one of my favorite Swedish bands.

"Anders said you needed this. I located it in Europe!"

Liv tossed back her head and giggled, and her face softened and spread into a more human countenance. Then she and Anders began to laugh like children, or adults on drugs. I watched them and smirked, fully aware that they were trying to break down my resistance, but the dark power and spirit had made me formidable! Through a careful regimen of self-control I'd become fully immune to joy and could not be seduced by the playful laughter of my bandmates! Liv stumbled and collapsed on top of Anders. Despite the dirt, ash, and dried residue of various liquids on the floor, they began rolling around down there. I think they were having a tickle fight. Her miniskirt edged up and I glimpsed a flash of panty. The next thing I knew, Liv grabbed my leg and pulled me down.

I was beginning to think Liv might make an acceptable groupie, but she could never, ever play in our band.

At a meeting at Pepe Lou's, Anders, our trusted leader, solemnly declared Liv the newest member of Lords of Sludge. Max took the news calmly, grunting slightly and never pausing in his consumption of Tater Tots with ketchup. Max's English skills were rather poor and he rarely said anything anyway. I thought I detected a slight scowl on the face of Stefan, beneath the facial hair that had been spreading and spreading since the day we first met until it covered his entire face, from just below the eyes to the top of his collar. I found this facial hair very werewolf-like and antisocial and approved of it vigorously. As for myself, I sat silently, chewing iceberg lettuce with Russian dressing, rehearsing in my head all the reasons why Liv could not join the band and plotting a scathing delivery for my objections. But before I had a chance to actually offer them, Liv jumped up from the table and began dancing a heavy-metal victory dance, stomping her boots and flashing the double-eared sign of Satan with both hands. "Lords of Sludge," she hooted, "Lords of Sludge!" Her scrunched face turned red with enthusiasm. At the next table, an old lady began to blow a rape whistle.

Liv had a nest of hair in her armpits and I could see it well as she slid into the booth and draped her arm around the cringing crone. "What's wrong, little mother? Have I given you a fright?"

The lady shrank back with the whistle dangling from her mouth. It seemed she regarded Liv with deep suspicion. Max was laughing gleefully at this, as were Stefan and Anders, and I knew my chances of ousting Liv were fading.

"I want not to harm you," she said to the senior, "but to please you. May I kiss your cheek?"

"Don't you dare," the old lady hissed, edging away from the armpit.

"I won't kiss you then, mother. I'm from across the sea and my customs must seem strange."

"Get away," the elderly woman said, but something in her had calmed and she said it without conviction. She'd let the whistle fall back into her purse and started to nibble on her eggs. Liv removed her arm from around the woman and began to chat with her politely, hands clasped in front of her on the table. Like the Swedes, she had lovely manners, and in a few moments Liv had charmed her foe utterly. The two sat chatting softly about whatever it is women talk about; then they were exchanging phone numbers.

After a while Liv bounded back to our table, sprightly-go-lucky, bragging that she had subdued the old one. The Swedish men applauded with delight and piled their extra Tater Tots on Liv's plate. They began an animated discussion about walking clubs for the elderly in different European countries while I slumped in the corner, one lone man, fuming.

The forest is our mother, and we must destroy the forest! When I see pocked mountain slopes, clear-cut of trees, I feel virile, hulking, masterful. When I see the machines of my fellow men chewing through groves in which I played as a child, consuming glens in which I picnicked with my mother and sister when I was a boy, I feel enlarged. We are men, in charge, plowing our masculinity into the earth, and in my heart I'm gladdened those places are destroyed because then I'll never be tempted to return to the dimpled, the pink, the fluffy. A true metal head knows innocence is irretrievable.

And so, to me, it was obvious Liv's femininity would corrupt us, soften us, wash us out to shades of pastel, but I figured if I complained the guys would kick me out of the band. Then where would I be? I'd be a clerk in a copy shop without a band. I'd be another minimum-wage worker in a leather jacket popping into the convenience store on the way home to buy a twelve-pack of beer with wadded bills and a handful of change. I didn't want to leave the rock and roll life. It was just beginning to happen for us. We'd finally managed to schedule a gig, and I was looking forward to playing in front of an audience. Then there was the fact that I loved it. For me there was nothing more satisfying than our give-and-take of energy, the unselfish sharing of talent, skills, and inspiration. When everything was working right, when all of us were in harmony, it was beyond bitchin'.

I was also genuinely fond of the Swedish men and their messy hair and the sauna where we often spent the evenings. Liv began to join us in the sauna as well, and I admit I appreciated the chance to spend time next to a live, naked girl. Now and then she rubbed against me and laughed. She tugged at the towel around my waist and requested to see "the nature of my unit." Later, she and Anders traipsed off to the bedroom together while the rest of us watched television and snacked on pickled herring.

Many nights, after warming in the sauna, we'd go running naked through the woods behind the house. I knew that over the hill was a shopping mall, and next to that a plowed lot where they were putting in a parking tower, but from our vantage point it almost seemed like we were in a primeval forest. When we got tired of running we'd leap backward into the drifts and thrash about, making angels in the snow. Of course, my angel and the angels of the Swedish men were dark and brooding, fallen soldiers of Satan. Twigs, piss, and pine branches helped the effect. But Liv's angels were luminous. No matter how hard she tried to thrash out something sinister, her angels were always feathery. They seemed to float on the snow, and cupped the moonlight like a silver goblet.

"Liv," said I, "you must be a Stardust Woman. You are not of the darkness like us."

Liv laughed and made the double-eared sign of Satan in the air. "You are mistaken, Gabe [for Gabe is my name], I am quite badly bitchin'!" Her silver laughter clogged the air like bubbles. "Dark power," she sang, prancing in the snow. "Dark power to all the children!"

"No," I replied. "Look at your angels. They look real. You are full of light, Liv. You are a good witch."

"She is full of hatred!" Anders insisted, smashing a fist into his palm.

Liv looked at the two of us, then threw her head back and laughed, her short, bleached hair catching the moon-light like a piece of dandelion fluff.

"I do not think," I said, very quietly, shivering in the drifts, "that she is full of hatred."

It was a frosty night, and soon the other men fled back to the sauna. Liv, though, seemed immune to temperature.

She bounced around, licking snow off tree branches, her tiny hands clasped under her chin like a kangaroo. Kangaroos look cuddly but in fact are vicious fighters. I was freezing and my toes were turning blue but I couldn't stop watching her. I admit I sort of liked being alone with her, naked. She had a chance to take a look at the nature of my unit if she wanted, but she seemed more intent on eating snow. The unit was pretty shrunk up from the cold anyway.

Liv bounded between the pines. "I'm pollinating," She said. "I take the snow from tree to tree. I am a pollinator."

"Liv," said I, "you are a freak!"

She bounced over and poked me in the stomach. "You small turd," she whispered. "You are a turd, and I'm a turd too!"

"I beg your pardon?"

"Ha! You try to act mean, but I see what a dumpling you are!"

What an odd, odd, odd, feeling Liv gave me—for a second, when she pronounced the word "dumpling," I was overwhelmed by an urge to grab her hand and skip off into one of those red, dripping sunsets they have on seventies greeting cards. It was an electric, honeymoon feeling, full of fun and frolic and utterly devoid of evil, loathing, or resentment. It was what I feared most—that deep down, in my core of being, I harbored a little flame of light.

I've always wanted desperately to be bad. I've always wanted to be extremely evil, full of hatred. I've always wanted people to exclaim, when I walk into a room: *Look at that fellow! He is truly bad!* Instead of saying what they usually say, which is nothing, or at most *Look at that fellow, he has one of those pointy devil beards like our friend Skizz.* Skizz is not bad; Skizz is a nice guy. I've tried to be self-centered and an asshole; I've tried to follow the path of Satan; I've tried to absorb all the meager boredom and antipathy that's been thrown my way by coaches, teachers, and popular girls and radiate it back, larger, grander, and more corrosive than ever, but I have a set of reflexes I can't control. I have an overwhelming desire to help those in trouble, or to talk to a person at a party if they seem to feel out of place, or to take stray animals home and love them. But I still feel a heavy sense of rejection and ugliness around my person. No one ever talks to me at a party if I feel out of place. No one ever wants to take me home and love me.

Heathens, take heart! Remember, the Vikings sailed the seas to find fresh, new places to invade! We must push ourselves daily to be worthy of the Dark Lord! As I trudged home that dark night from the house of the Swedish men, my boots crunching through the virgin snow, I rededicated myself to the task of corruption. I made a resolution to be as bad as possible. I would take the sparkly things of this world—including Liv, especially Liv—and muddy them. I would be smelly and dirty; of the dark, like a bat.

My resolve only grew stronger as the day approached when we were scheduled to play at Hole in One, a great Metal/Doom bar that had once been a great Golf/Sports bar. We had a show on a Friday night and were very stoked to play hellish great songs dedicated to Satan! In the weeks before the gig, our practices intensified. It became more important than ever that we work together. Hey, I'm no party pooper. I stashed my hatred; I nurtured it like a coal in a bucket of peat, saving it for later, when it would be most effective. This was the time to practice our Black/Doom metal music, including hellish great songs I'd written myself, like "The Bad Watcher Watches" and "Eater of My Soul." I observed Liv's luminous blond head bob and sway during practice; I listened to her synthesizer rumble and croak, and I waited. She would get hers, I thought. I'd really give it to her.

"More melody," Liv said, perched over her keyboard like a pretty songbird. "We must make our music fiery with melody!"

The Swedish men were in complete agreement. I, too, knew that the mighty power of Scandinavian metal music came from its ability to reconcile euphony with discord. Together, under Liv's guidance, we strengthened our songs, making them more tuneful. Liv designed vigorous, bold melodies on her keyboard; they were like the beams and rough-hewn buttresses on which our songs rested. Liv and I had to work especially closely, since lyric and melody go hand in hand. The Swedish musicians devised flourishes that enriched the whole. We started practice at five P.M. and played most nights until eleven. We improved steadily. We ordered pizza. After a while, even on days when we weren't practicing, our songs stuck in my head. It was happening. The Lords were mutating from a great band into an awesome one.

I would guess the Vikings had some sort of ritual they performed before going into battle. Perhaps they danced around a block of ice, or killed a she-goat. As modern-day warriors we had our own ritual of bodily adornment and preparation that we referred to as "getting ready for the gig." This took me quite some time, and it seemed to require a similar amount of effort for the Swedish men, because when I arrived at the club, there they all sat, on time as usual, with their hair teased and lacquered into various startling arrangements. Anders's tattoos were especially dark. His hair was shiny but stringier than ever and I thought I detected a touch of mascara. Stefan had combed his facial hair downward and looked more bestial than any human I'd ever seen; Max was clad entirely in black (okay, we all were) and had polished the silver pentagram around his neck. But of us all, Liv had been the most transformed by her preparations. She wore a boned, black bra that really showed off her figure. On her feet were pink go-go boots, and she'd painted a spiderweb across her cheek that completely camouflaged her canine quality. The truth is she looked beautiful.

I was almost swayed. It occurred to me that Liv was a nice girl with a good disposition and that I might this one time show some mercy—but in my heart I knew I must be fierce! Besides, I'd already decided how to strike. From my little sister I'd learned a foolproof way of wounding girls, and so, mustering all the darkness within me, all the hostility and thrashing evil, I turned to Liv, who was sitting by her synthesizer, polishing the keys, and said, "Wow. That outfit makes you look really fat."

For a moment Liv seemed taken aback. The spiderweb across her face curved downward while she took in my blackening evil countenance, the hatred spewing from within me. She looked at me with her muddy brown eyes, directly into my smoking core.

"Oh, Gabe! You had me going for a minute! Such a kidder! You're such a lamb." The spiderweb expanded when she giggled.

Then I was onstage, standing in a pool of hot light. I held a microphone in my fist and something was feeding back through the P.A. Anders fiddled with some knobs and the room grew silent except for the creaking of my leather trousers. I felt fuzzy and confused. I shaded my eyes and looked into the audience: not a bad turnout. Maybe a hundred metal heads slumped around in front of the stage; a few skinny girls, but mostly guys with bored faces and long, clean hair and freshly laundered, ripped T-shirts. They seemed to be in various stages of drunkenness. Behind me, Stefan crouched over his drum kit like a feral animal. To my right, Anders stood with his guitar hanging in front of his hips while Max waited expectantly behind his bass. At my side stood Liv, perched over her synthesizer with an elfin sparkle in her eye.

It was silent. I was waiting for something to happen, but nothing happened. I waited to feel malicious and potent but felt light and perky instead. Then, on Liv's count we sprang to life. Max plucked out the throbbing bass line to "The Bad Watcher Watches," an extremely Satanic song—this song makes "Parricide 2" seem like a trip to the petting zoo. Anders joined in with his growling but nonetheless buoyant guitar line.

Entwined between was Liv's lilting, sinister melody, which sounded a little like a calliope in a movie about a clown who eats children.

We sounded awesome. It was like we'd been practicing together our entire lives. Every part slid into place and blended with the others, without a thought. The crowd started to churn and wind around itself. I could feel the floorboards vibrating as we played louder, harder; my Satanic throat singing was really featured in this song and I felt the cells peeling off my larynx as I struggled to sing in a deeper, more frightening register: *He watches us / The bad watcher watches us / Ooooo / He watches us / Toil from the mountaintop...*

The crowd had begun to gyrate and shake. By the second chorus, they were going totally berserk. So many heads of hair were banging in front of me that the skirt of the stage looked like a field of wheat in a windstorm. I stepped out of the lights to give the other guys a chance to take their solos. Anders began wailing on his instrument as if it were a small animal he hoped to beat to death. He leaned forward and banged his head—his hair was actually getting caught in the strings of his guitar, but he didn't slow down—he was lost in the crunch of the music and the heat of the lights and the smell of the fans sweating below us. He was playing flourishes I'd never heard *anywhere* before, much less from Anders; wild, scrubbing riffs that were nevertheless melodic and tinged with sadness. That his guitar was merely an electrified construction of wire and wood and a couple of old pickups seemed unimaginable—it was more like a fallen angel spewing out the wickedest rock and roll from the lower intestine of hell! I closed my eyes. When I opened them, Anders's fingers were bleeding all over the pick guard.

Then Stefan took a drum solo. He was like a mutant woodland creature with advanced hand-eye coordination; his sticks flew over the kit so quickly they blurred. The kids in the audience stared at him with their mouths open. Then he stopped, hands raised, perspiration gushing down his ribs. All was silent. No one in the crowd so much as hooted. Slowly he brought both hands down at once; bam. Then up and down again. Bam. He was beating a slow rhythm with all his might on the snare, only the snare. Bam, bam, bam—it was trance inducing. It was like caveman music. The crowd loved it. We all loved it.

It was time for Liv to begin her synthesizer solo. Notes as soft as petals hung in the air beside the serrated snarls of a ruthless predator dismembering her prey. Liv's head drooped as her fingers leapt across the keys, urging forth a driving, overwhelming rock and roll moment. How could I have ever called the synthesizer a pansy instrument? The crowd roiled and churned. An odd tingling consumed me as I watched them, a kind of warm numbness. As Liv pushed the tune farther into the realm of the melodious, I began to feel almost ill with a kind of unpleasant pleasure, like being tickled. Something was happening—something was grasping at me; I had a sense it was grasping all of us. I was being swept up by a breezy, harmonious wave of major chords struck with pep. Then, after a weird, underwater period where I thought I might faint, my head cleared, and I understood what was happening.

A melody issued from Liv's organ, a melody effusive and irrepressible. It was contagious. It was sweet. It was Rodgers and Hammerstein's "Happy Talk," from the musical *South Pacific*, and *I* was belting it out. A rich, dulcet tenor sprang from my throat as helplessly I found myself constructing the musical question: *You've got to have a dream! If you don't have a dream! How you gonna have a dream come true?* My mind filled with all the Carpenters songs I had loved and I thought of how I always tried, as a boy singing in the shower, to get my vowels to sound as velvety and overstuffed as Karen Carpenter's did. I couldn't help it then; a tide of pent-up joy washed over me. It was uncontrollable, it was uncool and wrong, and I was so happy. I was so happy I felt sick. It was as though all the loathing and resentment I'd been nursing at least since I was a sophomore in high school had burst like a soap bubble, had been popped and defused and dried out, and all that was left inside me was a lather of pure euphoria. I was so happy I thought I might melt.

We were of the light, bedazzling all. Liv arched over her synthesizer, singing, while the Swedes strummed joyfully along. Anders banged out sweet, chiming chords on his guitar, an expression of blank rapture on his face. Max was laughing and bobbing from his knees. We were making something lovely. Together we praised the power of creation. Below, our fans stared, openmouthed with horror. Liv lifted her fingers from the keyboard and began to do the happy talkie dance with both hands.

Binocular Vision

EDITH PEARLMAN

For his fortieth birthday my father was given a pair of binoculars. His medical colleagues teamed up on the present. He was neither a bird-watcher nor a sports fan, so the glasses just lay on his dresser like a trophy.

They didn't tempt me at first. I had already been disappointed by his ophthalmoscope, which didn't magnify a thing. (I also didn't like the coin-operated telescope on our Connecticut city's twenty-four-story building, the tallest in New England; as soon as I managed to focus on something through the telescope, my nickel ran out.) But one December afternoon, wandering in an aimless, childish way around my parents' bedroom, I picked up the binoculars, took them to a window that looked out on the street, and directed them toward a leafless tree. I saw a brown blur, so I fiddled with the wheels on the instrument. Now the tree was hyper-clear, making my eyes ache. Finally, after more fiddling, I saw the tree plain and even vaguely menacing, like my great-uncle at the last family party who had leaned so close to me that his tie swayed in front of my eyes. But when I thoughtlessly reached out to touch the tree's bark, I touched instead the windowpane.

The side window in my parents' room, like the windows of the other bedrooms in our end-of-the-row house, looked out at the second-floor apartment next door, also brick, where the Simons lived.

With the aid of the binoculars, I projected myself into the Simons' living room. Their fireplace was as dark as a cave. On the mantel crouched a humpbacked clock. In one of the two chairs flanking the hearth sat Mrs. Simon herself, her gray head bent. She was crocheting. I could not see the pattern of the work, nor the pattern on her dress, but I could see that her green chair wore a lace antimacassar and that a flared lamp on a table cast its glow on a pile of magazines. There was no television, of course—only rich show-offs had televisions then.

I went into my own bedroom. From there I inspected the Simons' dining room. An empty silver bowl occupied pride of place on the table. Perhaps Mr. Simon's colleagues had given it to him when *he* turned forty. I went into my sister's bedroom. From her window I peered at the Simons' little kitchen. Two cups and two saucers lay on the drainboard. A calendar hung on the wall, but no matter how much I fiddled with the wheels of the binoculars I could not make out the Simons' appointments.

From our last bedroom, reserved for guests, I got a dark glimpse of the Simons' big bedroom. I knew there was a small bedroom, too, for my friend Elaine lived in an identical apartment down the street. The small bedroom faced the backyard, a skimpy strip of grass and six little garages, one each for the six apartments. I would never get to see that bedroom. The room I did see had a double bed with an afghan at its foot, folded into a perfect right triangle. This application of geometry to daily life gratified my critical ten-year-old self.

During that month, which included a school vacation, I discovered that Mrs. Simon was a great tidier. Often I would find her in the living room, readjusting an antimacassar or rearranging candy in a dish or polishing the glass door of the bookcase. Serious cleaning was done once a week by a regal mulatto woman, but sometimes Mrs. Simon would stand at the kitchen sink, her stubborn profile lowered, fiercely scrubbing something. Occasionally she lay down in the bedroom. And often she disappeared. Perhaps she was talking on the telephone in the hall, a windowless place my binoculars could not penetrate. Or perhaps she was walking a few blocks to Elm Street, as most of the women in our neighborhood did most days, in order to pick up some fish and vegetables, or a library book. Once in a while I ran into Mrs. Simon on just such an errand. We were the same height—I was a tall child and she a small and somewhat bent woman—and her expression was as steely as her curls. Our eyes met, with no mediating binoculars. "Hello," I'd whisper, suddenly shy. She never answered.

In the late afternoons, Mrs. Simon got busy. She stirred pots on the stove. She set the table in the dining room. She folded the evening paper several times, this way and that, and finally laid it on the arm of Mr. Simon's chair. Again she adjusted the antimacassars and arranged the candies.

Darkness came at 4:30. From the window of our spare bedroom, reading by flashlight, I kept track of the cars returning to the six garages. A floodlight illuminated the area. When Mr. Simon's car appeared, I would close my book, switch off my flashlight, and raise my binoculars.

Mr. Simon, a tall man, would unfold from his automobile. He'd pass a hand over his gray hair, raise the door of the garage, get back into the car, and drive it into the garage. He usually sat there for a while, giving me a chance to inspect his license plate, which had three numbers and two letters. I have forgotten them all. My eyes caressed the curve of his car trunk. I noticed the branch caught on the fender. Where had he been driving, to collect such a trophy? Was he a salesman? What did he do while Mrs. Simon and I were watching the clock for him?

In the midst of my musings, Mr. Simon would reappear, briefcase in hand, and roll down his garage door. That handkerchief, hanging from his overcoat pocket—might it slip out? Would the drop of the handkerchief be marked only by me, whose presence was as undetectable as God's? And if I alone saw cloth meet asphalt, could the handkerchief really be said to have fallen, or would it be like the tree I'd learned about in class, the tree that cracks unheard in the forest and thus provides a philosophical question for the ages? Surely Mrs. Simon, who sorted her laundry with as much finickiness as a forty-niner panning for gold, would notice a missing item. But the handkerchief clung to his pocket as Mr. Simon walked slowly across the backyard and toward the rear door of the apartment building.

I glided into my parents' dark bedroom. My mother was duplicating Mrs. Simon's activities in our kitchen downstairs, my father was saving people's vision in his office. I turned my magic glasses onto the Simons' bright living room, only a few yards away.

How I yearned to witness Mr. Simon's return. Alas, it always took place in that inner hall. It must be like my father's homecoming: the woman hurrying to the door; the man bringing in a gust of weather and excitement; the hug, affectionate and sometimes annoyingly long; and finally the separation, so that two little girls rushing downstairs could be caught in those overcoated arms. But at the Simons' there were no children. Perhaps the pair exchanged a dignified kiss.

Our dinner coincided with theirs. And then I had to help my mother with the dishes. It wasn't until evening that I saw the Simons again.

This was my favorite scene. The couple by the fireplace and the invisible guest. I could see how motionless Mr. Simon's long face was as he read the paper, page by slow page, and how stiffly he held his shoulders under the jacket he never took off. I could almost hear the tick of the mantelpiece clock.

I shifted my attention to Mrs. Simon. Cross and cross again went the needles. And up and down, up and down went the active lips, the unstoppable mouth, the mouth that never produced a word for me but spoke so easily and swiftly and continually when the beloved was home. Talking. Laughing. Talking again.

After vacation I visited the Simons less often. By the end of January I was dropping in only occasionally—for a moment at the end of an afternoon, say, to make sure that something was cooking on the stove.

Then, during breakfast one February morning, two policemen appeared at our back door. "Doctor, can you...?" My father did not pause even to put on his suit jacket; he just followed the sturdy officers into the yard, looking like their servant in his silk-backed waistcoat and his white shirtsleeves. They walked across the crusted snow and into the backyard of the apartment building next door. My mother stood at the kitchen window, her hand on her heart.

My father returned before we left for school. "It's Al Simon," he said to my mother. "He died during the night."

My sister continued to buckle her boots.

"Was he murdered?" I said.

"No," my father said. "What makes you ask?"

"The policemen."

My father sighed. Then, after a thoughtful pause, "Mr. Simon committed suicide," he told me. "In his car."

"Did he drive it off a cliff?"

My parents exchanged frowns and shrugs. Such a child, their looks said, all curiosity and no sympathy—and this the teachers call gifted? Then, still in a patient voice, my father explained that Mr. Simon had driven into his garage, closed the door from inside, stuffed the cracks with newspapers, reentered his car, and turned on the motor.

The next day in the obituary section I could find no hint of suicide, unless *suddenly* was the code word. But the final sentence was a shocker. "Mr. Simon, a bachelor, is survived by his mother."

I raced to my own mother. "I thought she was his wife!"

"So did she," my mother said, admitting me abruptly into the complicated world of adults, making me understand what I had until then only seen.

◙ ◙ ◙

Writing Exercises

1. *Story Trigger.* One way to test your skill in the use of concrete, significant detail is to create a reality that is convincing—and yet literally impossible. To begin, draft a three-to-five-page story in which a single impossible event happens in the everyday world. (For example, a dog tells fortunes, a secret message appears on a pizza, the radio announcer speaks in an ex-husband's voice—supermarket tabloids can be a good source of ideas.) First, focus on using detail to create the reality of both the normal world and the impossible event—the more believable the reality is, the more seamlessly readers will accept the magic.

2. Create metaphors as quickly as you can. Write down that one thing is another. Don't censor yourself—have fun. Start with a noun. (For instance, a house is a cake. A house is a flower. A house is the wind. A house is a clock. A house is a salesman.) See how many things one thing can become. Some of your metaphors are bound to be striking and useful. Try folding one or another of them into a scene you're working on.

3. Create similes. What is something like? Come up with a list of nouns as sentence subjects, then finish the sentences. (For example: His hair felt like _____. The dog looked like a _____. The room smelled like _____. The train sounded like _____. Etc.) Ask yourself which comparisons work. There should be some similarity in the things compared, more so than in metaphors, that changes one thing into another. Read your likenesses and assess them. Keep whatever works and use it in a story.

4. Write about something familiar from the point of view of a stranger—a foreigner, a time traveler from the past, a prisoner released after twenty years in jail, an orphan. Pick a situation that might seem commonplace to your readers and imagine how the stranger would perceive it through all her available senses. Send the urbanite to a small town in the Midwest, introduce the time traveler to his own future, have the ex-prisoner spend the evening in a karaoke bar, let the orphan be adopted by a previously childless couple. The goal is to make the everyday seem strange and new again. Avoid using familiar words (your character won't know them). You might even try not to *name* the situation but let your reader figure out where the character is through your use of sensory details.

3

BUILDING CHARACTER
Characterization, Part I

♦ *The Direct Methods of Character Presentation*

Human character is in the foreground of all fiction, however the humanity might be disguised. Attributing human characteristics to the natural world may be frowned on in science, but it is a literary necessity. Bugs Bunny isn't a rabbit; he's a plucky youth in ears. Peter Rabbit is a mischievous boy. Brer Rabbit is a sassy rebel. The romantic heroes of *Watership Down* are out of the Arthurian tradition, not out of the hutch.

Your fiction can be only as successful as the characters who move it and move within it. Whether they are drawn from life or are pure fantasy—and all fictional characters lie somewhere between the two—we must find them interesting, we must find them believable, and we must care about what happens to them.

YOU ARE GOING TO LOVE SOME OF YOUR CHARACTERS, because they are you or some facet of you, and you are going to hate some of your characters for the same reason. But no matter what, you are probably going to have to let bad things happen to some of the characters you love or you won't have much of a story. Bad things happen to good characters, because our actions have consequences, and we do not all behave perfectly all the time.

ANNE LAMOTT

The Direct Methods of Character Presentation

There are six basic methods of character presentation. There are four direct methods—*dialogue, appearance, action,* and *thought.* Dialogue will be discussed in this chapter because it plays such an essential role in bringing characters to life. The other direct methods, along with the indirect methods—*authorial interpretation* and *interpretation by another character*—will be discussed in Chapter 4. Employing a variety of these methods can help you create full characters.

DIALOGUE

Speech characterizes in a way that is different from appearance, because speech represents an effort, mainly voluntary, to externalize the internal and to manifest not merely taste or preference but also deliberated thought. Like fiction itself, human dialogue attempts to marry logic to emotion.

Summary, Indirect, and Direct Dialogue.   Speech can be conveyed in fiction with varying degrees of directness. It can be *summarized* as part of the narrative so that a good deal of conversation is condensed:

> At home in the first few months, he and Maizie had talked brightly about changes that would make the company more profitable and more attractive to a prospective buyer: new cuts, new packaging, new advertising, new incentives to make supermarkets carry the brand.
>
> Joan Wickersham, "Commuter Marriage"

It can be reported in the third person as *indirect speech* so that it carries, without actual quotation, the feel of the exchange:

> Had he brought the coffee? She had been waiting all day long for coffee. They had forgot it when they ordered at the store the first day.
>   Gosh, no, he hadn't. Lord, now he'd have to go back. Yes, he would if it killed him. He thought, though, he had everything else. She reminded him it was only because he didn't drink coffee himself. If he did he would remember it quick enough.
>
> Katherine Anne Porter, "Rope"

But usually when the exchange contains the possibility of discovery or decision, and therefore of dramatic action, it will be presented in *direct quotation:*

> "But I thought you hardly knew her, Mr. Morning."
>   He picked up a pencil and began to doodle on a notebook page. "Did I tell you that?"

"Yes, you did."

"It's true. I didn't know her well."

"What is it you're after, then? Who was this person you're investigating?"

"I would like to know that too."

Siri Hustvedt, "Mr. Morning"

These three methods of presenting speech can be used in combination to take advantage of the virtues of each:

They differed on the issue of the holiday, and couldn't seem to find a common ground. (*Summary.*) She had an idea: why not some Caribbean island over Christmas? Well, but his mother expected them for turkey. (*Indirect.*)

"Oh, lord, yes, I wouldn't want to go without a yuletide gizzard." (*Direct.*)

Summary and indirect speech are often useful to get us quickly to the core of the scene, or when, for example, one character has to inform another of events that we already know about, or when the emotional point of a conversation is that it has become tedious.

Carefully, playing down the danger, Len filled her in on the events of the long night.

Samantha claimed to be devastated. It was all very well if the Seversons wanted to let their cats run loose, but she certainly wasn't responsible for Lisbeth's parakeets, now was she?

But nothing is more frustrating to a reader than to be told that significant events are taking place in talk and to be denied the drama of the dialogue.

They whispered to each other all night long, and as he told her all about his past, she began to realize that she was falling in love with him.

Such a summary—it's *telling*—is a stingy way of treating the reader, who wants the chance to fall in love too.

Economy in Dialogue.   Because direct dialogue has a dual nature—emotion within a logical structure—its purpose in fiction is never merely to convey information. Dialogue may do that (although information often is more naturally conveyed in narration), but it needs simultaneously to characterize, provide exposition, set the scene, advance the action, foreshadow, and/or remind. William Sloane, in *The Craft of Writing*, says:

There is a tentative rule that pertains to all fiction dialogue. It must do more than one thing at a time or it is too inert for the purposes of fiction. This may sound harsh, but I consider it an essential discipline.

In considering Sloane's "tentative rule," I place the emphasis on *rule*. With dialogue as with significant detail, when you write you are constantly at pains to mean more than you say. If a significant detail must both call up a sense image and *mean*, then the character's words, which presumably mean something, should simultaneously suggest image, personality, or emotion.

Dialogue, therefore, is not simply transcribed speech, but distilled speech—the "filler" and inert small talk of real conversation is edited away, even as the weight of implication is increased. "You don't simply copy what you heard on the street," says fiction writer Alice LaPlante. "You want to make it *sound* natural, but that doesn't mean it *is* natural. It takes careful editing to create natural-sounding dialogue. Generally, that means keeping things brief, and paying attention to the rhythm of the sentences. Sentences are short. They're not particularly grammatically correct, but rather quirky and characteristic of the speaker."

As a general rule, distilling speech into dialogue means avoiding long monologues and keeping the sense of an exchange. A character who speaks several consecutive sentences might come across as either a windbag (which, of course, might be your intention) or the author's puppet. Often the first and last words, phrases, or sentences of a character's speech can be eliminated. In this way you are separating the wheat from the chaff. The characters' intentions and preoccupations can shine through because of the leaps the characters make in their dialogue and because of the spaces left within their dialogue. The things they can't bring themselves to say aloud are often as revealing, or more revealing, than those they do say.

Characterizing Dialogue. Even rote exchanges, however, can call up images. A character who says, "It is indeed a pleasure to meet you" carries his back at a different angle, dresses differently, from a character who says, "Hey, man, what's up?"

The three very brief speeches that follow portray three fictional men, sharply differentiated from each other not only by the content of what they say, but also by their diction (choice and use of words) and their syntax (the ordering of words in a sentence). Like appearance, these choices convey attributes of class, period, ethnicity, and so forth, as well as political or moral attitudes. How much do you know about each? How does each look?

> "I had a female cousin one time—a Rockefeller, as it happened—" said the Senator, "and she confessed to me that she spent the fifteenth, sixteenth and seventeenth years of her life saying nothing but, No, thank you.
> Which is all very well for a girl of that age and station. But it would have been a damned unattractive trait in a male Rockefeller."

Kurt Vonnegut, *God Bless You, Mr. Rosewater*

"You think you the only one ever felt this way?" he asked. "You think I never felt this way? You think she never felt this way? Every last one of them back there one time in they life wanted to give up. She want to give up now. You know that? You got any idea how sick she is? Soon after he go, she's going too. I won't give her another year. I want her to believe he'll be up there waiting for her. And you can help me do it. And you the only one."

Ernest Gaines, A *Lesson Before Dying*

The Knight looked surprised at the question. "What does it matter where my body happens to be?" he said. "My mind goes on working all the same. In fact, the more head downward I am, the more I keep inventing new things.

"Now, the cleverest thing of the sort that I ever did," he went on after a pause, "was inventing a new pudding during the meat course."

Lewis Carroll, *Through the Looking Glass*

There are forms of insanity that condemn people to hear voices against their will, but as writers we invite ourselves to hear voices without relinquishing our hold on reality or our right to control. The trick to writing good dialogue is hearing voice. The question is, what would he or she say? The answer is entirely in language. The choice of language reveals content, character, and conflict, as well as type.

It's logical that if you must develop voices in order to develop dialogue, you'd do well to start with monologue and develop voices one by one. Use your journal to experiment with speech patterns that will characterize. Some people speak in telegraphically short sentences missing various parts of speech. Some speak in convoluted eloquence or in rhythms tedious with qualifying phrases. Some rush headlong without a pause for breath until they're breathless; others are measured or terse or begrudge even forming a sentence. Trust your "inner ear" and use your journal to practice catching voices. Freewriting is invaluable to dialogue writing because it is the manner of composition closest to speech. There is no time to mull or edit. Any qualifications, corrections, and disavowals must be made part of the process and the text.

To increase your ability to "hear" dialogue, try carrying a small pocket notebook with you and noting, verbatim, vivid lines or exchanges of eavesdropped dialogue. At home, look back through your notebook for speech that interests you and freedraft a monologue passage of that speech in your writing journal. Don't look for words that seem right; just listen to the voice and let it flow. You'll begin to develop your own range of voices whether you catch a particular voice or not, and may even develop your ear by the very process of "hearing" it go wrong at times.

Other Uses of Dialogue.   You can also limber up in your journal by setting yourself deliberate exercises in making dialogue—or monologue—do more than one thing at a time. In addition to revealing character, dialogue can *set the scene*.

> "We didn't know no one was here. We thought hit a summer camp all closed up. Curtains all closed up. Nothing here. No cars or gear nor nothing. Looks closed to me, don't hit to you, J.J.?"
>
> Joy Williams, "Woods"

Dialogue can *set the mood*.

> "I have a lousy trip to Philadelphia, lousy flight back, I watch my own plane blow a tire on closed-circuit TV, I go to my office, I find Suzy in tears because Warren's camped in her one-room apartment. I come home and I find my wife hasn't gotten dressed in two days."
>
> Joan Didion, *Book of Common Prayer*

Dialogue can *reveal the theme* because, as William Sloane says, the characters talk about what the story is about.

> "You feel trapped, don't you?"
> Jane looks at her.
> "Don't you?"
> "No."
> "O.K.—You just have a headache."
> "I do."...
> Milly waits a moment and then clears her throat and says, "You know, for a while there after Wally and I were married, I thought maybe I'd made a mistake. I remember realizing that I didn't like the way he laughed. I mean, let's face it, Wally laughs like a hyena...."
>
> Richard Bausch, "The Fireman's Wife"

In all of the preceding passages, the dialogue fulfills Sloane's rule because, in addition to conveying its content, the dialogue either moves the story forward or enriches our understanding.

Dialogue is also one of the simplest ways to *reveal the past* (a fundamental playwriting device is to have a character who knows tell a character who doesn't know); and it is one of the most effective, because we get both the drama of the memory and the drama of the telling. Here is a passage from Toni Morrison's *The Bluest Eye* in which the past is evoked, the speaker characterized, the scene and mood set, and the theme revealed—all at the same time and in less than a dozen lines.

"The onliest time I be happy seem like was when I was in the picture show. Every time I got, I went. I'd go early, before the show started. They'd cut off the lights, and everything be black. Then the screen would light up, and I'd move right on in them pictures. White men taking such good care of they women, and they all dressed up in big clean houses with the bathtubs right in the same room with the toilet. Them pictures gave me a lot of pleasure, but it made coming home hard, and looking at Cholly hard. I don't know."

Be careful, however, that you don't succumb to the temptation to slip exposition into dialogue by allowing the characters to discuss things they both already know, just for the reader's benefit.

"I've missed you so much, Margie! It's been over a month since we ran into each other at the Farmer's Market. That was the day you told me that your grandson Eddie got into Julliard!"

"Yes, Suzie, and wasn't that right before the tornado came through town? We were so scared when that siren went off! Remember how we hid underneath the rickety table with the watermelons on it?"

This kind of dialogue is both ridiculous and tedious. If we really need to know about the Farmer's Market and Eddie and the tornado, tell us in exposition. Don't weigh your characters' dialogue down with such information.

Dialogue as Action. If the telling of a memory *changes the relationship* between the teller and the listener, then you have a scene of high drama, and the dialogue can *advance the action*.

This is an important device, because dialogue is most valuable to fiction when it is itself a means of telling the story.

In the following passage, for example, the mother of a seriously ill toddler looks anxiously to a radiologist for information:

"The surgeon will speak to you," says the Radiologist.

"Are you finding something?"

"The surgeon will speak to you," the Radiologist says again. "There seems to be something there, but the surgeon will talk to you about it."

"My uncle once had something on his kidney," says the Mother. "So they removed the kidney and it turned out the something was benign."

The Radiologist smiles a broad, ominous smile. "That's always the way it is," he says. "You don't know exactly what it is until it's in the bucket."

"In the bucket," the Mother repeats.

"That's doctor talk," the Radiologist says.

"It's very appealing," says the Mother. "It's a very appealing way to talk."

Lorrie Moore, "People Like That Are the Only People Here"

Here the radiologist's speech alters the mother's feeling toward him from hopeful to hostile in one short exchange. The level of fear for the child rises, and the dialogue itself has effected change.

A crucial (and sometimes difficult) distinction to make is between speech that is mere discussion or debate and speech that is drama or action. If in doubt, ask yourself: Can this conversation between characters really change anything? *Dialogue is action when it contains the possibility of change.* When two characters have made up their minds and know each other's positions on some political or philosophical matter, for instance, they may argue with splendid eloquence, but there will be no discovery and nothing to decide, and therefore no option for change. No matter how significant their topic, we are likely to find them wooden and uninteresting. The story's question *what happened next?* will suggest only *more talk:*

> "This has been the traditional fishing spot of the river people for a thousand years, and we have a moral responsibility to aid them in preserving their way of life. If you put in these rigs, it may undermine the ecosystem and destroy the aquifer of the entire county!"
> "Join the real world, Sybil. Free enterprise is based on this kind of technological progress, and without it we would endanger the economic base."

Ho-hum. In order to engage us emotionally in a disagreement, the characters must have an emotional stake in the outcome; we need to feel that, even if it's unlikely they would change their minds, they might change their lives.

> "If you sink that drill tomorrow morning, I'll be gone by noon."
> "Sybil, I have no choice."

Further, if you find your characters getting stuck in a repetitive conflict ("yes-you-are, no-I'm-not"), you can jump-start the action if you remember that people generally change their tactics—become charming, threatening, seductive, guilt-inducing, and so on—when they are not succeeding in getting what they badly want. And if *each* character in the scene wants something from the other, although it probably won't be the same thing, the momentum will build. It's much harder (although not impossible) to maintain dramatic energy when one of the characters simply wants to get off stage.

Text and Subtext.   Often the most forceful dialogue can be achieved by *not* having the characters say what they mean. People in extreme emotional states—whether of fear, pain, anger, or love—are at their least articulate. There is more narrative tension in a love scene where the lovers make anxious small talk, terrified of revealing their feelings, than in one where they hop into bed. A character who is able to say "I hate you!" hates less than one who bottles the fury and pretends to submit, unwilling to expose the truth.

Dialogue can fall flat if characters define their feelings too precisely and honestly, because often the purpose of human exchange is to conceal as well as to reveal—to impress, hurt, protect, seduce, or reject. Anton Chekhov believed that a line of dialogue should always leave the sense that more could have been said. Playwright David Mamet suggests that people may or may not say what they mean, but always say something designed to get what they want.

In this example from Alice Munro's "Before the Change," the daughter of a doctor who performed illegal abortions up until his recent death takes a phone call:

> A woman on the phone wants to speak to the doctor.
> "I'm sorry. He's dead."
> "Dr. Strachan. Have I got the right doctor?"
> "Yes but I'm sorry, he's dead."
> "Is there anyone—does he by any chance have a partner I could talk to? Is there anybody else there?"
> "No. No partner."
> "Could you give me any other number I could call? Isn't there some other doctor that can—"
> "No. I haven't any number. There isn't anybody that I know of."
> "You must know what this is about. It's very crucial. There are very special circumstances—"
> "I'm sorry."

It's clear here that neither woman is willing to mention abortion, and that the daughter will also not (and probably could not) speak about her complicated feelings toward her father and his profession. The exchange is rich with irony in that both women and also the reader know the "special circumstance" they are guardedly referring to; only the daughter and the reader are privy to the events surrounding the doctor's death and to the daughter's feelings.

Notice that this is not a very articulate exchange, but it does represent dramatic action, because for both women the stakes are high; they are both emotionally involved, but in ways that put them at cross-purposes.

In "Following the Notes" by Pia Z. Ehrhardt, a high school–age daughter has summoned her father to her place of work because her car battery is dead, but she slips up and reveals more to him than she means to. Her subterfuge and his understanding of it are both lurking in and between the lines of their exchange:

> "You left the headlights on?" he said.
> "The passenger light," I said, pointing at the back seat. "Door wasn't shut all the way."
> "Who was in the back?" he said. "I thought you were driving to work and home, only."

My daily comings and goings were charted in the kitchen, reviewed when I got back in the evening. I had the use of a Buick Century as long as I kept it filled with gas, washed it once a week in our driveway with mild detergent, and didn't joy ride with my friends.

"Sorry for the inconvenience," I said

"Don't be a smart-ass."

The idea of "reading between the lines" of dialogue is familiar to most people, for in life we tend to react more to what is implied in dialogue than to what is actually said. The linkage of text and subtext—that is, the surface, plot-related dialogue and its emotional undercurrent—was famously described by Ernest Hemingway with the analogy of an iceberg: "There is seven-eighths of it under water for every part that shows. Anything you know you can eliminate and it only strengthens your iceberg. It is the part that doesn't show."

When an unspoken subject remains unspoken, tension continues to build in a story. Often the crisis of a story occurs when the unspoken tension comes to the surface and an explosion results. "If you're trying to build pressure, don't take the lid off the pot," Jerome Stern suggests in his book *Making Shapely Fiction*. "Once people are really candid, once the unstated becomes stated, the tension is released and the effect is cathartic.... [Y]ou want to give yourself the space for a major scene. Here you do want to describe setting and action vividly, and render what they say fully. You've taken the lid off the pot and we want to feel the dialogue boil over."

IF YOU TAKE TWO STICKS AND HOLD THEM PARALLEL, you can capture that image in a photograph because it doesn't change. But if you rub those two sticks together, harder and harder, faster and faster, they will burst into flame—that's the kind of change you can capture in a story or on film. Friction is necessary for change to occur. But without the friction of conflict, there is no change. And without change, there is no story. A body at rest remains at rest unless it enters into conflict.

STEPHEN FISCHER

"No" Dialogue.   The previous Munro passage (page 75) also illustrates an essential element of conflict in dialogue: Tension and drama are heightened when characters are constantly (in one form or another) saying no to each other. In the following exchange from Ernest Hemingway's *The Old Man and the Sea*, the old man feels only love for his young protégé, and their conversation is a pledge of affection. Nevertheless, it is the old man's steady denial that lends the scene tension.

> "Can I go out and get sardines for you tomorrow?"
>
> "No. Go and play baseball. I can still row and Rogelio will throw the net."
>
> "I would like to go. If I cannot fish with you, I would like to serve in some way."
>
> "You brought me a beer," the old man said. "You are already a man."
>
> "How old was I when you first took me in a boat?"
>
> "Five and you were nearly killed when I brought the fish in too green and he nearly tore the boat to pieces. Can you remember?"
>
> "I can remember the tail slapping and banging and the thwart breaking and the noise of the clubbing. I can remember you throwing me into the bow where the wet coiled lines were and feeling the whole boat shiver and the noise of you clubbing him like chopping a tree down and the sweet blood smell all over me."
>
> "Can you really remember that or did I just tell it to you?"
>
> "I remember everything from when we first went together."
>
> The old man looked at him with his sunburned, confident loving eyes.
>
> "If you were my boy I'd take you out and gamble," he said. "But you are your father's and mother's and you are in a lucky boat."

Neither of these characters is consciously eloquent, and the dialogue is extremely simple. But look how much more it does than "one thing at a time"! It provides exposition on the beginning of the relationship, and it conveys the mutual affection of the two and the conflict within the old man between his love for the boy and his loyalty to the parents. It conveys the boy's eagerness to persuade and carries him into the emotion he had as a small child when the fish was clubbed. The dialogue represents a constant shift of power back and forth between the boy and the old man, as the boy, whatever else he is saying, continues to say *please*, and the old man, whatever else he is saying, continues to say *no*.

Another Hemingway story, "Hills Like White Elephants," also offers clear examples of "no" dialogue. Notice, however, that the conflict does not simply get stuck in a rut, because the characters continue to find new ways to ask and answer the questions as each tries to find the other's vulnerable points.

> "What should we drink?" the girl asked. She had taken off her hat and put it on the table.
>
> "It's pretty hot," the man said.
>
> "Let's drink beer."
>
> "Dos cervezas," the man said into the curtain.
>
> "Big ones?" a woman asked from the doorway.
>
> "Yes. Two big ones."

The woman brought two glasses of beer and two felt pads. She put the felt pads and the beer glasses on the table and looked at the man and the girl. The girl was looking off at the line of hills. They were white in the sun and the country was brown and dry.

"They look like white elephants," she said.

"I've never seen one," the man drank his beer.

"No, you wouldn't have."

"I might have," the man said. "Just because you say I wouldn't have doesn't prove anything."

The girl looked at the bead curtain. "They've painted something on it," she said. "What does it say?"

Specificity.   In dialogue, as in narrative, we will tend to believe a character who speaks in concrete details and to be skeptical of one who generalizes or delivers judgments unsupported by example. When the boy in the Hemingway passage protests, "I remember everything," we believe him because of the vivid details in his memory of the fish. If one character says, "It's perfectly clear from all his actions that he adores me and would do anything for me," and another says, "I had my hands all covered with the clay slick, and he just reached over to lift a lock of hair out of my eyes and tuck it behind my ear," which character do you believe is the more loved?

Similarly, in conflict dialogue, "details are the rocks characters throw at each other," says Stephen Fischer. Our memories for hurts and slights are sadly long, and an accusation that begins as a general blame—"You never think of my feelings"—is likely to be backed up with specific proof as the argument escalates—"You said you'd pick me up at seven New Year's Eve, but you left me waiting for an hour in the snow." "There's nothing generic in our lives," Fischer explains, "and the sparks given off in conflict may reveal all the facts we need to know about the characters."

It's interesting to observe that whereas in narrative you will demonstrate control if you state the facts and let the emotional value rise off of them, in dialogue you will convey information more naturally if the emphasis is on the speaker's feelings. "My brother is due to arrive at midafternoon and is bringing his four children with him" reads as bald exposition; whereas, "That idiot brother of mine thinks he can walk in in the middle of the afternoon and plunk his four kids in my lap!" or, "I can't wait till my brother gets here at three! You'll see—those are the four sweetest kids this side of the planet" will sound like talk and will slip us the information sideways.

Examine your dialogue to see if it does more than one thing at a time. Do the sound and syntax characterize by region, education, attitude? Do the choice of words and their syntax reveal that the character is stiff, outgoing, stifling anger, ignorant of the facts, perceptive, bigoted, afraid? Is the conflict advanced by "no" dialogue in which the characters say no to each other in different ways? Is the drama heightened by the characters' inability or unwillingness to tell the whole truth?

Once you are comfortable with the voice of your character, it is well to acknowledge that everyone has many voices and that what that character says will be, within his or her verbal range, determined by the character *to whom* it is said. All of us have one sort of speech for the vicar and another for the man who pumps the gas. Huck Finn, whose voice is idiosyncratically his own, says, "Yes, sir" to the judge and "Maybe I am, maybe I ain't" to his degenerate dad.

Pacing. Economy in dialogue—distilling it, avoiding the rehash of what the reader already knows, making sure that it does more than one job at a time—is an important part of pacing. At the same time, it's important not to hurry over the unfolding drama that takes place in an exchange of speech.

One reason why readers enjoy dialogue is that it's the most direct experience of the characters we get in fiction, the only time they express themselves without any authorial interference. Therefore, it's important when writing dialogue not to race through it quickly with an end in mind. You might think you know what the outcome of a conversation is going to be, but dialogue is always more fun to write, and to read, if the characters surprise you. When writing dialogue, take your time and listen closely to what your characters might say, based on who they are and what they want, rather than foisting your own agenda on them.

For instance, you may begin writing a scene with a plan to get in and out quickly. You may decide that this will be the scene where he breaks up with her.

"I've stopped by to tell you that it's over. I've had enough. We're finished."
"Fine. There's the door. Goodbye."

This quick exchange wouldn't allow you to discover the depth of the characters, with the consequence that the reader is cheated of the real drama. The characters come off sounding flat and unreal, whereas if you're aware as you're writing that both characters have their own desires and conflicting emotions, if you allow them to reveal some of their feelings and hide others, they will become authentic and believable. The subtext will be revealed. In a situation such as this, it's important to remember that the character being abandoned is not a passive sounding board or a mere echo.

"You still need to fix that porch light. Wow, don't you look nice."
"I've got three minutes to get downtown. Jake's waiting for me. What's up?"

This dialogue is more specific and the characters are at odds, but what exactly is going to happen isn't clear. He's trying to be nonchalant, a little bit aggressive but still kind; she seems to know why he's come and has already found someone else. Or at least wants him to think so. What if he insists on coming in for three minutes? This scene wants to be longer. Keep the talkers talking. Maybe they won't break up after all—not tonight, anyway.

There are additional ways to pace yourself when writing dialogue. Timing, as it is in stand-up comedy, is crucial. Vary your sentences and the placement of your dialogue tags. Decide where you want the reader to pause, what you want to emphasize.

In this excerpt from Tobias Wolff's "Hunters in the Snow," Wolff structures the paragraph so that the reader gets the full benefit of Frank's zinger.

> Frank had his fingers fanned out, tips against the bark of the stump where he'd laid his foot. His knuckles were hairy. He wore a heavy wedding band and on his right pinky another gold ring with a flat face and an "F" in what looked like diamonds. He turned the ring this way and that. "Tub," he said, "you haven't seen your own balls in years."

In Hemingway's "Hills Like White Elephants," the silences and interruptions say as much about the characters and their conflict as their words do.

> "I don't want you to do anything that you don't want to do—"
> "Nor that isn't good for me," she said. "I know. Could we have another beer?"
> "All right, but you've got to realize—"
> "I realize," said the girl. "Can't we maybe stop talking?"

Repetition is another way to vary pace and emphasize certain words and emotions. It becomes clear that the wife in Raymond Carver's "Cathedral" worries that her guest, Robert, the blind man, will sense her husband's hostility. The husband, who is the narrator, is listening to this exchange, which is really directed at him.

> My wife covered her mouth, and then she yawned. She stretched. She said, "I think I'll go upstairs and put on my robe. I think I'll change into something else. Robert, you make yourself comfortable," she said.
> "I'm comfortable," the blind man said.
> "I want you to feel comfortable in this house," she said.
> "I am comfortable," the blind man said.

With each repetition the word *comfortable* takes on a slightly different meaning.

Fiction writers generally manage the pace of a scene by blending dialogue with description, action, and the main character's thoughts. These are also direct ways to present character and will be discussed in the next chapter.

Format and Style.   The *format and style of dialogue*, like punctuation, has as its goal to be invisible; and though there may be occasions when departing from the rules is justified by some special effect, it's best to consider such occasions rare. Here are some basic guidelines:

What a character says aloud should be in quotation marks; thoughts should not. This helps clearly differentiate between the spoken and the internal, especially by acknowledging that speech is more deliberately formulated. If you feel that thoughts need to be set apart from narrative, use italics instead of quotation marks.

Begin the dialogue of each new speaker as a new paragraph. This helps orient the reader and keep clear who is speaking. If an action is described between the dialogue lines of two speakers, put that action in the paragraph of the speaker it describes:

> "I wish I'd taken that picture." Larry traced the horizon with his index finger.
>
> Janice snatched the portfolio away. "You've got chicken grease on your hands," she said, "and this is the only copy!"

Notice that the punctuation goes inside the quotation marks.

A dialogue tag tells us who has spoken—*John said, Mary said, Tim announced.* When a tag is used, it is connected to the dialogue line with a comma, even though the dialogue line may sound like a full sentence: *"I'm paying tonight," Mary said.* (Misusing a period in place of the comma with a tag is one of the most common mistakes in dialogue format.)

Avoid overusing the name of the person being spoken to in dialogue—it doesn't sound conversational.

> "For God sake, Benji, my job's more important than our marathon Monopoly game."
>
> "Ah, Mom, you're always taking things the wrong way."
>
> "Benji, you know that's not true."
>
> "Yup, true, Mom, every time."

Like a luggage tag or a nametag, a dialogue tag is for the purpose of identification, and *said* is usually adequate to the task. People also *ask* and *reply* and occasionally *add, recall, remember,* or *remind.* But sometimes an unsure writer will strain for emphatic synonyms: *She gasped, he whined, they chorused, John snarled, Mary spat.* This is unnecessary and obtrusive, because although unintentional repetition usually makes for awkward style, the word *said* is as invisible as punctuation. When reading we're scarcely aware of it, whereas we are forced to be aware of *she wailed.* If it's clear who is speaking without any dialogue tag at all, don't use one. Usually an identification at the beginning of a dialogue passage and an occasional reminder are sufficient. If the speaker is inherently identified in the speech pattern, so much the better.

Similarly, tonal dialogue tags should be used sparingly: *he said with relish; she added limply.* Such phrases are blatant "telling," and chances are that good dialogue will convey its own tone. *"Get off my case!" she said angrily.* We do not need to be told that she said this angrily. If she said it sweetly, then we would probably need to be told. If the dialogue does not give us a clue to the manner in which it is said, an action will often do so better than an adverb. *"I'll have a word with Mr. Ritter about it,"* he said with finality is weaker than *"I'll have a word with Mr. Ritter about it,"* he said, and picked up his hat.

It helps to make the dialogue tag unobtrusive if it comes within the spoken line: *"Don't give it a second thought,"* he said. *"I was just going anyway."* (A midline tag has the added benefit of helping readers hear a slight pause or change in the speaker's inflection.) A tag that comes at the beginning of the line may look too much like a play script: *He said, "Don't give it a second thought..."* And a tag that comes after too much speech becomes confusing or superfluous: *"Don't give it a second thought. I was going anyway, and I'll just take these and drop them at the copy shop on the way,"* he said. If we didn't know who was speaking long before this tag appears, it's too late to be of use and simply calls attention to itself.

Vernacular. *Vernacular* is a tempting, and can be an excellent, means of characterizing, but it is difficult to do well and easy to overdo. Dialect, re-gionality, and childhood should be achieved by word choice and syntax. Misspellings should be kept to a minimum because they distract and slow the reader, and worse, they tend to make the character seem stupid. There is no point in spelling phonetically any word as it is ordinarily pronounced: Almost all of us say things such as "fur" for *for,* "uv" for *of,* "wuz" for *was,* "an" for *and,* and "sez" for *says.* It's common to drop the g in words ending in *ing.* When you misspell these words in dialogue, you indicate that the speaker is ignorant enough to spell them that way when writing. Even if you want to indicate ignorance, you may alienate the reader by the means you choose to do so. John Updike puts this point well when he complains of a Tom Wolfe character:

> [His] pronunciations are steadfastly spelled out—'sump'm' for 'something,' 'far fat' for 'fire fight'—in a way that a Faulkner character would be spared. For Faulkner, Southern life was life; for Wolfe it is a provincial curiosity....

It is largely to avoid the charge of creating "provincial curiosities" that most fiction writers now avoid misspellings.

It can be even trickier catching the voice of a foreigner with imperfect English, because everyone has a native language, and when someone whose native language is French or Ibu starts to learn English, the grammatical mistakes he or she makes will be based on the grammatical structure of the native language. Unless you know French or Ibu, you will make the wrong sort of mistake, and your dialogue is likely to sound as if it came from second-rate sitcoms.

In vernacular or standard English, the bottom-line rule is that dialogue must be speakable. If it isn't speakable, it isn't dialogue.

> "Certainly I had had a fright I wouldn't soon forget," Reese would say later, "and as I slipped into bed fully dressed except for my shoes, which I flung God-knows-where, I wondered why I had subjected myself to a danger only a fool would fail to foresee for the dubious pleasure of spending one evening in the company of a somewhat-less-than-brilliant coed."

Nobody would say this because it can't be said. It is not only convoluted beyond reason, but it also stumbles over its alliteration, "only a fool would fail to foresee for," and takes more breath than the human lungs can hold.

Read your dialogue aloud and make sure it is comfortable to the mouth, the breath, and the ear. False, flabby, do-nothing dialogue will reveal itself, as will places that drag or seem rushed. This is the best way possible to tell if it's all coming together.

DIALOGUE TIPS

1. Have your characters speak no more than three sentences at a time—unless you have a good reason to do otherwise.

2. Dialogue is more interesting when characters are saying no to each other.

3. Keep exposition out of dialogue

4. Let your characters sometimes conceal or avoid instead of saying exactly what they mean.

5. Use "said" as a dialogue tag whenever possible.

6. Use an action rather than a modifier to show how a character is feeling.

7. Cut to the chase. Don't use dialogue that doesn't move the story forward and reveal character.

8. Don't let your characters be too articulate. Fragments are fine. Don't force conversations to follow a logical order (question followed by answer). No need to stay on the same subject or include clear transitions from one subject to another.

9. Vernacular is best conveyed by word choice and syntax as opposed to misspellings.

Fiesta, 1980

JUNOT DÍAZ

Mami's youngest sister—my tía Yrma—finally made it to the United States that year. She and tío Miguel got themselves an apartment in the Bronx, off the Grand Concourse and everybody decided that we should have a party. Actually, my pops decided, but everybody—meaning

Mami, tía Yrma, tío Miguel and their neighbors—thought it a dope idea. On the afternoon of the party Papi came back from work around six. Right on time. We were all dressed by then, which was a smart move on our part. If Papi had walked in and caught us lounging around in our underwear, he would have kicked our asses something serious.

He didn't say nothing to nobody, not even my moms. He just pushed past her, held up his hand when she tried to talk to him and headed right into the shower. Rafa gave me the look and I gave it back to him; we both knew Papi had been with that Puerto Rican woman he was seeing and wanted to wash off the evidence quick.

Mami looked really nice that day. The United States had finally put some meat on her; she was no longer the same flaca who had arrived here three years before. She had cut her hair short and was wearing tons of cheapass jewelry which on her didn't look too lousy. She smelled like herself, like the wind through a tree. She always waited until the last possible minute to put on her perfume because she said it was a waste to spray it on early and then have to spray it on again once you got to the party.

We—meaning me, my brother, my little sister and Mami—waited for Papi to finish his shower. Mami seemed anxious, in her usual dispassionate way. Her hands adjusted the buckle of her belt over and over again. That morning, when she had gotten us up for school, Mami told us that she wanted to have a good time at the party. I want to dance, she said, but now, with the sun sliding out of the sky like spit off a wall, she seemed ready just to get this over with.

Rafa didn't much want to go to no party either, and me, I never wanted to go anywhere with my family. There was a baseball game in the parking lot outside and we could hear our friends, yelling, Hey, and, Cabrón, to one another. We heard the pop of a ball as it sailed over the cars, the clatter of an aluminium bat dropping to the concrete. Not that me or Rafa loved baseball; we just liked playing with the local kids, thrashing them at anything they were doing. By the sounds of the shouting, we both knew the game was close, either of us could have made a difference. Rafa frowned and when I frowned back, he put up his fist. Don't you mirror me, he said.

Don't you mirror me, I said.

He punched me—I would have hit him back but Papi marched into the living room with his towel around his waist, looking a lot smaller than he did when he was dressed. He had a few strands of hair around his nipples and a surly closed-mouth expression, like maybe he'd scalded his tongue or something.

Have they eaten? he asked Mami.

She nodded. I made you something.

You didn't let him eat, did you?

Ay, Dios mío, she said, letting her arms fall to her side.

Ay, Dios mío is right, Papi said.

I was never supposed to eat before our car trips, but earlier, when she had put out our dinner of rice, beans and sweet platanos, guess who had been the first one to clean his plate? You couldn't blame Mami really, she had been busy—cooking, getting ready, dressing my sister Madai. I should have reminded her not to feed me but I wasn't that sort of son.

Papi turned to me. Coño, muchacho, why did you eat?

Rafa had already started inching away from me. I'd once told him I considered him a low-down chickenshit for moving out of the way every time Papi was going to smack me.

Collateral damage, Rafa had said. Ever heard of it?

No.

Look it up.

Chickenshit or not, I didn't dare glance at him. Papi was old-fashioned; he expected your undivided attention when you were getting your ass whupped. You couldn't look him in the eye either—that wasn't allowed. Better to stare at his belly button, which was perfectly round and immaculate. Papi pulled me to my feet by my ear.

If you throw up—

I won't, I cried, tears in my eyes, more out of reflex than pain.

Ya, Ramón, ya. It's not his fault, Mami said.

They've known about this party forever. How did they think we were going to get there? Fly?

He finally let go of my ear and I sat back down. Madai was too scared to open her eyes. Being around Papi all her life had turned her into a major-league wuss. Anytime Papi raised his voice her lip would start trembling, like some specialized tuning fork. Rafa pretended that he had knuckles to crack and when I shoved him, he gave me a *Don't start* look. But even that little bit of recognition made me feel better.

I was the one who was always in trouble with my dad. It was like my God-given duty to piss him off, to do everything the way he hated. Our fights didn't bother me too much. I still wanted him to love me, something that never seemed strange or contradictory until years later, when he was out of our lives.

By the time my ear stopped stinging Papi was dressed and Mami was crossing each one of us, solemnly, like we were heading off to war. We said, in turn, Bendición, Mami, and she poked us in our five cardinal spots while saying, Que Dios te bendiga.

This was how all our trips began, the words that followed me every time I left the house.

None of us spoke until we were inside Papi's Volkswagen van. Brand-new, lime-green and bought to impress. Oh, we were impressed, but me, every time I was in that VW and Papi went above twenty miles an hour,

I vomited. I'd never had trouble with cars before—that van was like my curse. Mami suspected it was the upholstery. In her mind, American things—appliances, mouthwash, funny-looking upholstery—all seemed to have an intrinsic badness about them. Papi was careful about taking me anywhere in the VW, but when he had to, I rode up front in Mami's usual seat so I could throw up out a window.

¿Cómo te sientes? Mami asked over my shoulder when Papi pulled onto the turnpike. She had her hand on the base of my neck. One thing about Mami, her palms never sweated.

I'm OK, I said, keeping my eyes straight ahead. I definitely didn't want to trade glances with Papi. He had this one look, furious and sharp, that always left me feeling bruised.

Toma. Mami handed me four mentas. She had thrown three out her window at the beginning of our trip, an offering to Eshú; the rest were for me.

I took one and sucked it slowly, my tongue knocking it up against my teeth. We passed Newark Airport without any incident. If Madai had been awake she would have cried because the planes flew so close to the cars.

How's he feeling? Papi asked.

Fine, I said. I glanced back at Rafa and he pretended like he didn't see me. That was the way he was, at school and at home. When I was in trouble, he didn't know me. Madai was solidly asleep, but even with her face all wrinkled up and drooling she looked cute, her hair all separated into twists.

I turned around and concentrated on the candy. Papi even started to joke that we might not have to scrub the van out tonight. He was beginning to loosen up, not checking his watch too much. Maybe he was thinking about that Puerto Rican woman or maybe he was just happy that we were all together. I could never tell. At the toll, he was feeling positive enough to actually get out of the van and search around under the basket for dropped coins. It was something he had once done to amuse Madai, but now it was habit. Cars behind us honked their horns and I slid down in my seat. Rafa didn't care; he grinned back at the other cars and waved. His actual job was to make sure no cops were coming. Mami shook Madai awake and as soon as she saw Papi stooping for a couple of quarters she let out this screech of delight that almost took off the top of my head.

That was the end of the good times. Just outside the Washington Bridge, I started feeling woozy. The smell of the upholstery got all up inside my head and I found myself with a mouthful of saliva. Mami's hand tensed on my shoulder and when I caught Papi's eye, he was like, No way. Don't do it.

The first time I got sick in the van Papi was taking me to the library. Rafa was with us and he couldn't believe I threw up. I was famous for my steel-lined stomach. A third-world childhood could give you that. Papi was worried enough that just as quick as Rafa could drop off the books we were on our way home. Mami fixed me one of her honey-and-onion concoctions and that made my stomach feel better. A week later we tried the library again and on this go-around I couldn't get the window open in time. When Papi got me home, he went and cleaned out the van himself, an expression of *askho* on his face. This was a big deal, since Papi almost never cleaned anything himself. He came back inside and found me sitting on the couch feeling like hell.

It's the car, he said to Mami. It's making him sick.

This time the damage was pretty minimal, nothing Papi couldn't wash off the door with a blast of the hose. He was pissed, though; he jammed his finger into my cheek, a nice solid thrust. That was the way he was with his punishments: imaginative. Earlier that year I'd written an essay in school called "My Father the Torturer," but the teacher made me write a new one. She thought I was kidding.

We drove the rest of the way to the Bronx in silence. We only stopped once, so I could brush my teeth. Mami had brought along my toothbrush and a tube of toothpaste and while every car known to man sped by us she stood outside with me so I wouldn't feel alone.

Tío Miguel was about seven feet tall and had his hair combed up and out, into a demi-fro. He gave me and Rafa big spleen-crushing hugs and then kissed Mami and finally ended up with Madai on his shoulder. The last time I'd seen Tío was at the airport, his first day in the United States. I remembered how he hadn't seemed all that troubled to be in another country.

He looked down at me. Carajo, Yunior, you look horrible!

He threw up, my brother explained.

I pushed Rafa. Thanks a lot, ass-face.

Hey, he said. Tío asked.

Tío clapped a bricklayer's hand on my shoulder. Everybody gets sick sometimes, he said. You should have seen me on the plane over here. Dios mio! He rolled his Asian-looking eyes for emphasis. I thought we were all going to die.

Everybody could tell he was lying. I smiled like he was making me feel better.

Do you want me to get you a drink? Tío asked. We got beer and rum.

Miguel, Mami said. He's young.

Young? Back in Santo Domingo, he'd be getting laid by now.

Mami thinned her lips, which took some doing.

Well, it's true, Tío said.

So, Mami, I said. When do I get to go visit the D.R.?

That's enough, Yunior.

It's the only pussy you'll ever get, Rafa said to me in English.

Not counting your girlfriend, of course.

Rafa smiled. He had to give me that one.

Papi came in from parking the van. He and Miguel gave each other the sort of handshakes that would have turned my fingers into Wonder bread.

Coño, compa'i, ¿cómo va todo? they said to each other.

Tía came out then, with an apron on and maybe the longest Lee Press-On Nails I've ever seen in my life. There was this one guru motherfucker in the *Guinness Book of World Records* who had longer nails, but I tell you, it was close. She gave everybody kisses, told me and Rafa how guapo we were—Rafa, of course, believed her—told Madai how bella she was, but when she got to Papi, she froze a little, like maybe she'd seen a wasp on the tip of his nose, but then kissed him all the same.

Mami told us to join the other kids in the living room. Tío said, Wait a minute, I want to show you the apartment. I was glad Tía said, Hold on, because from what I'd seen so far, the place had been furnished in Contemporary Dominican Tacky. The less I saw, the better. I mean, I liked plastic sofa covers but damn, Tío and Tía had taken it to another level. They had a disco ball hanging in the living room and the type of stucco ceilings that looked like stalactite heaven. The sofas all had golden tassels dangling from their edges. Tía came out of the kitchen with some people I didn't know and by the time she got done introducing everybody, only Papi and Mami were given the guided tour of the four-room third-floor apartment. Me and Rafa joined the kids in the living room. They'd already started eating. We were hungry, one of the girls explained, a pastelito in hand. The boy was about three years younger than me but the girl who'd spoken, Leti, was my age. She and another girl were on the sofa together and they were cute as hell.

Leti introduced them: the boy was her brother Wilquins and the other girl was her neighbor Mari. Leti had some serious tetas and I could tell that my brother was going to gun for her. His taste in girls was predictable. He sat down right between Leti and Mari and by the way they were smiling at him I knew he'd do fine. Neither of the girls gave me more than a cursory one-two, which didn't bother me. Sure, I liked girls but I was always too terrified to speak to them unless we were arguing or I was calling them stupidos, which was one of my favorite words that year. I turned to Wilquins and asked him what there was to do around here. Mari, who had the lowest voice I'd ever heard, said, He can't speak.

What does that mean?

He's mute.

I looked at Wilquins incredulously. He smiled and nodded, as if he'd won a prize or something.

Does he understand? I asked.

Of course he understands, Rafa said. He's not dumb.

I could tell Rafa had said that just to score points with the girls. Both of them nodded. Low-voice Mari said, He's the best student in his grade.

I thought, Not bad for a mute. I sat next to Wilquins. After about two seconds of TV Wilquins whipped out a bag of dominos and motioned to me. Did I want to play? Sure. Me and him played Rafa and Leti and we whupped their collective asses twice, which put Rafa in a real bad mood. He looked at me like maybe he wanted to take a swing, just one to make him feel better. Leti kept whispering into Rafa's ear, telling him it was OK.

In the kitchen I could hear my parents slipping into their usual modes. Papi's voice was loud and argumentative; you didn't have to be anywhere near him to catch his drift. And Mami, you had to put cups to your ears to hear hers. I went into the kitchen a few times—once so the tíos could show off how much bullshit I'd been able to cram in my head the last few years; another time for a bucket-sized cup of soda. Mami and Tía were frying tostones and the last of the pastelitos. She appeared happier now and the way her hands worked on our dinner you would think she had a life somewhere else making rare and precious things. She nudged Tía every now and then, shit they must have been doing all their lives. As soon as Mami saw me though, she gave me the eye. Don't stay long, that eye said. Don't piss your old man off.

Papi was too busy arguing about Elvis to notice me. Then somebody mentioned María Montez and Papi barked, María Montez? Let me tell *you* about María Montez, compa'i.

Maybe I was used to him. His voice—louder than most adults'—didn't bother me none, though the other kids shifted uneasily in their seats. Wilquins was about to raise the volume on the TV, but Rafa said, I wouldn't do that. Muteboy had balls, though. He did it anyway and then sat down. Wilquins's pop came into the living room a second later, a bottle of Presidente in hand. That dude must have had Spider-senses or something. Did you raise that? he asked Wilquins and Wilquins nodded.

Is this your house? his pops asked. He looked ready to beat Wilquins silly but he lowered the volume instead.

See, Rafa said. You nearly got your ass *kicked.*

I met the Puerto Rican woman right after Papi had gotten the van. He was taking me on short trips, trying to cure me of my vomiting. It wasn't really working but I looked forward to our trips, even though at the end of each one I'd be sick. These were the only times me and Papi did anything together. When we were alone he treated me much better, like maybe I was his son or something.

Before each drive Mami would cross me.

Bendición, Mami, I'd say.

She'd kiss my forehead. Que Dios te bendiga. And then she would give me a handful of mentas because she wanted me to be OK. Mami didn't think these excursions would cure anything, but the one time she had brought it up to Papi he had told her to shut up, what did she know about anything anyway?

Me and Papi didn't talk much. We just drove around our neighborhood. Occasionally he'd ask, How is it?

And I'd nod, no matter how I felt.

One day I was sick outside of Perth Amboy. Instead of taking me home he went the other way on Industrial Avenue, stopping a few minutes later in front of a light blue house I didn't recognize. It reminded me of the Easter eggs we colored at school, the ones we threw out the bus windows at other cars.

The Puerto Rican woman was there and she helped me clean up. She had dry papery hands and when she rubbed the towel on my chest, she did it hard, like I was a bumper she was waxing. She was very thin and had a cloud of brown hair rising above her narrow face and the sharpest blackest eyes you've ever seen.

He's cute, she said to Papi.

Not when he's throwing up, Papi said.

What's your name? she asked me. Are you Rafa?

I shook my head.

Then it's Yunior, right?

I nodded.

You're the smart one, she said, suddenly happy with herself. Maybe you want to see my books?

They weren't hers. I recognized them as ones my father must have left in her house. Papi was a voracious reader, couldn't even go cheating without a paperback in his pocket.

Why don't you go watch TV? Papi suggested. He was looking at her like she was the last piece of chicken on earth.

We got plenty of channels, she said. Use the remote if you want.

The two of them went upstairs and I was too scared of what was happening to poke around. I just sat there, ashamed, expecting something big and fiery to crash down on our heads. I watched a whole hour of the news before Papi came downstairs and said, Let's go.

About two hours later the women laid out the food and like always nobody but the kids thanked them. It must be some Dominican tradition or something. There was everything I liked—chicharrones, fried chicken, tostones, sancocho, rice, fried cheese, yuca, avocado, potato salad, a meteor-sized hunk of pernil, even a tossed salad which I could do without—but when I joined the other kids around the serving table, Papi said, Oh no you don't, and took the paper plate out of my hand. His fingers weren't gentle.

What's wrong now? Tía asked, handing me another plate.

He ain't eating, Papi said. Mami pretended to help Rafa with the pernil.

Why can't he eat?

Because I said so.

The adults who didn't know us made like they hadn't heard a thing and Tío just smiled sheepishly and told everybody to go ahead and eat. All the kids—about ten of them now—trooped back into the living room with their plates a-heaping and all the adults ducked into the kitchen and the dining room, where the radio was playing loud-ass bachatas. I was the only one without a plate. Papi stopped me before I could get away from him. He kept his voice nice and low so nobody else could hear him.

If you eat anything, I'm going to beat you. ¿Entiendes?

I nodded.

And if your brother gives you any food, I'll beat him too. Right here in front of everybody. ¿Entiendes?

I nodded again. I wanted to kill him and he must have sensed it because he gave my head a little shove.

All the kids watched me come in and sit down in front of the TV.

What's wrong with your dad? Leti asked.

He's a dick, I said.

Rafa shook his head. Don't say that shit in front of people.

Easy for you to be nice when you're eating, I said.

Hey, if I was a pukey little baby, I wouldn't get no food either.

I almost said something back but I concentrated on the TV. I wasn't going to start it. No fucking way. So I watched Bruce Lee beat Chuck Norris into the floor of the Colosseum and tried to pretend that there was no food anywhere in the house. It was Tía who finally saved me. She came into the living room and said, since you ain't eating, Yunior, you can at least help me get some ice.

I didn't want to, but she mistook my reluctance for something else.

I already asked your father.

She held my hand while we walked; Tía didn't have any kids but I could tell she wanted them. She was the sort of relative who always remembered your birthday but who you only went to visit because you had to. We didn't get past the first-floor landing before she opened her pocketbook and handed me the first of three pastelitos she had smuggled out of the apartment.

Go ahead, she said. And as soon as you get inside make sure you brush your teeth.

Thanks a lot, Tía, I said.

Those pastelitos didn't stand a chance.

She sat next to me on the stairs and smoked her cigarette. All the way down on the first floor and we could still hear the music and the adults and the television. Tía looked a ton like Mami; the two of them were both short and light-skinned. Tía smiled a lot and that was what set them apart the most.

How is it at home, Yunior?

What do you mean?

How's it going in the apartment? Are you kids OK?

I knew an interrogation when I heard one, no matter how sugar-coated it was. I didn't say anything. Don't get me wrong, I loved my tía, but something told me to keep my mouth shut. Maybe it was family loyalty, maybe I just wanted to protect Mami or I was afraid that Papi would find out—it could have been anything really.

Is your mom all right?

I shrugged.

Have there been lots of fights?

None, I said. Too many shrugs would have been just as bad as an an-swer. Papi's at work too much.

Work, Tía said, like it was somebody's name she didn't like.

Me and Rafa, we didn't talk much about the Puerto Rican woman. When we ate dinner at her house, the few times Papi had taken us over there, we still acted like nothing was out of the ordinary. Pass the ketchup, man. No sweat, bro. The affair was like a hole in our living room floor, one we'd gotten so used to circumnavigating that we sometimes forgot it was there.

By midnight all the adults were crazy dancing. I was sitting outside Tía's bedroom—where Madai was sleeping—trying not to attract atten-tion. Rafa had me guarding the door; he and Leti were in there too, with some of the other kids, getting busy no doubt. Wilquins had gone across the hall to bed so I had me and the roaches to mess around with.

Whenever I peered into the main room I saw about twenty moms and dads dancing and drinking beers. Every now and then somebody yelled, ¡Quisqueya! And then everybody else would yell and stomp their feet. From what I could see my parents seemed to be enjoying themselves.

Mami and Tía spent a lot of time side by side, whispering, and I kept expecting something to come of this, a brawl maybe. I'd never once been out with my family when it hadn't turned to shit. We weren't even theatrical or straight crazy like other families. We fought like sixth-graders, without any real dignity. I guess the whole night I'd been wait-ing for a blowup, something between Papi and Mami. This was how I always figured Papi would be exposed, out in public, where everybody would know.

You're a cheater!

But everything was calmer than usual. And Mami didn't look like she was about to say anything to Papi. The two of them danced every now and then but they never lasted more than a song before Mami joined Tía again in whatever conversation they were having.

I tried to imagine Mami before Papi. Maybe I was tired, or just sad, thinking about the way my family was. Maybe I already knew how it would all end up in a few years, Mami without Papi, and that was why I did it. Picturing her alone wasn't easy. It seemed like Papi had always been with her, even when we were waiting in Santo Domingo for him to send for us.

The only photograph our family had of Mami as a young woman, before she married Papi, was the one that somebody took of her at an election party that I found one day while rummaging for money to go to the arcade. Mami had it tucked into her immigration papers. In the photo, she's surrounded by laughing cousins I will never meet, who are all shiny from dancing, whose clothes are rumpled and loose. You can tell it's night and hot and that the mosquitos have been biting. She sits straight and even in a crowd she stands out, smiling quietly like maybe she's the one everybody's celebrating. You can't see her hands but I imagined they're knotting a straw or a bit of thread. This was the woman my father met a year later on the Malecón, the woman Mami thought she'd always be.

Mami must have caught me studying her because she stopped what she was doing and gave me a smile, maybe her first one of the night. Suddenly I wanted to go over and hug her, for no other reason than I loved her, but there were about eleven fat jiggling bodies between us. So I sat down on the tiled floor and waited.

I must have fallen asleep because the next thing I knew Rafa was kicking me and saying, Let's go. He looked like he'd been hitting those girls off; he was all smiles. I got to my feet in time to kiss Tía and Tío good-bye. Mami was holding the serving dish she had brought with her.

Where's Papi? I asked.

He's downstairs, bringing the van around. Mami leaned down to kiss me.

You were good today, she said.

And then Papi burst in and told us to get the hell downstairs before some pendejo cop gave him a ticket. More kisses, more handshakes and then we were gone.

I don't remember being out of sorts after I met the Puerto Rican woman, but I must have been because Mami only asked me questions when she thought something was wrong in my life. It took her about ten passes but finally she cornered me one afternoon when we were alone in the apartment. Our upstairs neighbors were beating the crap out of their kids, and me and her had been listening to it all afternoon. She put her hand on mine and said, Is everything OK, Yunior? Have you been fighting with your brother?

Me and Rafa had already talked. We'd been in the basement, where our parents couldn't hear us. He told me that yeah, he knew about her.

Papi's taken me there twice now, he said.

Why didn't you tell me? I asked.

What the hell was I going to say? *Hey, Yunior, guess what happened yesterday? I met Papi's sucia!*

I didn't say anything to Mami either. She watched me, very very closely. Later I would think, maybe if I had told her, she would have confronted him, would have done something, but who can know these things? I said I'd been having trouble in school and like that everything was back to normal between us. She put her hand on my shoulder and squeezed and that was that.

We were on the turnpike, just past Exit 11, when I started feeling it again. I sat up from leaning against Rafa. His fingers smelled and he'd gone to sleep almost as soon as he got into the van. Madai was out too but at least she wasn't snoring.

In the darkness, I saw that Papi had a hand on Mami's knee and that the two of them were quiet and still. They weren't slumped back or anything; they were both wide awake, bolted into their seats. I couldn't see either of their faces and no matter how hard I tried I couldn't imagine their expressions. Neither of them moved. Every now and then the van was filled with the bright rush of somebody else's headlights. Finally I said, Mami, and they both looked back, already knowing what was happening.

Every Tongue Shall Confess

ZZ PACKER

As Pastor Everett made the announcements that began the service, Clareese Mitchell stood with her choir members, knowing that once again she had to Persevere, put on the Strong Armor of God, the Breastplate of Righteousness, but she was having her monthly womanly troubles and all she wanted to do was curse the Brothers' Church Council of Greater Christ Emmanuel Pentecostal Church of the Fire Baptized, who'd decided that the Sisters had to wear *white* every Missionary Sunday, which was, of course, the day of the month when her womanly troubles were always at their absolute worst! And to think that the Brothers' Church Council of Greater Christ Emmanuel Pentecostal Church of the Fire Baptized had been the first place she'd looked for guidance and companionship nearly ten years ago when her aunt Alma had fallen ill. And why not? They were God-fearing, church-going men; men like Deacon Julian Jeffers, now sitting in the first row of pews, closest to the altar, right under the leafy top of the corn plant she'd brought in to make the sanctuary more homey. Two months ago she'd been reading the book of Micah and posed the idea of a Book of Micah discussion group to the Deacon Jeffers and he'd said, "Oh, Sister Clareese! We should make *you* a deacon!" Which of course they didn't. Deacons, like pastors, were men—not that she was complaining. But it still rankled that Jeffers had said he'd get back to her about the Micah discussion group and he never had.

Clareese's cross-eyes roved to the back of the church where Sister Drusella and Sister Maxwell sat, resplendent in their identical wide-brimmed, purple-flowered hats, their unsaved guests sitting next to them. The guests wore frightened smiles, and Clareese tried to shoot them reassuring looks. The gold-lettered banner behind them read: "We Are More Than Conquerors in Christ Our Lord," and she tried to use this as a focal point. But her cross-eyes couldn't help it; they settled, at last, on Deacon McCreedy, making his way down the aisle for the second time. Oh, how she hated him!

She would never forget—never, never, never—the day he came to the hospital where she worked; she was still wearing her white nurse's uniform and he'd said he was concerned about her spiritual well-being— *Liar!*—then drove her to where she lived with her aunt Alma, whose room resounded with perpetual snores and hacking and wheezing—as if Clareese didn't have enough of this at the hospital—and while Alma slept, Clareese poured Deacon McCreedy some fruit punch, which he drank between forkfuls of chicken, plus half their pork roast. No sooner than he'd wiped his hands on the napkin—didn't bother using a fork—he stood and walked behind her, covering her cross-eyes as though she were a child, as though he were about to give her a gift—a Bible with her very own name engraved on it, perhaps—but he didn't give her anything, he'd just covered her wandering eyes and said, "Sing 'On Christ the Solid Rock I Stand.' Make sure to do the Waterfall." And she was happy to do it, happy to please Deacon McCreedy, so she began singing in her best, cleanest voice until she felt his hand slide up the scratchy white pantyhose of her nurse's uniform and up toward the control-top of her pantyhose. Before she could stop him, one finger was wriggling around inside, and by then it was too late to tell him she was having her monthly womanly troubles. He drew back in disgust—no, *hatred*— then rinsed his hand in the kitchen sink and left without saying a word, not a thanks for the chicken or the pork roast or her singing. Not a single word of apology for anything. But she could have forgiven him—if Sisters could even forgive Deacons—for she could have understood that an unmarried man might have *needs,* but what really bothered her was how he ignored her. How a few weeks later she and Aunt Alma had been waiting for the bus after Wednesday-night prayer meeting and he *drove past.* That's right. No offer of a ride, no slowing down, no nothing. Aunt Alma was nearly blind and couldn't even see it was him, but Clareese recognized his car at once.

Yes, she wanted to curse the Brothers' Church Council of Greater Christ Emmanuel Pentecostal Church of the Fire Baptized, but Sisters and Brothers could not curse, could not even swear or take an oath, for *neither shalt thou swear by thy head, because thou canst not make one hair white or black.* So no oath, no swearing, and of course no betting— an extension of swearing—which was why she'd told the other nurses at University Hospital that she would not join their betting pool to predict who would get married first, Patty or Edwina. She told them about the black and white hairs and all Nurse Holloway did was clomp her pumps—as if she was too good for the standard orthopedically correct shoes—down the green tiles of the hall and shout behind her back, "Somebody sure needs to get laid." Oh, how the other RNs tittered in their gossipy way.

Now everyone applauded when Pastor Everett announced that Sister Nina would be getting married to Harold, one of the Brothers from Broadway Tongues of Spirit Church. Then Pastor Everett said, "Sister Nina will be holding a Council so we can get husbands for the rest of the hardworking Sisters." Like Sister Clareese, is what he meant. The congregation laughed at the joke. Ha ha. And perhaps the joke *was* on her. If she'd been married, Deacon McCreedy wouldn't have dared do what he did; if she'd been married perhaps she'd also be working fewer shifts at the hospital, perhaps she would have never met that patient—that man—who'd almost gotten her fired! And at exactly that moment, it hit her, right below the gut, a sharp pain, and she imagined her uterus, that Texas-shaped organ, the Rio Grande of her monthly womanly troubles flushing out to the Gulf.

Pastor Everett had finished the announcements. Now it was time for testimony service. She tried to distract herself by thinking of suitable testimonies. Usually she testified about work. Last week, she'd testified about the poor man with a platelet count of seven, meaning he was a goner, and how Nurse Holloway had told him, "We're bringing you more platelets," and how he'd said, "That's all right. God sent me more." No one at the nurses' station—to say nothing of those atheist doctors— believed him. But when Nurse Holloway checked, sure enough, Glory be to God, he had a count of sixteen. Clareese told the congregation how she knelt on the cold tiled floor of University Hospital's corridor, right then and there, arms outstretched to Glory. And what could the other nurses say to that? Nothing, that's what.

She remembered her testimony from a month ago, how she'd been working the hotline, and a mother had called to say that her son had eaten ants, and Sister Clareese had assured the woman that ants were God's creatures, and though disturbing, they wouldn't harm the boy. But the Lord told Clareese to stay on the line with the mother, not to rush the way other nurses often did, so Clareese stayed on the line. And Glory be to God that she did! Once the mother had calmed down she'd said, "Thank goodness. The insecticide I gave Kevin must have worked." Sister Clareese had stayed after her shift to make sure the woman brought her boy into Emergency. Afterward she told the woman to hold hands with Kevin and give God the Praise he deserved.

But she had told these stories already. As she fidgeted in her choir-mistress's chair, she tried to think of new ones. The congregation wouldn't care about how she had to stay on top of codes, or how she had to triple-check patients' charts. The only patients who stuck in her mind were Mrs. Geneva Bosma, whose toe was rotting off, and Mr. Toomey, who had prostate cancer. And, of course, Mr. Cleophus Sanders, the cause of all her current problems. Cleophus was an amputee who liked to turn the volume of his television up so high that his channel-surfing sounded as if someone were being electrocuted, repeatedly. At the nurses' station she'd overheard that Cleophus Sanders was once a musician who in his heyday went by the nickname "Delta Sweetmeat." But he'd gone in and out of the music business, sometimes taking construction jobs. A crane had fallen on his leg and he'd been amputated from below the knee. No, none of these cases was Edifying in God's sight. Her run-in with Cleophus had been downright un-Edifying

When Mr. Sanders had been moved into Mr. Toomey's room last Monday, she'd told them both, "I hope everyone has a blessed day!" She'd made sure to say this only after she was safely inside with the door closed behind her. She had to make sure she didn't mention God until the door was closed *behind* her, because Nurse Holloway was always clomping about, trying to say that this was a *university* hospital, as well as a *research* hospital, one at the very *forefront* of medicine, and didn't Registered Nurse Clareese Mitchell recognize and *respect* that not everyone shared her beliefs? That the hospital catered not only to Christians, but to people of the Jewish faith? To Muslims, Hindus, and agnostics? Atheists, even?

This Clareese knew only too well, which was why it was all the more important for her to Spread the Gospel. So she shut the door, and said to Mr. Toomey, louder this time, "I HOPE EVERYONE HAS A BLESSED DAY!"

Mr. Toomey grunted. Heavy and completely white, he reminded Sister Clareese of a walrus: everything about him drooped, his eyes like twin frowns, his nose, perhaps even his mouth, though it was hard to make out because of his frowning blond mustache. Well, Glory be to God, she expected something like a grunt from him, she couldn't say she was surprised: junkies who detox scream and writhe before turning clean; the man with a hangover does not like to wake to the sun. So it was with sinners exposed to the harsh, curing Light of the Lord.

"Hey, sanctified lady!" Cleophus Sanders called from across the room. "He got cancer! Let the man alone."

"I *know* what he *has*," Sister Clareese said. "I'm his *nurse*." This wasn't how she wanted the patient-RN relationship to begin, but Cleophus had gotten the better of her. Yes, that was the problem, wasn't it? *He'd* gotten the better of *her*. This was how Satan worked, throwing you off a little at a time. She would have to Persevere, put on the Strong Armor of God. She tried again.

"My name is Sister Clareese Mitchell, your assigned registered nurse. I can't exactly say that I'm pleased to meet you, because that would be a lie and 'lying lips are an abomination to the Lord.' I will say that I am pleased to do my duty and help you recover."

"*Me oh my!*" Cleophus Sanders said, and he laughed big and long, the kind of laughter that could go on and on, rising and rising, restarting itself if need be, like yeast. He slapped the knee of his amputated leg, the knee that would probably come off if his infection didn't stop eating away at it. But Cleophus Sanders didn't care. He just slapped that infected knee, hooting all the while in an ornery, backwoods kind of way that made Clareese want to hit him. But of course she would never, never do that.

She busied herself by changing Mr. Toomey's catheter, then remaking his bed, rolling the walrus of him this way and that, with little help on his part. As soon as she was done with Mr. Toomey, he turned on the Knicks game. The whole time she'd changed Mr. Toomey's catheter, however, Cleophus had watched her, laughing under his breath, then outright, a waxing and waning of hilarity as if her every gesture were laughably prim and proper.

"Look, Mr. *Cleophus Sanders*," she said, glad for the chance to bite on the ridiculous name, "I am a professional. You may laugh at what I do, but in doing so you laugh at the Almighty who has given me the breath to do it!"

She'd steeled herself for a vulgar reply. But no. Mr. Toomey did the talking.

"I tell *you* what!" Mr. Toomey said, pointing his remote at Sister Clareese, "I'm going to sue this hospital for lack of peace and quiet. All your Almighty this' and 'Oh Glory that' is keeping me from watching the game!"

So Sister Clareese murmured her apologies to Mr. Toomey, the whole while Cleophus Sanders put on an act of restraining his amusement, body and bed quaking in seizure-like fits.

Now sunlight filtered through the yellow-tinted windows of Greater Christ Emmanuel Pentecostal Church of the Fire Baptized, lighting Brother Hopkins, the organist, with a halo-like glow. The rest of the congregation had given their testimonies, and it was now time for the choir members to testify, starting with Clareese. Was there any way she could possibly turn her incident with Cleophus Sanders into an edifying testimony experience? Just then, another hit, and she felt a cramping so hard she thought she might double over. It was her turn. Cleophus's laughter and her cramping womb seemed one and the same; he'd inhabited her body like a demon, preventing her from thinking up a proper testimony. As she rose, unsteadily, to her feet, all she managed to say was, "Pray for me."

It was almost time for Pastor Everett to preach his sermon. To introduce it, Sister Clareese had the choir sing "Every Knee Shall Bow, Every Tongue Shall Confess." It was an old-fashioned hymn, unlike the hopped-up gospel songs churches were given to nowadays. And she liked the slow unfolding of its message: how without people uttering a word, all their hearts would be made plain to the Lord; that He would know you not by what you said or did, but by what you'd hoped and intended. The teens, however, mumbled over the verses, and older choir members sang without vigor. The hymn ended up sounding like the national anthem at a school assembly: a stouthearted song rendered in monotone.

"Thank you, thank you, thank you, Sister Clareese," Pastor Everett said, looking back at her, "for that wonderful tune."

Tune? She knew that Pastor Everett thought she was not the kind of person a choirmistress should be; she was quiet, nervous, skinny in all the wrong places, and completely cross-eyed. She knew he thought of her as something worse than a spinster, because she wasn't yet old.

Pastor Everett hunched close to the microphone, as though about to begin a forlorn love song. From the corners of her vision she saw him smile—only for a second but with every single tooth in his mouth. He was yam-colored, and given to wearing epaulets on the shoulders of his robes and gold braiding all down the front. Sister Clareese felt no attraction to him, but she seemed to be the only one who didn't; even the Sisters going on eighty were charmed by Pastor Everett, who, though not entirely handsome, had handsome moments.

"Sister Clareese," he said, turning to where she stood with the choir. "Sister Clareese, I know y'all just sang for us, but I need some *more* help. Satan got these Brothers and Sisters putting m'Lord on hold!"

Sister Clareese knew that everyone expected her and her choir to begin singing again, but she had been alerted to what he was up to; he had called her yesterday. He had thought nothing of asking her to unplug her telephone—her *only* telephone, her *private* line—to bring it to church so that he could use it in some sermon about call-waiting. Hadn't even asked her how she was doing, hadn't bothered to pray over her aunt Alma's sickness. Nevertheless, she'd said, "Why certainly, Pastor Everett. Anything I can do to help."

Now Sister Clareese produced her Princess telephone from under her seat and handed it to the Pastor. Pastor Everett held the telephone aloft, shaking it as if to rid it of demons. "How many of y'all—Brothers and Sisters—got telephones?" the Pastor asked.

One by one, members of the congregation timidly raised their hands.

"All right," Pastor Everett said, as though this grieved him, "almost all of y'all." He flipped through his huge pulpit Bible. "How many of y'all—Brothers and Sisters—got call-waiting?" He turned pages quickly, then stopped, as though he didn't need to search the scripture after all. "Let me tell ya," the Pastor said, nearly kissing the microphone, "there is *Someone!* Who won't *accept* your call-waiting! There is *Someone!* Who won't *wait,* when you put Him on hold!" Sister Nancy Popwell and Sister Drusella Davies now had their eyes closed in concentration, their hands waving slowly in the air in front of them as though they were trying to make their way through a dark room.

The last phone call Sister Clareese had made was on Wednesday, to Mr. Toomey. She knew both he and Cleophus were likely to reject the Lord, but she had a policy of sorts, which was to call patients who'd been in her care for at least a week. She considered it her Christian duty to call—even on her day off—to let them know that Jesus cared, and that she cared. The other RNs resorted to callous catchphrases that they bandied about the nurses' station: "Just because I care *for* them doesn't mean I have to care *about* them," or, "I'm a nurse, not a nursery." Not Clareese. Perhaps she'd been curt with Cleophus Sanders, but she had been so in defense of God. Perhaps Mr. Toomey had been curt with her, but he was going into O.R. soon, and grouchiness was to be expected.

Nurse Patty had been switchboard operator that night and Clareese had had to endure her sighs before the girl finally connected her to Mr. Toomey.

"Praise the Lord, Mr. Toomey!"

"Who's this?"

"This is your nurse, Sister Clareese, and I'm calling to say that Jesus will be with you through your surgery."

"Who?"

"Jesus," she said.

She thought she heard the phone disconnect, then, a voice. Of course. Cleophus Sanders.

"Why ain't you called *me*?" Cleophus said.

Sister Clareese tried to explain her policy, the thing about the week.

"So you care more about some white dude than you care about good ol' Cleophus?"

"It's not that, Mr. Sanders, God cares for white and black alike. Acts 10:34 says, 'God is no respecter of persons.' Black or white. Red, purple, or green—he doesn't care, as long as you accept his salvation and live right." When he was silent on the other end she said, "It's that I've only known you for two days. I'll see you tomorrow."

She tried to hang up, but he said, "Let me play something for you. Something interesting, since all you probably listen to is monks chanting and such."

Before she could respond, there was a noise on the other end that sounded like juke music. Then he came back on the phone and said, "Like that, don't you?"

"I had the phone away from my ear."

"I thought you said 'lying is the abominable.' Do you like or do you don't?" When she said nothing he said, "Truth, now."

She answered yes.

She didn't want to answer yes. But she also didn't want to lie. And what was one to do in that circumstance? If God looked into your heart right then, what would He think? Or would He have to approve because He made your heart that way? Or were you obliged to train it against its wishes? She didn't know what to think, but on the other end Cleophus said, "What you just heard there was the blues. What you just heard there was me."

"...Let me tell ya!" Pastor Everett shouted, his voice hitting its highest octave, "*Jeeeee-zus*—did not *tell* his *Daddy*—'I'm sorry, Pops, but my girlfriend is on the other line'; *Jeeeee-zus*—never *told* the Omnipotent One, 'Can you wait a sec, I think I got a call from the electric company!' *Jeeeeeeee-zus*—never told Matthew, Mark, Luke, or John, 'I'm *sorry,* but I got to put you on hold; I'm sorry, Brother Luke, but I got some mac and cheese in the oven; I'm *sorry,* but I got to eat this fried chicken'"—and at this, Pastor Everett paused, grinning in anticipation of his own punch line—"'cause it's finger-licking good!"

Drops of sweat plunked onto his microphone.

Sister Clareese watched as the congregation cheered, the women flagging their Bibles in the air as though the Bibles were as light and yielding as handkerchiefs; their bosoms jouncing as though they were harboring sacks of potatoes in their blouses. They shook tambourines, scores of them all going at once, the sound of something sizzling and frying.

That was it? That was The Message? Of course, she'd only heard part of it, but still. Of course she believed that one's daily life shouldn't outstrip one's spiritual one, but there seemed no place for true belief at Greater Christ Emmanuel Pentecostal Church of the Fire Baptized. Everyone wanted flash and props, no one wanted the Word itself, naked in its fiery glory.

Most of the Brothers and Sisters were up on their feet. "Tell it!" yelled some, while others called out, "Go 'head on!" The organist pounded out the chords to what could have been the theme song of a TV game show.

She looked to see what Sister Drusella's and Sister Maxwell's unsaved guests were doing. Drusella's unsaved guest was her son, which made him easy to bring into the fold: he was living in her shed and had no car. He was busy turning over one of the cardboard fans donated by Hamblin and Sons Funeral Parlor, reading the words intently, then flipping it over again to stare at the picture of a gleaming casket and grieving family. Sister Donna Maxwell's guest was an ex-con she'd written to and tried to save while he was in prison. The ex-con seemed to watch the scene with approval, though one could never really know what was going on in the criminal mind. For all Sister Clareese knew, he could be counting all the pockets he planned to pick.

And they called themselves missionaries. Family members and ex-cons were easy to convince of God's will. As soon as Drusella's son took note of the pretty young Sisters his age, he'd be back. And everyone knew you could convert an ex-con with a few well-timed pecan pies.

Wednesday was her only day off besides Sunday, and though a phone call or two was her policy on days off, she very seldom visited the hospital. And yet, last Wednesday, she'd had to. The more she'd considered Cleophus's situation—his loss of limb, his devil's music, his unsettling laughter—the more she grew convinced that he was her Missionary Challenge. That he was especially in need of Saving.

Minutes after she'd talked with him on the phone, she took the number 42 bus and transferred to the crosstown H, then walked the rest of the way to the hospital.

Edwina had taken over for Patty as nurses' station attendant, and she'd said, "We have an ETOH in—where's your uniform?"

"It's not my shift," she called behind her as she rushed past Edwina and into Room 204.

She opened the door to find Cleophus sitting on the bed, still plucking chords on his unplugged electric guitar that she'd heard him playing over the phone half an hour earlier. Mr. Toomey's bed was empty; one of the nurses must have already taken him to O.R., so Cleophus had the room to himself. The right leg of Cleophus's hospital pants hung down limp and empty, and it was the first time she'd seen his guitar, curvy and shiny as a sportscar. He did not acknowledge her when she entered. He was still picking away at his guitar, singing a song about a man whose woman had left him so high and dry, she'd taken the car, the dog, the furniture. Even the wallpaper. Only when he'd strummed the final chords did Cleophus look up, as if noticing her for the first time.

"Sister *Clare-reeeese!*" He said it as if he were introducing a showgirl.

"It's your soul," Clareese said. "God wants me to help save your soul." The urgency of God's message struck her so hard, she felt the wind knocked out of her. She sat on the bed next to him.

"Really?" he said, cocking his head a little.

"Really and truly," Clareese said, "I know I said I liked your music, but I said it because God gave you that gift for you to use. For Him."

"Uhnn-huh," Cleophus said. "How about this, little lady. How about if God lets me keep this knee, I'll come to church with you. We can go out and get some dinner afterwards. Like a proper couple."

She tried not to be flattered. "The Lord does *not make* deals, Mr. Sanders. But I'm sure the Lord would love to see you in church regardless of what happens to your knee."

"Well, since you seem to be His receptionist, how about you ask the Lord if he can give you the day off. I can take you out on the town. See, if I go to church, I *know* the Lord won't show. But I'm positive you will."

"Believe you me, Mr. Sanders, the Lord is at every service. *Where two or three are gathered together in my name, there am I in the midst of them.*" She sighed, trying to remember what she came to say. "*He is the Way, the Truth and the Life. No man—*"

"*...cometh to the father,*" Cleophus said, "*but by me.*"

She looked at him. "You know your Bible."

"Naw. You were speaking and I just heard it." He absently strummed his guitar. "You were talking, saying that verse, and the rest of it came to me. Not even a voice," he said, "more like...kind of like music."

She stared. Her hands clapped his, preventing him from playing further. For a moment, she was breathless. He looked at her, suddenly seeming to comprehend what he'd just said, that the Lord had actually spoken to him. For a minute, they sat there, both overjoyed at what the Lord had done, but then he had to go ruin it. He burst out laughing his biggest, most sinful laugh yet.

"Awww!" he cried, doubled over, and then flopped backward onto his hospital bed. Then he closed his eyes, laughing without sound.

She stood up, chest heaving, wondering why she even bothered with him.

"Clareese," he said, trying to clear his voice of any leftover laughter, "don't go." He looked at her with pleading eyes, then patted the space beside him on the bed.

She looked around the room for some cue. Whenever she needed an answer, she relied on some sign from the Lord; a fresh beam of sunlight through the window, the hands of a clock folded in prayer, or the flush of a commode. These were signs that whatever she was thinking of doing was right. If there was a storm cloud, or something in her path, then that was a bad sign. But nothing in the room gave her any indication whether she should stay and witness to Mr. Sanders, or go.

"What, Mr. Sanders, do you want from me? It's my day off. I decided to come by and offer you an invitation to my church because God has given you a gift. A musical gift." She dug into her purse, then pulled out a pocket-sized Bible. "But I'll leave you with this. If you need to find us— our church—the name and number is printed inside."

He took the Bible with a little smile, turning it over, then flipping through it, as if some money might be tucked away inside. "Seriously, though," he'd said, "let me ask you a question that's gonna seem dumb. Childish. Now, I want you to think long and hard about it. Why the hell's there so much suffering in the world if God's doing his job? I mean, look at me. Take old Toomey, too. We done anything *that* bad to deserve all this put on us?"

She sighed. "Because of people, that's why. Not God. It's *people* who allow suffering, people who create it. Perpetrate it."

"Maybe that explains Hitler and all them others, but I'm talking about—" He gestured at the room, the hospital in general.

Clareese tried to see what he saw when he looked at the room. At one time, the white and pale green walls of the hospital rooms had given her solace; the way everything was clean, clean, clean; the many patients that had been in each room, some nice, some dying, some willing to accept the Lord. But most, like Mr. Toomey, cast the Lord aside like wilted lettuce, and now the clean hospital room was just a reminder of the emptiness, the barrenness, of her patients' souls. Cleophus Sanders was just another patient who disrespected the Lord.

"Why does He allow natural disasters to kill people?" Clareese said, knowing that her voice was raised louder than what she meant it to be. "Why are little children born to get some rare blood disease and die? Why," she yelled, waving her arms, "does a crane fall on your leg and smash it? I don't know, Mr. Sanders. And I don't like it. But I'll say this! No one has a *right* to live! The only right we have is to die. That's it! If you get plucked out of the universe and given a chance to become a life, that's more than not having become anything at all, and for that, Mr. Sanders, you should be grateful!"

She had not known where this last bit had come from, and, she could tell, neither had he, but she could hear the other nurses coming down the hall to see who was yelling, and though Cleophus Sanders looked to have more pity on his face than true belief, he had come after her when she turned to leave. She'd heard the clatter of him gathering his crutches, and even when she heard the meaty weight of him slam onto the floor, she did not turn back. Then there it was. Pastor Everett's silly motion of cupping his hand to his ear, like he was eavesdropping on the choir, his signal that he was waiting for Sister Clareese to sing her solo, waiting to hear the voice that would send the congregation shouting "Thank you, Jesus, Blessed Savior!"

How could she do it. She thought of Cleophus on the floor and felt ashamed. She hadn't seen him since; her yelling had been brought to the attention of the administrators, and although the hospital was understaffed, the administration had suggested that she not return until next week. They handed her the card of the staff psychiatrist. She had not told anyone at church what had happened. Not even her aunt Alma.

She didn't want to sing. Didn't feel like it, but, she thought, *I will freely sacrifice myself unto Thee: I will praise Thy name, O Lord, for it is good.* Usually thinking of a scripture would give her strength, but this time it just made her realize how much strength she was always needing.

She didn't want to, but she'd do it. She'd sing a stupid solo part—the Waterfall, they called it—not even something she'd *invented* or *planned* to do who knows how many years ago when she'd had to sneeze her brains out, but oh no, she'd tried holding it in, and when she had to sing her solo, those years ago, her near-sneeze had made the words come out tumbling in a series of staccato notes that were almost fluid, and ever since then, she'd had to sing *all* solos that way, it was expected of her, everyone loved it, it was her trademark, she sang: "All-hall other-her her grooouund—is sink-king sand!"

The congregation applauded.

"Saints," the Pastor said, winding down, "you know this world will soon be *over!* Jesus will come back to this tired, sorry Earth in *a moment and a twinkling of an eye!* So you can't use call-waiting on the Lord! *Jeeee-zus,* my friends, does not accept conference calls! You are Children of God! You need to PRAY! Put down your phone! Say goodbye to AT&T! You cannot go in God's *direction,* without a little—*genuflection!*"

The congregation went wild, clapping and banging tambourines, whirling in the aisles. But the choir remained standing in case Pastor Everett wanted another song. For the first time, Clareese found that her monthly troubles had settled down. And now that she had the wherewithal to concentrate, she couldn't. Her cross-eyes wouldn't keep steady, they roamed like the wheels of a defective shopping cart, and from one roving eye she saw her aunt Alma, waving her arms as though listening to leftover strains of Clareese's solo.

What would she do? She didn't know if she'd still have her job when she went back on Monday, didn't know what the staff psychiatrist would try to pry out of her. More important, she didn't know what her aunt Alma would do without the special medical referrals Clareese could get her. What was a Sister to do?

Clareese's gaze must have found him just a moment after everyone else's had. A stranger at the far end of the aisle, standing directly opposite Pastor Everett as though about to engage him in a duel. There was Cleophus Sanders with his crutches, the right leg of his pinstriped pants hollow, wagging after him. Over his shoulder was a strap, attached to which was his guitar. Even Deacon McCreedy was looking.

What in heaven's name was Cleophus doing here? To bring his soul to salvation? To ridicule her? For another argument? Perhaps the doctors had told him he did not need the operation after all, and Cleophus was keeping his end of the deal with God. But he didn't seem like the type to keep promises. She saw his eyes search the congregation, and when he saw her, they locked eyes as if he had come to claim her. He did not come to get Saved, didn't care about his soul in that way, all he cared about was—

Now she knew why he'd come. He'd come for her. He'd come *despite* what she'd told him, despite his disbelief. Anyhow, she disapproved. It was God he needed, not her. Nevertheless, she remained standing for a few moments, even after the rest of the choir had already seated themselves, waving their cardboard fans to cool their sweaty faces.

Emergency

DENIS JOHNSON

I'd been working in the emergency room for about three weeks, I guess. This was in 1973, before the summer ended. With nothing to do on the overnight shift but batch the insurance reports from the daytime shifts, I just started wandering around, over to the coronary-care unit, down to the cafeteria, et cetera, looking for Georgie, the orderly, a pretty good friend of mine. He often stole pills from the cabinets.

He was running over the tiled floor of the operating room with a mop.

"Are you still doing that?" I said.

"Jesus, there's a lot of blood here," he complained.

"Where?" The floor looked clean enough to me.

"What the hell were they doing in here?" he asked me.

"They were performing surgery, Georgie," I told him.

"There's so much goop inside of us, man," he said, "and it all wants to get out." He leaned his mop against a cabinet.

"What are you crying for?" I didn't understand.

He stood still, raised both arms slowly behind his head, and tightened his ponytail. Then he grabbed the mop and started making broad random arcs with it, trembling and weeping and moving all around the place really fast. "What am I *crying* for?" he said.

"Jesus. Wow, oh boy, perfect."

I was hanging out in the ER with fat, quivering Nurse. One of the Family Service doctors that nobody liked came in looking for Georgie to wipe up after him. "Where's Georgie?" this guy asked.

"Georgie's in OR," Nurse said.

"Again?"

"No," Nurse said. "Still."

"Still? Doing what?"

"Cleaning the floor."

"Again?"

"No," Nurse said again. "Still."

Back in OR, Georgie dropped his mop and bent over in the posture of a child soiling its diapers. He stared down with his mouth open in terror.

He said, "What am I going to do about these fucking *shoes*, man?"

"Whatever you stole," I said, "I guess you already ate it all, right?"

"Listen to how they squish," he said, walking around carefully on his heels.

"Let me check your pockets, man."

He stood still a minute, and I found his stash. I left him two of each, whatever they were. "Shift is about half over," I told him.

"Good. Because I really, really, really need a drink," he said.

"Will you please help me get this blood mopped *up*?"

Around 3:30 A.M. a guy with a knife in his eye came in, led by Georgie.

"I hope *you* didn't do that to him," Nurse said.

"Me?" Georgie said. "No. He was like this."

"My wife did it," the man said. The blade was buried to the hilt in the outside corner of his left eye. It was a hunting knife kind of thing.

"Who brought you in?" Nurse said.

"Nobody. I just walked down. It's only three blocks," the man said.

Nurse peered at him. "We'd better get you lying down."

"Okay, I'm certainly ready for something like that," the man said.

She peered a bit longer into his face. "Is your other eye," she said, "a glass eye?"

"It's plastic, or something artificial like that," he said.

"And you can see out of *this* eye?" she asked, meaning the wounded one.

"I can see. But I can't make a fist out of my left hand because this knife is doing something to my brain."

"My God," Nurse said.

"I guess I'd better get the doctor," I said.

"There you go," Nurse agreed.

They got him lying down, and Georgie says to the patient, "Name?"

"Terrence Weber."

"Your face is dark. I can't see what you're saying."

"Georgie," I said.

"What are you saying, man? I can't see."

Nurse came over, and Georgie said to her, "His face is dark."

She leaned over the patient. "How long ago did this happen, Terry?" she shouted down into his face.

"Just a while ago. My wife did it. I was asleep," the patient said.

"Do you want the police?"

He thought about it and finally said, "Not unless I die."

Nurse went to the wall intercom and buzzed the doctor on duty, the Family Service person. "Got a surprise for you," she said over the intercom. He took his time getting down the hall to her, because he knew she hated Family Service and her happy tone of voice could only mean something beyond his competence and potentially humiliating.

He peeked into the trauma room and saw the situation: the clerk—that is, me—standing next to the orderly, Georgie, both of us on drugs, looking down at a patient with a knife sticking up out of his face.

"What seems to be the trouble?" he said.

The doctor gathered the three of us around him in the office and said, "Here's the situation. We've got to get a team here, an entire team. I want a good eye man. A great eye man. The best eye man. I want a brain surgeon. And I want a really good gas man, get me a genius. I'm not touching that head. I'm just going to watch this one. I know my limits. We'll just get him prepped and sit tight. Orderly!"

"Do you mean me?" Georgie said. "Should I get him prepped?"

"Is this a hospital?" the doctor asked. "Is this the emergency room? Is that a patient? Are you the orderly?"

I dialed the hospital operator and told her to get me the eye man and the brain man and the gas man.

Georgie could be heard across the hall, washing his hands and singing a Neil Young song that went "Hello cowgirl in the sand. Is this place at your command?"

"That person is not right, not at all, not one bit," the doctor said.

"As long as my instructions are audible to him it doesn't concern me," Nurse insisted, spooning stuff up out of a little Dixie cup.

"I've got my own life and the protection of my family to think of."

"Well, okay, okay. Don't chew my head off," the doctor said.

The eye man was on vacation or something. While the hospital's operator called around to find someone else just as good, the other specialists were hurrying through the night to join us. I stood around looking at charts and chewing up more of Georgie's pills. Some of them tasted the way urine smells, some of them burned, some of them tasted like chalk. Various nurses, and two physicians who'd been tending somebody in ICU, were hanging out down here with us now.

Everybody had a different idea about exactly how to approach the problem of removing the knife from Terrence Weber's brain. But when Georgie came in from prepping the patient—from shaving the patient's eyebrow and disinfecting the area around the wound, and so on—he seemed to be holding the hunting knife in his left hand.

The talk just dropped off a cliff.

"Where," the doctor asked finally, "did you get that?"

Nobody said one thing more, not for quite a long time.

After a while, one of the ICU nurses said, "Your shoelace is untied." Georgie laid the knife on a chart and bent down to fix his shoe.

There were twenty more minutes left to get through.

"How's the guy doing?" I asked.

"Who?" Georgie said.

It turned out that Terrence Weber still had excellent vision in the one good eye, and acceptable motor and reflex, despite his earlier motor complaint. "His vitals are normal," Nurse said. "There's nothing wrong with the guy. It's one of those things."

After a while you forget it's summer. You don't remember what the morning is. I'd worked two doubles with eight hours off in between, which I'd spent sleeping on a gurney in the nurses' station. Georgie's pills were making me feel like a giant helium-filled balloon, but I was wide awake. Georgie and I went out to the lot, to his orange pickup.

We lay down on a stretch of dusty plywood in the back of the truck with the daylight knocking against our eyelids and the fragrance of alfalfa thickening on our tongues.

"I want to go to church," Georgie said.

"Let's go to the county fair."

"I'd like to worship. I would."

"They have these injured hawks and eagles there. From the Humane Society," I said.

"I need a quiet chapel about now."

Georgie and I had a terrific time driving around. For a while the day was clear and peaceful. It was one of the moments you stay in, to hell with all the troubles of before and after. The sky is blue, and the dead are coming back. Later in the afternoon, with sad resignation, the county fair bares its breasts. A champion of the drug LSD, a very famous guru of the love generation, is being interviewed amid a TV crew off to the left of the poultry cages. His eyeballs look like he bought them in a joke shop. It doesn't occur to me, as I pity this extraterrestrial, that in my life I've taken as much acid as he has.

After that, we got lost. We drove for hours, literally hours, but we couldn't find the road back to town.

Georgie started to complain. "That was the worst fair I've been to. Where were the rides?"

"They had rides," I said.

"I didn't see one ride."

A jackrabbit scurried out in front of us, and we hit it.

"There was a merry-go-round, a Ferris wheel, and a thing called the Hammer that people were bent over vomiting from after they got off," I said. "Are you completely blind?"

"What was that?"

"A rabbit."

"Something thumped."

"You hit him. *He* thumped."

Georgie stood on the brake pedal. "Rabbit stew."

He threw the truck in reverse and zigzagged back toward the rabbit. "Where's my hunting knife?" He almost ran over the poor animal a second time.

"We'll camp in the wilderness," he said. "In the morning we'll breakfast on its haunches." He was waving Terrence Weber's hunting knife around in what I was sure was a dangerous way.

In a minute he was standing at the edge of the fields, cutting the scrawny little thing up, tossing away its organs. "I should have been a doctor," he cried.

A family in a big Dodge, the only car we'd seen for a long time, slowed down and gawked out the windows as they passed by. The father said, "What is it, a snake?"

"No, it's not a snake," Georgie said. "It's rabbit with babies inside it."

"Babies!" the mother said, and the father sped the car forward, over the protests of several little kids in the back.

Georgie came back to my side of the truck with his shirtfront stretched out in front of him as if he were carrying apples in it, or some such, but they were, in fact, slimy miniature bunnies. "No way I'm eating those things," I told him.

"Take them, take them. I gotta drive, take them," he said, dumping them in my lap and getting in on his side of the truck. He started driving along faster and faster, with a look of glory on his face. "We killed the mother and saved the children," he said.

"It's getting late," I said. "Let's get back to town."

"You bet." Sixty, seventy, eighty-five, just topping ninety.

"These rabbits better be kept warm." One at a time I slid the little things in between my shirt buttons and nestled them against my belly. "They're hardly moving," I told Georgie.

"We'll get some milk and sugar and all that, and we'll raise them up ourselves. They'll get as big as gorillas."

The road we were lost on cut straight through the middle of the world. It was still daytime, but the sun had no more power than an ornament or a sponge. In this light the truck's hood, which had been bright orange, had turned a deep blue.

Georgie let us drift to the shoulder of the road, slowly, slowly, as if he'd fallen asleep or given up trying to find his way.

"What is it?"

"We can't go on. I don't have any headlights," Georgie said.

We parked under a strange sky with a faint image of a quarter-moon superimposed on it.

There was a little wood beside us. This day had been dry and hot, the buck pines and what all simmering patiently, but as we sat there smoking cigarettes it started to get very cold.

"The summer's over," I said.

That was the year when arctic clouds moved down over the Midwest, and we had two weeks of winter in September.

"Do you realize it's going to snow?" Georgie asked me.

He was right, a gun-blue storm was shaping up. We got out and walked around idiotically. The beautiful chill! That sudden crispness, and the tang of evergreen stabbing us!

The gusts of snow twisted themselves around our heads while the night fell. I couldn't find the truck. We just kept getting more and more lost. I kept calling, "Georgie, can you see?" and he kept saying, "See what? See what?"

The only light visible was a streak of sunset flickering below the hem of the clouds. We headed that way.

We bumped softly down a hill toward an open field that seemed to be a military graveyard, filled with rows and rows of austere, identical markers over soldiers' graves. I'd never before come across this cemetery. On the farther side of the field, just beyond the curtains of snow, the sky was torn away and the angels were descending out of a brilliant blue summer, their huge faces streaked with light and full of pity. The sight of them cut through my heart and down the knuckles of my spine, and if there'd been anything in my bowels I would have messed my pants from fear.

Georgie opened his arms and cried out, "It's the drive-in, man!"

"The drive-in . . ." I wasn't sure what these words meant.

"They're showing movies in a fucking bizzard!" Georgie screamed.

"I see. I thought it was something else," I said.

We walked carefully down there and climbed through the busted fence and stood in the very back. The speakers, which I'd mistaken for grave markers, muttered in unison. Then there was tinkly music, of which I could very nearly make out the tune. Famous movie stars rode bicycles beside a river, laughing out of their gigantic lovely mouths. If anybody had come to see this show, they'd left when the weather started. Not one car remained, not even a broken-down one from last week, or one left here because it was out of gas. In a couple of minutes, in the middle of a whirling square dance, the screen turned black, the cinematic summer ended, the snow went dark, there was nothing but my breath.

"I'm starting to get my eyes back," Georgie said in another minute.

A general grayness was giving birth to various shapes, it was true. "But which ones are close and which ones are far off?" I begged him to tell me.

By trial and error, with a lot of walking back and forth in wet shoes, we found the truck and sat inside it, shivering.

"Let's get out of here," I said.

"We can't go anywhere without headlights."

"We've gotta get back. We're a long way from home."

"No, we're not."

"We must have come 300 miles."

"We're right outside town, Fuckhead. We've just been driving around and around."

"This is no place to camp. I hear the interstate over there."

"We'll just stay here till it gets late. We can drive home late. We'll be invisible."

We listened to the big rigs going from San Francisco to Pennsylvania along the interstate, like shudders down a long hacksaw blade, while the snow buried us.

Eventually Georgie said, "We better get some milk for those bunnies."

"We don't have *milk*," I said.

"We'll mix sugar up with it."

"Will you forget about this milk all of a sudden?"

"They're mammals, man."

"Forget about those rabbits."

"Where are they, anyway?"

"You're not listening to me. I said, 'Forget the rabbits.'"

"Where are they?"

The truth was I'd forgotten all about them, and they were dead.

"They slid around behind me and got squashed," I said tearfully.

"They slid around *behind*?"

He watched while I pried them out from behind my back.

I picked them out one at a time and held them in my hands and we looked at them. There were eight. They weren't any bigger than my fingers, but everything was there.

Little feet! Eyelids! Even whiskers! "Deceased," I said.

Georgie asked, "Does everything you touch turn to shit? Does this happen to you every time?"

"No wonder they call me Fuckhead."

"It's a name that's going to stick."

"I realize that."

"'Fuckhead' is gonna ride you to your grave."

"I just said so. I agreed with you in advance," I said.

Or maybe that wasn't the time it snowed. Maybe it was the time we slept in the truck and I rolled over on the bunnies and flattened them. It doesn't matter. What's important for me to remember now is that early the next morning the snow was melted off the windshield and the daylight woke me up. A mist covered everything, and with the sunshine, was beginning to grow sharp and strange. The bunnies weren't a problem yet, or they'd already been a problem and were already forgotten, and there was nothing on my mind. I felt the beauty of the morning. I could understand how a drowning man might suddenly feel a deep thirst being quenched. Or how the slave might become a friend to his master. Georgie slept with his face right on the steering wheel.

I saw bits of snow resembling an abundance of blossoms on the stems of the drive-in speakers—no, revealing the blossoms that were always there. A bull elk stood still in the pasture beyond the fence giving off an air of authority and stupidity. And a coyote jogged across the pasture and faded away among the saplings.

That afternoon we got back to work in time to resume everything as if it had never stopped happening and we'd never been anywhere else.

"The Lord," the intercom said, "is my shepherd." It did that each evening because this was a Catholic hospital. "Our Father who art in Heaven," and so on.

"Yeah, yeah," Nurse said.

The man with the knife in his head, Terrence Weber, was released around suppertime. They'd kept him overnight and given him an eyepatch—all for no reason, really.

He stopped off at ER to say good-bye. "Well, those pills they gave me make everything taste terrible," he said.

"It could have been worse," Nurse said.

"Even my tongue."

"It's just a miracle you didn't end up sightless or at least dead," she reminded him.

The patient recognized me. He acknowledged me with a smile.

"I was peeping on the lady next door while she was out there sunbathing," he said. "My wife decided to blind me."

He shook Georgie's hand. Georgie didn't know him. "Who are you supposed to be?" he asked Terrence Weber.

Some hours before that, Georgie had said something that had suddenly and completely explained the difference between us. We'd been driving back toward town, along the Old Highway, through the flatness. We picked up a hitchhiker, a boy I knew. We stopped the truck and the boy climbed slowly up out of the fields as out of the mouth of a volcano. His name was Hardee. He looked even worse than we probably did.

"We got messed up and slept in the truck all night," I told Hardee.

"I had a feeling," Hardee said. "Either that or, you know, driving 1,000 miles."

"That, too," I said.

"Or you're sick or diseased or something."

"Who's this guy?" Georgie asked.

"This is Hardee. He lived with me last summer. I found him on the doorstep. What happened to your dog?" I asked Hardee.

"He's still down there."

"Yeah, I heard you went to Texas."

"I was working on a bee farm," Hardee said.

"Wow. Do those things sting you?"

"Not like you'd think," Hardee said. "You're part of their daily drill. It's all part of a harmony."

Outside, the same identical stretch of ground repeatedly rolled past our faces. The day was cloudless, blinding. But Georgie said, "Look at that," pointing straight ahead of us.

One star was so hot it showed, bright and blue, in the empty sky.

"I recognized you right away," I told Hardee. "But what happened to your hair? Who chopped it off?"

"I hate to say."

"Don't tell me."

"They drafted me."

"Oh no."

"Oh yeah. I'm AWOL. I'm bad AWOL. I got to get to Canada."

"Oh, that's terrible," I said to Hardee.

"Don't worry," Georgie said. "We'll get you there."

"How?"

"Somehow. I think I know some people. Don't worry. You're on your way to Canada."

That world! These days it's all been erased and they've rolled it up like a scroll and put it away somewhere. Yes, I can touch it with my fingers. But where is it?

After a while Hardee asked Georgie, "What do you do for a job?" and Georgie said, "I save lives."

Writing Exercises

1. Go to a mall, park, restaurant, or some other public place and eavesdrop. In your notebook, write down some lines of dialogue you overhear—anything that captures your attention. Bring your notebook to class, pick your favorite line or two, and write them on the board. Once everyone in class has done this, you can each pick a line from the board and use it to begin a scene. Somewhere along the line, incorporate at least three more lines of dialogue from the board into the scene. Write quickly, and have fun!

2. Often we fight about the small things because the big things are too big and scary, too likely to get out of hand. Write a scene between two characters almost having a big fight, but not quite. Have the real tension be about something bigger than the trivial issue at hand (e.g., it's not really about the remote control but rather about control and being remote and power and who has it in the relationship).

3. Put two characters together who have just found themselves to be at two different crossroads. I just got fired. You just landed a new job. Now what?

4. Have a character say something that reveals him or her in a new light. Maybe the revelation was meant to shock: "You're having an affair with your dentist?!" Maybe the revelation was unwitting and inadvertent: "Whoa, wait a minute, you did *what?*"

5. Flirtation. Two people are feeling each other out, not sure how far to go in revealing their feelings, not sure if the other person is just being friendly or is really interested, not sure whether to play hard to get, not sure...not sure.

6. Have one character *imagine* a conversation with another. The conversation he or she is anticipating (and, in some sense, rehearsing for) should be unavoidable. It could, however, be one of two types: a conversation your character is dreading (a shameful admission, breaking some bad news, etc.) or one your character is looking forward to (revealing a new promotion or raise, a declaration of love, etc.).

4

THE FLESH MADE WORD
Characterization, Part II

The Direct Methods of Character Presentation

APPEARANCE

Of the four methods of direct presentation—dialogue (discussed in the previous chapter), appearance, action, and thought—appearance is especially important because our eyes are our most highly developed means of perception, and we therefore receive more nonsensuous information by sight than by any other sense. Beauty is only skin deep, but people are embodied, and whatever beauty—or ugliness—there is in them must somehow surface in order for us to perceive it. Such surfacing involves speech and action as well as appearance, but it is appearance that prompts our first reaction to people, and everything they wear and own presents some aspect of their inner selves.

Concerned to see beyond mere appearances, writers are sometimes inclined to neglect this power of the visible. In fact, much of the tension and conflict in character does proceed from the truth that appearance is not reality. But in order to know this, we must see the appearance first. Features, shape, style, clothing, and objects can make statements of internal values that are political, religious, social, intellectual, and essential. The man in the Ultrasuede jacket is making a different statement from the one in the holey sweatshirt. The woman with the cigarette holder is telling us something different from the one with the palmed joint. Even a person who has forsaken our materialistic society altogether, sworn off supermarkets, and gone to the country to grow organic potatoes has a special relationship with his or her hoe. However indifferent we may be to our looks, that indifference is the result of experiences with our bodies. A twenty-two-year-old Apollo who has been handsome since he was six is a very different person from the man who spent his childhood cocooned in fat and burst the chrysalis at age sixteen.

Following are two very brief portraits of women. Each is mainly characterized by such trivialities as fabric, furnishings, and cosmetics. It would nevertheless be impossible to mistake the essential nature of the one for that of the other.

How beautiful Helen is, how elegant, how timeless: how she charms Esther Songford and how she flirts with Edwin, laying a scarlet fingernail on his dusty lapel, mesmerizing.

She comes in a chauffeured car. She is all cream and roses. Her stockings are purest silk; her underskirt, just briefly showing, is lined with lace.

Fay Weldon, *Female Friends*

As soon as I entered the room, a pungent odor of phosphorus told me she'd taken rat poison. She lay groaning between the quilts. The tatami by the bed was splashed with blood, her waved hair was matted like rope waste, and a bandage tied round her throat showed up unnaturally white.... The painted mouth in her waxen face created a ghastly effect, as though her lips were a gash open to the ears.

Masuji Ibuse, "Tajinko Village"

Vividness and richness of character are created in these two passages, which use nothing more than appearance to characterize.

Note that sense impressions other than sight are still a part of the way a character "appears." A limp handshake or a soft cheek; an odor of Chanel, oregano, or decay—these sense impressions can characterize much the way looks do if the narrative allows the reader to touch, smell, or taste a character.

The sound and associations of a character's name, too, can give a clue to personality: The affluent Mr. Chiddister in Chapter 2 is automatically a more elegant sort than the affluent Mr. Strum; Huck Finn must have a different life from that of the Marquis of Lumbria. Although names with a blatant meaning—Joseph Surface, Billy Pilgrim, Martha Quest—tend to stylize a character and should be used sparingly, if at all, ordinary names can hint at traits you mean to heighten, and it is worth combing any list of names, including the telephone book, to find suggestive sounds. My own telephone book yields, at a glance this morning, Linda Holladay, Marvin Entzminger, and Melba Peebles, any one of which might set me to speculating on a character.

Sound also characterizes as a part of "appearance" insofar as sound represents timbre, tenor, or quality of noise and speech; the characterizing reediness or gruffness of a voice; the lift of laughter or stiffness of delivery.

The way a character physically moves is yet another form of "appearance." It is important to understand the difference between *movement* and *action*, however, for these terms are not synonymous. Physical movement—the way he crosses his legs, the way she charges down the hall—characterizes without necessarily moving the plot forward. Often movement is part of the setup of the scene, a way of establishing the situation before change-producing action begins.

ACTION

The significant characters of a fiction must be both capable of causing an action and capable of being changed by it.

WHAT'S VITAL FOR THE FICTION WRITER to remember is that the wicked, the violent, and the stupid do also love, in their way. Just as humble and loving and thoughtful people also hate. Hate humbly, hate lovingly, hate thoughtfully, and so on.

DOUG BAUER

If we accept that a story records a process of change, how is this change brought about? Basically, human beings face chance and choice, or discovery and decision—the first of each pair involuntary and the second voluntary.

Translated into action, this means that a character driven by desire takes an action with an expected result, but something intervenes. Some force outside the character presents itself, in the form of information or accident or the behavior of others or the elements. The unknown becomes known, and then the discoverer must either take action or deliberately not take action, involving readers in the tension of the narrative query: And then what happens?

Here is a passage from Toni Morrison's "Recitatif" that demonstrates first movement, then discovery, then decision:

> It was August and a bus crowd was just unloading. They would stand around a long while: going to the john, and looking at gifts and junk-for-sale machines, reluctant to sit down so soon. Even to eat. I was trying to fill the coffeepots and get them all situated on the electric burners when I saw her. She was sitting in a booth smoking a cigarette with two guys smothered in head and facial hair. Her own hair was so big and wild I could hardly see her face. But the eyes. I would know them anywhere. She had on a powder-blue halter and shorts outfit and earrings the size of bracelets. Talk about lipstick and eyebrow pencil. She made the big girls look like nuns. I couldn't get off the counter until seven o'clock, but I kept watching the booth in case they got up to leave before that. My replacement was on time for a change, so I counted and stacked my receipts as fast as I could and signed off. I walked over to the booth....

Here, unloading, milling around, and filling coffeepots is *movement* that represents scene-setting and characterization. The significant *action* begins with the discovery, "I saw her." Notice that "she" is characterized directly by appearance, whereas the narrator is mainly characterized by her movements (expressed in active verbs)—*watching, counting, stacking, signing off*—until the moment when she acts on her decision. At the points of both the discovery and the decision we anticipate the possibility of change: What happens next?

In the next passage, from John Cheever's "The Cure," the initial movement is seemingly innocuous before abruptly shifting toward suspense:

> I turned on a light in the living room and looked at Rachel's books. I chose one by an author named Lin Yutang and sat down on a sofa under a lamp. Our living room is comfortable. The book seemed interesting. I was in a neighborhood where most of the front doors were unlocked, and on a street that is very quiet on a summer night. All the animals are domesticated, and the only night birds that I've ever heard are some owls way down by the railroad track. So it was very quiet. I heard the Barstows' dog bark, briefly, as if he had been waked by a nightmare, and then the barking stopped. Everything was quiet again. Then I heard, very close to me, a footstep and a cough.

I felt my flesh get hard—you know that feeling—but I didn't look up from my book, although I felt that I was being watched.

This scene is set with movement and one choice—that book—that offers no particular opportunity for change and no particular dramatic force. With the moment "Then I heard," however, a discovery or realization of a different sort occurs, and there is suddenly the possibility of real change and so, suddenly, real dramatic tension. Notice that in the second paragraph the narrator discovers a familiar and entirely involuntary reaction—"I felt my flesh get hard"—followed by the decision *not* to take what would be the instinctive action. In fiction as in life, restraint, the decision to do nothing, is fraught with possible tension.

In most cases, writers do not want their technique to be too conspicuous, so they usually conceal the decision and discovery structure. In the next example, from Raymond Carver's "Neighbors," the pattern of change—Bill Miller's gradual intrusion into his neighbor's house—is based on a series of decisions that Carver does not explicitly state. The passage ends with a turning point, a moment of discovery.

When he returned to the kitchen the cat was scratching in her box. She looked at him steadily for a minute before she turned back to the litter. He opened all the cupboards and examined the canned goods, the cereals, the packaged foods, the cocktail and wine glasses, the china, the pots and pans. He opened the refrigerator. He sniffed some celery, took two bites of cheddar cheese, and chewed on an apple as he walked into the bedroom. The bed seemed enormous, with a fluffy white bedspread draped to the floor. He pulled out a nightstand drawer, found a half-empty package of cigarettes and stuffed them into his pocket. Then he stepped to the closet and was opening it when the knock sounded at the front door.

There is hardly grand larceny being committed here, but the actions build toward tension through two distinct techniques. The first is that they do actually "build": At first Bill only "examines." The celery he only sniffs, whereas he takes two bites of the cheese, then a whole apple, then half a pack of cigarettes. He moves from the kitchen to the bedroom, which is a clearer invasion of privacy, and from cupboard to refrigerator to nightstand to closet, each a more intimate intrusion than the last.

The second technique is that the narrative subtly hints at Bill's own sense of stealth. It would be easy to imagine a vandal who performed the same actions with complete indifference. But Bill thinks the cat looks "steadily" at him, which is hardly of any importance except that he feels it to be. His awareness of the enormous white bed hints at sexual guilt. When the knock at the front door sounds, we start, as he must, in a clear sense of getting caught.

Thus it turns out that the internal or mental moment of change is where the action lies. Much movement in a story is mere event, and this is why descriptions of actions, like stage directions in a dull play, sometimes add little or nothing. When the wife picks up a cup of coffee, that is mere event. If she finds that the lipstick on the cup is not her shade, that is a dramatic event, a discovery; it makes a difference. She makes a decision to fling it at the woman with the Cherry Ice mouth. Flinging it is an action, but the dramatic change occurs with the second character's realization (discovery) that she has been hit—and so on.

Every story is a pattern of change (events connected, as the author E. M. Forster observed, primarily by cause and effect) in which small and large changes are made through discovery and decision.

THOUGHT

Fiction has a flexibility denied to film and drama, where everything the spectator knows must be shown. In fiction you have the privilege of entering a character's mind, sharing at its source internal conflict, reflection, and the crucial processes of decision and discovery. Like speech, a character's thought can be offered in summary (*He hated the way she ate*), or as indirect thought (*Why did she hold her fork straight up like that?*), or directly, as if we are overhearing the character's own mind (*My God, she's going to drop the yolk!*). As with speech, the three methods can be alternated in the same paragraph to achieve at once immediacy and pace.

Methods of presenting a character's thought will be more fully discussed in Chapter 8 on point of view. What's most important to characterization is that thought, like speech, reveals more than information. It can also set mood, reveal or betray desires, develop theme, and so forth.

The territory of a character's mind is above all likely to be the center of the action. Aristotle says that a man "is his desire"; that is, his character is defined by his ultimate purpose, good or bad. *Thought*, says Aristotle, is the process by which a person works backward in his mind from his goal to determine what action he can take toward that goal at a given moment.

It is not, for example, your ultimate desire to read this book. Very likely you don't even "want" to read it; you'd rather be sleeping or jogging or making love. But your ultimate goal is, say, to be a rich, respected, and famous writer. In order to attain this goal, you reason, you must know as much about the craft as you can learn. To do this, you would like to take a graduate degree at the Writer's Workshop in Iowa. To do that, you must take an undergraduate degree in _____, where you now find yourself, and must get an A in Ms. or Mr. _____'s creative writing course. To do that, you must produce a character sketch from one of the assignments at the end of this chapter by a week from Tuesday. To do so, you must sit here reading this chapter now instead of sleeping, jogging, or making love. Your ultimate motive has led you logically backward to a deliberate "moral" decision on the action you can take at this minor crossroad. In fact, it turns out that you want to be reading after all.

The relationship that Aristotle perceives among desire, thought, and action seems to me a very useful one for an author, both in structuring plot and in creating character. What does this protagonist want to happen in the last paragraph of this story? What is the particular thought process by which this person works backward to determine what she or he will do now, in the situation that presents itself on page one?

> I was on my way to what I hoped would be *the* romantic vacation of my life, off to Door County for a whole week of sweet sane rest. More rest. I needed more rest.
>
> David Haynes, *All American Girls*

The action, of course, may be the wrong one. Thought thwarts us, because it leads to a wrong choice, or because thought is full of conflicting desires and consistent inconsistencies, or because there is enormous human tension between suppressed thought and expressed thought:

> When he shuts off the shower, the phone is ringing. A sense that it has been ringing for a long time—can a mechanical noise have a quality of desperation?—propels him naked and dripping into the living room. He picks up the phone and his caller, as he has suspected, is Mieko.... He is already annoyed after the first hello. Mieko's voice is sharp, high, very Japanese, although she speaks superb English. He says, "Hello, Mieko," and he sounds annoyed.
>
> Jane Smiley, "Long Distance"

A person, a character, can't do much about what he or she wants; it just is (which is another way of saying that character is desire). What we can deliberately choose is our behavior, the action we take in a given situation. Achievement of our desire would be easy if the thought process between desire and act were not so faulty and so wayward, or if there were not such an abyss between the thoughts we think and those that we are willing and able to express.

The four methods of direct characterization are forms of "showing" that bring character vividly alive. But there may also be times that you wish to shape our knowledge of and reaction to your characters by "telling" us about them, judging and interpreting for the reader.

The Indirect Methods of Character Presentation

There are two methods of indirect characterization—indirect in the sense that, rather than being presented directly to our sight and hearing, the character is described in summarized, abstract, or judgmental terms by either the author or another speaker. Both of these methods are forms of "telling," and both may shape our overall view.

AUTHORIAL INTERPRETATION

The first indirect method of presenting a character is authorial interpretation—"telling" us the character's background, motives, values, virtues, and the like. The advantages of this indirect method are enormous, for its use leaves you free to move in time and space; to know anything you choose to know whether the character knows it or not; and, godlike, to tell us what we are to feel. The indirect method allows you to convey a great deal of information in a short time.

> The most excellent Marquis of Lumbria lived with his two daughters, Caroline, the elder, and Luisa; and his second wife, Doña Vicente a woman with a dull brain, who, when she was not sleeping, was complaining of everything, especially the noise....
>
> The Marquis of Lumbria had no male children, and this was the most painful thorn in his existence. Shortly after having become a widower, he had married Doña Vicente, his present wife, in order to have a son, but she proved sterile.
>
> The Marquis' life was as monotonous and as quotidian, as unchanging and regular, as the murmur of the river below the cliff or as the liturgic services in the cathedral.
>
> Miguel de Unamuno, *The Marquis of Lumbria*

The disadvantage of this indirect method is that it distances the reader as all generalizations and abstractions tend to do. Indeed, in the passage above, it may well be part of Unamuno's purpose to convey the "monotonous" and "quotidian" quality of the Marquis' life by this summarized and distanced rehearsal of facts, motives, and judgments. Nearly every author will use the indirect method occasionally, and you may find it useful when you want to cover the exposition quickly. However, direct presentation of the characters—showing them in action and allowing readers to draw their own conclusions—will more actively engage the reader.

INTERPRETATION BY ANOTHER CHARACTER

A character may also be presented through the opinions of other characters, which may be considered a second indirect method. When this method is employed, however, the second character must give his or her opinions in speech, action, or thought. In the process, the observing character is inevitably also characterized. Whether we accept the opinion depends on what we think of that character as he or she is thus directly characterized. In this scene from Jane Austen's *Mansfield Park*, for example, the busybody Mrs. Norris gives her opinion of the heroine.

> "... [T]here is something about Fanny, I have often observed it before,—she likes to go her own way to work; she does not like to be dictated to;

she takes her own independent walk whenever she can; she certainly has a little spirit of secrecy, and independence, and nonsense, about her, which I would advise her to get the better of."

As a general reflection on Fanny, Sir Thomas thought nothing could be more unjust, though he had been so lately expressing the same sentiments himself, and he tried to turn the conversation, tried repeatedly before he could succeed.

Here Mrs. Norris's opinion is directly presented in her speech and Sir Thomas's in his thoughts, each of them being characterized in the process. It is left to the reader to decide (without much difficulty) whose view of Fanny is the more reliable.

Similarly, in Clyde Edgerton's contemporary novel *Raney*, the opposing outlooks of a newlywed "odd couple" are dramatized through their contradictory characterizations of a lonely and preoccupied neighbor.

"Charles," I said, "you'd rather sit down back there in the bedroom and read a book than talk to a live human being like Mrs. Moss."

"I'm not so sure I agree with your assessment of Mrs. Moss," he says.

"What do you mean by that?"

"It means I have had one conversation with Mrs. Moss and one conversation with Mrs. Moss is enough. I am not interested in her falling off the commode and having a hairline rib fracture. I am not interested in her cataract operation. Mrs. Moss is unable to comprehend anything beyond her own problems and you know it."

"... Mrs. Moss does talk about herself right much. She'll come over in her apron to borrow a cup of something. One Sunday she borrowed a cup of flour after I saw a bag of Red Band in her shopping cart—on top—at the Piggly Wiggly on Saturday. But the way I figure it is this: Mrs. Moss has had a lifetime of things happening to her and all along she's had these other people—her husband and children—to watch these things happen. So she didn't ever have to *tell* anybody. Then her husband died and her children left and there was nobody around to watch these things happen anymore, so she don't have any way to share *except* to tell. So the thing to do is listen. It's easy to cut her off when she just goes on and on. You just start talking about something else. She follows right along."

Set halfway through the novel, this argument confirms the reader's view of Charles as an urban liberal who is broad-minded in abstract principles yet impatient with actual people, while Raney, the small-town narrator, tends to be narrow-minded in the abstract but compassionate with individuals, at least those long familiar to her. What is crystallized about this couple through their argument is even more important than what is learned about the incidental character of the neighbor.

Conflict Between Methods of Presentation

The conflict that is the essence of character can be effectively (and, if it doesn't come automatically, quite consciously) achieved in fiction by producing a conflict between methods of presentation. A character can be directly revealed to us through *appearance, dialogue, action,* and *thought.* If you set one of these methods (most frequently *thought*) at odds with the others, then dramatic tension will be produced. Imagine, for example, a character who is impeccably and expensively dressed, who speaks eloquently, who acts decisively, and whose mind is revealed to us as full of order and determination. He is inevitably a flat character. But suppose that he is impeccable, eloquent, decisive, and that his mind is a mess of wounds and panic. He is at once interesting.

Here is the opening passage of Saul Bellow's *Seize the Day,* in which appearance and action are blatantly at odds with thought. Notice that it is the tension between suppressed thought and what is expressed through appearance and action that produces the rich character conflict.

> When it came to concealing his troubles, Tommy Wilhelm was not less capable than the next fellow. So at least he thought, and there was a certain amount of evidence to back him up. He had once been an actor—no, not quite, an extra—and he knew what acting should be. Also, he was smoking a cigar, and when a man is smoking a cigar, wearing a hat, he has an advantage: it is harder to find out how he feels. He came from the twenty-third floor down to the lobby on the mezzanine to collect his mail before breakfast, and he believed—he hoped—he looked passably well: doing all right.

Tommy Wilhelm is externally composed but mentally anxious, mainly anxious about looking externally composed. By contrast, in the next passage, from Samuel Beckett's *Murphy,* the landlady, Miss Carridge, who has just discovered a suicide in one of her rooms, is anxious in speech and action but is mentally composed.

> She came speeding down the stairs one step at a time, her feet going so fast that she seemed on little caterpillar wheels, her forefinger sawing horribly at her craw for Celia's benefit. She slithered to a stop on the steps of the house and screeched for the police. She capered in the street like a consternated ostrich, with strangled distracted rushes towards the York and Caledonian Roads in turn, embarrassingly equidistant from the tragedy, tossing up her arms, undoing the good work of the samples, screeching for police aid. Her mind was so collected that she saw clearly the impropriety of letting it appear so.

In this third example, from Zora Neale Hurston's "The Gilded Six-Bits," it is the very intensity of the internal that both prevents and dictates action:

> Missie May was sobbing. Wails of weeping without words. Joe stood, and after a while he found out that he had something in his hand. And then he stood and felt without thinking and without seeing with his natural eyes. Missie May kept on crying and Joe kept on feeling so much, and not knowing what to do with all his feelings, he put Slemmon's watch charm in his pants pocket and took a good laugh and went to bed.

I have said that thought is most frequently at odds with one or more of the other three methods of direct presentation—reflecting the difficulty we have expressing ourselves openly or accurately—but this is by no means always the case. A character may be successfully, calmly, even eloquently expressing fine opinions while betraying himself by pulling at his ear, or herself by crushing her skirt. Captain Queeg of Herman Wouk's *The Caine Mutiny* is a memorable example of this, maniacally clicking the steel balls in his hand as he defends his disciplinary code.

Often we are not privy to the thoughts of a character at all, so that the conflicts must be expressed in a contradiction between the external methods of direct presentation, appearance, speech, and action. Character A may be speaking floods of friendly welcome but betraying his real feeling by backing steadily away. Character B, dressed in taffeta ruffles and ostrich plumes, may wail pityingly over the miseries of the poor. Notice that the notion of betraying oneself is important here: We're more likely to believe the evidence unintentionally given than deliberate expression.

A classic example of such self-betrayal is found in Leo Tolstoy's *The Death of Ivan Ilyich*, where the widow confronts her husband's colleague at the funeral.

> … [N]oticing that the table was endangered by his cigarette ash, she immediately passed him an ashtray, saying as she did so: "I consider it an affectation to say that my grief prevents my attending to practical affairs. On the contrary, if anything can—I won't say console me, but— distract me, it is seeing to everything concerning him." She again took out her handkerchief as if preparing to cry, but suddenly, as if mastering her feeling, she shook herself and began to speak calmly. "But there is something I want to talk to you about."

It is no surprise either to the colleague or to us that Praskovya Fedorovna wants to talk about getting money.

Finally, character conflict can be expressed by creating a tension between the direct and the indirect methods of presentation, and this is a source of much irony. The author presents us with a judgment of the character and then lets him or her speak, appear, act, and/or think in contradiction to this judgment.

Sixty years had not dulled his response; his physical reactions, like his moral ones were guided by his will and strong character, and these could be seen plainly in his features. He had a long tube-like face with a long rounded open jaw and a large depressed nose.

Flannery O'Connor, "The Artificial Nigger"

What we see here in the details of Mr. Head's features are not will and strong character but grimly unlikable qualities. "Tube-like" is an ugly image; an "open jaw" suggests stupidity; and "depressed" connotes more than shape, while dogged repetition of "long" stretches the face grotesquely.

THE OLDER WE GET, THE MORE ... you realize there's a whole range of things that you will never do, of things and people you will never be. As life becomes more and more limiting, there is something wonderful about being able to get inside the skin of people unlike yourself.

LEE SMITH

The Universal Paradox

Though critics often praise literature for exhibiting characteristics of the *individual*, the *typical*, and the *universal* all at the same time, I don't think this is of much use to the practicing writer. For though you may labor to create an individual character, and you may make that character a credible example of type, I don't think you can *set out to be* "universal."

It is true, I believe, that if literature has any social justification or use it is that readers can identify the common humanity in, and can therefore identify with, characters vastly different from themselves in century, geography, gender, culture, and beliefs; and that this enhances the scope of the reader's sympathy. Yet, paradoxically, if you aim for the universal, you're likely to achieve the pompous, whereas if you aim for the individual, you're more apt to create a character in whom a reader can see aspects of himself or herself.

Imagine this scene: The child chases a ball into the street. The tires screech, the bumper thuds, the blood geysers into the air, the pulp of the small body lies inert on the asphalt. How would a bystander react? (Is it universal?) How would a passing doctor react? (Is it typical?) How would Dr. Henry Lowes, just coming from the maternity ward of his own hospital, where his wife has had her fourth miscarriage, react? (Is it individual?) Each question narrows the range of convincing reaction, and as a writer you want to convince in each range. If you succeed in the third, you are likely to have succeeded in the other two.

My advice then is to labor in the range of the particular. If you aim for a universal character, you may end up with a vague or dull or windy one. On the other hand, if you set out to write a typical character, you're likely to produce a caricature, because people are typical only in the generalized qualities that lump them together. *Typical* is the most provincial adjective in a writer's vocabulary, signaling that you're writing only for those who share your assumptions. A "typical" schoolgirl in Dar es Salaam is a very different type from one in San Francisco. Furthermore, every person is typical of many things, successively or simultaneously. She may be in turn a "typical" schoolgirl, bride, divorcée, and feminist. He may be at one and the same time a "typical" New Yorker, math professor, doting father, and adulterer. It is in the confrontation and convolution of types that much of our individuality is produced.

Writing in generalities and typicalities is akin to bigotry—we see only what's alike about people, not what's unique. When effective, a description of type blames the character for the failure to individualize, and if an author sets out deliberately to produce types rather than individuals, then that author invariably wants to condemn or ridicule those types. Mark Helprin, in "The Schreuderspitze," takes the ridicule of type to comic extreme:

> In Munich are many men who look like weasels. Whether by genetic accident, meticulous crossbreeding, an early and puzzling migration, coincidence, or a reason that we do not know, they exist in great numbers. Remarkably, they accentuate this unfortunate tendency by wearing mustaches, Alpine hats, and tweed. A man who resembles a rodent should never wear tweed.

This is not to say that all characters must be fully drawn or *round*. *Flat* characters—who exist only to exhibit a function or a single characteristic—are useful and necessary. Eric Bentley suggests in *The Life of the Drama* that if a messenger's function in a play is to deliver his message, it would be very tedious to stop and learn about his psychology. Nevertheless, onstage even a flat character has a face and a costume, and in fiction detail can give even a flat character a few angles and contours. The servant classes in the novels of Henry James are notoriously absent as individuals because they exist only in their functions (*that excellent creature had already assembled the baggage*, etc.), whereas Charles Dickens, who peoples his novels with dozens of flat characters, brings even these alive in detail.

> And Mrs. Miff, the wheezy little pew opener—a mighty dry old lady, sparely dressed, with not an inch of fullness anywhere about her—is also here.

Dombey and Son

To borrow a notion from George Orwell's *Animal Farm*, all good characters are created round, but some are created rounder than others.

Credibility

Though you aim at individuality and not typicality in characters, your characters will exhibit typicality in the sense of "appropriateness." A Baptist Texan behaves differently from an Italian nun; a rural schoolboy behaves differently from a professor emeritus at Harvard. If you are to succeed in creating an individual character, particular and alive, you will also inevitably know what is appropriate to that sort of person and will let us know as much as we need to know to feel the appropriateness of the behavior.

For instance, we need to know soon, preferably in the first paragraph, the character's gender, age, and race or nationality. We need to know something of his or her class, period, and region. A profession (or the clear lack of it) and a marital status help too. *Almost any reader can identify with almost any character; what no reader can identify with is confusion.* When some or several of the fundamentals of type are withheld from us—when we don't know whether we're dealing with a man or a woman, an adult or a child—the process of identifying cannot begin, and the story is slow to move us.

None of the information need come as information; it can be implied by appearance, tone, action, or detail. In the next example, Barbara Kingsolver plunges the character of Leah Price and her family into a new life for which they are clearly ill-prepared, practically and politically. Although they are focused on their destination, by the end of the first two paragraphs, we know a lot about the family and the culture they carry with them.

> We came from Bethlehem, Georgia, bearing Betty Crocker cake mixes into the jungle. My sisters and I were all counting on having one birthday apiece during our twelve-month mission. "And heaven knows," our mother predicted, "they won't have Betty Crocker in the Congo."
>
> "Where we are headed, there will *be* no buyers and sellers at all," my father corrected. His tone implied that Mother failed to grasp our mission, and that her concern with Betty Crocker confederated her with the coin-jingling sinners who vexed Jesus till he pitched a fit and threw them out of the church. "Where we are headed," he said, to make things perfectly clear, "not so much as a Piggly Wiggly." Evidently Father saw this as a point in the Congo's favor. I got the most spectacular chills, just from trying to imagine.

> *The Poisonwood Bible*

We know that the family is Southern, not only because their town of origin is named, but also from expressions such as "vexed" and "pitched a fit," as well as from mention of the Piggly Wiggly grocery chain. Not only do we know that they are missionaries, but further, we hear the father's sermonizing voice through his repetition of the phrase "where we are headed," preaching that is echoed in the implication that the mother is "confederated" with "the coin-jingling sinners." We also hear hints of the harsh pleasure the father will take in the family's hardship. The Betty Crocker mixes tell us that the women are trying to hang on to a little bit of home comfort, yet at the same time they are taking all-American '50s culture to a place where it is irrelevant and ultimately destructive—indeed, the cake mixes are quickly ruined by jungle humidity. And although we don't know the exact age of the narrator, she seems to be a teenager old enough to hear the subtext of her father's reprovals and to relish the false sophistication of phrases such as "the most spectacular chills" and "imagine." In a very short space, Kingsolver has sketched the family, their dangerous ignorance, and the father's divisive, single-minded determination.

The following passage is an even more striking example of implied information.

> Every time the same story. Your Barbie is roommates with my Barbie, and my Barbie's boyfriend comes over and your Barbie steals him, okay? Kiss kiss kiss. Then the two Barbies fight. You dumbbell! He's mine. Oh no he's not, you stinky! Only Ken's invisible, right? Because we don't have money for a stupid-looking boy doll when we'd both rather ask for a new Barbie outfit next Christmas. We have to make do with your mean-eyed Barbie and my bubblehead Barbie and our one outfit apiece not including the sock dress.
>
> Sandra Cisneros, "Barbie-Q"

Here there is no description whatever of the characters, and no direct reference to them except for the designations *you* and *I*. What do we nevertheless know about their gender, their age, their financial status, the period in which they live, their personalities, their attitudes, their relationship, the narrator's emotions?

Students of writing are sometimes daunted by the need to give so much information immediately. The thing to remember is that credibility consists in the combination of appropriateness and specificity. The trick is to find telling details that will convey the information while our attention remains on the desire or emotion of the character. Nobody wants to read a story that begins:

> She was a twenty-eight-year-old suburban American woman, relatively affluent, who was extremely distressed when her husband, Peter, left her.

But most of that, and much more besides, could be contained in a few details.

> After Peter left with the DVD player, the microwave, and the key to the garage, she went down to the kitchen and ate three jars of peanut butter without tasting a single spoonful.

I don't mean to imply that it is necessarily easy to signal the essentials of type immediately. It would be truer to say that it is necessary and hard. The opening paragraph of a story is its second-strongest statement (the final paragraph is the strongest) and sets the tone for all that follows. If the right words don't come to you as a gift, you may have to sit sifting and discarding the inadequate ones for a long time before you achieve both clarity and interest.

Purpose

Your character's purpose—that is, the desire that impels her or him to action—will determine our degree of identification and sympathy on the one hand, or judgment on the other.

Aristotle, in *The Poetics*, says that "there will be an element of character if what a person says or does reveals a certain moral purpose; and a good element of character, if the purpose so revealed is good." It might seem that the antiheroes, brutes, hoods, whores, perverts, and bums who people modern literature do very little in the way of revealing good moral purpose. The history of Western literature shows a movement downward and inward: downward through society from royalty to gentry to the middle classes to the lower classes to the dropouts; inward from heroic action to social drama to individual consciousness to the subconscious to the unconscious. What has remained consistent is that, while the reader is in the author's world, we understand and identify with the protagonist or protagonists, we "see their point of view"; and the fiction succeeds largely because we are willing to grant them a goodness that we would not grant them in life. While you read, you expand your mental scope by identifying with, temporarily "becoming," a character, borrowing a different mind. Fiction, as critic Laurence Gonzales says of rock music, "lets you wander around in someone else's hell for a while and see how similar it is to your own."

Complexity

If the characters of your story are credible through being appropriate and individual, and if they invite identification or judgment through a sense of their purpose, they also need to be complex. They need to exhibit enough conflict and contradiction that we can recognize them as belonging to the contradictory human race; and they should exhibit a range of possibility so that a shift of power in the plot can also produce a shift of purpose or morality. That is, they need to be capable of change.

Conflict is at the core of character, as it is of plot. If plot begins with trouble, then character begins with a person in trouble; and trouble most dramatically occurs because we all have traits, tendencies, and desires that are at war, not simply with the world and other people, but with other traits, tendencies, and desires of our own. All of us probably know a woman of the strong, striding, independent sort, attractive only to men who like a strong and striding woman. And when she falls in love? She becomes a clinging sentimentalist. All of us know a father who is generous, patient, and dependable. And when the children cross the line? He smashes crockery and wields a strap. All of us are gentle, violent; logical, schmaltzy; tough, squeamish; lusty, prudish; sloppy, meticulous; energetic, apathetic; manic, depressive. Perhaps you don't fit that particular list of contradictions, but you are sufficiently in conflict with yourself that as an author you have characters enough in your own psyche to people the work of a lifetime if you will identify, heighten, and dramatize these conflicts within character, which Aristotle called "consistent inconsistencies."

UNLIKE EVEN THOSE CLOSEST TO US IN REAL LIFE—our spouses, our lovers, our kin, whom we can never know completely—fictional people retain only as much privacy and secrecy as those who create them decide to let them keep.

DOUG BAUER

If you think of the great characters of literature, you can see how inner contradiction—consistent inconsistency—brings each to a crucial dilemma. Hamlet is a strong and decisive man who procrastinates. Dorothea Brooke of *Middlemarch* is an idealistic and intellectual young woman, a total fool in matters of the heart. Ernest Hemingway's Francis Macomber wants to test his manhood against a lion and cannot face the test. Here, in a moment of crisis from *Mom Kills Self and Kids*, Alan Saperstein reveals with great economy the consistent inconsistency of his protagonist, a man who hadn't much time for his family until their absence makes clear how dependent he has been on them.

> When I arrived home from work I found my wife had killed our two sons and taken her own life.
>   I uncovered a blast of foul, black steam from the pot on the stove and said, "Hi, hon, what's for dinner?" But she did not laugh. She did not bounce to her feet and pirouette into the kitchen to greet me. My little one didn't race into my legs and ask what I brought him. The seven-year-old didn't automatically beg me to play a game knowing my answer would be a tired, "Maybe later."

In "The Self as Source," Cheryl Moskowitz proposes a fiction technique that relies specifically on identifying conflicting parts of the writer's personality. She points to Robert Louis Stevenson's *The Strange Case of Dr. Jekyll and Mr. Hyde* as a fairly blatant model for such fiction, and quotes from Dr. Jekyll:

> ...I thus drew steadily nearer to that truth...that man is not truly one, but two. I say two, because the state of my own knowledge does not pass beyond that point....I hazard the guess that man will ultimately be known for a mere polity of multifarious, incongruous and independent denizens.

It is, of course, impossible to know to what degree Shakespeare, Eliot, Hemingway, or Saperstein have self-consciously used their own inner contradictions to build and dramatize their characters. An author works not only from his or her own personality but also from observation and imagination, and I fully believe that you are working at full stretch only when all three are involved. The question of autobiography is a complicated one, and as writer you frequently won't know yourself how much you have experienced, how much you have observed, and how much you have invented. Actress Mildred Dunnock once observed that drama is possible "because people can feel what they haven't experienced," an observation that surely extends to the writing and reading of fiction. If you push yourself to write at the outer edge of your emotional experience—what you can imagine yourself doing, even if you might not risk such actions in life—then all your writing is autobiographical in the sense that it must have passed through your mind.

Change

In a story, as opposed to a sketch or anecdote, says poet and novelist Al Young, "stuff happens, people *change*, situations *change*, there is no standing still." Certainly the easiest way to check the plot of your story is to ask, "Does my character change from opening to end? Do I give the sense that his or her life will never be quite the same again?"

Often the notion of change is mistaken by new writers to mean change that is abrupt and contrived—for instance from Scrooge to St. Nick—yet this rarely happens in life or in realistic fiction. Rather, change can be as subtle as a step in a new direction, a slight shift in belief, or a willingness to question a rigid view or recognize unseen value in a person or situation. Our society's belief in the power of change is reaffirmed each New Year's Day, and one of the vicarious pleasures fiction offers is the chance to experience the workings of change within a character's consciousness.

John L'Heureux offers a psychological framework for viewing change: "A story is about a single moment in a character's life when a definitive choice is made, after which nothing is the same."

The "integrity" of good fiction is a concept L'Heureux emphasizes, for the decision made in that "single moment" shows the essential integrity of the main character. He uses integrity in its primal sense of "wholeness," since at the moment of choice the character elects to live either more in harmony or more at odds with his or her best self. The decision made in that moment affects the character's relationship with the self forever.

"What we do determines what we become," fiction writer Nancy Huddleston Packer affirms. "Because character and event are interlocked, stories don't end in accident; rather, the consequences of the story come from the character who determines events. Our decisions make us who we are forever afterward."

Reinventing Character

There are a few other ways you can try to make a character fresh and forceful in your mind before you start writing.

If the character is based on you or on someone you know, drastically alter the model in some external way: Change blond hair to dark or thin to thick; imagine the character as the opposite gender, or radically alter the setting in which the character must act. Part of the trouble with writing directly from experience is that you know too much about it—what "they" did, how you felt. Under such circumstances it's hard to know whether everything in your mind is getting onto the page. An external alteration forces you to resee, and so to see more clearly, and so to convey more clearly what you see.

On the other hand, if the character is created primarily out of your observation or invention and is unlike yourself, try to find an internal area that you have in common with the character. If you are a blond, slender young woman and the character is a fat, balding man, do you nevertheless have in common a love of French *haute cuisine*? Are you haunted by the same sort of dream? Do you share a fear of public performance or a susceptibility to fine weather?

I can illustrate these techniques only from my own writing, because I am the only author whose self I can identify with any certainty in fictional characters. In one novel, I wanted to open with a scene in which the heroine buries a dog in her backyard. I had recently buried a dog in my backyard. I wanted to capture the look and feel of red Georgia earth at sunrise, the tangle of roots, and the smell of decay. But I knew that I was likely to make the experience too much my own, too little my character's. I set about to make her not-me. I have long dark hair and an ordinary figure, and I tend to live in Levi's. I made Shaara Soole

> ... big boned, lanky, melon-breasted, her best feature was a head of rusty barbed-wire hair that she tried to control with a wardrobe of scarves and headband things. Like most costume designers, she dressed with more originality than taste, usually on the Oriental or Polynesian side,

sometimes with voluminous loops of thong and matte metal over an
ordinary shirt. This was somewhat eccentric in Hubbard, Georgia, but
Shaara may have been oblivious to her eccentricity, being so concerned to
keep her essential foolishness in check.

Having thus separated Shaara from myself, I was able to bury the dog
with her arms and through her eyes rather than my own. On the other
hand, a few pages later I was faced with the problem of introducing her
ex-husband, Boyd Soole. I had voluminous notes on this character, and
I knew that he was almost totally unlike me: a man, to begin with, and
a huge man, a theater director with a natural air of power and authority
and very little interest in domestic affairs. I sat at my desk for several days,
unable to make him move convincingly. My desk oppressed me, and I felt
trapped and uncomfortable, my work thwarted, it seemed, by the very chair
and typewriter. Then it occurred to me that Boyd was *also* sitting at a desk
trying to work.

The dresser at the Travelodge was some four inches too narrow and three
inches too low. If he set his feet on the floor his knees would sit free of the
drawer but would be awkwardly constricted left and right. If he crossed
his legs, he could hook his right foot comfortably outside the left of the
knee-hole but would bruise his thigh at the drawer. If he shifted back he
was placed at an awkward distance from his script. And in this position he
could not work.

This passage did not instantly allow me to live inside Boyd Soole's skin, nor
did it solve all my problems with his characterization. But it did let me get on
with the story, and it gave me a flash of sympathy for him that later grew much
more profound than I had foreseen.

Often, identifying what you have in common with the feelings of your
character will also clarify what is important about her or him to the story—
why, in fact, you chose to write about such a person at all. Even if the character is presented as a villain, you have something in common, and I don't mean
something forgivable. If he or she is intolerably vain, watch your own private
gestures in front of the mirror and borrow them. If he or she is cruel, remember
how you enjoyed hooking the worm.

There is no absolute requirement that a writer need behave honestly in life;
there is absolutely no such requirement. Great writers have been public hams,
domestic dictators, emotional con artists, and Nazis. What is required for fine
writing is honesty on the page—not how the characters *should* react at the
funeral, at the surprise party, in bed, but how they *would*. In order to develop
such honesty of observation on the page, you must begin with a willing honesty of observation (though mercifully not of behavior) in yourself.

Creating a Group or Crowd

Sometimes it is necessary to introduce several or many people in the same scene, and this needn't present a problem, because the principle is pretty much the same in every case, and is the same as in film: pan, then close-up. In other words, give us a sense of the larger scene first, then a few details to characterize individuals. If you begin by concentrating too long on one character only, we will tend to see that person as being alone.

> Herm peered through the windshield and eased his foot up off the gas. Damn, he thought, it's not going to let up. The yellow lights made slick pools along the shoulder. He fiddled with the dial, but all he could get was blabber-radio and somebody selling vinyl siding. His back ached. His eyes itched. A hundred and forty miles to go.

At this point, if you introduce a wife, two children, and a dog to the scene, we will have to make rapid and uncomfortable adjustments in our mental picture. Better to begin with the whole carful and then narrow it down to Herm:

> Herm peered through the windshield and glanced over at Inga, who was snoring lightly against the window. The kids hadn't made a sound for about half an hour either, and only Cheza was wheezing dogbreath now and then on the back of his neck. He eased his foot up off the gas. Damn, he thought ...

If the action involves several characters who therefore need to be seen right away, introduce them as a group and then give us a few characterizing details:

> All the same there were four guns on him before he'd focused enough to count. "Peace," he said again. There were three old ones, one of them barely bigger than a midget, and the young one was fat. One of the old ones had on a uniform jacket much too big for him, hanging open on his slack chest. The young one spun a string of their language at him.

If the need is to create a crowd, it is still important, having established that there is a crowd, to give us a few details. We will believe more thoroughly in large numbers of people if you offer example images for us. Here, for example, is a passage from *Underworld* in which Don LeLillo introduces two parts of a crowd, the boys who are waiting to sneak into the ballpark and the last legitimate arrivals:

> ... they have found one another by means of slidy looks that detect the fellow foolhard and here they stand, black kids and white kids up from the subways or off the local Harlem streets, bandidos, fifteen in all, and according to topical legends maybe four will get through for every one that's caught.

They are waiting nervously for the ticket holders to clear the turnstiles, the last loose cluster of fans, the stragglers and loiterers. They watch the late-arriving taxis from downtown and the brilliantined men stepping dapper to the windows, policy bankers and supper club swells and Broadway hotshots, high aura'd, picking lint off their sleeves.

THE CHARACTER JOURNAL

Whether indirect, direct, or, most commonly, both direct and indirect methods are used, a full and rich fictional character will need to be both credible and complex, will show purpose (and that purpose will reveal something about his or her morality), and in the course of the story will undergo some, perhaps small but nonetheless significant, change. In order to explore these elements of character, your journal can be an invaluable help.

As a writer you may have the lucky, facile sort of imagination to which characters spring full-blown, complete with gestures, histories, and passions. Or it may be that you need to explore in order to exploit, to draw your characters out gradually and coax them into being. That can be lucky too.

For either kind of writer, but especially the latter, the journal lets you coax and explore without committing yourself to anything or anyone. It allows you to know everything about your character whether you use it or not. Before you put a character in a story, know how well that character sleeps, what he eats for lunch, what she buys, and how the bills get paid. Know how your character would prefer to spend evenings and weekends and why such plans get thwarted, what memories the character has of pets and parents, cities, snow, or school. You may end up using none of this information, but knowing it may teach you how your bookperson taps a pencil or twists a lock of hair, and when and why. When you know these things, you will have taken a step past invention toward the moment of imagination in which you become your character, live in his or her skin, and produce an action that, for the reader, rings universally true.

Use the journal to note your observations of people. Try writing down your impressions of the library assistant who annoys you or the loner at the bar who intrigues you. Try to capture a gesture or the messages that physical features and clothing send. Invent a reason for that harshness or that loneliness; invent a past. Then try taking the character out of context and setting her or him in another. Get your character in trouble, and you may be on your way to a short story.

Character: A Summary

It may be helpful to summarize the practical advice on character from this chapter and the previous one.

1. Be aware of the four methods of direct character presentation—appearance, speech, action, and thought—and of the indirect methods, authorial interpretation and the presentation by another character.

2. Reveal the character's conflicts by presenting attributes in at least one of these methods that contrasts with attributes you present in the others.

3. Focus sharply on how the character looks, on what she or he wears and owns, and on how she or he moves. Let us focus on it too.

4. Examine the character's speech to make sure it does more than convey information. Does it characterize, accomplish exposition, and reveal emotion, intent, or change? Does it advance the conflict through "no" dialogue? Speak it aloud: Does it "say"?

5. Build action by making your characters discover and decide. Make sure that what happens is action and not mere event or movement—that is, that it contains the possibility for human change.

6. Use your journal to explore and build ideas for characters.

7. Know the details of your character's life: what he or she does during every part of the day, thinks about, remembers, wants, likes and dislikes, eats, says, means.

8. Know all the influences that go into the making of your character's type: age, gender, race, nationality, marital status, region, education, religion, profession.

9. Know what your character wants, both generally out of life and specifically in the context of the story. Keeping that desire in mind, "think backward" with the character to decide what he or she would do in any situation presented.

10. Identify, heighten, and dramatize consistent inconsistencies. What does your character want that is at odds with whatever else she wants? What patterns of thought and behavior work against his primary goal?

11. If the character is based on a real model, including yourself, make a dramatic external alteration.

12. If the character is imaginary or alien to you, identify a mental or emotional point of contact.

Bullet in the Brain

TOBIAS WOLFF

Anders couldn't get to the bank until just before it closed, so of course the line was endless and he got stuck behind two women whose loud, stupid conversation put him in a murderous temper. He was never in the best of tempers anyway, Anders—a book critic known for the weary, elegant savagery with which he dispatched almost everything he reviewed.

With the line still doubled around the rope, one of the tellers stuck a "POSITION CLOSED" sign in her window and walked to the back of the bank, where she leaned against a desk and began to pass the time with a man shuffling papers. The women in front of Anders broke off their conversation and watched the teller with hatred. "Oh, that's nice," one of them said. She turned to Anders and added, confident of his accord, "One of those little human touches that keep us coming back for more."

Anders had conceived his own towering hatred of the teller, but he immediately turned it on the presumptuous crybaby in front of him. "Damned unfair," he said, "Tragic, really. If they're not chopping off the wrong leg, or bombing your ancestral village, they're closing their positions."

She stood her ground. "I didn't say it was tragic," she said, "I just think it's a pretty lousy way to treat your customers."

"Unforgivable," Anders said. "Heaven will take note."

She sucked in her cheeks but stared past him and said nothing. Anders saw that the other woman, her friend, was looking in the same direction. And then the tellers stopped what they were doing, and the customers slowly turned, and silence came over the bank. Two men wearing black ski masks and blue business suits were standing to the side of the door. One of them had a pistol pressed against the guard's neck. The guard's eyes were closed, and his lips were moving. The other man had a sawed-off shotgun. "Keep your big mouth shut!" the man with the pistol said, though no one had spoken a word. "One of you tellers hits the alarm, you're all dead meat. Got it?"

The tellers nodded.

"Oh, bravo," Anders said. *"Dead meat."* He turned to the woman in front of him. "Great script, eh? The stern, brass-knuckled poetry of the dangerous classes."

She looked at him with drowning eyes.

The man with the shotgun pushed the guard to his knees. He handed the shotgun to his partner and yanked the guard's wrists up behind his back and locked them together with a pair of handcuffs. He toppled him onto the floor with a kick between the shoulder blades. Then he took his shotgun back and went over to the security gate at the end of the counter. He was short and heavy and moved with peculiar slowness, even torpor. "Buzz him in," his partner said. The man with the shotgun opened the gate and sauntered along the line of tellers, handing each of them a Hefty bag. When he came to the empty position he looked over at the man with the pistol, who said, "Whose slot is that?"

Anders watched the teller. She put her hand to her throat and turned to the man she'd been talking to. He nodded. "Mine," she said.

"Then get your ugly ass in gear and fill that bag."

"There you go," Anders said to the woman in front of him. "Justice is done."

"Hey! Bright boy! Did I tell you to talk?"

"No," Anders said.

"Then shut your trap."

"Did you hear that?" Anders said. "'Bright boy.' Right out of 'The Killers.'"

"Please be quiet," the woman said.

"Hey, you deaf or what?" The man with the pistol walked over to Anders. He poked the weapon into Anders' gut. "You think I'm playing games?"

"No," Anders said, but the barrel tickled like a stiff finger and he had to fight back the titters. He did this by making himself stare into the man's eyes, which were clearly visible behind the holes in the mask: pale blue and rawly red-rimmed. The man's left eyelid kept twitching. He breathed out a piercing, ammoniac smell that shocked Anders more than anything that had happened, and he was beginning to develop a sense of unease when the man prodded him again with the pistol.

"You like me, bright boy!" he said. "You want to suck my dick!"

"No," Anders said.

"Then stop looking at me."

Anders fixed his gaze on the man's shiny wing-tip shoes.

"Not down there. Up there." He stuck the pistol under Anders' chin and pushed it upward until Anders was looking at the ceiling.

Anders had never paid much attention to that part of the bank, a pompous old building with marble floors and counters and pillars, and gilt scrollwork over the tellers' cages. The domed ceiling had been decorated with mythological figures whose fleshy, toga-draped ugliness Anders had taken in at a glance many years earlier and afterward declined to notice. Now he had no choice but to scrutinize the painter's work. It was even worse than he remembered, and all of it executed with the utmost gravity. The artist had a few tricks up his sleeve and used them again and again—a certain rosy blush on the underside of the clouds, a coy backward glance on the faces of the cupids and fauns. The ceiling was crowded with various dramas, but the one that caught Anders' eye was Zeus and Europa—portrayed, in this rendition, as a bull ogling a cow from behind a haystack. To make the cow sexy, the painter had canted her hips suggestively and given her long, droopy eyelashes through which she gazed back at the bull with sultry welcome. The bull wore a smirk and his eyebrows were arched. If there'd been a bubble coming out of his mouth, it would have said, "Hubba hubba."

"What's so funny, bright boy?"

"Nothing."

"You think I'm comical? You think I'm some kind of clown?"

"No."

"You think you can fuck with me?"

"No."

"Fuck with me again, you're history. *Capiche?*"

Anders burst out laughing. He covered his mouth with both hands and said, "I'm sorry, I'm sorry," then snorted helplessly through his fingers and said, "*Capiche*—oh, God, *capiche*," and at that the man with the pistol raised the pistol and shot Anders right in the head.

The bullet smashed Anders' skull and ploughed through his brain and exited behind his right ear, scattering shards of bone into the cerebral cortex, the corpus callosum, back toward the basal ganglia, and down into the thalamus. But before all this occurred, the first appearance of the bullet in the cerebrum set off a crackling chain of iron transports and neuro-transmissions. Because of their peculiar origin these traced a peculiar pattern, flukishly calling to life a summer afternoon some forty years past, and long since lost to memory. After striking the cranium the bullet was moving at 900 feet per second, a pathetically sluggish, glacial pace compared to the synaptic lightning that flashed around it. Once in the brain, that is, the bullet came under the mediation of brain time, which gave Anders plenty of leisure to contemplate the scene that, in a phrase he would have abhorred, "passed before his eyes."

It is worth noting what Anders did not remember, given what he did remember. He did not remember his first lover, Sherry, or what he had most madly loved about her, before it came to irritate him—her unembarrassed carnality, and especially the cordial way she had with his unit, which she called Mr. Mole, as in, "Uh-oh, looks like Mr. Mole wants to play," and, "let's hide Mr. Mole!" Anders did not remember his wife, whom he had also loved before she exhausted him with her predictability, or his daughter, now a sullen professor of economics at Dartmouth. He did not remember standing just outside his daughter's door as she lectured her bear about his naughtiness and described the truly appalling punishments Paws would receive unless he changed his ways. He did not remember a single line of the hundreds of poems he had committed to memory in his youth so that he could give himself the shivers at will— not "Silent, upon a peak in Darien," or "My God, I heard this day," or "All my pretty ones? Did you say all? O hell-kite! All?" None of these did he remember; not one. Anders did not remember his dying mother saying of his father, "I should have stabbed him in his sleep."

He did not remember Professor Josephs telling his class how Athenian prisoners in Sicily had been released if they could recite Aeschylus, and then reciting Aeschylus himself, right there, in the Greek. Anders did not remember how his eyes had burned at those sounds. He did not remember the surprise of seeing a college classmate's name on the jacket of a novel not long after they graduated, or the respect he had felt after reading the book. He did not remember the pleasure of giving respect.

Nor did Anders remember seeing a woman leap to her death from the building opposite his own just days after his daughter was born. He did not remember shouting, "Lord have mercy!" He did not remember deliberately crashing his father's car into a tree, or having his ribs kicked in by three policemen at an anti-war rally, or waking himself up with laughter. He did not remember when he began to regard the heap of books on his desk with boredom and dread, or when he grew angry at writers for writing them. He did not remember when everything began to remind him of something else.

This is what he remembered. Heat. A baseball field. Yellow grass, the whirr of insects, himself leaning against a tree as the boys of the neighborhood gather for a pickup game. He looks on as the others argue the relative genius of Mantle and Mays. They have been worrying this subject all summer, and it has become tedious to Anders; an oppression, like the heat.

Then the last two boys arrive, Coyle and a cousin of his from Mississippi. Anders has never met Coyle's cousin before and will never see him again. He says hi with the rest but takes no further notice of him until they've chosen sides and someone asks the cousin what position he wants to play. "Shortstop," the boy says. "Short's the best position they is." Anders turns and looks at him. He wants to hear Coyle's cousin repeat what he's just said, but he knows better than to ask. The others will think he's being a jerk, ragging the kid for his grammar. But that isn't it, not at all—it's that Anders is strangely roused, elated, by those final two words, their pure unexpectedness and their music. He takes the field in a trance, repeating them to himself.

The bullet is already in the brain; it won't be outrun forever, or charmed to a halt. In the end it will do its work and leave the troubled skull behind, dragging its comet's tail of memory and hope and talent and love into the marble hall of commerce. That can't be helped. But for now Anders can still make time. Time for the shadows to lengthen on the grass, time for the tethered dog to bark at the flying ball, time for the boy in right field to smack his sweat-blackened mitt and softly chant, *They is, they is, they is.*

Tandolfo the Great

RICHARD BAUSCH

"Tandolfo," he says to his own image in the mirror over the bathroom sink. "She loves you not, you goddam fool."

He's put the makeup on, packed the bag of tricks—including the rabbit, whom he calls Chi-Chi; and the bird, attention-getter, which he calls Witch. He's to do a birthday party on the other side of the river. Some five-year-old, and so this is going to be one of those tough ones, a crowd of babies, and all the adults waiting around for him to screw up.

He has fortified himself with something, and he feels ready. He isn't particularly worried about it. But there's a little something else he has to do, first. Something on the order of the embarrassingly ridiculous: he has to make a small delivery.

This morning, at the local bakery, he picked up a big pink wedding cake, with its six tiers and its scalloped edges and its little bride and groom on top. He'd ordered it on his own: he'd taken the initiative, planning to offer it to a young woman of his acquaintance. He managed somehow to set the thing on the backseat of the car and when he got home he found a note from her announcing, all excited and happy, that she's engaged. The man she'd had such trouble with has had a change of heart; he wants to get married after all. She's going to Houston to live. She loves her dear old Tandolfo with a big kiss and a hug always, and she knows he'll have every happiness. She's so thankful for his friendship. Her magic man. He's her sweet clown. She has actually driven over here and, finding him gone, left the note for him, folded under the door knocker—her pink notepaper, with the little tangle of flowers at the top. She wants him to call her, come by as soon as he can to help celebrate. *Please,* she says. *I want to give you a big hug.* He read this and then walked out to stand on the sidewalk and look at the cake in its place on the backseat of the car.

"Good God," he said. He'd thought he would put the clown outfit on, deliver the cake in person in the evening; an elaborate proposal to a girl he's never even kissed. He's a little unbalanced, and he knows it. Over the months of their working together for the county government, he's built up tremendous feelings of loyalty and yearning toward her. He thought she felt something, too. He interpreted gestures—her hand lingering on his shoulder when he made her laugh; her endearments to him, tinged as they seemed to be with a kind of sadness, as if she were afraid for what the world might do to someone so romantic.

"You sweet clown," she said. And she said it a lot. And she talked to him about her ongoing trouble, the guy she'd been in love with who kept waffling about getting married. He wanted no commitments. Tandolfo, aka Rodney Wilbury, told her that he hated men who weren't willing to run the risks of love. Why, he personally was the type who'd always believed in marriage and children, lifelong commitments. He had caused difficulties for himself and life was a disappointment so far, but he believed in falling in love and starting a family. She didn't hear him. It all went right through her like white noise on the radio. For weeks he had come around to visit her, had invited her to watch him perform. She confided in him, and he thought of movies where the friend sticks around and is a good listener, and eventually gets the girl. They fall in love. He put his hope in that. He was optimistic; he'd ordered and bought the cake. Apparently the whole time, all through the listening and being noble with her, she thought of it as nothing more than friendship, accepting it from him because she was accustomed to being offered friendship.

Now he leans close to the mirror to look at his own eyes through the makeup. They look clear enough. "Loves you absolutely not. You must be crazy. You must be the great Tandolfo."

Yes.

Twenty-six-year-old, out-of-luck Tandolfo. In love. With a great oversized cake in the backseat of his car. It's Sunday, a cool April day. He's a little inebriated. That's the word he prefers. It's polite; it suggests something faintly silly. Nothing could be sillier than to be dressed like this in the broad daylight, and to go driving across the bridge into Virginia to put on a magic show. Nothing could be sillier than to have spent all that money on a completely useless purchase—a cake six tiers high. Maybe fifteen pounds of sugar.

When he has made his last check of the clown face in the mirror, and the bag of tricks and props, he goes to his front door and stands at the screen looking out at the architectural shadow of it in the backseat. The inside of the car will smell like icing for days. He'll have to keep the windows open even if it rains; he'll go to work smelling like confectionery delights. The whole thing makes him laugh. A wedding cake. He steps out of the house and makes his way in the late-afternoon sun down the sidewalk to the car. As if they have been waiting for him, three boys come skating down from the top of the hill. He has the feeling that if he tried to sneak out like this at two in the morning, someone would come by and see him anyway. "Hey, Rodney," one boy says. "I mean Tandolfo."

Tandolfo recognizes him. A neighborhood boy, a tough. Just the kind to make trouble, just the kind with no sensitivity to the suffering of others. "Leave me alone or I'll turn you into spaghetti," he says.

"Hey, guys—it's Tandolfo the Great." The boy's hair is a bright blond color, and you can see through it to his scalp.

"Scram," Tandolfo says. "Really."

"Aw, what's your hurry, man?"

"I've just set off a nuclear device," Tandolfo says with grave seriousness. "It's on a timer. Poof."

"Do a trick for us," the blond one says. "Where's that scurvy rabbit of yours?"

"I gave it the week off." Someone, last winter, poisoned the first Chi-Chi. He keeps the cage indoors now. "I'm in a hurry. No rabbit to help with the driving."

But they're interested in the cake now. "Hey, what's that in your car? Is that what I think it is?"

"Just stay back."

"Is that a cake, man? Is that real?"

Tandolfo gets his cases into the trunk, and hurries to the driver's side door. The three boys are peering into the backseat.

"Hey, man. A cake. Can we have a piece of cake?"

"Back off," Tandolfo says.

The white-haired one says, "Come on, Tandolfo."

"Hey, Tandolfo, I saw some guys looking for you, man. They said you owed them money."

He gets in, ignoring them. He starts the car.

"You sucker," one of them says.

"Hey, man. Who's the cake for?"

He drives away, thinks of himself leaving them in a cloud of exhaust. Riding through the green shade, he glances in the rear-view mirror and sees the clown face, the painted smile. It makes him want to laugh. He tells himself he's his own cliché—a clown with a broken heart. Looming behind him is the cake, like a passenger in the backseat.

He drives slow. He has always believed viscerally that gestures mean everything. When he moves his hands and brings about the effects that amaze little children, he feels larger than life, unforgettable. He learned the magic while in high school, as a way of making friends, and though it didn't really make him any friends, he's been practicing it ever since. It's an extra source of income, and lately income has had a way of disappearing too quickly. He's been in some trouble—betting the horses; betting the sports events. He's hungover all the time. There have been several polite warnings at work. He's managed so far to tease everyone out of the serious looks, the cool evaluative study of his face. The fact is, people like him in an abstract way, the way they like distant clownish figures: the comedian whose name they can't remember. He can see it in their eyes. Even the rough characters after his loose change have a certain sense of humor about it. He's a phenomenon, a subject of conversation.

There's traffic on Key Bridge, and he's stuck for a while. It becomes clear that he'll have to go straight to the birthday party. Sitting behind the wheel of the car with his cake on the backseat, he becomes aware of people in other cars noticing him. In the car to his left, a girl stares, chewing gum. She waves, rolls her window down. Two others are with her, one in the backseat. "Hey," she says. He nods. Smiles inside what he knows is the painted smile. His teeth will look dark against the makeup.

"Where's the party?" she says.

But the traffic moves again. He concentrates. The snarl is on the other side of the bridge—construction of some kind. He can see the cars lined up, waiting to go up the hill into Roslyn and beyond. Time is beginning to be a consideration. In his glove box, he has a flask of bourbon. He reaches over and takes it out, looks around himself. No police anywhere. Just the idling cars and people tuning their radios or arguing or simply staring out as if at some distressing event. The smell of the cake is making him woozy. He takes a swallow of the bourbon, then puts it back. The car with the girls in it goes by him in the left lane, and they are not even looking at him. He watches them go on ahead. He's in the wrong lane again; he can't remember a time when his lane was the only one moving. He told her once that he considered himself in the race of people who gravitate to the nonmoving lanes of highways, and who cause traffic lights to turn yellow by approaching them. She took the idea and carried it out a little—saying she was of the race of people who emitted enzymes which instilled a sense of impending doom in marriageable young men, and made them wary of long-term relationships.

"No," Tandolfo/Rodney said. "I'm living proof that isn't so. I have no such fear, and I'm with you."

"But you're of the race of people who make mine relax all the enzymes."

"You're not emitting the enzymes now, I see."

"No," she said. "It's only with marriageable young men."

"I emit enzymes that prevent people like you from seeing that I'm a marriageable young man."

"I'm too relaxed to tell," she said, and touched his shoulder. A plain affectionate moment that gave him tossing nights and fever.

Because of the traffic, he arrives late at the birthday party. He gets out of the car and two men come down from the house to greet him. He keeps his face turned away, remembering too late the breath mints in his pocket.

"Jesus," one of the men says. "Look at this. Hey—who comes out of the cake? This is a kid's birthday party."

"The cake stays."

"What does he mean, it stays? Is that a trick?"

They're both looking at him. The one spoken to must be the birthday boy's father—he's wearing a party cap that says DAD. He has long dirty-looking strands of blond hair jutting out from the cap, and there are streaks of sweaty grit on the sides of his face. "So you're the Great Tandolfo," he says, extending a meaty red hand. "Isn't it hot in that makeup?"

"No, sir."

"We've been playing volleyball."

"You've exerted yourselves."

They look at him. "What do you do with the cake?" the one in the DAD cap asks.

"Cake's not part of the show, actually."

"You just carrying it around with you?"

The other man laughs. He's wearing a T-shirt with a smile face on the chest. "This ought to be some show," he says.

They all make their way across the street and the lawn, to the porch of the house. It's a big party—bunting everywhere and children gathering quickly to see the clown.

"Ladies and gentlemen," says the man in the DAD cap. "I give you Tandolfo the Great."

Tandolfo isn't ready yet. He's got his cases open, but he needs a table to put everything on. The first trick is where he releases the bird. He'll finish with the best trick, in which the rabbit appears as if from a pan of flames: it always draws a gasp, even from the adults; the fire blooms in the pan, down goes the "lid"—it's the rabbit's tight container—the latch is tripped, and the skin of the "lid" lifts off. *Voilà!* Rabbit. The fire is put out by the fireproof cage bottom. He's gotten pretty good at making the switch, and if the crowd isn't too attentive—as children often are not—he can perform certain hand tricks with some style. But he needs a table, and he needs time to set up.

The whole crowd of children is seated in front of the door into the house. He's standing here on the porch, his back to the stairs, and he's been introduced.

"Hello, boys and girls," he says, and bows. "Tandolfo needs a table."

"A table," one of the women says. All the adults are ranged against the porch wall, behind the children. He sees light sweaters, shapely hips, and wild tresses; he sees beer cans in tight fists and heavy jowls, bright ice-blue eyes. A little row of faces, and one elderly face. He feels more inebriated than he likes now, and he tries to concentrate.

"Mommy, I want to touch him," one child says.

"Look at the cake," says another, who's sitting on the railing to Tandolfo's right, with a new pair of shiny binoculars trained on the car. "Do we get some cake?"

"There's cake," says the man in the DAD cap. "But not that cake. Get down, Ethan."

"I want that cake."

"Get down. This is Teddy's birthday."

"Mommy, I want to touch him."

"I need a table, folks. I told somebody that over the telephone."

"He did say he needed a table. I'm sorry," says a woman who is probably the birthday boy's mother. She's quite pretty, leaning in the doorframe with a sweater tied to her waist.

"A table," says another woman. Tandolfo sees the birthmark on her mouth, which looks like a stain. He thinks of this woman as a child in school, with this difference from other children, and his heart goes out to her.

"I need a table," he says to her, his voice as gentle as he can make it.

"What's he going to do, perform an operation?" says DAD.

It amazes Tandolfo how easily people fall into talking about him as though he were an inanimate object, or something on a television screen. "The Great Tandolfo can do nothing until he gets a table," he says, with as much mysteriousness and drama as he can muster under the circumstances.

"I want that cake out there," says Ethan, still perched atop the porch railing. The other children start talking about cake and ice cream, and the big cake Ethan has spotted; there's a lot of confusion, and restlessness. One of the smaller children, a girl in a blue dress, comes forward and stands gazing at Tandolfo. "What's your name?" she says, swaying slightly, her hands behind her back.

"Go sit down," he says to her. "We have to sit down or Tandolfo can't do his magic."

In the doorway, two of the men are struggling with a folding card table. It's one of those rickety ones with the skinny legs, and it won't do.

"That's kind of rickety, isn't it?" says the woman with the birthmark.

"I said Tandolfo needs a sturdy table, boys and girls."

There's more confusion. The little girl has come forward and taken hold of his pant leg. She's just standing there holding it, looking at him. "We have to go sit down," he says, bending to her, speaking sweetly, clownlike. "We have to do what Tandolfo wants."

Her small mouth opens wide, as if she's trying to yawn, and with pale blue eyes quite calm and staring she emits a screech, an ear-piercing, nonhuman shriek that brings everything to a stop. Tandolfo/Rodney steps back, with his amazement and his inebriate heart, and now everyone's gathering around the girl, who continues to scream, less piercing now, her hands fisted at her sides, those blue eyes closed tight.

"What happened?" the man in the DAD cap wants to know. "Where the hell's the magic tricks?"

"I told you all I needed a *table.*"

"Whud you say to her to make her cry?" He indicates the little girl, who is not merely crying but is giving forth a series of broken, grief-stricken howls.

"I want magic tricks," the birthday boy says, loud. "Where's the magic tricks?"

"Perhaps if we moved the whole thing inside," the woman with the birthmark says, fingering her left ear and making a face.

The card table has somehow made its way to Tandolfo, through the confusion and grief. The man in the DAD cap sets it down and opens it.

"There," he says, as if his point is made.

In the next moment, Tandolfo realizes that someone's removed the little girl. Everything's relatively quiet again, though her cries are coming through the walls of one of the rooms inside the house. There are perhaps fifteen children, mostly seated before him; five or six men and women behind them, or kneeling with them. "Okay, now," DAD says. "Tandolfo the Great."

"Hello, little boys and girls," Tandolfo/Rodney says. "I'm happy to be here. Are you glad to see me?" A general uproar goes up. "Well, good," he says. "Because just look what I have in my magic bag." And with a flourish, he brings out the hat from which he will release Witch. The bird is encased inside a fold of shiny cloth, pulsing there. He can feel it. He rambles on, talking fast, or trying to, and when the time comes to reveal the bird, he almost flubs it. But Witch flaps his wings and makes enough of a commotion to distract even the adults, who applaud now, and get the children to applaud. "Isn't that wonderful," Tandolfo hears. "Where did that bird come from?"

"He had it hidden away," says the birthday boy.

"Now," Tandolfo says, "for my next spell, I need a little friend from the audience." He looks right at the birthday boy—round face, short nose, freckles. Bright red hair. Little green eyes. The whole countenance speaks of glutted appetites and sloth. This kid could be on Roman coins, an emperor. He's not used to being compelled to do anything, but he seems eager for a chance to get into the act. "How about you?" Tandolfo says to him.

The others, led by their parents, cheer.

The birthday boy gets to his feet and makes his way over the bodies of the other children to stand with Tandolfo. In order for the trick to work, Tandolfo must get everyone watching the birthday boy, and there's a funny hat he keeps in the bag for this purpose. "Now," he says to the boy, "since you're part of the show, you have to wear a costume." He produces the hat as if from behind the boy's ear. Another cheer goes up. He puts the hat on his head and adjusts it, crouching down. The green eyes stare impassively at him; there's no hint of awe or fascination in them. "There we are," he says. "What a handsome fellow."

But the birthday boy takes the hat off.

"No, no. We have to wear the hat to be onstage."

"Ain't a stage," the boy says.

"Well, but hey," Tandolfo says for the benefit of the adults. "Didn't you know that all the world's a stage?" He tries to put the hat on again, but the boy moves from under his reach and slaps his hand away. "We have to wear the hat," Tandolfo says, trying to control his anger. "We can't do the magic without our magic hats." He tries once more, and the boy waits until the hat is on, then simply removes it and holds it behind him, shying away when Tandolfo tries to retrieve it. The noise of the others now sounds like the crowd at a prizefight; there's a contest going on, and they're enjoying it. "Give Tandolfo the hat now. We want magic, don't we?"

"Do the magic," the boy demands.

"I'll do the magic if you give me the hat."

"I won't."

Nothing. No support from the adults. Perhaps if he weren't a little tipsy, perhaps if he didn't feel ridiculous and sick at heart and forlorn, with his wedding cake and his odd mistaken romance, his loneliness, which he has always borne gracefully and in humor, and his general dismay; perhaps if he were to find it in himself to deny the sudden, overwhelming sense of the unearned affection given this little slovenly version of stupid complacent spoiled satiation standing before him—he might've simply gone on to the next trick.

Instead, he leans down and in the noise of the moment, says to the boy, "Give me the hat, you little prick."

The green eyes widen slightly.

It grows quiet. Even the small children can tell that something's happened to change everything.

"Tandolfo has another trick," Rodney says, "where he makes the birthday boy pop like a balloon. Especially if he's a fat birthday boy."

A stirring among the adults.

"Especially if he's an ugly little slab of flesh like this one here."

"Now just a minute," says DAD.

"Pop," Rodney says to the birthday boy, who drops the hat and then, seeming to remember that defiance is expected, makes a face. Sticks out his tongue. Rodney/Tandolfo is quick with his hands by training, and he grabs the tongue.

"Awk," the boy says. "Aw-aw-aw."

"Abracadabra." Rodney lets go, and the boy falls backward into the lap of one of the older children. "Whoops, time to sit down," says Rodney.

Very quickly, he's being forcibly removed. They're rougher than gangsters. They lift him, punch him, tear at his costume—even the women. Someone hits him with a spoon. The whole scene boils out onto the lawn, where someone has released the case that Chi-Chi was in. Chi-Chi moves about wide-eyed, hopping between running children, evading them, as Tandolfo the Great cannot evade the adults. He's being pummeled, because he keeps trying to return for his rabbit. And the adults won't let him off the curb.

"Okay," he says finally, collecting himself. He wants to let them know he's not like this all the time; wants to say it's circumstances, grief, personal pain hidden inside seeming brightness and cleverness; he's a man in love, humiliated, wrong about everything. He wants to tell them, but he can't speak for a moment, can't even quite catch his breath. He stands in the middle of the street, his funny clothes torn, his face bleeding, all his magic strewn everywhere. "I would at least like to collect my rabbit," he says, and is appalled at the absurd sound of it—its huge difference from what he intended to say. He straightens, pushes the hair out of his eyes, adjusts the clown nose, and looks at them. "I would say that even though I wasn't as patient as I could've been, the adults have not comported themselves well here," he says.

"Drunk," one of the women says.

Almost everyone's chasing Chi-Chi now. One of the older boys approaches him, carrying Witch's case. Witch looks out the air hole, impervious, quiet as an idea. And now one of the men, someone Tandolfo hasn't noticed before, an older man clearly wearing a hairpiece, brings Chi-Chi to him. "Bless you," Rodney says, staring into the man's sleepy, deploring gaze.

"I don't think we'll pay you," the man says. The others are all filing back into the house, herding the children before them.

Rodney speaks to the man. "The rabbit appears out of fire."

The man nods. "Go home and sleep it off, kid."

"Right, thank you."

He puts Chi-Chi in his compartment, stuffs everything in its place in the trunk. Then he gets in and drives away. Around the corner he stops, wipes off what he can of the makeup; it's as if he's trying to remove the grime of bad opinion and disapproval. Nothing feels any different. He drives to the little suburban street where she lives with her parents, and by the time he gets there it's almost dark. The houses are set back in the trees; he sees lighted windows, hears music, the sound of children playing in the yards. He parks the car and gets out. A breezy April dusk.

"I am Tandolfo the soft-hearted," he says. "Hearken to me." Then he sobs. He can't believe it. "Jeez," he says. "Goddam."

He opens the back door of the car, leans in to get the cake. He'd forgotten how heavy it is. Staggering with it, making his way along the sidewalk, intending to leave it on her doorstep, he has an inspiration. Hesitating only for the moment it takes to make sure there are no cars coming, he goes out and sets it down in the middle of the street.

Part of the top sags slightly, from having bumped his shoulder as he pulled it off the backseat of the car. The bride and groom are almost supine, one on top of the other. He straightens them, steps back, and looks at it. In the dusky light, it looks blue. It sags just right, with just the right angle, expressing disappointment and sorrow.

Yes, he thinks. This is the place for it. The aptness of it, sitting out like this, where anyone might come by and splatter it all over creation, actually makes him feel some faint sense of release, as if he were at the end of a story. Everything will be all right if he can think of it that way. He's wiping his eyes, thinking of moving to another town. There are money troubles and troubles at work, and failures beginning to catch up to him, and he's still aching in love. He thinks how he has suffered the pangs of failure and misadventure, but in this painful instance there's symmetry, and he will make the one eloquent gesture—leaving a wedding cake in the middle of the road, like a sugar-icinged pylon. Yes.

He walks back to the car, gets in, pulls it around, and backs into the driveway of the house across the street. Leaving the engine idling, he rolls the window down and rests his arm on the sill, gazing at the incongruous shape of it there in the falling dark. He feels almost glad, almost—in some strange inexpressible way—vindicated, and he imagines what she might do if she saw him here. In a moment he's fantasizing that she comes running from her house, calling his name, looking at the cake and admiring it. This fantasy gives way to something else: images of destruction, flying sugar and candy debris. He's quite surprised to find that he wants her to stay where she is, doing whatever she's doing. He realizes with a feeling akin to elation that what he really wants—and for the moment all he really wants—is what he now has: a perfect vantage point from which to watch oncoming cars.

Turning the engine off, he waits, concentrating on the one thing, full of anticipation—dried blood and grime on his face, his hair all on end, his eyes glazed with rage and humiliation—a man imbued with interest, and happily awaiting the results of his labor.

Eleven

SANDRA CISNEROS

What they don't understand about birthdays and what they never tell you is that when you're eleven, you're also ten, and nine, and eight, and seven, and six, and five, and four, and three, and two, and one. And when you wake up on your eleventh birthday you expect to feel eleven, but you don't. You open your eyes and everything's just like yesterday, only it's today. And you don't feel eleven at all. You feel like you're still ten. And you are—underneath the year that makes you eleven.

Like some days you might say something stupid, and that's the part of you that's still ten. Or maybe some days you might need to sit on your mama's lap because you're scared, and that's the part of you that's five. And maybe one day when you're all grown up maybe you will need to cry like if you're three, and that's okay. That's what I tell Mama when she's sad and needs to cry. Maybe she's feeling three.

Because the way you grow old is kind of like an onion or like the rings inside a tree trunk or like my little wooden dolls that fit one inside the other, each year inside the next one. That's how being eleven years old is.

You don't feel eleven. Not right away. It takes a few days, weeks even, sometimes even months before you say eleven when they ask you.

And you don't feel smart eleven, not until you're almost twelve. That's the way it is. Only today I wish I didn't have only eleven years rattling inside me like pennies in a tin Band-Aid box. Today I wish I was one hundred and two instead of eleven because if I was one hundred and two I'd have known what to say when Mrs. Price put the red sweater on my desk. I would've known how to tell her it wasn't mine instead of just sitting there with that look on my face and nothing coming out of my mouth.

"Whose is this?" Mrs. Price says, and she holds the red sweater up in the air for all the class to see. "Whose? It's been sitting in the coatroom for a month."

"Not mine," says everybody. "Not mine."

"It has to belong to somebody," Mrs. Price keeps saying, but nobody can remember. It's an ugly sweater with red plastic buttons and a collar and sleeves all stretched out like you could use it for a jump rope. It's maybe a thousand years old and even if it belonged to me I wouldn't say so.

Maybe because I'm skinny, maybe because she doesn't like me, that stupid Sylvia Saldivar says, "I think it belongs to Rachel." An ugly sweater like that, all raggedy and old, but Mrs. Price believes her. Mrs. Price takes the sweater and puts it right on my desk, but when I open my mouth nothing comes out.

"That's not, I don't, you're not ... Not mine," I finally say in a little voice that was maybe me when I was four.

"Of course it's yours," Mrs. Price says. "I remember you wearing it once." Because she's old and the teacher, she's right and I'm not.

Not mine, not mine, not mine, but Mrs. Price is already turning to page thirty-two, and math problem number four. I don't know why but all of a sudden I'm feeling sick inside, like the part of me that's three wants to come out of my eyes, only I squeeze them shut tight and bite down on my teeth really hard and try to remember today when I am eleven, eleven. Mama is making a cake for me tonight, and when Papa comes home everybody will sing Happy Birthday, Happy Birthday to you.

But when the sick feeling goes away and I open my eyes, the red sweater's still sitting there like a big red mountain. I move the red sweater to the corner of my desk with my ruler. I move my pencil and books and eraser as far from it as possible. I even move my chair a little to the right. Not mine, not mine, not mine.

In my head I'm thinking how long till lunchtime, how long till I can take the red sweater and throw it over the schoolyard fence, or leave it hanging on a parking meter, or bunch it up into a little ball and toss it in the alley. Except when math period ends Mrs. Price says loud and in front of everybody, "Now, Rachel, that's enough," because she sees I've shoved the red sweater to the tippy-tip corner of my desk and it's hanging all over the edge like a waterfall, but I don't care.

"Rachel," Mrs. Price says. She says it like she's getting mad. "You put that sweater on right now and no more nonsense."

"But it's not—"

"Now!" Mrs. Price says. This is when I wish I wasn't eleven, because all the years inside of me—ten, nine, eight, seven, six, five, four, three, two, one—are pushing at the back of my eyes when I put one arm through one sleeve of the sweater that smells like cottage cheese, and then the other arm through the other and stand there with my arms apart like if the sweater hurts me and it does, all itchy and full of germs that aren't even mine.

That's when everything I've been holding in since this morning, since when Mrs. Price put the sweater on my desk, finally lets go, and all of a sudden I'm crying in front of everybody. I wish I was invisible but I'm not. I'm eleven and it's my birthday today and I'm crying like I'm three in front of everybody. I put my head down on the desk and bury my stupid clown-sweater arms. My face all hot and spit coming out of me, until there aren't any more tears left in my eyes, and it's just my body shaking like when you have the hiccups, and my whole head hurts like when you drink milk too fast.

But the worst part is right before the bell rings for lunch. That stupid Phyllis Lopez, who is even dumber than Sylvia Saldivar, says she remembers the red sweater is hers! I take it off right away and give it to her, only Mrs. Price pretends like everything's okay.

Today I'm eleven. There's a cake Mama's making for tonight, and when Papa comes home from work we'll eat it. There'll be candles and presents and everybody will sing Happy Birthday, Happy Birthday to you, Rachel, only it's too late.

I'm eleven today. I'm eleven, ten, nine, eight, seven, six, five, four, three, two, and one, but I wish I was one hundred and two. I wish I was anything but eleven, because I want today to be far away already, far away like a runaway balloon, like a tiny o in the sky, so tiny-tiny you have to close your eyes to see it.

◙ ◙ ◙

Writing Exercises

1. Sometimes our characters are too closely based on real-life people or parts of ourselves. We identify so closely with them that we are unwilling to let them get into any serious trouble, and trouble is what a story is all about. Write a scene in which your character gets into trouble. How might you have her mess up? Perhaps she makes a fool of herself by saying or doing the wrong thing, or is stubborn even though she is dead wrong

about something. Maybe someone else is at fault, maybe she's chosen to do something downright bad. An indiscretion? An "experiment"? An immoral act?

2. Write two versions of an opening paragraph of a story that introduces a character indirectly—one in which you (as the author) describe her and a second in which another character in the story does the describing.

   In your first version, tell the reader some of the basics (gender, age, race/nationality, class, region, period, etc.), but go further as well, revealing some details about the character's personality and desires, values and emotions. In your second version, let another character introduce that character. What is this second character's attitude toward the first? What does he or she know, guess, conclude?

3. Every family has one—a black sheep, an eccentric, an embarrassment. For a page or two describe that person in your own family. It may well be someone others talk about and disapprove of but whom you find intriguing. Is there the germ of a story in the rumors, the envy, and the half-told tales? Or, perhaps the story grows out of the actual encounters you or others have had with this person.

4. Have a character write a letter to someone with whom she's had a misunderstanding or disagreement, but have her do this *without addressing the problem directly*. Perhaps she's being polite, perhaps she's trying to protect herself; but in any case, she dances around the main issue in the letter, which is nevertheless clearly revealed. In the course of this letter, she will be telling us something about the second character, the one with whom she has the problem, but inadvertently she will be telling us even more about herself—about her own prejudices, biases, insecurities, jealousies, and fears.

5

FAR, FAR AWAY
Fictional Place

+ *Place and Atmosphere*

+ *Harmony and Conflict Between Character and Place*

+ *Place and Character*

+ *Place and Emotion*

+ *Symbolic and Suggestive Place*

+ *Alien and Familiar Place*

+ *An Exercise in Place*

"It's the job of the writer to create a world that entices you in and shows you what's at stake there," says fiction writer Nancy Huddleston Packer. For some writers, that world itself may inspire the story, while others will tend to focus on setting and atmosphere during the revision process. Still, even from the first, raw draft, it is important to remember Elizabeth Bowen's maxim that "nothing happens nowhere" and Jerome Stern's further admonition that a scene that seems to happen nowhere often seems not to happen at all. The failure to create an atmosphere, to establish a sense of where or when the story takes place, will leave readers bored or confused. And just as the rhythm of your prose must work with and not against your intention, so the use of place must work with and not against your ultimate meaning. Setting helps define a story's dimensions. Setting grounds a story in place.

Like dialogue, setting must do more than one thing at once, from illuminating the story's symbolic underpinnings to such practical kinds of "showing" as reflecting emotion or revealing subtle aspects of a character's life. Yet just as character and plot are interlinked, so character itself is a product of place and culture. We need not only know a character's gender, race, and age, but also in what atmosphere she or he operates to understand the significance of the action. For instance, could you imagine Scarlett O'Hara from *Gone with the Wind* without her plantation? Scarlett O'Hara acts as she does because she's a product of the Old South. The setting in which she's always lived defines and helps to explain her.

Sister Clareese in ZZ Packer's story "Every Tongue Shall Confess" doesn't challenge the hypocritical and sexist deacons of the Greater Christ Emmanuel Pentecostal Church of the Fire Baptized, because her church, with its familiar roles and expectations, is comforting and the most important thing in her life. The two bickering old women in Eudora Welty's story "A Visit of Charity" behave the way they do because they've been forgotten by the outside world, forced to live out their last days together in the cold, dark nursing home. In "St. Lucy's Home for Girls Raised by Wolves" feral girls are rehabilitated by nuns in a strict, proper setting which puts the wolf girls to the ultimate test. And finally, setting itself may give rise to an external conflict—one as big as the Vietnam War in "The Things They Carried" or as small as the disrupted birthday party in "Tandolfo the Great." The setting need not seem scary or even problematic to us as readers (a child's birthday party seems harmless enough) but if the character (in this case a drunk, enraged, humiliated clown) finds the setting to be hostile, then a conflict is born.

WHEN I WAS WRITING *Searches and Seizure,* I was living in London, and I needed to describe a hotel room. I've been in lots of hotel rooms, of course, but I didn't want to depend upon my memory. And so I went to the Royal Garden Hotel in Kensington and rented a room, simply to study the furniture there, to feel the glossy top of the wood that is almost not wood, to get the smell of the shower, the textures in the bath, to look at the rhetoric on the cards on top of the television set. This is stuff that I could not invent, and it was important to me to have it down very, very accurately. So I took notes. Somebody watching me would have thought I was a madman.

STANLEY ELKIN

But realistic settings constructed from memory or research are only part of the challenge, for an intensely created fantasy world makes new boundaries for the mind. *Once upon a time, long ago and far away, a dream, hell, heaven, a garbage shaft, Middle Earth, Hogwarts boarding school,* and *the subconscious* all have been the settings of excellent fiction. Even Utopian fiction, set *Nowhere* with a capital *N* (or *nowhere* spelled backward, as Samuel Butler had it in *Erehwon*), happens in a nowhere with distinct physical characteristics. Outer space is an exciting setting precisely because its physical boundary is the outer edge of our familiar world. Obviously this does not absolve the writer from the necessity of giving outer space its own characteristics, atmosphere, and logic. If anything, these must be more intensely realized within the fiction, since we have less to borrow from in our own experience.

> The westering sun shining in on his face woke Shevek as the dirigible, clearing the last high pass of the Ne Theras, turned south.... He pressed his face to the dusty window, and sure enough, down there between two low rusty ridges was a great walled field, the Port. He gazed eagerly, trying to see if there was a spaceship on the pad. Despicable as Urras was, still it was another world; he wanted to see a ship from another world, a voyager across the dry and terrible abyss, a thing made by alien hands. But there was no ship in the Port.
>
> Ursula K. Le Guin, *The Dispossessed*

We may be in outer space, but we are on a planet that shares certain aspects with our own—a westering sun, a mountain pass, and a walled field with two low rusty ridges—disappointingly empty. We've gone some place specific and real, and it is that reality and specificity that allow us to get lost in the story.

But what ingredients, when mixed together, make a setting? Is setting simply a description of the current weather conditions and the sights and smells and sounds immediately in the foreground of your story? Not necessarily. Fiction writer Michael Martone says that a truly effective evocation of fictional setting might resemble those old painted murals in post offices from the 1930s and early '40s. Any one of the figures in the mural has his or her own story, while at the same time those stories are embedded in the larger story of the whole painting. As we stand there observing the figures, we may see the social interactions between them, but at the same time we also observe the layers of history and social forces around these characters, as evidenced in their buildings, their inventions, their appliances, their transportation, their agriculture, their efforts to tame and control nature.

"These murals attempt," says Martone, "by the design of hundreds of details, to convey the simultaneous presence of history and social life of the greater community along with the personal specific struggle of a protagonist. Purely as a practical matter, placing stories in such a fertile media will make it easy for things to happen [in a story], for characters to do things."

To illustrate this, Martone refers to a story by Rick DeMarinis titled "Under the Wheat," about a construction worker who is building nuclear silos in a nearly deserted North Dakota town. As Martone points out, the character in this story is always looking up or down through various membranes of time and space. He is dwarfed by the constructed and the natural features of the place. Here he is fishing on the still surface of the lake created by a nearby dam:

Something takes my hook and strips off ten yards of line and then stops dead. Snag. I reel it in. The pole is bent double and the line is singing. Then something lets go but it isn't the line because I'm still snagged. It breaks the surface, a lady's shoe. It's brown and white with a short heel. I toss it into the bottom of the boat. The water is shallow here, and clear. There's something dark and wide under me like a shadow on the water. An old farmhouse, submerged when the dam filled. There's a deep current around the structure. I can see fence, tires, an old truck, feed pens. There is a fat farmer in the yard looking up at me, checking the weather, and I jump away from him, almost tipping the boat. My heart feels tangled in my ribs. But it is only a stump with arms. The current takes my boat in easy circles. A swimmer would be in serious trouble. I crank up the engine and head back. No fish today. So be it. Sometimes you come home empty-handed. The shoe is new, stylish and was made in Spain.

Setting can be rich and layered with many relics from the past—the barn, the fence, the truck. And it can be ominous—where did that lady's shoe come from?

Place and Atmosphere

Your fiction must have an *atmosphere* because without it your characters will be unable to breathe.

Part of the atmosphere of a scene or story is its setting, including the locale, period, weather, and time of day. Part of the atmosphere is its *tone*, an attitude taken by the narrative voice that can be described in terms of a quality—sinister, facetious, formal, solemn, wry. The two facets of atmosphere, setting and tone, are often inextricably mixed in the ultimate effect. A sinister atmosphere might be achieved partly by syntax, rhythm, and word choice; partly by darkness, dampness, and a desolate landscape, as is shown in the first line of Edgar Allan Poe's "The Fall of the House of Usher":

During the whole of a dull, dark, and soundless day in the autumn of the year, when the clouds hung oppressively low in the heavens, I had been passing alone, on horseback, through a singularly dreary tract of country; and at length found myself, as the shades of the evening drew on, within view of the melancholy House of Usher.

In Annie Proulx's story "What Kind of Furniture Would Jesus Pick?" we can feel the extent of a beleaguered housewife's oppression when we read this description of the wind attacking her Wyoming ranch:

> The house lay directly in line with a gap in the encircling hills to the northwest, and through this notch the prevailing winds poured, falling on the house with ferocity. The house shuddered as the wind punched it and slid along its sides like a released torrent from a broken dam. Week after week in winter it sank and rose, attacked and feinted. When she put her head down and went out to the truck it yanked at her clothing, shot up her sleeves, whisked her hair into a raveled fright wig.

The words *encircling hills*, *prevailing winds*, *falling*, *ferocity*, *shuddered*, *punched*, *released torrent*, *broken dam*, *week after week*, *sank and rose*, *attacked and feinted*, *put her head down*, *yanked*, *shot*, *whisked*, and *raveled fright wig* leave no doubt as to how she's feeling, not only about the wind, but about her life in general.

You can orient your reader in a place with straight information (*On the southern bank of the Bayou Teche...*), but as with the revelation of character, you may more effectively reveal place through concrete detail (*The bugs hung over the black water in clusters of a steady hum*). Stuart Dybek offers another set of evocative details in his story "Breasts": *Joe's bedroom window was open too, and a breeze that tingled the blinds they hadn't bothered to draw seemed tinted with the glow of the new arc lights the city had erected.* In both of these examples the information is indirect. We aren't sure yet what to make of the clusters of bugs or the open blinds, but they reveal an attitude toward the setting, and we seem to experience it firsthand.

Harmony and Conflict Between Character and Place

If character is the foreground of fiction, setting is the background, and as in a painting's composition, the foreground may be in harmony or in conflict with the background. If we think of the Impressionist paintings of the late nineteenth century, we think of the harmony of, say, women with light-scattering parasols strolling against summer landscapes of light-scattering trees. By contrast, the Spanish painter José Cortijo has a portrait of a girl on her Communion day; she sits curled and ruffled, in a lace mantilla, on an ornately carved Mediterranean throne against a backdrop of stark, harshly lit, poverty-stricken shacks.

Likewise, the setting and characters of a story may be in harmony:

> The Bus to St. James's—a Protestant Episcopal school for boys and girls—started its round at eight o'clock in the morning, from a corner of Park Avenue in the Sixties. The earliness of the hour meant that some of the parents who took their children there were sleepy and still without coffee,

but with a clear sky the light struck the city at an extreme angle, the air was fresh, and it was an exceptionally cheerful time of day. It was the hour when cooks and doormen walk dogs, and when porters scrub the lobby floor mats with soap and water.

John Cheever, "The Bus to St. James's"

Contentment, regularity, and peace are suggested by this passage. For the parents and the students of St. James, all is right with the world.

Or there can be an inherent conflict between the background and foreground:

...He opened the door himself and started down the walk to get her going. The sky was a dying violet and the houses stood out darkly against it, bulbous liver-colored monstrosities of a uniform ugliness though no two were alike. Since this had been a fashionable neighborhood forty years ago, his mother persisted in thinking they did well to have an apartment in it. Each house had a narrow collar of dirt around it in which sat, usually, a grubby child. Julian walked with his hands in his pockets, his head down and thrust forward and his eyes glazed with the determination to make himself completely numb during the time he would be sacrificed to her pleasure.

Flannery O'Connor, "Everything That Rises Must Converge"

Notice how images of the time of day work with concrete details of place to create very different atmospheres—on the one hand *morning, Park Avenue, earliness, clear sky, light, extreme angle, air, fresh, cheerful, dogs, scrub, soap, water*; and on the other *dying violet, darkly, bulbous liver-colored monstrosities, uniform ugliness, narrow, dirt, grubby child*. Notice also that where conflict occurs, there is already "narrative content," or the makings of a story. We might reasonably expect that in the Cheever story, where the characters are in apparent harmony with their background, there is or will be conflict in the foreground between or among those children, parents, and perhaps the servitors who keep their lives so well scrubbed. It won't surprise us when the peace and quiet of this world shatters and the weather gets downright dangerous by the end of the story.

Place and Character

One of the most economical means of sketching a character is simply to show readers a personal space that the character has created, be it a bedroom, locker, kitchen, hideout, office cubicle, or the interior of a car. This technique is illustrated in Elizabeth Tallent's story "Prowler," as Dennis, a divorced father, surveys his thirteen-year-old son's bedroom.

Dennis believes it tells everything about Kenny: photo-realist motorcycles, chrome and highly evolved threat, grace the walls, along with a frail Kafka razor-bladed from a library book, a sin so small and so unprecedented that Dennis uncharacteristically forgot to mention it to him. If Kenny's motorcycle paintings are depressing, surely jug-eared Kafka promises complexity, contradiction, hope?

Through the description of Kenny's room, we see that the boy is making a transition to the rocky years of adolescence, showing both a typical interest in fast, powerful, rebellious vehicles and also signs of more private teenage angst (and what is he doing with razor blades anyway?). Not every parent would interpret a Kafka portrait, much less a stolen one, as a sign of hope; in this case, the reflection may reveal as much about the observing father as about the indirectly observed son, adding a further layer of complexity.

Doug Coupland uses an even more self-conscious version of the same technique to create a quick portrait of the household of fanatical young Microsoft employees featured in his novel *Microserfs*:

> More details about our group house—Our House of Wayward Mobility.
> Because the house receives almost no sun, moss and algae tend to colonize what surfaces they can. There is a cherry tree, crippled by a fungus. The rear verandah, built of untreated 2×4's, has quietly rotted away, and the sliding door in the kitchen has been braced shut with a hockey stick to prevent the unwary from straying into the suburban abyss....
> Inside, each of us has a bedroom. Because of the McDonald's-like turnover in the house, the public rooms—the living room, kitchen, dining room, and basement—are bleak to say the least. The dormlike atmosphere precludes heavy-duty interior design ideas. In the living room are two velveteen sofas that were too big and too ugly for some long-gone tenants to take with them. Littered about the Tiki Green shag carpet are:
>
> - Two Microsoft Works PC inflatable beach cushions
> - One Mitsubishi 27-inch color TV
> - Various vitamin bottles
> - Several weight-gaining system cartons (mine)
> - 86 copies of MacWEEK arranged in chronological order by Bug Barbecue, who will go berserk if you so much as move one issue out of date
> - Bone-shaped chew toys for when Mishka visits
> - Two PowerBooks
> - Three IKEA mugs encrusted with last month's blender drink sensation
> - Two 12.5 pound dumbbells (Susan's)

- A Windows NT box
- Three baseball caps (two Mariners, one A's)
- Abe's Battlestar Galactica trading card album
- Todd's pile of books on how to change your life to win! (*Getting Past OK, 7 Habits of Highly Effective People…*)

The kitchen is stocked with ramshackle 1970s avocado green appliances. You can almost hear the ghost of Emily Hartley yelling "Hi, Bob!" every time you open the fridge door (a sea of magnets and 4×6-inch photos of last year's house parties). Our mail is in little piles by the front door: bills, Star Trek junk mail, and the heap-o-catalogues next to the phone.

I think we'd order our lives via 1-800 numbers if we could.

Like their mold-ravaged house, the Microserfs also receive almost no sun as they pursue their project shipping deadlines round the clock; the litter of objects listed gives clues to whatever thin slices of personality remain.

What generalizations might you make about the Microserfs after reading this passage? Are they self-absorbed? Driven? Wealthy? Immature? Focused? Sloppy? All these descriptions may apply, but they seem bland and inadequate when juxtaposed with the list of specific details that bring them to life in a way that mere adjectives never could.

Here is Michael Martone again: "The reader is to be pulled in by the preponderance of the evidence that he or she has been sifting through. As you read, the details fall like snow that suddenly is ash. The character is clearly visible once he is coated, like a statue in the town square after such a storm, with a film of detail."

SUPPOSE WE THINK OF A SCENE IN YOUR NOVEL as a scene in a play. Any scene in any play takes place on some sort of set. I feel that the sets in your play are quite wonderful, but you never let us see them. A spotlight follows every move the characters make and throws an almost blinding radiance on them, but it is a little like the spotlight a burglar uses when he is cracking a safe; it illuminates a small circle and the rest of the stage is in darkness most of the time….It would be better, I think, if you occasionally used a spotlight large enough to illuminate the corners of the room, for those corners have gone on existing all through the most dramatic moments.

CAROLINE GORDON TO FLANNERY O'CONNOR

Place and Emotion

Our relation to place, time, and weather, like our relation to clothes and other objects, is charged with emotion more or less subtle, more or less profound. It is filled with judgment mellow or harsh. And it alters according to what happens to us. In some rooms you are always trapped; you enter them with grim purpose and escape them as soon as you can. Others invite you to settle in, to nestle or carouse. Some landscapes lift your spirits; others depress you. Cold weather gives you energy and bounce, or else it clogs your head and makes you huddle, struggling. You describe yourself as a night person or a morning person. The house you loved as a child now makes you, precisely because you were once happy there, think of loss and death. It is central to fiction that all such emotion be used or heightened (or invented) to dramatic effect.

Imagine experiencing a thunderstorm when in the throes of a new love: The rain might seem to glitter, the lightning to sizzle, the thunder to rumble with anticipation. The downpour would refresh and exhilarate, nourishing the newly budding violets. Then imagine how the very same storm would feel in the midst of a lousy romantic breakup: The raindrops would be thick and cold, almost greasy; the lightning would slash at the clouds; the thunder would growl. Torrents of rain would beat the delicate tulips to the ground.

Because we have all had the experience of seeing our inner emotional states reflected by the outer world, we instinctively understand that setting can serve as a mirror of emotion. Seen through the eyes of a character, setting is never neutral.

In Frederick Busch's story "Ralph the Duck," the narrator thinks back on a troubling incident that had taken place during his rounds at the local college that evening. He sits with a "king-sized drink composed of sour mash whiskey and ice" and

> In our back room, which is on the northern end of the house, and cold for sitting in that close to dawn, I sat and watched the texture of the sky change. It was going to snow, and I wanted to see the storm come up the valley.

He seems to sense that there is worse trouble to come, and in fact it later arrives in the middle of an ice storm. Yet by the story's end, when he is feeling some relief and hope (to which the laconic narrator himself would never admit), we see these feelings mirrored in a very different view of the same landscape.

> I was at the northern windows, looking through the mullions down the valley to the faint red line along the mounds and little peaks of the ridge beyond the valley. The sun was going to come up, and I was looking for it.

Setting can help to portray a swirl of emotion, as in this moment from Joyce Carol Oates's story "Where Are You Going, Where Have You Been?" in which Arnold Friend's attempts to disorient and terrorize Connie are succeeding, and she is losing her grasp on all that is familiar, even as she feels nostalgic for the home she is leaving:

> The kitchen looked like a place she had never seen before, some room she had run inside but which wasn't good enough, wasn't going to help her. The kitchen window had never had a curtain, after three years, and there were dishes in the sink for her to do—probably—and if you ran your hand across the table you'd probably feel something sticky there.

Emotion is conveyed in these and similar passages, even as the story is being anchored in place. When a reader senses that setting is being used to reveal something important, there is no danger of its being what one student calls "the stuff you skip."

What do we skip? Self-indulgent description of setting that seems to exist only as an excuse for flowery, inflated language: "The majestic mountains rose like great behemoths above the grassy plains, and the plains themselves rolled away like a great and endless ocean." Description of setting that feels forced—an overly fastidious catalog of details, often awkwardly placed: "The dead man's pantry was stocked with canisters of oatmeal, Cream of Wheat, cornmeal, flour (white and whole wheat), rice (brown and white), couscous, instant grits, and Wheatena, and bottles of various cooking oils—corn, olive, canola, sunflower, and vegetable." Description that is generic and perfunctory, lacking in emotional significance or authorial judgment: "Robert's farm consisted of 1,276 acres of land, most of which was tillable, but seventy-seven acres of which was made up of woodlots and inaccessible bottomland along three different creeks."

Michael Martone, in a lecture on setting, noted: "In many stories I read, [household] appliances are often deployed neutrally, used mainly…as a way to fill up space, background things merely to run or handle, props, business for the character to perform when the real action is happening between people."

When we read any nonessential description, our eyes and minds will glaze over and we'll either skip ahead to "the good parts" or stop reading altogether.

"SWALLOWS, FLITTING OVER THE SURFACE OF THE WATER, twittered gaily"—eliminate such commonplaces. You have to choose small details in describing nature, grouping them in such a way that if you close your eyes after reading it you can picture the whole thing. For example, you'll get a picture of a moonlit night if you write that on the dam of the mill a piece of broken bottle flashed like a bright star and the black shadow of a dog or a wolf rolled by like a ball, etc.

ANTON CHEKHOV TO HIS BROTHER ALEXANDER

Symbolic and Suggestive Place

Ever since the rosy-fingered dawn came over the battlefield of Homer's *Iliad* (and no doubt well before that), poets and writers have used the context of history, night, storm, stars, sea, city, and plain to give their stories a sense of reaching out toward the universe. Sometimes the universe resonates with an answer, and in his plays Shakespeare consistently drew parallels between the conflicts of the heavenly bodies and the conflicts of nations and characters.

In "The Life You Save May Be Your Own," Flannery O'Connor uses the elements in a conscious Shakespearean way, letting the setting reflect and affect the theme.

> The old woman and her daughter were sitting on their own porch when Mr. Shiflet came up their road for the first time. The old woman slid to the edge of her chair and leaned forward, shading her eyes from the piercing sunset with her hand. The daughter could not see far in front of her and continued to play with her fingers. Although the old woman lived in this desolate spot with only her daughter, and she had never seen Mr. Shiflet before, she could tell, even from a distance, that he was a tramp and no one to be afraid of. His left coat sleeve was folded up to show there was only half an arm in it and his gaunt figure listed lightly to the side as if the breeze were pushing him. He had on a black town suit and a brown felt hat that was turned up in the front and down in the back and he carried a tin tool box by a handle. He came on at an amble, up her road, his face turned toward the sun which appeared to be balancing itself on the peak of a small mountain.

The focus in this opening paragraph of the story is on the characters and their actions, and the setting is economically, almost incidentally, established: *porch, road, sunset, breeze, peak, small mountain*. What the passage gives us is a type of landscape, rural and harsh; the only adjectives in the description of the setting are *piercing, desolate,* and *small*. But this general background works together with details of action, thought, and appearance to establish a great deal more that is both informational and emotional. The old woman's peering suggests that people on the road are not only unusual but suspicious. On the other hand, that she is reassured to see a tramp suggests both a period and a set of assumptions about country life. That Mr. Shiflet wears a town suit establishes him as a stranger to this set of assumptions. That the sun appears to be balancing itself (we are not sure whether it is the old woman's observation or the author's) leaves us, at the end of the paragraph, with a sense of anticipation and tension.

Now, what happens in the story is this: Mr. Shiflet repairs the old woman's car and (in order to get the car) marries her retarded daughter. He abandons the daughter on their honeymoon and picks up a hitchhiker, who insults both Mr. Shiflet and the memory of his mother. The hitchhiker jumps out. Mr. Shiflet curses and drives on.

Throughout the story, as in the first paragraph, the focus remains on the characters and their actions. Yet the landscape and the weather make their presence felt, subtly commenting on attitudes and actions. As Mr. Shiflet's fortunes wax promising and he expresses satisfaction with his own morality, "A fat yellow moon appeared in the branches of the fig tree as if it were going to roost there with the chickens." When, hatching his plot, he sits on the steps with the mother and daughter, "The old woman's three mountains were black against the sky." Once he has abandoned the girl, the weather grows "hot and sultry, and the country had flattened out. Deep in the sky a storm was preparing very slowly and without thunder." Once more there is a sunset, but this time the sun "was a reddening ball that through his windshield was slightly flat on the bottom and top," and this deflated sun reminds us of the "balanced" one about to be punctured by the peak in its inevitable decline. When the hitchhiker has left him, a cloud covers the sun, and Mr. Shiflet in his fury prays for the Lord to "break forth and wash the slime from this earth!" His prayer is apparently answered.

After a few minutes there was a guffawing peal of thunder from behind and fantastic raindrops, like tin-can tops, crashed over the rear of Mr. Shiflet's car. Very quickly he stepped on the gas and with his stump sticking out the window he raced the galloping shower to Mobile.

The setting in this story, as this bald summary emphasizes, is deliberately used as a comment on the actions. The behavior of the weather, in ironic juxtaposition to the title, "The Life You Save May Be Your Own," makes clear that the "slime" Mr. Shiflet has damned may be himself. Yet the reader is never aware of this as a symbolic intrusion. The setting remains natural and realistically convincing, an incidental backdrop, until the heavens are ready to make their guffawing comment.

Robert Coover's settings rarely present a symbolic or sentient universe, but they produce in us an emotionally charged expectation of what is likely to happen here. The following passages are the opening paragraphs of three short stories from a single collection, *Pricksongs and Descants*. Notice how the three different settings are achieved not only by imagery and content, but also by the very different rhythms of the sentence structure.

A pine forest in the midafternoon. Two children follow an old man, dropping breadcrumbs, singing nursery tunes. Dense earthy greens seep into the darkening distance, flecked and streaked with filtered sunlight. Spots of red, violet, pale blue, gold, burnt orange. The girl carries a basket for gathering flowers. The boy is occupied with the crumbs. Their song tells of God's care for little ones.

"The Gingerbread House"

Situation: television panel game, live audience. Stage strobelit and cameras insecting about. Moderator, bag shape corseted and black suited behind desk/rostrum, blinking mockmodesty at lens and lamps, practised pucker on his soft mouth and brows arched in mild goodguy astonishment. Opposite him, the panel: Aged Clown, Lovely Lady and Mr. America, fat as the continent and bald as an eagle. There is an empty chair between Lady and Mr. A, which is now filled, to the delighted squeals of all, by a spectator dragged protesting from the Audience, nondescript introduced as Unwilling Participant, or more simply, Bad Sport. Audience: same as ever, docile, responsive, good-natured, terrifying. And the Bad Sport, you ask, who is he? fool! thou art!

"Panel Game"

She arrives at 7:40, ten minutes late, but the children, Jimmy and Bitsy, are still eating supper, and their parents are not ready to go yet. From the other rooms come the sounds of a baby screaming, water running, a television musical (no words: probably a dance number—patterns of gliding figures come to mind). Mrs. Tucker sweeps into the kitchen, fussing with her hair, and snatches a baby bottle full of milk out of a pan of warm water, rushes out again. Harry! she calls. The babysitter's here already!

"The Babysitter"

Here are three quite familiar places: a fairy-tale forest, a television studio, and a suburban house. In at least the first two selections, the locale is more consciously and insistently set than in the O'Connor opening, yet all three remain suggestive backdrops rather than active participants—no guffawing or galloping here. Coover directs our attitude toward these places through imagery and tone.

In "The Gingerbread House," the forest is a neverland, and the time is once upon a time, though there are grimmer-than-Grimm hints of violence about it. Simple sentence structure helps establish the childlike quality appropriate to a fairy tale. But a more complex sentence intervenes, with surprising intensity of imagery: *dense, earthy, seep, darkening, flecked, streaked, filtered.* Because of this, the innocence of the tone is set askew, so that by the time we hear of God's care for little ones, we fully and accurately expect a brutal disillusionment.

Setting can often, and in a variety of ways, arouse reader expectation and foreshadow events to come. In "The Gingerbread House," there is an implied conflict between character and setting, between the sentimentality of the children's flowers and nursery tunes and the threatening forest, so that we are immediately aware of the central conflict of the story: innocence versus violence. As in the Cheever story "The Bus to St. James's," anticipation can also be aroused by an insistent single attitude toward setting, and in this case the reader, being a contrary sort of person, is likely to anticipate a change or paradox.

Where conflict between character and setting is immediately introduced, as it is in both "The Gingerbread House" and "Panel Game," it is usually because the character is unfamiliar with, or uncomfortable in, the setting. In "Panel Game" it's both. The television studio is a place of hysteria, chaos, and hypocrisy (as evidenced by the moderator's mockmodesty and practiced pucker). The television studio, which is in fact a familiar and unthreatening place to most of us, has been made mad. This is achieved partly by violating expected grammar. The sentences are not sentences. They are missing vital verbs and logical connectives, so that the images are squashed against each other. The prose is cluttered, effortful, negative; as a result, as reader you know "the delighted squeals of all" do not include your own, and you're ready to sympathize with the unwilling central character (you!).

In "The Babysitter," notice that the setting is ordinary and is presented as ordinary. The sentences have standard and rather leisurely syntax; neither form nor image startles. Details are generic, not specific: the house is presented without a style; the children are named but not seen; Mrs. Tucker behaves in a way predictable and familiar to most anyone in contemporary America. What Coover has in fact done is to present us with a setting so usual, so "typical," that we begin to suspect that something unusual is afoot.

Indeed, the Tuckers, their house, their children, their car, their night out, and their babysitter remain unvaryingly typical throughout all the external actions in the course of the evening. Against this relentlessly wholesome backdrop play the individual fantasies of the characters—brilliant, brutal, sexual, dangerous, and violent—that provide the conflict of the story.

Alien and Familiar Place

Many poets and novelists have observed that the function of literature is to make the ordinary fresh and strange. F. Scott Fitzgerald, on the other hand, advised a young writer that reporting extreme things as if they were ordinary was the starting point of fiction. Both of these views are true, and they are particularly true of setting. Whether a place is familiar or unfamiliar, comfortable or discomfiting in fiction has nothing to do with whether the reader actually knows the place and feels good there. It is an attitude taken, an assumption made. In his detective novels, Ross Macdonald assumes a familiarity toward California that is translatable into any language ("I turned left off the highway and down an old switchback blacktop to a dead end"), whereas even the natives of North Hollywood must feel alien on Tom Wolfe's version of their streets:

> ...endless scorched boulevards lined with one-story stores, shops, bowling alleys, skating rinks, taco drive-ins, all of them shaped not like rectangles but like trapezoids, from the way the roofs slant up from the back and

the plate-glass fronts slant out as if they're going to pitch forward on the sidewalk and throw up.

The Kandy-Kolored Tangerine-Flake Streamline Baby

The prose of Tom Wolfe, whether about rural North Carolina, Fifth Avenue, or Cape Kennedy, lives in a tone of constant breathless astonishment. By contrast, Ray Bradbury's outer space is pure down-home.

It was quiet in the deep morning of Mars, as quiet as a cool black well, with stars shining in the canal waters, and, breathing in every room, the children curled with their spiders in closed hands.

The Martian Chronicles

One great advantage of being a writer is that you may create the world. Places and the elements have the significance and the emotional effect you give them in language. As a person you may be depressed by rain, but as an author you are free to make rain mean freshness, growth, bounty, and God. You may choose; the only thing you are not free to do is not to choose.

As with character, the first requisite of effective setting is to know it fully, to experience it mentally, and the second is to create it through significant detail. What sort of place is this, and what are its peculiarities? What is the weather like, the light, the season, the time of day? What are the contours of the land and architecture? What are the social assumptions of the inhabitants, and how familiar and comfortable are the characters with this place and its lifestyle? These things are not less important in fiction than in life, but more so, since their selection inevitably takes on significance.

And as in the stories at the end of this chapter—"St. Lucy's Home for Girls Raised by Wolves," "The Flowers," and "A Visit of Charity"—setting may become a character itself.

In Eudora Welty's "A Visit of Charity," a young girl must visit a home for old people, what we now call an assisted-care facility. She will find it hard to enter and harder to leave. Here is the opening paragraph:

It was mid-morning—a very cold, bright day. Holding a potted plant before her, a girl of fourteen jumped off the bus in front of the Old Ladies' Home, on the outskirts of town. She wore a red coat, and her straight yellow hair was hanging down loose from the pointed white cap all the little girls were wearing that year. She stopped for a moment beside one of the prickly dark shrubs with which the city had beautified the Home, and then proceeded slowly toward the building, which was of whitewashed brick and reflected the winter sunlight like a block of ice. As she walked vaguely up the steps she shifted the small pot from hand to hand; then she had to set it down and remove her mittens before she could open the heavy door.

An Exercise in Place

Here is a series of passages about war, set in different periods and places. The first is in Russia during the campaign of Napoleon, the second on the island of Pianosa during World War II, and the third in a post-Holocaust future.

> Several tens of thousands of the slain lay in diverse postures and various uniforms. Over the whole field, previously so gaily beautiful with the glitter of bayonets and cloudlets of smoke in the morning sun, there now spread a mist of damp and smoke and a strange acid smell of saltpeter and blood. Clouds gathered and drops of rain began to fall on the dead and wounded, on the frightened, exhausted, and hesitating men, as if to say: Enough, men! Enough! Cease! Bethink yourselves! What are you doing?
>
> Leo Tolstoy, *War and Peace*

> Their only hope was that it would never stop raining, and they had no hope because they all knew it would. When it did stop raining in Pianosa, it rained in Bologna. When it stopped raining in Bologna, it began again in Pianosa. If there was no rain at all, there were freakish, inexplicable phenomena like the epidemic of diarrhea or the bomb line that moved. Four times during the first six days they were assembled and briefed and then sent back. Once, they took off and were flying in formation when the control tower summoned them down. The more it rained, the worse they suffered. The worse they suffered, the more they prayed that it would continue raining.
>
> Joseph Heller, *Catch-22*

> She liked the wild, quatrosyllabic lilt of the word, Barbarian. Then, looking beyond the wooden fence, she saw a trace of movement in the fields beyond. It was not the wind among the young corn; or, if it was wind among the young corn, it carried her the whinny of a raucous horse. It was too early for poppies but she saw a flare of scarlet. She ceased to watch the Soldiers; instead she watched the movement flow to the fences and crash through them and across the tender wheat. Bursting from the undergrowth came horseman after horseman. They flashed with curious curved plates of metal dredged up from the ruins. Their horses were bizarrely caparisoned with rags, small knives, bells and chains dangling from manes and tails, and man and horse together, unholy centaurs crudely daubed with paint, looked twice as large as life. They fired long guns. Confronted with the terrors of the night in the freshest hours of the morning, the gentle crowd scattered, wailing.
>
> Angela Carter, *Heroes and Villains*

Compare the settings. How do climate, period, imagery, and language contribute to each? To what degree is place a sentient force? Is there conflict between character and setting? How does setting affect and/or reveal the attitude taken toward the war? What mood, what emotions are implied?

St. Lucy's Home for Girls Raised by Wolves

KAREN RUSSELL

Stage 1: The initial period is one in which everything is new, exciting, and interesting for your students. It is fun for your students to explore their new environment.

—from *The Jesuit Handbook on Lycanthropic Culture Shock*

At first, our pack was all hair and snarl and floor-thumping joy. We forgot the barked cautions of our mothers and fathers, all the promises we'd made to be civilized and ladylike, couth and kempt. We tore through the austere rooms, overturning dresser drawers, pawing through the neat piles of the Stage 3 girls' starched underwear, smashing lightbulbs with our bare fists. Things felt less foreign in the dark. The dim bedroom was windowless and odorless. We remedied this by spraying exuberant yellow streams all over the bunks. We jumped from bunk to bunk, spraying. We nosed each other midair, our bodies buckling in kinetic laughter. The nuns watched us from the corner of the bedroom, their tiny faces pinched with displeasure.

"*Ay caramba,*" Sister Maria de la Guardia sighed. "*Que barbaridad!*" She made the Sign of the Cross. Sister Maria came to St. Lucy's from a halfway home in Copacabana. In Copacabana, the girls are fat and languid and eat pink slivers of guava right out of your hand. Even at Stage 1, their pelts are silky, sun-bleached to near invisibility. Our pack was hirsute and sinewy and mostly brunette. We had terrible posture. We went knuckling along the wooden floor on the calloused pads of our fists, baring row after row of tiny, wood-rotted teeth. Sister Josephine sucked in her breath. She removed a yellow wheel of floss from under her robes, looping it like a miniature lasso.

"The girls at our facility are *backwoods,*" Sister Josephine whispered to Sister Maria de la Guardia with a beatific smile. "You must be patient with them." I clamped down on her ankle, straining to close my jaws around the woolly XXL sock. Sister Josephine tasted like sweat and freckles. She smelled easy to kill.

We'd arrived at St. Lucy's that morning, part of a pack fifteen-strong. We were accompanied by a mousy, nervous-smelling social worker; the baby-faced deacon; Bartholomew, the blue wolfhound; and four burly woodsmen. The deacon handed out some stale cupcakes and said a quick prayer. Then he led us through the woods. We ran past the wild apiary, past the felled oaks, until we could see the white steeple of St. Lucy's rising out of the forest. We stopped short at the edge of a muddy lake. Then the deacon took our brothers. Bartholomew helped him to herd the boys up the ramp of a small ferry. We girls ran along the shore, tearing at our new jumpers in a plaid agitation. Our brothers stood on the deck, looking small and confused.

Our mothers and fathers were werewolves. They lived an outsider's existence in caves at the edge of the forest, threatened by frost and pitchforks. They had been ostracized by the local farmers for eating their silled fruit pies and terrorizing the heifers. They had ostracized the local wolves by having sometimes-thumbs, and regrets, and human children. (Their condition skips a generation.) Our pack grew up in a green purgatory. We couldn't keep up with the purebred wolves, but we never stopped crawling. We spoke a slab-tongued pidgin in the cave, inflected with frequent howls. Our parents wanted something better for us; they wanted us to get braces, use towels, be fully bilingual. When the nuns showed up, our parents couldn't refuse their offer. The nuns, they said, would make us naturalized citizens of human society. We would go to St. Lucy's to study a better culture. We didn't know at the time that our parents were sending us away for good. Neither did they.

That first afternoon, the nuns gave us free rein of the grounds. Everything was new, exciting, and interesting. A low granite wall surrounded St. Lucy's, the blue woods humming for miles behind it. There was a stone fountain full of delectable birds. There was a statue of St. Lucy. Her marble skin was colder than our mother's nose, her pupilless eyes rolled heavenward. Doomed squirrels gamboled around her stony toes. Our diminished pack threw back our heads in a celebratory howl—an exultant and terrible noise, even without a chorus of wolf brothers in the background. There were holes everywhere!

We supplemented these holes by digging some of our own. We interred sticks, and our itchy new jumpers, and the bones of the friendly, unfortunate squirrels. Our noses ached beneath an invisible assault. Everything was smudged with a human odor: baking bread, petrol, the nuns' faint woman-smell sweating out beneath a dark perfume of tallow and incense. We smelled one another, too, with the same astounded fascination. Our own scent had become foreign in this strange place.

We had just sprawled out in the sun for an afternoon nap, yawning into the warm dirt, when the nuns reappeared. They conferred in the shadow of the juniper tree, whispering and pointing. Then they started towards us. The oldest sister had spent the past hour twitching in her sleep, dreaming of fatty and infirm elk. (The pack used to dream the same dreams back then, as naturally as we drank the same water and slept on the same red scree.) When our oldest sister saw the nuns approaching, she instinctively bristled. It was an improvised bristle, given her new, human limitations. She took clumps of her scraggly, nut-brown hair and held it straight out from her head.

Sister Maria gave her a brave smile.

"And what is your name?" she asked.

The oldest sister howled something awful and inarticulable, a distil-late of hurt and panic, half-forgotten hunts and eclipsed moons. Sister Maria nodded and scribbled on a yellow legal pad. She slapped on a name tag: HELLO, MY NAME IS _____! "Jeanette it is."

The rest of the pack ran in a loose, uncertain circle, torn between our instinct to help her and our new fear. We sensed some subtler danger afoot, written in a language we didn't understand.

Our littlest sister had the quickest reflexes. She used her hands to flatten her ears to the side of her head. She backed towards the far cor-ner of the garden, snarling in the most menacing register that an eight-year-old wolf-girl can muster. Then she ran. It took them two hours to pin her down and tag her: HELLO, MY NAME IS MIRABELLA!

"Stage 1," Sister Maria sighed, taking careful aim with her tranquil-izer dart. "It can be a little overstimulating."

Stage 2: After a time, your students realize that they must work to adjust to the new culture. This work may be stressful and students may experience a strong sense of dislocation. They may miss certain foods. They may spend a lot of time daydreaming during this period. Many students feel isolated, irritated, bewildered, depressed, or generally uncomfortable.

Those were the days when we dreamed of rivers and meat. The full-moon nights were the worst! Worse than cold toilet seats and boiled tomatoes, worse than trying to will our tongues to curl around our false new names. We would snarl at one another for no reason. I remember how disorienting it was to look down and see two square-toed shoes instead of my own four feet. Keep your mouth shut, I repeated during our walking drills, staring straight ahead. Keep your shoes on your feet. Mouth shut, shoes on feet. Do not chew on your new penny loafers. Do not. I stumbled around in a daze, my mouth black with shoe pol-ish. The whole pack was irritated, bewildered, depressed. We were all uncomfortable, and between languages. We had never wanted to run away so badly in our lives; but who did we have to run back to? Only the curled black grimace of the mother. Only the father, holding his tawny head between his paws. Could we betray our parents by going back to them? After they'd given us the choicest part of the woodchuck, loved us at our hairless worst, nosed us across the ice floes and abandoned us at St. Lucy's for our own betterment?

Physically, we were all easily capable of clearing the low stone walls. Sister Josephine left the wooden gates wide open. They unslatted the windows at night so that long fingers of moonlight beckoned us from the woods. But we knew we couldn't return to the woods; not till we were civilized, not if we didn't want to break the mother's heart. It all felt like a sly, human taunt.

It was impossible to make the blank, chilly bedroom feel like home. In the beginning, we drank gallons of bathwater as part of a collaborative effort to mark our territory. We puddled up the yellow carpet of old newspapers. But later, when we returned to the bedroom, we were dismayed to find all trace of the pack musk had vanished. Someone was coming in and erasing us. We sprayed and sprayed every morning; and every night, we returned to the same ammonia eradication. We couldn't make our scent stick here; it made us feel invisible. Eventually we gave up. Still, the pack seemed to be adjusting on the same timetable. The advanced girls could already alternate between two speeds: "slouch" and "amble." Almost everybody was fully bipedal.

Almost.

The pack was worried about Mirabella.

Mirabella would rip foamy chunks out of the church pews and replace them with ham bones and girl dander. She loved to roam the grounds wagging her invisible tail. (We all had a hard time giving that up. When we got excited, we would fall to the ground and start pumping our backsides. Back in those days we could pump at rabbity velocities. *Que horror!* Sister Maria frowned, looking more than a little jealous.) We'd give her scolding pinches. "Mirabella," we hissed, imitating the nuns. "No." Mirabella cocked her ears at us, hurt and confused.

Still, some things remained the same. The main commandment of wolf life is Know Your Place, and that translated perfectly. Being around other humans had awakened a slavish-dog affection in us. An abasing, belly-to-the-ground desire to please. As soon as we realized that someone higher up in the food chain was watching us, we wanted only to be pleasing in their sight. Mouth shut, I repeated, shoes on feet. But if Mirabella had this latent instinct, the nuns couldn't figure out how to activate it. She'd go bounding around, gleefully spraying on their gilded statue of St. Lucy, madscratching at the virulent fleas that survived all of their powders and baths. At Sister Maria's tearful insistence, she'd stand upright for roll call, her knobby, oddly muscled legs quivering from the effort. Then she'd collapse right back to the ground with an ecstatic *oomph!* She was still loping around on all fours (which the nuns had taught us to see looked unnatural and ridiculous—we could barely believe it now, the shame of it, that we used to locomote like that!), her fists blue-white from the strain. As if she were holding a secret tight to the ground. Sister Maria de la Guardia would sigh every time she saw her. *"Caramba!"* She'd sit down with Mirabella and pry her fingers apart. "You see?" she'd say softly, again and again. "What are you holding on to? Nothing, little one. Nothing."

Then she would sing out the standard chorus, "Why can't you be more like your sister Jeanette?"

The pack hated Jeanette. She was the most successful of us, the one furthest removed from her origins. Her real name was GWARR!, but she wouldn't respond to this anymore. Jeanette spiffed her penny loafers until her very shoes seemed to gloat. (Linguists have since traced the colloquial origins of "goody two-shoes" back to our facilities.) She could even growl out a demonic-sounding precursor to "Pleased to meet you." She'd delicately extend her former paws to visitors, wearing white kid gloves.

"Our little wolf, disguised in sheep's clothing!" Sister Ignatius liked to joke with the visiting deacons, and Jeanette would surprise everyone by laughing along with them, a harsh, inhuman, barking sound. Her hearing was still twig-snap sharp. Jeanette was the first among us to apologize; to drink apple juice out of a sippy cup; to quit eyeballing the cleric's jugular in a disconcerting fashion. She curled her lips back into a cousin of a smile as the traveling barber cut her pelt into bangs. Then she swept her coarse black curls under the rug. When we entered a room, our nostrils flared beneath the new odors: onion and bleach, candle wax, the turnipy smell of unwashed bodies. Not Jeanette. Jeanette smiled and pretended like she couldn't smell a thing.

I was one of the good girls. Not great and not terrible, solidly middle of the pack. But I had an ear for languages, and I could read before I could adequately wash myself. I probably could have vied with Jeanette for the number one spot, but I'd seen what happened if you gave in to your natural aptitudes. This wasn't like the woods, where you had to be your fastest and your strongest and your bravest self. Different sorts of calculations were required to survive at the home.

The pack hated Jeanette, but we hated Mirabella more. We began to avoid her, but sometimes she'd surprise us, curled up beneath the beds or gnawing on a scapula in the garden. It was scary to be ambushed by your sister. I'd bristle and growl, the way that I'd begun to snarl at my own reflection as if it were a stranger.

"Whatever will become of Mirabella?" we asked, gulping back our own fear. We'd heard rumors about former wolf-girls who never adapted to their new culture. It was assumed that they were returned to our native country, the vanishing woods. We liked to speculate about this before bedtime, scaring ourselves with stories of catastrophic bliss. It was the disgrace, the failure that we all guiltily hoped for in our hard beds. Twitching with the shadow question: *Whatever will become of me?*

We spent a lot of time daydreaming during this period. Even Jeanette. Sometimes I'd see her looking out at the woods in a vacant way. If you interrupted her in the midst of one of these reveries, she would lunge at you with an elder-sister ferocity, momentarily forgetting her human catechism. We liked her better then, startled back into being foamy old Jeanette.

In school, they showed us the St. Francis of Assisi slide show, again and again. Then the nuns would give us bags of bread. They never announced these things as a test; it was only much later that I realized that we were under constant examination. "Go feed the ducks," they urged us. "Go practice compassion for all God's creatures." *Don't pair me with Mirabella*, I prayed, *anybody but Mirabella.* "Claudette"—Sister Josephine beamed—"why don't you and Mirabella take some pumpernickel down to the ducks?"

"Ohhkaaythankyou," I said. (It took me a long time to say anything; first I had to translate it in my head from the Wolf.) It wasn't fair. They knew Mirabella couldn't make bread balls yet. She couldn't even undo the twist tie of the bag. She was sure to eat the birds; Mirabella didn't even try to curb her desire to kill things—and then who would get blamed for the dark spots of duck blood on our Peter Pan collars? Who would get penalized with negative Skill Points? Exactly.

As soon as we were beyond the wooden gates, I snatched the bread away from Mirabella and ran off to the duck pond on my own. Mirabella gave chase, nipping at my heels. She thought it was a game. "Stop it," I growled. I ran faster, but it was Stage 2 and I was still unsteady on my two feet. I fell sideways into a leaf pile, and then all I could see was my sister's blurry form, bounding towards me. In a moment, she was on top of me, barking the old word for tug-of-war. When she tried to steal the bread out of my hands, I whirled around and snarled at her, pushing my ears back from my head. I bit her shoulder, once, twice, the only language she would respond to. I used my new motor skills. I threw dirt, I threw stones. "Get away!" I screamed, long after she had made a cringing retreat into the shadows of the purple saplings. "Get away, get away!"

Much later, they found Mirabella wading in the shallows of a distant river, trying to strangle a mallard with her rosary beads. I was at the lake; I'd been sitting there for hours. Hunched in the long cattails, my yellow eyes flashing, shoving ragged hunks of bread into my mouth.

I don't know what they did to Mirabella. Me they separated from my sisters. They made me watch another slide show. This one showed images of former wolf-girls, the ones who had failed to be rehabilitated. Long-haired, sad-eyed women, limping after their former wolf packs in white tennis shoes and pleated culottes. A wolf-girl bank teller, her makeup smeared in oily rainbows, eating a raw steak on the deposit slips while her colleagues looked on in disgust. Our parents. The final slide was a bolded sentence in St. Lucy's prim script: DO YOU WANT TO END UP SHUNNED BY BOTH SPECIES?

After that, I spent less time with Mirabella. One night she came to me, holding her hand out. She was covered with splinters, keening a high, whining noise through her nostrils. Of course I understood what she wanted; I wasn't that far removed from our language (even though I was reading at a fifth-grade level, halfway into Jack London's *The Son of the Wolf*).

"Lick your own wounds," I said, not unkindly. It was what the nuns had instructed us to say; wound licking was not something you did in polite company. Etiquette was so confounding in this country. Still, looking at Mirabella—her fists balled together like small, white porcupines, her brows knitted in animal confusion—I felt a throb of compassion. *How can people live like they do?* I wondered. Then I congratulated myself. This was a Stage 3 thought.

> Stage 3: It is common that students who start living in a new and different culture come to a point where they reject the host culture and withdraw into themselves. During this period, they make generalizations about the host culture and wonder how the people can live like they do. Your students may feel that their own culture's lifestyle and customs are far superior to those of the host country.

The nuns were worried about Mirabella, too. To correct a failing, you must first be aware of it as a failing. And there was Mirabella, shucking her plaid jumper in full view of the visiting cardinal. Mirabella, battling a raccoon under the dinner table while the rest of us took dainty bites of peas and borscht. Mirabella, doing belly flops into compost.

"You have to pull your weight around here," we overheard Sister Josephine saying one night. We paused below the vestry window and peered inside.

"Does Mirabella try to earn Skill Points by shelling walnuts and polishing Saint-in-the-Box? No. Does Mirabella even know how to say the word *walnut*? Has she learned how to say anything besides a sinful 'HraaaHA!' as she commits frottage against the organ pipes? No."

There was a long silence.

"Something must be done," Sister Ignatius said firmly. The other nuns nodded, a sea of thin, colorless lips and kettle-black brows. "Something must be done," they intoned. That ominously passive construction; a something so awful that nobody wanted to assume responsibility for it.

I could have warned her. If we were back home, and Mirabella had come under attack by territorial beavers or snow-blind bears, I would have warned her. But the truth is that by Stage 3 I wanted her gone. Mirabella's inability to adapt was taking a visible toll. Her teeth were ground down to nubbins; her hair was falling out. She hated the spongy, long-dead foods we were served, and it showed—her ribs were poking through her uniform. Her bright eyes had dulled to a sour whiskey color. But you couldn't show Mirabella the slightest kindness anymore—she'd never leave you alone! You'd have to sit across from her at meals, shoving her away as she begged for your scraps. I slept fitfully during that period, unable to forget that Mirabella was living under my bed, gnawing on my loafers.

It was during Stage 3 that we met our first purebred girls. These were girls raised in captivity, volunteers from St. Lucy's School for Girls. The apple-cheeked fourth-grade class came to tutor us in playing. They had long golden braids or short, severe bobs. They had frilly-duvet names like Felicity and Beulah; and pert, bunny noses; and terrified smiles. We grinned back at them with genuine ferocity. It made us nervous to meet new humans. There were so many things that we could do wrong! And the rules here were different depending on which humans we were with: dancing or no dancing, checkers playing or no checkers playing, pumping or no pumping.

The purebred girls played checkers with us.

"These girl-girls sure is dumb," my sister Lavash panted to me between games. "I win it again! Five to none."

She was right. The purebred girls were making mistakes on purpose, in order to give us an advantage. "King me," I growled, out of turn. "*I say king me!*" and Felicity meekly complied. Beulah pretended not to mind when we got frustrated with the oblique, fussy movement from square to square and shredded the board to ribbons. I felt sorry for them. I wondered what it would be like to be bred in captivity, and always homesick for a dimly sensed forest, the trees you've never seen.

Jeanette was learning how to dance. On Holy Thursday, she mastered a rudimentary form of the Charleston. "*Brava!*" The nuns clapped. "*Brava!*"

Every Friday, the girls who had learned how to ride a bicycle celebrated by going on chaperoned trips into town. The purebred girls sold seven hundred rolls of gift-wrap paper and used the proceeds to buy us a yellow fleet of bicycles built for two. We'd ride the bicycles uphill, a sanctioned pumping, a grim-faced nun pedaling behind each one of us. "Congratulations!" the nuns would huff. "Being human is like riding this bicycle. Once you've learned how, you'll never forget." Mirabella would run after the bicycles, growling out our old names. HWRAA! GWARR! TRRRRRRR! We pedaled faster.

At this point, we'd had six weeks of lessons, and still nobody could do the Sausalito but Jeanette. The nuns decided we needed an inducement to dance. They announced that we would celebrate our successful rehabilitations with a Debutante Ball. There would be brothers, ferried over from the Home for Man-Boys Raised by Wolves. There would be a photographer from the *Gazette Sophisticate*. There would be a three-piece jazz band from West Toowoomba, and root beer in tiny plastic cups. The brothers! We'd almost forgotten about them. Our invisible tails went limp. I should have been excited; instead, I felt a low mad anger at the nuns. They knew we weren't ready to dance with the brothers; we weren't even ready to talk to them. Things had been so much simpler in the woods. That night I waited until my sisters were asleep. Then I slunk into the closet and practiced the Sausalito two-step in secret, a private mass of twitch and foam. Mouth shut—shoes on feet! Mouth shut—shoes on feet! Mouthshutmouthshut...

One night I came back early from the closet and stumbled on Jeanette. She was sitting in a patch of moonlight on the windowsill, reading from one of her library books. (She was the first of us to sign for her library card, too.) Her cheeks looked dewy.

"Why you cry?" I asked her, instinctively reaching over to lick Jeanette's cheek and catching myself in the nick of time.

Jeanette blew her nose into a nearby curtain. (Even her mistakes annoyed us—they were always so well intentioned.) She sniffled and pointed to a line in her book: "The lake-water was reinventing the forest and the white moon above it, and wolves lapped up the cold reflection of the sky." But none of the pack besides me could read yet, and I wasn't ready to claim a common language with Jeanette.

The following day, Jeanette golfed. The nuns set up a miniature putt-putt course in the garden. Sister Maria dug four sandtraps and got old Walter, the groundskeeper, to make a windmill out of a lawn mower engine. The eighteenth hole was what they called a "doozy," a minuscule crack in St. Lucy's marble dress. Jeanette got a hole in one.

On Sundays, the pretending felt almost as natural as nature. The chapel was our favorite place. Long before we could understand what the priest was saying, the music instructed us in how to feel. The choir director—aggressively perfumed Mrs. Valuchi, gold necklaces like pineapple rings around her neck—taught us more than the nuns ever did. She showed us how to pattern the old hunger into arias. Clouds moved behind the frosted oculus of the nave, glass shadows that reminded me of my mother. The mother, I'd think, struggling to conjure up a picture. A black shadow, running behind the watery screen of pines.

We sang at the chapel annexed to the home every morning. We understood that this was the humans' moon, the place for howling beyond purpose. Not for mating, not for hunting, not for fighting, not for

anything but the sound itself. And we'd howl along with the choir, hurl-
ing every pitted thing within us at the stained glass. "Sotto voce." The
nuns would frown. But you could tell that they were pleased.

Stage 4: As a more thorough understanding of the host culture is
acquired, your students will begin to feel more comfortable in their
new environment. Your students feel more at home, and their self-
confidence grows. Everything begins to make sense.

"Hey, Claudette," Jeanette growled to me on the day before the ball.
"Have you noticed that everything's beginning to make sense?"

Before I could answer, Mirabella sprang out of the hall closet and
snapped through Jeanette's homework binder. Pages and pages of
words swirled around the stone corridor, like dead leaves off trees.

"What about you, Mirabella?" Jeanette asked politely, stooping to
pick up her erasers. She was the only one of us who would still talk
to Mirabella; she was high enough in the rankings that she could afford
to talk to the scruggliest wolf-girl. "Has everything begun to make more
sense, Mirabella?"

Mirabella let out a whimper. She scratched at us and scratched at us,
raking her nails along our shins so hard that she drew blood. Then she
rolled belly-up on the cold stone floor, squirming on a bed of spelling-bee
worksheets. Above us, small pearls of light dotted the high, tinted window.

Jeanette frowned. "You are a late bloomer, Mirabella! Usually,
everything's begun to make more sense by Month Twelve at the latest."
I noticed that she stumbled on the word *bloomer*. HraaaHA! Jeanette
could never fully shake our accent. She'd talk like that her whole life,
I thought with a gloomy satisfaction, each word winced out like an apology for itself.

"Claudette, help me," she yelped. Mirabella had closed her jaws
around Jeanette's bald ankle and was dragging her towards the closet.
"Please. Help me to mop up Mirabella's mess."

I ignored her and continued down the hall. I had only four more
hours to perfect the Sausalito. I was worried only about myself. By that
stage, I was no longer certain of how the pack felt about anything.

At seven o'clock on the dot, Sister Ignatius blew her whistle and frog-
marched us into the ball. The nuns had transformed the rectory into a
very scary place. Purple and silver balloons started popping all around
us. Black streamers swooped down from the eaves and got stuck in
our hair like bats. A full yellow moon smirked outside the window. We
were greeted by blasts of a saxophone, and fizzy pink drinks, and the
brothers.

The brothers didn't smell like our brothers anymore. They smelled like
pomade and cold, sterile sweat. They looked like little boys. Someone had

washed behind their ears and made them wear suspendered dungarees. Kyle used to be a blustery alpha male, BTWWWR!, chewing through rattlesnakes, spooking badgers, snatching a live trout out of a grizzly's mouth. He stood by the punch bowl, looking pained and out of place.

"My stars!" I growled. "What lovely weather we've been having!"

"Yeees," Kyle growled back. "It is beginning to look a lot like Christmas." All around the room, boys and girls raised by wolves were having the same conversation. Actually, it had been an unseasonably warm and brown winter, and just that morning a freak hailstorm had sent Sister Josephina to an early grave. But we had only gotten up to Unit 7: Party Dialogue; we hadn't yet learned the vocabulary for Unit 12: How to Tactfully Acknowledge Disaster. Instead, we wore pink party hats and sucked olives on little sticks, inured to our own strangeness.

The nuns swept our hair back into high, bouffant hairstyles. This made us look more girlish and less inclined to eat people, the way that squirrels are saved from looking like rodents by their poofy tails. I was wearing a white organdy dress with orange polka dots. Jeanette was wearing a mauve organdy dress with blue polka dots. Linette was wearing a red organdy dress with white polka dots. Mirabella was in a dark corner, wearing a muzzle. Her party culottes were duct-taped to her knees. The nuns had tied little bows on the muzzle to make it more festive. Even so, the jazz band from West Toowoomba kept glancing nervously her way.

"You smell astoooounding!" Kyle was saying, accidentally stretching the diphthong into a howl and then blushing. "I mean—"

"Yes, I know what it is that you mean," I snapped. (That's probably a little narrative embellishment on my part; it must have been months before I could really "snap" out words.) I didn't smell astounding. I had rubbed a pumpkin muffin all over my body earlier that morning to mask my natural, feral scent. Now I smelled like a purebred girl, easy to kill. I narrowed my eyes at Kyle and flattened my ears, something I hadn't done for months. Kyle looked panicked, trying to remember the words that would make me act like a girl again. I felt hot, oily tears squeezing out of the red corners of my eyes. *Shoesonfeet!* I barked at myself. I tried again. "My! What lovely weather—"

The jazz band struck up a tune.

"The time has come to do the Sausalito," Sister Maria announced, beaming into the microphone. "Every sister grab a brother!" She switched on Walter's industrial flashlight, struggling beneath its weight, and aimed the beam in the center of the room.

Uh-oh. I tried to skulk off into Mirabella's corner, but Kyle pushed me into the spotlight. "No," I moaned through my teeth, "nooooooo." All of a sudden the only thing my body could remember how to do was pump and pump. In a flash of white-hot light, my months at St. Lucy's had vanished, and I was just a terrified animal again. As if of their own accord, my feet started to wiggle out of my shoes. *Mouth shut*, I gasped, staring down at my naked toes, *mouthshutmouthshut*.

"Ahem. The time has come," Sister Maria coughed, "to do the Sausalito." She paused. "The Sausalito," she added helpfully, "does not in any way resemble the thing that you are doing."

Beads of sweat stood out on my forehead. I could feel my jaws gaping open, my tongue lolling out of the left side of my mouth. What were the steps? I looked frantically for Jeanette; she would help me, she would tell me what to do.

Jeanette was sitting in the corner, sipping punch through a long straw and watching me pant. I locked eyes with her, pleading with the mute intensity that I had used to beg her for weasel bones in the forest. "What are the steps?" I mouthed.

"The steps!"

"The steps?" Then Jeanette gave me a wide, true wolf smile. For an instant, she looked just like our mother. "Not for you," she mouthed back.

I threw my head back, a howl clawing its way up my throat. I was about to lose all my Skill Points, I was about to fail my Adaptive Dancing test. But before the air could burst from my lungs, the wind got knocked out of me. *Oomph!* I fell to the ground, my skirt falling softly over my head. Mirabella had intercepted my eye-cry for help. She'd chewed through her restraints and tackled me from behind, barking at unseen cougars, trying to shield me with her tiny body. *"Caramba!"* Sister Maria squealed, dropping the flashlight. The music ground to a halt. And I have never loved someone so much, before or since, as I loved my littlest sister at that moment. I wanted to roll over and lick her ears, I wanted to kill a dozen spotted fawns and let her eat first.

But everybody was watching; everybody was waiting to see what I would do. "I wasn't talking to you," I grunted from underneath her. "I didn't want your help. Now you have ruined the Sausalito! You have ruined the ball!" I said more loudly, hoping the nuns would hear how much my enunciation had improved.

"You have ruined it!" my sisters panted, circling around us, eager to close ranks. "Mirabella has ruined it!" Every girl was wild-eyed and itching under her polka dots, punch froth dribbling down her chin. The pack had been waiting for this moment for some time. "Mirabella cannot adapt! Back to the woods, back to the woods!"

The band from West Toowoomba had quietly packed their instruments into black suitcases and were sneaking out the back. The boys had fled back towards the lake, bow ties spinning, snapping suspenders in their haste. Mirabella was still snarling in the center of it all, trying to figure out where the danger was so that she could defend me against it. The nuns exchanged glances.

In the morning, Mirabella was gone. We checked under all the beds. I pretended to be surprised. I'd known she would have to be expelled the minute I felt her weight on my back. Walter came and told me this in secret after the ball, "So you can say yer good-byes." I didn't want to face Mirabella. Instead, I packed a tin lunch pail for her: two jelly sandwiches on saltine crackers, a chloroformed squirrel, a gilt-edged placard of St. Bolio. I left it for her with Sister Ignatius, with a little note: "Best wishes!" I told myself I'd done everything I could.

"Hooray!" the pack crowed. "Something has been done!"

We raced outside into the bright sunlight, knowing full well that our sister had been turned loose, that we'd never find her. A low roar rippled through us and surged up and up, disappearing into the trees. I listened for an answering howl from Mirabella, heart thumping—what if she heard us and came back? But there was nothing.

We graduated from St. Lucy's shortly thereafter. As far as I can recollect, that was our last communal howl.

Stage 5: At this point your students are able to interact effectively in the new cultural environment. They find it easy to move between the two cultures.

One Sunday, near the end of my time at St. Lucy's, the sisters gave me a special pass to go visit the parents. The woodsman had to accompany me; I couldn't remember how to find the way back on my own. I wore my best dress and brought along some prosciutto and dill pickles in a picnic basket. We crunched through the fall leaves in silence, and every step made me sadder. "I'll wait out here," the woodsman said, leaning on a blue elm and lighting a cigarette.

The cave looked so much smaller than I remembered it. I had to duck my head to enter. Everybody was eating when I walked in. They all looked up from the bull moose at the same time, my aunts and uncles, my sloe-eyed, lolling cousins, the parents. My uncle dropped a thighbone from his mouth. My littlest brother, a cross-eyed wolf-boy who has since been successfully rehabilitated and is now a dour, balding children's book author, started whining in terror. My mother recoiled from me, as if I was a stranger. TRRR? She sniffed me for a long moment. Then she sank her teeth into my ankle, looking proud and sad. After all the tail wagging and perfunctory barking had died down, the parents sat back on their hind legs. They stared up at me expectantly, panting in the cool gray envelope of the cave, waiting for a display of what I had learned.

"So," I said, telling my first human lie. "I'm home."

The Flowers

ALICE WALKER

It seemed to Myop as she skipped lightly from hen house to pigpen to smokehouse that the days had never been as beautiful as these. The air held a keenness that made her nose twitch. The harvesting of the corn and cotton, peanuts and squash, made each day a golden surprise that caused excited little tremors to run up her jaws.

Myop carried a short, knobby stick. She struck out at random at chickens she liked, and worked out the beat of a song on the fence around the pigpen. She felt light and good in the warm sun. She was ten, and nothing existed for her but her song, the stick clutched in her dark brown hand, and the tat-de-ta-ta-ta of accompaniment.

Turning her back on the rusty boards of her family's sharecropper cabin, Myop walked along the fence till it ran into the stream made by the spring. Around the spring, where the family got drinking water, silver ferns and wildflowers grew. Along the shallow banks pigs rooted. Myop watched the tiny white bubbles disrupt the thin black scale of soil and the water that silently rose and slid away down the stream.

She had explored the woods behind the house many times. Often, in late autumn, her mother took her to gather nuts among the fallen leaves. Today she made her own path, bouncing this way and that way, vaguely keeping an eye out for snakes. She found, in addition to various common but pretty ferns and leaves, an armful of strange blue flowers with velvety ridges and a sweet suds bush full of the brown, fragrant buds.

By twelve o'clock, her arms laden with sprigs of her findings, she was a mile or more from home. She had often been as far before, but the strangeness of the land made it not as pleasant as her usual haunts. It seemed gloomy in the little cove in which she found herself. The air was damp, the silence close and deep.

Myop began to circle back to the house, back to the peacefulness of the morning. It was then she stepped smack into his eyes. Her heel became lodged in the broken ridge between brow and nose, and she reached down quickly, unafraid, to free herself. It was only when she saw his naked grin that she gave a little yelp of surprise.

He had been a tall man. From feet to neck covered a long space. His head lay beside him. When she pushed back the leaves and layers of earth and debris Myop saw that he'd had large white teeth, all of them cracked or broken, long fingers, and very big bones. All his clothes had rotted away except some threads of blue denim from his overalls. The buckles of the overall had turned green.

Myop gazed around the spot with interest. Very near where she'd stepped into the head was a wild pink rose. As she picked it to add to her bundle she noticed a raised mound, a ring, around the rose's root. It was the rotted remains of a noose, a bit of shredding plowline, now blending benignly into the soil. Around an overhanging limb of a great spreading oak clung another piece. Frayed, rotted, bleached, and frazzled—barely there—but spinning restlessly in the breeze. Myop laid down her flowers.

And the summer was over.

A Visit of Charity

EUDORA WELTY

It was mid-morning—a very cold, bright day. Holding a potted plant before her, a girl of fourteen jumped off the bus in front of the Old Ladies' Home, on the outskirts of town. She wore a red coat, and her straight yellow hair was hanging down loose from the pointed white cap all the little girls were wearing that year. She stopped for a moment beside one of the prickly dark shrubs with which the city had beautified the Home, and then proceeded slowly toward the building, which was of whitewashed brick and reflected the winter sunlight like a block of ice. As she walked vaguely up the steps she shifted the small pot from hand to hand; then she had to set it down and remove her mittens before she could open the heavy door.

"I'm a Campfire Girl...I have to pay a visit to some old lady," she told the nurse at the desk. This was a woman in a white uniform who looked as if she were cold; she had close-cut hair which stood up on the very top of her head exactly like a sea wave. Marian, the little girl, did not tell her that this visit would give her a minimum of only three points in her score.

"Acquainted with any of our residents?" asked the nurse. She lifted one eyebrow and spoke like a man.

"With any old ladies? No—but—that is, any of them will do," Marian stammered. With her free hand she pushed her hair behind her ears, as she did when it was time to study Science.

The nurse shrugged and rose. "You have a nice *multiflora cineraria* there," she remarked as she walked ahead down the hall of closed doors to pick out an old lady.

There was loose, bulging linoleum on the floor. Marian felt as if she were walking on the waves, but the nurse paid no attention to it. There was a smell in the hall like the interior of a clock. Everything was silent until, behind one of the doors, an old lady of some kind cleared her throat like a sheep bleating. This decided the nurse. Stopping in her tracks, she first extended her arm, bent her elbow, and leaned forward from the hips—all to examine the watch strapped to her wrist; then she gave a loud double-rap on the door.

"There are two in each room," the nurse remarked over her shoulder.

"Two what?" asked Marian without thinking. The sound like a sheep's bleating almost made her turn around and run back.

One old woman was pulling the door open in short, gradual jerks, and when she saw the nurse a strange smile forced her old face dangerously awry. Marian, suddenly propelled by the strong, impatient arm of the nurse, saw next the side-face of another old woman, even older, who was lying flat in bed with a cap on and a counterpane drawn up to her chin.

"Visitor," said the nurse, and after one more shove she was off up the hall.

Marian stood tongue-tied; both hands held the potted plant. The old woman, still with that terrible, square smile (which was a smile of welcome) stamped on her bony face, was waiting....Perhaps she said something. The old woman in bed said nothing at all, and she did not look around.

Suddenly Marian saw a hand, quick as a bird claw, reach up in the air and pluck the white cap off her head. At the same time, another claw to match drew her all the way into the room, and the next moment the door closed behind her.

"My, my, my," said the old lady at her side.

Marian stood enclosed by a bed, a washstand and a chair; the tiny room had altogether too much furniture. Everything smelled wet—even the bare floor. She held on to the back of the chair, which was wicker and felt soft and damp. Her heart beat more and more slowly, her hands got colder and colder, and she could not hear whether the old women were saying anything or not. She could not see them very clearly. How dark it was! The window shade was down, and the only door was shut. Marian looked at the ceiling....It was like being caught in a robbers' cave, just before one was murdered.

"Did you come to be our little girl for a while?" the first robber asked.

Then something was snatched from Marian's hand—the little potted plant.

"Flowers!" screamed the old woman. She stood holding the pot in an undecided way. "Pretty flowers," she added.

Then the old woman in bed cleared her throat and spoke. "They are not pretty," she said, still without looking around, but very distinctly.

Marian suddenly pitched against the chair and sat down in it.

"Pretty flowers," the first old woman insisted. "Pretty—pretty…"

Marian wished she had the little pot back for just a moment—she had forgotten to look at the plant herself before giving it away. What did it look like?

"Stinkweeds," said the other old woman sharply. She had a bunchy white forehead and red eyes like a sheep. Now she turned them toward Marian. The fogginess seemed to rise in her throat again, and she bleated, "Who—are—you?"

To her surprise, Marian could not remember her name. "I'm a Campfire Girl," she said finally.

"Watch out for the germs," said the old woman like a sheep, not addressing anyone.

"One came out last month to see us," said the first old woman.

A sheep or a germ? wondered Marian dreamily, holding on to the chair.

"Did not!" cried the other old woman.

"Did so! Read to us out of the Bible, and we enjoyed it!" screamed the first.

"Who enjoyed it!" said the woman in bed. Her mouth was unexpectedly small and sorrowful, like a pet's.

"We enjoyed it," insisted the other. "You enjoyed it—I enjoyed it."

"We all enjoyed it," said Marian, without realizing that she had said a word.

The first old woman had just finished putting the potted plant high, high on the top of the wardrobe, where it could hardly be seen from below. Marian wondered how she had ever succeeded in placing it there, how she could ever have reached so high.

"You mustn't pay any attention to old Addie," she now said to the little girl. "She's ailing today."

"Will you shut your mouth?" said the woman in bed. "I am not."

"You're a story."

"I can't stay but a minute—really, I can't," said Marian suddenly. She looked down at the wet floor and thought that if she were sick in here they would have to let her go.

With much to-do the first old woman sat down in a rocking chair—still another piece of furniture!—and began to rock. With the fingers of one hand she touched a very dirty cameo pin on her chest. "What do you do at school?" she asked.

"I don't know…" said Marian. She tried to think but she could not.

"Oh, but the flowers are beautiful," the old woman whispered. She seemed to rock faster and faster; Marian did not see how anyone could rock so fast.

"Ugly," said the woman in bed.

"If we bring flowers—" Marian began, and then fell silent. She had almost said that if Campfire Girls brought flowers to the Old Ladies' Home, the visit would count one extra point, and if they took a Bible with them on the bus and read it to the old ladies, it counted double. But the old woman had not listened, anyway; she was rocking and watching the other one, who watched back from the bed.

"Poor Addie is ailing. She has to take medicine—see?" she said, pointing a horny finger at a row of bottles on the table, and rocking so high that her black comfort shoes lifted off the floor like a little child's.

"I am no more sick than you are," said the woman in bed.

"Oh, yes you are!"

"I just got more sense than you have, that's all," said the other old woman, nodding her head.

"That's only the contrary way she talks when *you all* come," said the first old lady with sudden intimacy. She stopped the rocker with a neat pat of her feet and leaned toward Marian. Her hand reached over—it felt like a petunia leaf, clinging and just a little sticky.

"Will you hush! Will you hush!" cried the other one.

Marian leaned back rigidly in her chair.

"When I was a little girl like you, I went to school and all," said the old woman in the same intimate, menacing voice. "Not here—another town…"

"Hush!" said the sick woman. "You never went to school. You never came and you never went. You never were anything—only here. You never were born! You don't know anything. Your head is empty, your heart and hands and your old black purse are all empty, even that little old box that you brought with you you brought empty—you showed it to me. And yet you talk, talk, talk, talk, talk all the time until I think I'm losing my mind! Who are you? You're a stranger—a perfect stranger! Don't you know you're a stranger? Is it possible that they have actually done a thing like this to anyone—sent them in a stranger to talk, and rock, and tell away her whole long rigmarole? Do they seriously suppose that I'll be able to keep it up, day in, day out, night in, night out, living in the same room with a terrible old woman—forever?"

Marian saw the old woman's eyes grow bright and turn toward her. This old woman was looking at her with despair and calculation in her face. Her small lips suddenly dropped apart, and exposed a half circle of false teeth with tan gums.

"Come here, I want to tell you something," she whispered. "Come here!"

Marian was trembling, and her heart nearly stopped beating altogether for a moment.

"Now, now, Addie," said the first old woman. "That's not polite. Do you know what's really the matter with old Addie today?" She, too, looked at Marian; one of her eyelids dropped low.

"The matter?" the child repeated stupidly. "What's the matter with her?"

"Why, she's mad because it's her birthday!" said the first old woman, beginning to rock again and giving a little crow as though she had answered her own riddle.

"It is not, it is not!" screamed the old woman in bed. "It is not my birthday, no one knows when that is but myself, and will you please be quiet and say nothing more, or I'll go straight out of my mind!" She turned her eyes toward Marian again, and presently she said in the soft, foggy voice, "When the worst comes to the worst, I ring this bell, and the nurse comes." One of her hands was drawn out from under the patched counterpane—a thin little hand with enormous black freckles. With a finger which would not hold still she pointed to a little bell on the table among the bottles.

"How old are you?" Marian breathed. Now she could see the old woman in bed very closely and plainly, and very abruptly, from all sides, as in dreams. She wondered about her—she wondered for a moment as though there was nothing else in the world to wonder about. It was the first time such a thing had happened to Marian.

"I won't tell!"

The old face on the pillow, where Marian was bending over it, slowly gathered and collapsed. Soft whimpers came out of the small open mouth. It was a sheep that she sounded like—a little lamb. Marian's face drew very close, the yellow hair hung forward.

"She's crying!" She turned a bright, burning face up to the first old woman.

"That's Addie for you," the old woman said spitefully.

Marian jumped up and moved toward the door. For the second time, the claw almost touched her hair, but it was not quick enough. The little girl put her cap on.

"Well, it was a real visit," said the old woman, following Marian through the doorway and all the way out into the hall. Then from behind she suddenly clutched the child with her sharp little fingers. In an affected, high-pitched whine she cried, "Oh, little girl, have you a penny to spare for a poor old woman that's not got anything of her own? We don't have a thing in the world—not a penny for candy—not a thing! Little girl, just a nickel—a penny—".

Marian pulled violently against the old hands for a moment before she was free. Then she ran down the hall, without looking behind her and without looking at the nurse, who was reading *Field & Stream* at her desk. The nurse, after another triple motion to consult her wrist watch, asked automatically the question put to visitors in all institutions: "Won't you stay and have dinner with *us*?"

Marian never replied. She pushed the heavy door open into the cold air and ran down the steps.

Under the prickly shrub she stooped and quickly, without being seen, retrieved a red apple she had hidden there.

Her yellow hair under the white cap, her scarlet coat, her bare knees all flashed in the sunlight as she ran to meet the big bus rocketing through the street.

"Wait for me!" she shouted. As though at an imperial command, the bus ground to a stop.

She jumped on and took a big bite out of the apple.

◙ ◙ ◙

Writing Exercises

1. This exercise involves two steps. First, describe a public place from your own childhood that continues to evoke powerful, emotional memories. It could be a movie theater, shopping mall, ballpark, the parking lot at your high school, or even the town dump. Now set a scene in this location. Use dialogue, description, action, and the thoughts of at least one of your characters. The scene should involve at least two characters, both of whom are uncomfortable in this setting.

2. Have your character accept a ride from someone she doesn't know well. Describe the ride and the car, particularly its interior. Instead of naming or generalizing about your character's feelings, focus on the details and let them reveal her emotional state and comfort level. Let the details tell us whether the car is luxurious, pristine, a family runabout, a mess. You're the author and so may know the future. Will the character's impressions of the owner, based on the car's condition, prove accurate?

3. Put a character in conflict with a setting. Imagine a character who misunderstands the nature of the place, or overlooks something important, or is oblivious of the danger suggested by certain details. Or imagine a character whose reaction to a place is the opposite of what we would expect: She is carefree in a dark urban alley; he is tranquil and reflective at the shoo ting range; he is contented in the funeral home.

4. Describe a place where a character feels trapped. It could be obvious (a jail cell, dentist's chair, elevator, or orphanage), but it might be less obvious (an RV, an amusement park, a wedding rehearsal, or a library). Use sensory details to suggest your character's discomfort, claustrophobia, and dread.

5. Photographers and filmmakers use a technique called depth of field. So do fiction writers. Write a scene in which you move back and forth between two "fields of action." Have two things going at once—one involving your characters in the foreground and a second having to do with the background. For instance, you might give us some dialogue among the characters on a picnic, then a paragraph about that storm brewing on the horizon, then back to the picnic, and so on. Don't worry too much about making explicit connections or creating transitions between paragraphs. In time, the two strands will figure out their own way of interweaving.

6

LONG AGO
Fictional Time

• *Summary and Scene*

• *Revising Summary and Scene*

• *Flashback*

• *Slow Motion*

Literature is, by virtue of its nature and subject matter, tied to time in a way the other arts are not. A painting represents a frozen instant that viewers experience at a time of their own choosing. Music bridges a span of time, which also dictates tempo and rhythm, but the time scheme is self-enclosed and makes no reference to time in the world outside itself. In fiction, the concern is *content time*, the period covered in the story. It is quite possible to write a story that takes about twenty minutes to read and covers about twenty minutes of action (Jean-Paul Sartre performed experiments in this *durational realism*), but no one has suggested such a correspondence as a requirement for fiction. Sometimes the time period covered is telescoped, sometimes stretched. Sometimes time becomes elastic and reconceived in new ways. "Currents," a story of fewer than a thousand words, tells the story of a summer day, starting with the present and moving backward through time. The history of the world up until now can be covered in a sentence; four seconds of crisis may take a chapter. It's even possible to do both at once: William Golding's entire novel *Pincher Martin* takes place between the time the drowning protagonist begins to take off his boots and the moment he dies with his boots still on. But when asked by a student, "How long does it really take?" Golding replied, "Eternity."

Summary and Scene

Summary and *scene* are methods of treating time in fiction. A summary covers a relatively long period of time in relatively short compass; a scene deals at length with a relatively short period of time.

Summary narration is a useful and often necessary device: It may give information, fill in a character's background, let us understand a motive, alter pace, create a transition, leap moments or years. For example, early in *The Poisonwood Bible*, summary is used both to fast-forward through time to the story's present moment and to set the political context:

> In the year of our Lord 1960 a monkey barreled through space in an American rocket; a Kennedy boy took the chair out from under a fatherly general named Ike; and the whole world turned on an axis called the Congo. The monkey sailed right overhead, and on a more earthly plane men in locked rooms bargained for the Congo's treasure. But I was there. Right on the head of that pin.

In the following example from Ian McEwan's *Enduring Love*, the narrator is preparing to pick up his wife at the airport. The summary leading up to their reunion doesn't tell us every single thing he did that morning (information we don't really need) but gives us enough description of his preparations to let us know how eagerly he's looking forward to his wife's return:

> On the way out to Heathrow I had made a detour into Covent Garden and found a semilegal place to park, near Carluccio's. I went in and put together a picnic whose centerpiece was a great ball of mozzarella, which the assistant fished out of an earthenware vat with a wooden claw. I also bought black olives, mixed salad, and focaccia. Then I hurried up Long Acre to Rota's to take delivery of Clarissa's birthday present. Apart from the flat and our car, it was the most expensive single item I had ever bought. The rarity of this little book seemed to give off a heat I could feel through the thick brown wrapping paper as I walked back up the street. Forty minutes later I was scanning the screens for arrival information.

Short bits of summary often come in the middle of a scene, as in this excerpt from Alice Munro's story "Hateship, Friendship, Courtship, Loveship, Marriage." The main character, Johanna, is trying on potential wedding dresses in a clothing store, and the summary explores her reasons for having blurted out her secret to the saleswoman:

> "It's likely what I'll get married in," said Johanna.
>   She was surprised at that coming out of her mouth. It wasn't a major error—the woman didn't know who she was and would probably not be

talking to anybody who did know. Still, she had meant to keep absolutely quiet. She must have felt she owed this person something—that they'd been through the disaster of the green suit and the discovery of the brown dress together and that was a bond. Which was nonsense. The woman was in the business of selling clothes, and she'd succeeded in doing just that.

"Oh!" the woman cried out. "How wonderful!"

Even the history of a relationship can be given in summary, as seen in this paragraph from Munro's "What Is Remembered":

Pierre and Jonas had grown up together in West Vancouver—they could remember it before the Lion's Gate Bridge was built, when it seemed like a small town. Their parents were friends. When they were eleven or twelve years old they had built a rowboat and launched it at Dundarave Pier. At the university they had parted company for awhile—Jonas was studying to be an engineer, while Pierre was enrolled in the Classics, and the Arts and Engineering students traditionally despised each other. But in the years since then the friendship had to some extent been revived. Jonas, who was not married, came to visit Pierre and Meriel, and sometimes stayed with them for a week at a time.

All four of these summaries use concrete details to engage the reader—the monkey barreling through space, a giant ball of mozzarella, the disaster of the green suit, launching a rowboat. Vivid and specific summary is enlightening and enjoyable to read. On the other hand, a general, perfunctory summary— "They met a few years ago and fell in love. He thought she was beautiful; she thought he was cute. They had many lively dates together before they got engaged"—is likely to be one of those passages that readers skip.

Summary can be called the mortar of the story, but scenes are the building blocks. Scene is the crucial means of allowing your reader to experience the story with the characters. Basically defined, a scene is dialogue and action that take place between two or more characters over a set period of "real" time. Like a story, on its own small scale, a scene has a turning point or mini-crisis that propels the story forward toward its conclusion. Scene is *always* necessary to fiction, for it allows readers to see, hear, and sense the story's drama moment to moment. Jerome Stern, in *Making Shapely Fiction*, astutely observes that like a child in a tantrum, when you want everyone's full attention you "make a scene," using the writer's full complement of "dialogue, physical reactions, gestures, smells, sounds, and thoughts." A confrontation, a turning point, or a crisis occurs at given moments that take on significance as moments and cannot be summarized. The form of a story requires confrontations, turning points, and crises—and therefore requires scenes.

It is quite possible to write a short story in a single scene, with hardly any summary at all, as demonstrated by "A Visit of Charity" (included at the end of

Chapter 5) and "Mud" by Geoffrey Forsyth (included at the end of Chapter 7). The interplay between scene and summary can move so rapidly that a story may seem to be nothing but summary, but a closer look usually reveals at least some use of scene. Take, for example, Hannah Bottomy Voskuil's very short story "Currents" (included at the end of this chapter). What seems to be nothing but summary is really a collection of mini-scenes or moments that include action, drama, telling details, and even dialogue. It is nearly impossible, however, to write a successful story entirely in summary. One of the most common errors beginning fiction writers make is to summarize events rather than realize them as moments.

Here is a moment in the story "Tandolfo the Great," which I've summarized to show the limitations of summary. The clown, Rodney, has just called the birthday boy a name. "Then Rodney decides to insult the boy further, and when the boy sticks out his tongue, Rodney grabs it and lets go, causing the boy to sit down hard. The boy's parents and their friends roughly remove Rodney, take him outside, and prevent him from rescuing his rabbit. He tries to stick up for himself, but nobody takes him seriously."

This summary keeps us at a distance from the action and characters, just when we expect, and need, to be up close. This particular moment is a turning point, and in the scene as Richard Bausch actually wrote it, we are right there, experiencing everything along with Rodney, delighting in his attack on the birthday boy, suffering his humiliation when he's manhandled, feeling his need to rescue Chi-Chi the rabbit, squirming in discomfort when he reveals his drunken state:

It grows quiet. Even the small children can tell that something's happened to change everything.

"Tandolfo has another trick," Rodney says, "where he makes the birthday boy pop like a balloon. Especially if he's a fat birthday boy."

A stirring among the adults.

"Especially if he's an ugly little slab of flesh like this one here."

"Now just a minute," says DAD.

"Pop," Rodney says to the birthday boy, who drops the hat and then, seeming to remember that defiance is expected, makes a face. Sticks out his tongue. Rodney/Tandolfo is quick with his hands by training, and he grabs the tongue.

"Awk," the boy says. "Aw-aw-aw."

"Abracadabra." Rodney lets go, and the boy falls backward into the lap of one of the older children. "Whoops, time to sit down," says Rodney.

Very quickly, he's being forcibly removed. They're rougher than gangsters. They lift him, punch him, tear at his costume—even the women. Someone hits him with a spoon. The whole scene boils out onto the lawn, where someone has released the cage that Chi-Chi was in. Chi-Chi moves about wide-eyed, hopping between running children, evading them, as Tandolfo the Great cannot evade the adults. He's being pummeled, because he keeps trying to return for his rabbit. And the adults won't let him off the curb....

He straightens, pushes the hair out of his eyes, adjusts the clown nose, and looks at them. "I would say that even though I wasn't as patient as I could've been, the adults have not comported themselves well here," he says.

"Drunk," one of the women says.

Transitions between summary and scene must also be carefully crafted. In the following paragraph from Margaret Atwood's *Lady Oracle*, the narrator has been walking home from her Brownie troop with older girls who tease and terrify her with threats of a bad man. The first paragraph of this quotation summarizes the way things were over a period of a few months and then makes a transition to a specific afternoon:

The snow finally changed to slush and then to water, which trickled down the hill of the bridge in two rivulets, one on either side of the path; the path itself turned to mud. The bridge was damp, it smelled rotten, the willow branches turned yellow, the skipping ropes came out. It was light again in the afternoons, and on one of them, when for a change Elizabeth hadn't run off but was merely discussing the possibilities with the others, a real man actually appeared.

The second paragraph, the beginning of a scene, specifies a particular moment:

He was standing at the far side of the bridge, a little off the path, holding a bunch of daffodils in front of him. He was a nice-looking man, neither old nor young, wearing a good tweed coat, not at all shabby or disreputable. He didn't have a hat on, his taffy-colored hair was receding and the sunlight gleamed on his high forehead.

Notice that the scene is introduced when an element of conflict and confrontation occurs. That the threatened bad man does appear and that he is surprisingly innocuous promises a turn of events and a change in the relationship among the girls. We need to see the moment when this change occurs.

Throughout *Lady Oracle*, a typical pattern recurs: a summary leading up to, and followed by, a scene that represents a turning point. Here is another example—one with a different setting and characters—from later in the novel:

My own job was fairly simple. I stood at the back of the archery range, wearing a red leather change apron, and rented out the arrows. When the barrels of arrows were almost used up, I'd go down to the straw targets. The difficulty was that we couldn't make sure all the arrows had actually been shot before we went down to clear the targets. Rob would shout, Bows DOWN, please, arrows OFF the string, but occasionally someone would let an arrow go, on purpose or by accident. This was how I got shot. We'd pulled the arrows and the men were carrying the barrels back to the line; I was replacing a target face, and I'd just bent over.

To get comfortable with this pattern of storytelling, it may help to think of your own past as a movement through time: *I was born in Arizona and lived there with my parents until I was eighteen; then I spent three years in New York before going on to England.* Or you might instead remember the way things were during a period of that time: *In New York we used to go down Broadway for a midnight snack, and Judy would always dare us to do some nonsense or other before we got back.* But when you think of the events that significantly altered your life, your mind will present you with a scene: *Then one afternoon Professor Bovie stopped me in the hall after class and wagged his glasses at me. "Have you thought about studying in England?"*
The moments that altered your life you remember at length and in detail; your memory tells you your story, and it is a great natural storyteller.

A STORY ISN'T ABOUT A MOMENT IN TIME, a story is about *the* moment in time.

W. D. WETHERELL

Scene and summary are often intermixed, of course, and summary may serve precisely to heighten scene.
As we saw in a previous example from the Munro story about the women in the clothing store, summary used within a scene can suggest contrast with the past, intensify mood, or delay while creating suspense about what will happen next. This example from Rosellen Brown's *Before and After*—in which a father, disturbed by reports of a young girl's murder, is checking out his son's car in a dark garage—does all three.

The snow was lavender where the light came down on it, like the weird illumination you see in planetariums that changes every color and makes white electric blue. Jacob and I loved to go to the science museum in Boston—not that long ago he had been at that age when the noisy saga of whirling planets and inexplicable anti-gravitational feats, narrated by a man with a deep official-facts voice, was thrilling. He was easily, unstintingly thrilled, or used to be. Not now, though.

Notice how Brown uses brief summaries both of the way things used to be and the way things have changed over time—as well as images of time, weather, and even the whirling cosmos—to rouse our fear toward the "instant" in which major change occurs:

> At the last instant I thought I'd look at the trunk. I was beginning to feel relief wash over me like that moon-white air outside—a mystery still, where he might be, but nothing suspicious. The trunk snapped open and rose with the slow deliberation of a drawbridge, and then I thought I'd fall over for lack of breath. Because I knew I was looking at blood.

In this excerpt from *Saturday* by Ian McEwan, a novel that takes place on one Saturday, the main character, a neurosurgeon, has awakened in the middle of the night and is staring out the window at the street below. A bit of summary in this scene lets us know how things appear outside his window right now, as opposed to how they usually look. Notice the smooth transitions between the time periods and how the sensory descriptions ground us in both:

> He leans forward, pressing his weight onto his palms against the sill, exulting in the emptiness and clarity of the scene. His vision—always good—seems to have sharpened. He sees the paving stone mica glistening in the pedestrianised square, pigeon excrement hardened by distance and cold into something almost beautiful, like a scattering of snow. He likes the symmetry of black cast-iron posts and their even darker shadows, and the lattice of cobbled gutters. The overfull litter baskets suggest abundance rather than squalor; the vacant benches set around the circular gardens look benignly expectant of their daily traffic—cheerful lunchtime office crowds, the solemn, studious boys from the Indian hostel, lovers in quiet raptures or crisis, the crepuscular drug dealers, the ruined old lady with her wild haunting calls. Go away! She'll shout for hours at a time, and squawk harshly, sounding like some marsh bird or zoo creature.
> Standing here, as immune to the cold as a marble statue, gazing towards Charlotte Street, towards a foreshortened jumble of facades, scaffolding and pitched roofs, Henry thinks the city is a success....

The movements between scene and summary can be quite fluid—you can move in and out and back and forth between them quite easily as long as the reader is not confused, and as long as both scene and summary seem relevant and engaging.

It is crucial that a fiction writer understand the difference between the two and know when and how to best use each of them.

ONE SIMPLE TRICK TO HELP YOU CONCENTRATE ON writing a scene at a specific time in a specific location is to state, right away, something like this: 10 A.M., NYC Athletic Club, Jim and John. If you know when, where, and how, you could probably jump in, and if not, add one more element: what. What are they competing for? What are they in conflict about?

JOSIP NOVAKOVICH

Revising Summary and Scene

Some writers have a tendency to oversummarize, racing through more time and more events than are necessary to tell the story. The danger there is lack of depth. Other writers undersummarize, finding it difficult to deal with quick leaps and transitions, dwelling at excessive length on every scene, including the scenes of the past. The danger of such writing is that readers may not sense which scenes are more important than others. The writer seems not to have made this decision himself or herself. Reluctant to do the writer's job, a reader may lose patience.

After you have written (and especially workshopped) a few stories, you will know which sort of writer you are, and in which direction you need to work.

Following are some comments you may hear in workshop—and suggestions for revising your story accordingly:

- If people say *you have enough material for a novel*, then you have probably not distilled your material down to the very few scenes that contain the significance you seek.

  —Pick one event of all those you have included that contains a moment of crucial change in your character. Write *that* scene in detail, moment by moment. Take time to create the place and the period. Make us see, taste, smell. Let characters speak. Is there a way to indicate, sketch, contain—or simply omit—all that earlier life you raced through in summary? If this proves too difficult, have you really found out yet what your story is about? Explore the scene, rather than the summary, for clues.

  —Try condensing an unnecessary scene to a sentence. Every scene should feel necessary to the story. Each one should build on the one before, and in each scene something surprising should happen—the conflict should escalate. Scenes in which nothing important happens can be summarized. For instance, this exchange of information between the characters does not merit a scene: "Suzie stopped by her parents' house to talk to her mother about the missing money, but her father told her that her mother had gone to visit a sick friend. Suzie said she'd call later and went back to her apartment."

—Try fusing two or even three such scenes into one. Ask yourself what is being accomplished in each scene, and try to determine whether or not one scene could do the work for all of them. For instance, in the previous example, you might have a scene following the one where Suzie visits her parents' house in which, back at her apartment, Suzie's boyfriend tells her that her mother has called and wants to speak to her right away. Another scene might include a telephone call between Suzie and her mother, in which her mother asks her to come to the casino and bring her credit card. And then, finally, you may have a scene where Suzie enters the casino and finds her mother standing, zombie-like, in front of the slot machines. This final scene is likely to be the only one that's really necessary. There might be some summary of the visit with her father and the telephone call with her mother, or Suzie might mention some or all of these things to her mother when she sees her in the casino—perhaps this is the third time in a week that her mother has called in a panic, which upsets not only Suzie but her boyfriend too. And why is her mother continuing to lie to Suzie's father? Sick friend, indeed.

This scene-combining may seem impossible at first, and it may involve sacrificing a delicious phrase or a nifty nuance, but it is simply the necessary work of plotting.

- If your critics say *you write long* or *your story really begins on page three* (or *six*, or *eleven*), have you indulged yourself in setting things up, or dwelt on the story's past at the expense of its present? Where the writer begins writing the story is not necessarily where the final version of the story will begin. Look through your story for a better place to begin.

Chekhov advised his fellow writers to tear the story in half and begin in the middle; in fact, most stories begin as close to the end as possible. Nancy Huddleston Packer says: "The first line of a story should hook readers' attention and pull them into the middle of the action. You want readers to feel like the train is leaving without them, so they'd better get on board and keep reading as fast as they can."

John Gardner described a story as being a "vivid and continuous dream" that the writer creates in the mind of the reader. John L'Heureux applies this notion to the opening of a story, saying that the first paragraph should be designed to help readers "sink into the dream of the story." Like the opening frame of a movie, the opening paragraph entices readers into the story-dream, economically setting the tone; establishing the world, level of reality, and point of view; indirectly conveying information; and "promising" that certain concerns will be dealt with over the course of the story. Often the possible ground for some change or reversal is established in the opening as well.

- If your readers are *confused by what happens at the end*, it may very well be that you have summarized the crisis instead of realizing it in a scene. The crisis moment in a story *must always be presented as a scene*. This is the moment we have been waiting for. This is the payoff when the slipper fits. We want to be there. We want to feel the moment that change happens, hear it, taste it, see it in color in close-up on the wide screen of our minds. This is also a hard job, sometimes the hardest a writer has to do. It's draining to summon up all that emotion in all its intensity. And there isn't always a glass slipper handy when you need one; it may be difficult enough to identify the moment when you need that scene.

Many writers avoid writing crisis scenes in early drafts, perhaps because in fiction, as in our lives, we often try to avoid intense conflict. In order to write a vivid close-up scene for the reader, a writer must first fully imagine that scene, must place him- or herself in it and emotionally experience it, moment by moment. Many writers find it necessary to take it a step further, as Dan Chaon did when he wrote the crisis moment of "Big Me," in which the protagonist, Andy, has been caught trespassing in the home of his creepy neighbor Mr. Mickleson:

I'll also tell you that the hardest part of the story for me—the final confrontation between Andy and Mickleson—was ultimately written as I actually acted out the scene late at night. Imagine our poor neighbor lady glancing over and seeing me prancing around my study, gesticulating and saying things like "Hold still, I'll whisper," and then writing wildly on a legal pad. My neighbor closed her curtain discreetly, as I suppose I should have as well.

It is often the case that such scenes, even in the imagination, are uncomfortable places to be. However, your job as a writer is to recognize the need for such a scene and to try to overcome your squeamishness about going there.

So when is the right time to end your story? As the following writers suggest, the best place to look for an answer to this question is the story itself.

It will turn out that your first page has a lot to do with your last page. Just as in a poem, the first line has a lot to do with the last line, even though you didn't know what it was going to be.

Doris Betts

An ending that seems unsatisfactory might actually be fine. The trouble with the ending might be that the beginning or the middle doesn't set up the ending. A problem scene may not be a problem because of the way it is written. The revision of the ending might need to be carried out back in the beginning of the story.... You start writing the ending when you write your first word.

Jerome Stern, *Making Shapely Fiction*

The climax is that major event, usually toward the end, that brings all the tunes you have been playing so far into one major chord, after which at least one of your people is profoundly changed. If someone isn't changed, then what is the point of your story? For the climax, there must be a killing or a healing or a domination. It can be a real killing, a murder, or it can be a killing of the spirit, or of something terrible inside one's soul, or it can be a killing of a deadness within, after which the person becomes alive again. The healing may be about union, reclamation, the rescue of a fragile prize. But whatever happens, we need to feel that it was inevitable, that even though we may be amazed, it feels absolutely right, that of course things would come to this, of course they would shake down in this way.

Anne Lamott, Bird by Bird

I don't like endings that feel like they've got a big bow or THE END sign. What I really like in an ending is to feel satisfied that there was completion within the story, and yet, in some way, the story is still open.

Jill McCorkle

Flashback

Flashback—in either scene or summary—is one of the most magical of fiction's contrivances, easier and more effective in this medium than in any other, because the reader's mind is a swifter mechanism for getting into the past than anything that has been devised for stage or even film. In fiction you can give the reader a smoothly worded transition into the past, and the force of the story will be time-warped to whenever and wherever you want it.

Nevertheless, many beginning writers use unnecessary flashbacks. While flashback can be a useful way to provide background to character or the history of events—the information that screenwriters call *backstory*—it isn't the only way. Rather, dialogue, brief summary, a reference, or detail can often tell us all we need to know.

If you are tempted to use flashback to fill in the whole past, try using your journal for exploring background. Write down everything, fast. Then take a hard look at it to decide just how *little* of it you can use, how much of it the reader can infer, how you can sharpen an image to imply a past incident or condense a grief into a line of dialogue. Trust the reader's experience of life to understand events from attitudes. And keep the present of the story moving.

For instance, when thinking about the backstory for the scene involving Suzie and her gambling-addicted mother, you might write in your journal about the escalation of Suzie's mother's problem with money—how it started when Suzie's older sister ran away from home, how her mother began buying gadgets and appliances she saw on TV, how Suzie came home one day to find her mother rearranging brand-new living room furniture, the "old" furniture she'd bought six months ago already sitting out in the yard. Then riverboat casinos came to Davenport, and when her mother's friends decided to go there on a lark, only Suzie's mother stayed all night, Suzie and her father were frantic with worry, etc., etc.

When looking at all this material, you might be tempted to use some of it in flashbacks—a scene when Suzie and her parents discover that their older daughter has run away? Or when Suzie finds her mother rearranging the furniture? Or when the mother stays out all night at the casino and Suzie and her father are calling everyone they know? But should you interrupt the present story for any of these potential flashbacks? Are they worth bringing it to a halt? I'd say no, except for possibly the first example—the aftermath of the older daughter's disappearance. That scene could have deep emotional resonance and help us better understand the mother's problems. The other examples could appear in the story in summary form, if they need to appear at all.

Writing out all of this background material is never a waste of time. Even if most of it is never mentioned in either scene or summary, it will inform your understanding of the characters and allow you to understand their problems and empathize with them, helping you to create a fuller, richer, more plausible story.

Flashback is effectively used in fiction to *reveal* at the *right point*. It does not so much distract us from, as contribute to, the central action of the story, deepening our understanding of character and theme. If you find that you do need to use a flashback to reveal, at some point, why the character reacts as she does, or how totally he is misunderstood by those around him, or some other point of emotional significance, then there are several ways to help the reader make that leap in time.

- Provide a smooth, clear transition between present and past. A connection between what's happening in the present and what happened in the past will often best transport the reader, just as it does the character. But avoid overly blatant transitions such as "Henry thought back to the time" and "I drifted back in memory." Assume the reader's intelligence and ability to follow a leap back. For example:

  The kid in the Converse high-tops lifted off on the tips of his toes and slam-dunked it in.
  Joe'd done that once, in the lot off Seymour Street, when he was still four inches shorter than Ruppert and had already started getting zits. It was early fall, and...

- A graceful transition to the past allows you to summarize necessary background quickly, as in this example from James W. Hall's *Under Cover of Daylight*.

  Thorn watched as Sugarman made a quick inspection of the gallery. Thorn sat on the couch where he'd done his homework as a boy, the one that looked out across the seawall toward Carysfort light.

That was how his nights had been once, read a little Thoreau, do some algebra, and look up, shifting his body so he could see through the louvers the fragile pulse of that marker light, and let his mind roam, first out the twelve miles to the reef and then pushing farther, out past the shipping lanes into a world he pictured as gaudy and loud, chaotic. Bright colors and horns honking, exotic vegetables and market stalls, and water, clear and deep and shadowy, an ocean of fish, larger and more powerful than those he had hauled to light. Beyond the reef.

- If you are writing in the past tense, begin the flashback in the past perfect (*she had driven; he had worked*) and use the construction "had + (verb)" two or three times more. Then switch to the simple past (*he raced; she crept*); the reader will be with you. If you are writing in the present tense, you may want to keep the whole flashback in the past tense.

- Try to avoid a flashback within a flashback. If you find yourself tempted by this awkward shape, it probably means you're trying to let flashback carry too much of the story.

- When the flashback ends, be very clear that you are catching up to the present again. Repeat an action or image that the reader will remember belonging to the basic time period of the story. For instance, if in the present time of the story the characters are eating dinner in a fancy restaurant, you could bring us back into the present by mentioning some of the sights and smells of the place—the sight of the annoying waiter coming toward them again, the delicious smell of the coffee in the cup your character is savoring. Or you could have the character set down his fork and glance at the other character across the table. However you decide to do it, you must place the reader firmly where he or she belongs. Often simply beginning the paragraph with "Now..." will accomplish the reorientation.

Slow Motion

Flashback is a term borrowed from film, and I want to borrow another—*slow motion*—to point out a correlation between narrative time and significant detail.

When people experience moments of great intensity, their senses become especially alert and they register, literally, more than usual. In extreme crisis people have the odd sensation that time is slowing down, and they see, hear, smell, and remember ordinary sensations with extraordinary clarity. This psychological fact can work artistically in reverse: You can create the intensity by using detail with special focus and precision. The phenomenon is so universal that it has become a standard film technique to register a physical blow, a gunshot, sexual passion, or extreme fear in slow motion. The technique works forcefully in fiction as well.

Ian McEwan, in *A Child in Time*, demonstrates the technique:

...He was preparing to overtake when something happened—he did not quite see what—in the region of the lorry's wheels, a hiatus, a cloud of dust, and then something black and long snaked through a hundred feet towards him. It slapped the windscreen, clung there a moment and was whisked away before he had time to understand what it was. And then— or did this happen in the same moment?—the rear of the lorry made a complicated set of movements, a bouncing and swaying, and slewed in a wide spray of sparks, bright even in sunshine. Something curved and metallic flew off to one side. So far Stephen had had time to move his foot towards the brake, time to notice a padlock swinging on a loose flange, and 'Wash me please' scrawled in grime. There was a whinnying of scraped metal and new sparks, dense enough to form a white flame which seemed to propel the rear of the lorry into the air.

Anyone who has faced some sort of accident can identify with the experience of sensuous slowdown McEwan records. But the slow-motion technique works also with experiences most of us have not had and to which we must submit in imagination:

Blood was spurting from an artery in my left leg. I could not see it, and I do not recall how I knew it...for a short time I was alone with Patrick. I told myself I was in good hands, but I did not do this with words; I surrendered myself. I focused on breathing. I slowed my breathing, and tried to remain absolutely in the present, in each moment...waiting to die or stay alive was like getting an injection as a child, when you first learned not to think, but to gather yourself into the present, to breathe slowly, to relax your muscles, even your arm as the nurse swabbed it with alcohol, to feel the cool alcohol, to smell it, to feel your feet on the floor and see the color of the wall, and nothing else as your slow breathing opened you up to the incredible length and breadth and depth of one second.

Andre Dubus, "Breathing"

And the technique will work when the intensity or trauma of the moment is not physical but emotional:

They were in the deep sleep of midnight when Pauline came quietly into her son's room and saw that there were two in his bed. She turned on the light. The room was cold and stuffy; warm in the core of it was the smell of a body she had known since she gave birth to him, unmistakable to her as the scent that leads a bitch to her puppy, and it was mingled with the scents of sexuality caressed from the female nectary. The cat was a rolled fur glove in an angle made by Sasha's bent knees. The two in the bed opened their eyes; they focussed out of sleep and saw Pauline. She was looking at them, at their naked shoulders above the covers....

Nadine Gordimer, *A Sport of Nature*

Central to this technique are the alert but matter-of-fact acceptance of the event and the observation of small, sometimes apparently random, details. The characters do not say, "Oh my God, we're going to die!" or "What an outrage!" Instead they record a padlock swinging, the cool feel of an alcohol swab, a cat rolled into the angle of bent knees.

Beginning writers often overuse summary in their fiction because it seems to be the fastest and most direct way of getting information across. Often, however, we want the reader to linger awhile and experience certain moments along with the characters. Once you become adept at the skill of manipulating time in fiction, you will find that the necessity of setting your story at some specific time is a liberating opportunity.

IN OUR EFFORT TO KEEP THE ACTION FROM lagging, we hurry the reader over crucial moments. But anything that is very exciting can't be taken in hurriedly. If somebody is killed in an automobile accident, people who were involved in the accident or who merely witnessed it will be busy for days afterwards piecing together a picture of what happened. They simply couldn't take it all in at that time. When we are writing fiction, we have to give the reader ample time to take in what is happening, particularly if it is very important.

CAROLINE GORDON TO FLANNERY O'CONNER

You're Ugly, Too

LORRIE MOORE

You had to get out of them occasionally, those Illinois towns with the funny names: Paris, Oblong, Normal. Once, when the Dow-Jones dipped two hundred points, the Paris paper boasted a banner headline: NORMAL MAN MARRIES OBLONG WOMAN. They knew what was important. They did! But you had to get out once in a while, even if it was just across the border to Terre Haute, for a movie.

Outside of Paris, in the middle of a large field, was a scatter of brick buildings, a small liberal arts college with the improbable name of Hilldale-Versailles. Zoë Hendricks had been teaching American History there for three years. She taught "The Revolution and Beyond" to freshmen and sophomores, and every third semester she had the Senior Seminar for Majors, and although her student evaluations had been slipping in the last year and a half—*Professor Hendricks is often late for class and usually arrives with a cup of hot chocolate, which she offers the class sips of*—generally, the department of nine men was pleased to have her. They felt she added some needed feminine touch to the corridors—that faint trace of Obsession and sweat, the light, fast clicking of heels. Plus they had had a sex-discrimination suit, and the dean had said, well, it was time.

The situation was not easy for her, they knew. Once, at the start of last semester, she had skipped into her lecture hall singing "Getting to Know You"—both verses. At the request of the dean, the chairman had called her into his office, but did not ask her for an explanation, not really. He asked her how she was and then smiled in an avuncular way. She said, "Fine," and he studied the way she said it, her front teeth catching on the inside of her lower lip. She was almost pretty, but her face showed the strain and ambition of always having been close but not quite. There was too much effort with the eyeliner, and her earrings, worn no doubt for the drama her features lacked, were a little frightening, jutting out from the side of her head like antennae.

"I'm going out of my mind," said Zoë to her younger sister, Evan, in Manhattan. *Professor Hendricks seems to know the entire sound track to* The King and I. *Is this history?* Zoë phoned her every Tuesday.

"You always say that," said Evan, "but then you go on your trips and vacations and then you settle back into things and then you're quiet for a while and then you say you're fine, you're busy, and then after a while you say you're going crazy again, and you start all over." Evan was a part-time food designer for photo shoots. She cooked vegetables in green dye. She propped up beef stew with a bed of marbles and shopped for new kinds of silicone sprays and plastic ice cubes. She thought her life was "OK." She was living with her boyfriend of many years, who was independently wealthy and had an amusing little job in book publishing. They were five years out of college, and they lived in a luxury midtown high-rise with a balcony and access to a pool. "It's not the same as having your own pool," Evan was always sighing, as if to let Zoë know that, as with Zoë, there were still things she, Evan, had to do without.

"Illinois. It makes me sarcastic to be here," said Zoë on the phone. She used to insist it was irony, something gently layered and sophisticated, something alien to the Midwest, but her students kept calling it sarcasm, something they felt qualified to recognize, and now she had to agree. It wasn't irony. *What is your perfume?* a student once asked her. *Room freshener*, she said. She smiled, but he looked at her, unnerved.

Her students were by and large good Midwesterners, spacey with estrogen from large quantities of meat and cheese. They shared their parents' suburban values; their parents had given them things, things, things. They were complacent. They had been purchased. They were armed with a healthy vagueness about anything historical or geographic. They seemed actually to know very little about anything, but they were extremely good-natured about it. "All those states in the East are so tiny and jagged and bunched up," complained one of her undergraduates the week she was lecturing on "The Turning Point of Independence: The Battle at Saratoga." "Professor Hendricks, you're from Delaware originally, right?" the student asked her.

"Maryland," corrected Zoë.

"Aw," he said, waving his hand dismissively. "New England."

Her articles—chapters toward a book called *Hearing the One About: Uses of Humor in the American Presidency*—were generally well received, though they came slowly for her. She liked her pieces to have something from every time of day in them—she didn't trust things written in the morning only—so she reread and rewrote painstakingly. No part of a day, its moods, its light, was allowed to dominate. She hung on to a piece for over a year sometimes, revising at all hours, until the entirety of a day had registered there.

The job she'd had before the one at Hilldale-Versailles had been at a small college in New Geneva, Minnesota, Land of the Dying Shopping Mall. Everyone was so blond there that brunettes were often presumed to be from foreign countries. *Just because Professor Hendricks is from Spain doesn't give her the right to be so negative about our country*. There was a general emphasis on cheerfulness. In New Geneva you weren't supposed to be critical or complain. You weren't supposed to notice that the town had overextended and that its shopping malls were raggedy and going under. You were never to say you weren't fine thank you and yourself. You were supposed to be Heidi. You were supposed to lug goat milk up the hills and not think twice. Heidi did not complain. Heidi did not do things like stand in front of the new IBM photocopier, saying, "If this fucking Xerox machine breaks on me one more time, I'm going to slit my wrists."

But now, in her second job, in her fourth year of teaching in the Midwest, Zoë was discovering something she never suspected she had: a crusty edge, brittle and pointed. Once she had pampered her students, singing them songs, letting them call her at home, even, and ask personal questions. Now she was losing sympathy. They were beginning to seem different. They were beginning to seem demanding and spoiled.

"You act," said one of her Senior Seminar students at a scheduled conference, "like your opinion is worth more than everybody else's in the class."

Zoë's eyes widened. "I *am* the teacher," she said. "I *do* get paid to act like that." She narrowed her gaze at the student, who was wearing a big leather bow in her hair, like a cowgirl in a TV ranch show. "I mean, otherwise *everybody* in the class would have little offices and office hours." *Sometimes Professor Hendricks will take up the class's time just talking about movies she's seen.* She stared at the student some more, then added, "I bet you'd like that."

"Maybe I sound whiny to you," said the girl, "but I simply want my history major to mean something."

"Well, there's your problem," said Zoë, and with a smile, she showed the student to the door. "I like your bow," she added.

Zoë lived for the mail, for the postman, that handsome blue jay, and when she got a real letter, with a real full-price stamp, from someplace else, she took it to bed with her and read it over and over. She also watched television until all hours and had her set in the bedroom, a bad sign. *Professor Hendricks has said critical things about Fawn Hall, the Catholic religion, and the whole state of Illinois. It is unbelievable.* At Christmastime she gave twenty-dollar tips to the mailman and to Jerry, the only cabbie in town, whom she had gotten to know from all her rides to and from the Terre Haute airport, and who, since he realized such rides were an extravagance, often gave her cut rates.

"I'm flying in to visit you this weekend," announced Zoë.

"I was hoping you would," said Evan. "Charlie and I are having a party for Halloween. It'll be fun."

"I have a costume already. It's a bonehead. It's this thing that looks like a giant bone going through your head."

"Great," said Evan.

"It is, it's great."

"Alls I have is my moon mask from last year and the year before. I'll probably end up getting married in it."

"Are you and Charlie getting *married*?" Foreboding filled her voice.

"Hmmmmmmnnno, not immediately."

"Don't get married."

"Why?"

"Just not yet. You're too young."

"You're only saying that because you're five years older than I am and *you're* not married."

"*I'm* not married? Oh, my God," said Zoë. "I forgot to get married."

Zoë had been out with three men since she'd come to Hilldale-Versailles. One of them was a man in the Paris municipal bureaucracy who had fixed a parking ticket she'd brought in to protest and who then asked her to coffee. At first she thought he was amazing—at last, someone who did not want Heidi! But soon she came to realize that all men, deep down, wanted Heidi. Heidi with cleavage. Heidi with outfits. The parking ticket bureaucrat soon became tired and intermittent. One cool fall day, in his snazzy, impractical convertible, when she asked him what was wrong, he said, "You would not be ill-served by new clothes, you know." She wore a lot of gray-green corduroy. She had been under the impression that it brought out her eyes, those shy stars. She flicked an ant from her sleeve.

"Did you have to brush that off in the car?" he said, driving. He glanced down at his own pectorals, giving first the left, then the right, a quick survey. He was wearing a tight shirt.

"Excuse me?"

He slowed down at a yellow light and frowned. "Couldn't you have picked it up and thrown it outside?"

"The ant? It might have bitten me. I mean, what difference does it make?"

"It might have bitten you! Ha! How ridiculous! Now it's going to lay eggs in my car!"

The second guy was sweeter, lunkier, though not insensitive to certain paintings and songs, but too often, too, things he'd do or say would startle her. Once, in a restaurant, he stole the garnishes off her dinner plate and waited for her to notice. When she didn't, he finally thrust his fist across the table and said, "Look," and when he opened it, there was her parsley sprig and her orange slice, crumpled to a wad. Another time he described to her his recent trip to the Louvre. "And there I was in front of Géricault's *Raft of the Medusa*, and everyone else had wandered off, so I had my own private audience with it, all those painted, drowning bodies splayed in every direction, and there's this motion in that painting that starts at the bottom left, swirling and building, and building, and building, and going up to the right-hand corner, where there's this guy waving a flag, and on the horizon in the distance you could see this teeny tiny boat. . . ." He was breathless in the telling. She found this touching and smiled in encouragement. "A painting like that," he said, shaking his head. "It just makes you shit."

"I have to ask you something," said Evan. "I know every woman complains about not meeting men, but really, on my shoots, I meet a lot of men. And they're not all gay, either." She paused. "Not anymore."

"What are you asking?"

The third guy was a political science professor named Murray Peterson, who liked to go out on double dates with colleagues whose wives he was attracted to. Usually the wives would consent to flirt with him. Under the table sometimes there was footsie, and once there was even kneesie. Zoë and the husband would be left to their food, staring into their water glasses, chewing like goats. "Oh, Murray," said one wife, who had never finished her master's in physical therapy and wore great clothes. "You know, I know everything about you: your birthday, your license plate number. I have everything memorized. But then that's the kind of mind I have. Once at a dinner party I amazed the host by getting up and saying good-bye to every single person there, first *and* last names."

"I knew a dog who could do that," said Zoë, with her mouth full. Murray and the wife looked at her with vexed and rebuking expressions, but the husband seemed suddenly twinkling and amused. Zoë swallowed. "It was a Talking Lab, and after about ten minutes of listening to the dinner conversation this dog knew everyone's name. You could say, 'Bring this knife to Murray Peterson,' and it would."

"Really," said the wife, frowning, and Murray Peterson never called again.

"Are you seeing anyone?" said Evan. "I'm asking for a particular reason. I'm not just being like mom."

"I'm seeing my house. I'm tending to it when it wets, when it cries, when it throws up." Zoë had bought a mint-green ranch house near campus, though now she was thinking that maybe she shouldn't have. It was hard to live in a house. She kept wandering in and out of the rooms, wondering where she had put things. She went downstairs into the basement for no reason at all except that it amused her to own a basement. It also amused her to own a tree. The day she moved in, she had tacked to her tree a small paper sign that said *Zoë's Tree*.

Her parents, in Maryland, had been very pleased that one of their children had at last been able to afford real estate, and when she closed on the house they sent her flowers with a Congratulations card. Her mother had even UPS'd a box of old decorating magazines saved over the years, photographs of beautiful rooms her mother used to moon over, since there never had been any money to redecorate. It was like getting her mother's pornography, that box, inheriting her drooled-upon fantasies, the endless wish and tease that had been her life. But to her mother it was a rite of passage that pleased her. "Maybe you will get some ideas from these," she had written. And when Zoë looked at the photographs, at the bold and beautiful living rooms, she was filled with longing. Ideas and ideas of longing.

Right now Zoë's house was rather empty. The previous owner had wallpapered around the furniture, leaving strange gaps and silhouettes on the walls, and Zoë hadn't done much about that yet. She had bought furniture, then taken it back, furnishing and unfurnishing, preparing and shedding, like a womb. She had bought several plain pine chests to use as love seats or boot boxes, but they came to look to her more and more like children's coffins, so she returned them. And she had recently bought an Oriental rug for the living room, with Chinese symbols on it she didn't understand. The salesgirl had kept saying she was sure they meant *Peace* and *Eternal Life*, but when Zoë got the rug home, she worried. What if they didn't mean *Peace* and *Eternal Life*? What if they meant, say, *Bruce Springsteen*. And the more she thought about it, the more she became convinced she had a rug that said *Bruce Springsteen*, and so she returned that, too.

She had also bought a little baroque mirror for the front entryway, which she had been told, by Murray Peterson, would keep away evil spirits. The mirror, however, tended to frighten *her*, startling her with an image of a woman she never recognized. Sometimes she looked puffier and plainer than she remembered. Sometimes shifty and dark. Most times she just looked vague. *You look like someone I know,* she had been told twice in the last year by strangers in restaurants in Terre Haute. In fact, sometimes she seemed not to have a look of her own, or any look whatsoever, and it began to amaze her that her students and colleagues were able to recognize her at all. How did they know? When she walked into a room, how did she look so that they knew it was her? Like this? Did she look like this? And so she returned the mirror.

"The reason I'm asking is that I know a man I think you should meet," said Evan. "He's fun. He's straight. He's single. That's all I'm going to say."

"I think I'm too old for fun," said Zoë. She had a dark bristly hair in her chin, and she could feel it now with her finger. Perhaps when you had been without the opposite sex for too long, you began to resemble them. In an act of desperate invention, you began to grow your own. "I just want to come, wear my bonehead, visit with Charlie's tropical fish, ask you about your food shoots."

She thought about all the papers on "Our Constitution: How It Affects Us" she was going to have to correct. She thought about how she was going in for ultrasound tests on Friday, because, according to her doctor and her doctor's assistant, she had a large, mysterious growth in her abdomen. Gallbladder, they kept saying. Or ovaries or colon. "You guys practice medicine?" asked Zoë, aloud, after they had left the room. Once, as a girl, she brought her dog to a vet, who had told her, "Well, either your dog has worms or cancer or else it was hit by a car."

She was looking forward to New York.

"Well, whatever. We'll just play it cool. I can't wait to see you, hon. Don't forget your bonehead," said Evan.

"A bonehead you don't forget," said Zoë.

"I suppose," said Evan.

The ultrasound Zoë was keeping a secret, even from Evan. "I feel like I'm dying," Zoë had hinted just once on the phone.

"You're not dying," said Evan. "You're just annoyed."

"Ultrasound," Zoë now said jokingly to the technician who put the cold jelly on her bare stomach. "Does that sound like a really great stereo system, or what?" She had not had anyone make this much fuss over her bare stomach since her boyfriend in graduate school, who had hovered over her whenever she felt ill, waved his arms, pressed his hands upon her navel, and drawled evangelically, "Heal! Heal for thy Baby Jesus' sake!" Zoë would laugh and they would make love, both secretly hoping she would get pregnant. Later they would worry together, and he would sink a cheek to her belly and ask whether she was late, was she late, was she sure, she might be late, and when after two years she had not gotten pregnant, they took to quarreling and drifted apart.

"OK," said the technician absently.

The monitor was in place, and Zoë's insides came on the screen in all their gray and ribbony hollowness. They were marbled in the finest gradations of black and white, like stone in an old church or a picture of the moon. "Do you suppose," she babbled at the technician, "that the rise in infertility among so many couples in this country is due to completely different species trying to reproduce?" The technician moved the scanner around and took more pictures. On one view in particular, on Zoë's right side, the technician became suddenly alert, the machine he was operating clicking away.

Zoë stared at the screen. "That must be the growth you found there," suggested Zoë.

"I can't tell you anything," said the technician rigidly.

"Your doctor will get the radiologist's report this afternoon and will phone you then."

"I'll be out of town," said Zoë.

"I'm sorry," said the technician.

Driving home, Zoë looked in the rearview mirror and decided she looked—well, how would one describe it? A little wan. She thought of the joke about the guy who visits his doctor and the doctor says, "Well, I'm sorry to say you've got six weeks to live."

"I want a second opinion," says the guy. *You act like your opinion is worth more than everyone else's in the class.*

"You want a second opinion? OK," says the doctor. "You're ugly, too." She liked that joke. She thought it was terribly, terribly funny.

She took a cab to the airport, Jerry the cabbie happy to see her.

"Have fun in New York," he said, getting her bag out of the trunk. He liked her, or at least he always acted as if he did. She called him "Jare."

"Thanks, Jare."

"You know, I'll tell you a secret: I've never been to New York. I'll tell you two secrets: I've never been on a plane." And he waved at her sadly as she pushed her way in through the terminal door. "Or an escalator!" he shouted.

The trick to flying safe, Zoë always said, was never to buy a discount ticket and to tell yourself you had nothing to live for anyway, so that when the plane crashed it was no big deal. Then, when it didn't crash, when you had succeeded in keeping it aloft with your own worthlessness, all you had to do was stagger off, locate your luggage, and, by the time a cab arrived, come up with a persuasive reason to go on living.

"You're here!" shrieked Evan over the doorbell, before she even opened the door. Then she opened it wide. Zoë set her bags on the hall floor and hugged Evan hard. When she was little, Evan had always been affectionate and devoted. Zoë had always taken care of her, advising, reassuring, until recently, when it seemed Evan had started advising and reassuring *her*. It startled Zoë. She suspected it had something to do with Zoë's being alone. It made people uncomfortable. "How *are* you?"

"I threw up on on the plane. Besides that, I'm OK."

"Can I get you something? Here, let me take your suitcase. Sick on the plane. Eeeyew."

"It was into one of those sickness bags," said Zoë, just in case Evan thought she'd lost it in the aisle. "I was very quiet."

The apartment was spacious and bright, with a view all the way downtown along the East Side. There was a balcony and sliding glass doors. "I keep forgetting how nice this apartment is. Twentieth floor, doorman..." Zoë could work her whole life and never have an apartment like this. So could Evan. It was Charlie's apartment. He and Evan lived in it like two kids in a dorm, beer cans and clothes strewn around. Evan put Zoë's bag away from the mess, over by the fish tank. "I'm so glad you're here," she said. "Now what can I get you?"

Evan made them a snack—soup from a can, and saltines.

"I don't know about Charlie," she said, after they had finished. "I feel like we've gone all sexless and middle-aged already."

"Hmmm," said Zoë. She leaned back into Evan's sofa and stared out the window at the dark tops of the buildings. It seemed a little unnatural to live up in the sky like this, like birds that out of some wrongheaded derring-do had nested too high. She nodded toward the lighted fish tanks and giggled.

"I feel like a bird," she said, "with my own personal supply of fish."

Evan sighed. "He comes home and just sacks out on the sofa, watching fuzzy football. He's wearing the psychic cold cream and curlers, if you know what I mean."

Zoë sat up, readjusted the sofa cushions. "What's fuzzy football?"

"We haven't gotten cable yet. Everything comes in fuzzy. Charlie just watches it that way."

"Hmmm, yeah, that's a little depressing," Zoë said. She looked at her hands. "Especially the part about not having cable."

"This is how he gets into bed at night." Evan stood up to demonstrate. "He whips all his clothes off, and when he gets to his underwear, he lets it drop to one ankle. Then he kicks up his leg and flips the underwear in the air and catches it. I, of course, watch from the bed. There's nothing else. There's just that."

"Maybe you should just get it over with and get married."

"Really?"

"Yeah. I mean, you guys probably think living together like this is the best of both worlds, but . . ." Zoë tried to sound like an older sister; an older sister was supposed to be the parent you could never have, the hip, cool mom. ". . . I've always found that as soon as you think you've got the best of both worlds"—she thought now of herself, alone in her house; of the toad-faced cicadas that flew around like little caped men at night, landing on her screens, staring; of the size fourteen shoes she placed at the doorstep, to scare off intruders; of the ridiculous inflatable blow-up doll someone had told her to keep propped up at the breakfast table—"it can suddenly twist and become the worst of both worlds."

"Really?" Evan was beaming. "Oh, Zoë. I have something to tell you. Charlie and I *are* getting married."

"Really." Zoë felt confused.

"I didn't know how to tell you."

"Yes, well, I guess the part about fuzzy football misled me a little."

"I was hoping you'd be my maid of honor," said Evan, waiting. "Aren't you happy for me?"

"Yes," said Zoë, and she began to tell Evan a story about an award-winning violinist at Hilldale-Versailles, how the violinist had come home from a competition in Europe and taken up with a local man, who made her go to all his summer softball games, made her cheer for him from the stands, with the wives, until she later killed herself. But when she got halfway through, to the part about cheering at the softball games, Zoë stopped.

"What?" said Evan. "So what happened?"

"Actually, nothing," said Zoë lightly. "She just really got into softball. I mean, really. You should have seen her."

Zoë decided to go to a late-afternoon movie, leaving Evan to chores she needed to do before the party—*I have to do them alone*, she'd said, a little tense after the violinist story. Zoë thought about going to an art museum, but women alone in art museums had to look good. They always did. Chic and serious, moving languidly, with a great handbag. Instead, she walked over and down through Kips Bay, past an earring boutique called Stick It in Your Ear, past a beauty salon called Dorian Gray's. That was the funny thing about *beauty*, thought Zoë. Look it up in the yellow pages, and you found a hundred entries, hostile with wit, cutesy with warning. But look up *truth*—ha! There was nothing at all.

Zoë thought about Evan getting married. Would Evan turn into Peter Pumpkin Eater's wife? Mrs. Eater? At the wedding would she make Zoë wear some flouncy lavender dress, identical with the other maids'? Zoë hated uniforms, had even, in the first grade, refused to join Elf Girls, because she didn't want to wear the same dress as everyone else. Now she might have to. But maybe she could distinguish it. Hitch it up on one side with a clothespin. Wear surgical gauze at the waist. Clip to her bodice one of those pins that said in loud letters, SHIT HAPPENS.

At the movie—*Death by Number*—she bought strands of red licorice to tug and chew. She took a seat off to one side in the theater. She felt strangely self-conscious sitting alone and hoped for the place to darken fast. When it did, and the coming attractions came on, she reached inside her purse for her glasses. They were in a Baggie. Her Kleenex was also in a Baggie. So were her pen and her aspirin and her mints. Everything was in Baggies. This was what she'd become: *a woman alone at the movies with everything in a Baggie.*

At the Halloween party, there were about two dozen people. There were people with ape heads and large hairy hands. There was someone dressed as a leprechaun. There was someone dressed as a frozen dinner. Some man had brought his two small daughters: a ballerina and a ballerina's sister, also dressed as a ballerina. There was a gaggle of sexy witches—women dressed entirely in black, beautifully made up and jeweled. "I hate those sexy witches. It's not in the spirit of Halloween," said Evan. Evan had abandoned the moon mask and dolled herself up as a hausfrau, in curlers and an apron, a decision she now regretted. Charlie, because he liked fish, because he owned fish, collected fish, had decided to go as a fish. He had fins and eyes on the side of his head. "Zoë! How are you! I'm sorry I wasn't here when you first arrived!" He spent the rest of his time chatting up the sexy witches.

"Isn't there something I can help you with here?" Zoë asked her sister. "You've been running yourself ragged." She rubbed her sister's arm, gently, as if she wished they were alone.

"Oh, God, not at all," said Evan, arranging stuffed mushrooms on a plate. The timer went off, and she pulled another sheetful out of the oven. "Actually, you know what you can do?"

"What?" Zoë put on her bonehead.

"Meet Earl. He's the guy I had in mind for you. When he gets here, just talk to him a little. He's nice. He's fun. He's going through a divorce."

"I'll try." Zoë groaned. "OK? I'll try." She looked at her watch.

When Earl arrived, he was dressed as a naked woman, steel wool glued strategically to a body stocking, and large rubber breasts protruding like hams.

"Zoë, this is Earl," said Evan.

"Good to meet you," said Earl, circling Evan to shake Zoë's hand. He stared at the top of Zoë's head. "Great bone."

Zoë nodded. "Great tits," she said. She looked past him, out the window at the city thrown glitteringly up against the sky; people were saying the usual things: how it looked like jewels, like bracelets and necklaces unstrung. You could see Grand Central station, the clock of the Con Ed building, the red-and-gold-capped Empire State, the Chrysler like a rocket ship dreamed up in a depression. Far west you could glimpse the Astor Plaza, its flying white roof like a nun's habit. "There's beer out on the balcony, Earl—can I get you one?" Zoë asked.

"Sure, uh, I'll come along. Hey, Charlie, how's it going?"

Charlie grinned and whistled. People turned to look. "Hey, Earl," someone called, from across the room. "Va-va-va-voom."

They squeezed their way past the other guests, past the apes and the sexy witches. The suction of the sliding door gave way in a whoosh, and Zoë and Earl stepped out onto the balcony, a bonehead and a naked woman, the night air roaring and smoky cool. Another couple was out here, too, murmuring privately. They were not wearing costumes. They smiled at Zoë and Earl. "Hi," said Zoë. She found the plastic-foam cooler, dug into it, and retrieved two beers.

"Thanks," said Earl. His rubber breasts folded inward, dimpled and dented, as he twisted open the bottle.

"Well," sighed Zoë anxiously. She had to learn not to be afraid of a man, the way, in your childhood, you learned not to be afraid of an earthworm or a bug. Often, when she spoke to men at parties, she rushed things in her mind. As the man politely blathered on, she would fall in love, marry, then find herself in a bitter custody battle with him for the kids and hoping for a reconciliation, so that despite all his betrayals she might no longer despise him, and in the few minutes remaining, learn, perhaps, what his last name was and what he did for a living, though probably there was already too much history between them. She would nod, blush, turn away.

"Evan tells me you're a professor. Where do you teach?"

"Just over the Indiana border into Illinois."

He looked a little shocked. "I guess Evan didn't tell me that part."

"She didn't?"

"No."

"Well, that's Evan for you. When we were kids we both had speech impediments."

"That can be tough," said Earl. One of his breasts was hidden behind his drinking arm, but the other shone low and pink, full as a strawberry moon.

"Yes, well, it wasn't a total loss. We used to go to what we called peach pearapy. For about ten years of my life I had to map out every sentence in my mind, way ahead, before I said it. That was the only way I could get a coherent sentence out."

Earl drank from his beer. "How did you do that? I mean, how did you get through?"

"I told a lot of jokes. Jokes you know the lines to already—you can just say them. I love jokes. Jokes and songs."

Earl smiled. He had on lipstick, a deep shade of red, but it was wearing off from the beer. "What's your favorite joke?"

"Uh, my favorite joke is probably...OK, all right. This guy goes into a doctor's office and—"

"I think I know this one," interrupted Earl, eagerly. He wanted to tell it himself. "A guy goes into a doctor's office, and the doctor tells him he's got some good news and some bad news—that one, right?"

"I'm not sure," said Zoë. "This might be a different version."

"So the guy says, 'Give me the bad news first,' and the doctor says, 'OK. You've got three weeks to live.' And the guy cries, 'Three weeks to live! Doctor, what is the good news?' And the doctor says, 'Did you see that secretary out front? I finally fucked her.' "

Zoë frowned.

"That's not the one you were thinking of?"

"No." There was accusation in her voice. "Mine was different."

"Oh," said Earl. He looked away and then back again. "You teach history, right? What kind of history do you teach?"

"I teach American, mostly—eighteenth and nineteenth century." In graduate school, at bars, the pickup line was always: "So what's your century?"

"Occasionally I teach a special theme course," she added, "say, 'Humor and Personality in the White House.' That's what my book's on." She thought of something someone once told her about bowerbirds, how they build elaborate structures before mating.

"Your book's on *humor*?"

"Yeah, and, well, when I teach a theme course like that, I do all the centuries." *So what's your century?*

"All three of them."

"Pardon?" The breeze glistened her eyes. Traffic revved beneath them. She felt high and puny, like someone lifted into heaven by mistake and then spurned.

"Three. There's only three."

"Well, four, really." She was thinking of Jamestown, and of the Pilgrims coming here with buckles and witch hats to say their prayers.

"I'm a photographer," said Earl. His face was starting to gleam, his rouge smearing in a sunset beneath his eyes.

"Do you like that?"

"Well, actually I'm starting to feel it's a little dangerous."

"Really?"

"Spending all your time in a darkroom with that red light and all those chemicals. There's links with Parkinson's, you know."

"No, I didn't."

"I suppose I should wear rubber gloves, but I don't like to. Unless I'm touching it directly, I don't think of it as real."

"Hmmm," said Zoë. Alarm buzzed through her, mildly, like a tea.

"Sometimes, when I have a cut or something, I feel the sting and think, *Shit.* I wash constantly and just hope. I don't like rubber over the skin like that."

"Really."

"I mean, the physical contact. That's what you want, or why bother?"

"I guess," said Zoë. She wished she could think of a joke, something slow and deliberate, with the end in sight. She thought of gorillas, how when they had been kept too long alone in cages, they would smack each other in the head instead of mating.

"Are you...in a relationship?" Earl suddenly blurted.

"Now? As we speak?"

"Well, I mean, I'm sure you have a relationship to your *work.*" A smile, a weird one, nestled in his mouth like an egg. She thought of zoos in parks, how when cities were under siege, during world wars, people ate the animals. "But I mean, with a *man.*"

"No, I'm not in a relationship with a *man.*" She rubbed her chin with her hand and could feel the one bristly hair there. "But my last relationship was with a very sweet man," she said. She made something up. "From Switzerland. He was a botanist—a weed expert. His name was Jerry. I called him 'Jare.' He was so funny. You'd go to the movies with him and all he would notice were the plants. He would never pay attention to the plot. Once, in a jungle movie, he started rattling off all these Latin names, out loud. It was very exciting for him." She paused, caught her breath. "Eventually he went back to Europe to, uh, study the edelweiss." She looked at Earl. "Are you involved in a relationship? With a *woman?*"

Earl shifted his weight, and the creases in his body stocking changed, splintering outward like something broken. His pubic hair slid over to one hip, like a corsage on a saloon girl. "No," he said, clearing his throat. The steel wool in his underarms was inching toward his biceps. "I've just gotten out of a marriage that was full of bad dialogue, like 'You want more *space?* I'll give you more space!' *Clonk.* Your basic Three Stooges."

Zoë looked at him sympathetically. "I suppose it's hard for love to recover after that."

His eyes lit up. He wanted to talk about love. "But *I* keep thinking love should be like a tree. You look at trees and they've got bumps and

scars from tumors, infestations, what have you, but they're still growing. Despite the bumps and bruises, they're...straight."

"Yeah, well," said Zoë, "where I'm from, they're all married or gay.
Did you see that movie *Death by Number*?"

Earl looked at her, a little lost. She was getting away from him. "No,"
he said.

One of his breasts had slipped under his arm, tucked there like a
baguette. She kept thinking of trees, of gorillas and parks, of people in
wartime eating the zebras. She felt a stabbing pain in her abdomen.

"Want some hors d'oeuvres?" Evan came pushing through the sliding
door. She was smiling, though her curlers were coming out, hanging
bedraggled at the ends of her hair like Christmas decorations, like food
put out for the birds. She thrust forward a plate of stuffed mushrooms.

"Are you asking for donations or giving them away," said Earl, wit-
tily. He liked Evan, and he put his arm around her.

"You know, I'll be right back," said Zoë.

"Oh," said Evan, looking concerned.

"Right back. I promise."

Zoë hurried inside, across the living room, into the bedroom, to the
adjoining bath. It was empty; most of the guests were using the half
bath near the kitchen. She flicked on the light and closed the door.
The pain had stopped and she didn't really have to go to the bathroom,
but she stayed there anyway, resting. In the mirror above the sink she
looked haggard beneath her bonehead, violet grays showing under the
skin like a plucked and pocky bird. She leaned closer, raising her chin
a little to find the bristly hair. It was there, at the end of the jaw, sharp
and dark as a wire. She opened the medicine cabinet, pawed through
it until she found some tweezers. She lifted her head again and poked
at her face with the metal tips, grasping and pinching and missing.
Outside the door she could hear two people talking low. They had come
into the bedroom and were discussing something. They were sitting on
the bed. One of them giggled in a false way. She stabbed again at her
chin, and it started to bleed a little. She pulled the skin tight along the
jawbone, gripped the tweezers hard around what she hoped was the
hair, and tugged. A tiny square of skin came away with it, but the hair
remained, blood bright at the root of it. Zoë clenched her teeth. "Come
on," she whispered. The couple outside in the bedroom were now telling
stories, softly, and laughing. There was a bounce and squeak of mat-
tress, and the sound of a chair being moved out of the way. Zoë aimed
the tweezers carefully, pinched, then pulled gently away, and this time
the hair came, too, with a slight twinge of pain and then a great flood of
relief. "Yeah!" breathed Zoë. She grabbed some toilet paper and dabbed
at her chin. It came away spotted with blood, and so she tore off some
more and pressed hard until it stopped. Then she turned off the light

and opened the door, to return to the party. "Excuse me," she said to the couple in the bedroom. They were the couple from the balcony, and they looked at her, a bit surprised. They had their arms around each other, and they were eating candy bars.

Earl was still out on the balcony, alone, and Zoë rejoined him there.

"Hi," she said. He turned around and smiled. He had straightened his costume out a bit, though all the secondary sex characteristics seemed slightly doomed, destined to shift and flip and zip around again any moment.

"Are you OK?" he asked. He had opened another beer and was chugging.

"Oh, yeah. I just had to go to the bathroom." She paused. "Actually I have been going to a lot of doctors recently."

"What's wrong?" asked Earl.

"Oh, probably nothing. But they're putting me through tests." She sighed. "I've had sonograms. I've had mammograms. Next week I'm going in for a candygram." He looked at her worriedly. "I've had too many gram words," she said.

"Here, I saved you these." He held out a napkin with two stuffed mushroom caps. They were cold and leaving oil marks on the napkin.

"Thanks," said Zoë, and pushed them both in her mouth. "Watch," she said, with her mouth full. "With my luck, it'll be a gallbladder operation."

Earl made a face. "So your sister's getting married," he said, changing the subject. "Tell me, really, what you think about love."

"*Love?*" Hadn't they done this already? "I don't know." She chewed thoughtfully and swallowed. "All right. I'll tell you what I think about love. Here is a love story. This friend of mine—"

"You've got something on your chin," said Earl, and he reached over to touch it.

"*What?*" said Zoë, stepping back. She turned her face away and grabbed at her chin. A piece of toilet paper peeled off it, like tape. "It's nothing," she said. "It's just—it's nothing."

Earl stared at her.

"At any rate," she continued, "this friend of mine was this award-winning violinist. She traveled all over Europe and won competitions; she made records, she gave concerts, she got famous. But she had no social life. So one day she threw herself at the feet of this conductor she had a terrible crush on. He picked her up, scolded her gently, and sent her back to her hotel room. After that she came home from Europe. She went back to her old hometown, stopped playing the violin, and took up with a local boy. This was in Illinois. He took her to some Big Ten bar every night to drink with his buddies from the team. He used to say things like "Katrina here likes to play the violin," and then he'd pinch her cheek. When she once suggested that they go home, he said, 'What, you think you're too famous for a place like this? Well, let me tell you something. You may think you're famous, but you're not *famous* famous.' Two famouses. 'No one here's ever heard of you.' Then he went up and bought a round of drinks for everyone but her. She got her coat, went home, and shot a gun through her head."

Earl was silent.

"That's the end of my love story," said Zoë.

"You're not at all like your sister," said Earl.

"Ho, really," said Zoë. The air had gotten colder, the wind singing minor and thick as a dirge.

"No." He didn't want to talk about love anymore. "You know, you should wear a lot of blue—blue and white—around your face. It would bring out your coloring." He reached an arm out to show her how the blue bracelet he was wearing might look against her skin, but she swatted it away.

"Tell me, Earl. Does the word *fag* mean anything to you?"

He stepped back, away from her. He shook his head in disbelief. "You know, I just shouldn't try to go out with career women. You're all stricken. A guy can really tell what life has done to you. I do better with women who have part-time jobs."

"Oh, yes?" said Zoë. She had once read an article entitled "Professional Women and the Demographics of Grief." Or no, it was a poem: *If there were a lake, the moonlight would dance across it in conniptions.* She remembered that line. But perhaps the title was "The Empty House: Aesthetics of Barrenness." Or maybe "Space Gypsies: Girls in Academe." She had forgotten.

Earl turned and leaned on the railing of the balcony. It was getting late. Inside, the party guests were beginning to leave. The sexy witches were already gone. "Live and learn," Earl murmured.

"Live and get dumb," replied Zoë. Beneath them on Lexington there were no cars, just the gold rush of an occasional cab. He leaned hard on his elbows, brooding.

"Look at those few people down there," he said. "They look like bugs. You know how bugs are kept under control? They're sprayed with bug hormones, female bug hormones. The male bugs get so crazy in the presence of this hormone, they're screwing everything in sight: trees, rocks—everything but female bugs. Population control. That's what's happening in this country," he said drunkenly. "Hormones sprayed around, and now men are screwing rocks. Rocks!"

In the back the Magic Marker line of his buttocks spread wide, a sketchy black on pink like a funnies page. Zoë came up, slow, from behind and gave him a shove. His arms slipped forward, off the railing, out over the city below. Beer spilled out of his bottle, raining twenty stories down to the street.

"Hey, what are you doing?!" he said, whipping around. He stood straight and readied and moved away from the railing, sidestepping Zoë. "What the *hell* are you doing?"

"Just kidding," she said. "I was just kidding." But he gazed at her, appalled and frightened, his Magic Marker buttocks turned away now toward all of downtown, a naked pseudo-woman with a blue bracelet at the wrist, trapped out on a balcony with—with *what? "Really, I was just kidding!"* Zoë shouted. The wind lifted the hair up off her head, skyward in spines behind the bone. If there were a lake, the moonlight would dance across it in conniptions. She smiled at him, and wondered how she looked.

The Fun House

SHERMAN ALEXIE

In the trailer by Tshimikain Creek where my cousins and I used to go crazy in the mud, my aunt waited. She sewed to pass the time, made beautiful buckskin outfits that no one could afford, and once she made a full-length beaded dress that was too heavy for anyone to wear.

"It's just like the sword in the stone," she said. "When a woman comes along who can carry the weight of this dress on her back, then we'll have found the one who will save us all."

One morning she sewed while her son and husband watched television. It was so quiet that when her son released a tremendous fart, a mouse, startled from his hiding place beneath my aunt's sewing chair, ran straight up her pant leg.

She pulled her body into the air, reached down her pants, unbuttoned them, tried to pull them off, but they stuck around the hips.

"Jesus, Jesus," she cried while her husband and son rolled with laughter on the floor.

"Get it out, get it out," she yelled some more while her husband ran over and smacked her legs in an effort to smash the mouse dead.

"Not that way," she cried again and again.

All the noise and laughter and tears frightened the mouse even more, and he ran down my aunt's pant leg, out the door and into the fields.

In the aftermath, my aunt hiked her pants back up and cursed her son and husband.

"Why didn't you help me?" she asked.

Her son couldn't stop laughing.

"I bet when that mouse ran up your pant leg, he was thinking, *What in the hell kind of mousetraps do they got now?*" her husband said.

"Yeah," her son agreed. "When he got up there, he probably said to himself, *That's the ugliest mousetrap I've ever seen!*"

"Stop it, you two," she yelled. "Haven't you got any sense left?"

"Calm down," my uncle said. "We're only teasing you."

"You're just a couple of ungrateful shits," my aunt said. "Where would you be if I didn't cook, if my fry bread didn't fill your stomachs every damn night?"

"Momma," her son said. "I didn't mean it."

"Yeah," she said. "And I didn't mean to give birth to you. Look at you. Thirty years old and no job except getting drunk. What good are you?"

"That's enough," her husband yelled.

"It's never enough," my aunt said and walked outside, stood in the sun, and searched the sky for predators of any variety. She hoped some falcon or owl would find the mouse and she hoped some pterodactyl would grab her husband and son.

Bird feed, she thought. *They'd make good bird feed.*

In the dark my aunt and her husband were dancing. Thirty years ago and they two-stepped in an Indian cowboy bar. So many Indians in one place and it was beautiful then. All they needed to survive was the drive home after closing time.

"Hey, Nezzy," a voice cried out to my aunt. "You still stepping on toes?"

My aunt smiled and laughed. She was a beautiful dancer, had given lessons at the Arthur Murray Dance Studio to pay her way through community college. She had also danced topless in a Seattle bar to put food in her child's stomach.

There are all kinds of dancing.

"Do you love me?" my aunt asked her husband.

He smiled. He held her closer, tighter. They kept dancing.

After closing time, they drove home on the back roads.

"Be careful," my aunt told her husband. "You drank too much tonight."

He smiled. He put his foot to the fire wall and the pickup staggered down the dirt road, went on two wheels on a sharp corner, flipped, and slid into the ditch.

My aunt crawled out of the wreck, face full of blood, and sat on the roadside. Her husband had been thrown out of the pickup and lay completely still in the middle of the road.

"Dead? Knocked out? Passed out?" my aunt asked herself.

After a while, another car arrived and stopped. They wrapped an old shirt around my aunt's head and loaded her husband into the backseat.

"Is he dead?" my aunt asked.

"Nah, he'll be all right."

They drove that way to the tribal hospital. My aunt bled into the shirt; her husband slept through his slight concussion. They kept him overnight for observation, and my aunt slept on a cot beside his bed. She left the television on with the volume turned off.

At sunrise my aunt shook her husband awake.

"What?" he asked, completely surprised. "Where am I?"

"In the hospital."

"Again?"

"Yeah, again."

Thirty years later and they still hadn't paid the bill for services rendered.

My aunt walked down her dirt road until she was dizzy. She walked until she stood on the bank of Tshimikain Creek. The water was brown, smelled a little of dead animal and uranium. My cousins and I dove into these waters years ago to pull colored stones from the muddy bottom and collect them in piles beside the creek. My aunt stood beside one of those ordinary monuments to childhood and smiled a little, cried a little.

"One dumb mouse tears apart the whole damn house," she said. Then she stripped off her clothes, kept her shoes on for safety, and dove naked into the creek. She splashed around, screamed in joy as she waded through. She couldn't swim but the creek was shallow, only just past her hips. When she sat down the surface rested just below her chin, so whenever she moved she swallowed a mouthful of water.

"I'll probably get sick," she said and laughed just as her husband and son arrived at the creek, out of breath.

"What the hell are you doing?" her husband asked.

"Swimming."

"But you don't know how to swim."

"I do now."

"Get out of there before you drown," her husband said. "And get some clothes on."

"I'm not coming out until I want to," my aunt said, and she floated up on her back for the first time.

"You can't do that," her son yelled now. "What if somebody sees you?"

"I don't care," my aunt said. "They can all go to hell, and you two can drive the buses that get them there."

Her husband and son threw their hands up in surrender, walked away.

"And cook your own damn dinner," my aunt yelled at their backs.

She floated on the water like that for hours, until her skin wrinkled and her ears filled with water. She kept her eyes closed and could barely hear when her husband and son came back every so often to plead with her.

"One dumb mouse tore apart the whole damn house. One dumb mouse tore apart the whole damn house," she chanted at them, sang it like a nursery rhyme, like a reservation Mother Goose.

The delivery room was a madhouse, a fun house. The Indian Health Service doctor kept shouting at the nurses.

"Goddamn it," he yelled. "I've never done this before. You've got to help me."

My aunt was conscious, too far into delivery for drugs, and she was screaming a little bit louder than the doctor.

"Shit, shit, fuck," she yelled and grabbed onto the nurses, the doctors, kicked at her stirrups. "It hurts, it hurts, it hurts!"

Her son slid out of her then and nearly slipped through the doctor's hands. The doctor caught him by an ankle and held on tightly.

"It's a boy," he said. "Finally."

A nurse took the baby, held it upside down as she cleared his mouth, wiped his body almost clean. My aunt took her upside-down son with only one question: *Will he love to eat potatoes?*

While my aunt held her baby close to her chest, the doctor tied her tubes, with the permission slip my aunt signed because the hospital administrator lied and said it proved her Indian status for the BIA.

"What are you going to name it?" a nurse asked my aunt.

"Potatoes," she said. "Or maybe Albert."

When the sun went down and the night got too cold, my aunt finally surrendered the water of Tshimikain Creek, put clothes on her damp and tired body, and walked up her road toward home. She looked at the bright lights shining in the windows, listened to the dogs bark stupidly, and knew that things had to change.

She walked into the house, didn't say a word to her stunned husband and son, and pulled that heaviest of beaded dresses over her head. Her knees buckled and she almost fell from the weight; then she did fall.

"No," she said to her husband and son as they rose to help her.

She stood, weakly. But she had the strength to take the first step, then another quick one. She heard drums, she heard singing, she danced.

Dancing that way, she knew things were beginning to change.

Currents

HANNAH BOTTOMY VOSKUIL

Gary drank single malt in the night, out on the porch that leaned toward the ocean. His mother, distracted, had shut off the floodlights and he did not protest against the dark.

Before that, his mother, Josey, tucked in her two shivering twelve-year-old granddaughters.

"I want you both to go swimming first thing tomorrow. Can't have two seals like you afraid of the water."

Before that, one of the girls held the hand of a wordless Filipino boy. His was the first hand she'd ever held. They were watching the paramedics lift the boy's dead brother into an ambulance.

At this time, the other girl heaved over a toilet in the cabana.

Before that, the girl who would feel nauseated watched as the drowned boy's hand slid off the stretcher and bounced along the porch rail. Nobody placed the hand back on the stretcher, and it bounced and dragged and bounced.

Before that, Gary saw the brown hair sink and resurface as the body bobbed. At first he mistook it for seaweed.

Before that, thirty-five people struggled out of the water at the Coast Guard's command. A lifeguard shouted over Jet Ski motors about the increasing strength of the riptide.

Before that the thirty-five people, including Gary and the two girls, formed a human chain and trolled the waters for the body of a Filipino boy. The boy had gone under twenty minutes earlier and never come back up.

Before that, a lifeguard sprinted up the beach, shouting for volunteers. The two girls, resting lightly on their sandy bodyboards, stood up to help.

Before that, a Filipino boy pulled on the torpid lifeguard's ankle and gestured desperately at the waves. My brother, he said.

Before that, it was a simple summer day.

◨ ◨ ◨

Writing Exercises

1. Make a list of activities that take place over a brief period of time, a few hours at most. Choose one of these and write a short (five-page) story confined within that period of time.

2. Imagine an accident. It might be minor—a finger cut, a knocked-over vase. Or it might be major—a car wreck, a fire. Now, write several versions of the accident: a one-sentence summary, a one-paragraph summary, a full scene, and finally, a slo-o-o-o-wed down version of the scene. It may help to think of filmmaking. Begin with a panoramic establishing shot and let the camera keep zooming in, closer and closer, to an extreme close-up.

3. Write a story that takes place over a fairly long period of time (at least six months, perhaps several years). Make a list of possible events in the story;

you may even want to draw a time line. Sketch out your story, bearing in mind that you will have to cover great stretches of time. What will you show in scenes? What can be summarized? For common or everyday experiences, can one scene or summary suggest the rest? (A single scene of newlyweds fighting can convey the nature of all their arguments. Likewise, a summary of a specific/generalized day at the office can give a sense of a character's everyday life.)

4. Write a very short (two- to three-page) story in which you use (in miniature) scene, summary, flashback, and slow motion.

7

THE TOWER AND THE NET
Story Form, Plot, and Structure

What makes you want to write?

It seems likely that the earliest storytellers—in the tent or the harem, around the campfire or on the Viking ship—distracted their listeners from a dull or dangerous evening with tales of suspenseful heroic exploits. They did this with heroic exploits and a skill at creating suspense: What happened next? And after that? And then what happened?

Natural storytellers are still around, and a few of them are very rich. Some are on the best-seller list; more are in television and film. But it's probable that your impulse to write has little to do with the desire or the skill to work out a plot. On the contrary, you want to write because you are a sensitive observer. You have something to say that does not answer the question *What happened next?* You share with most—and the best—contemporary fiction writers a sense of the injustice, the absurdity, and the beauty of the world; and you want to register your protest, your laughter, and your affirmation.

Yet readers still want to wonder what happened next, and unless you make them wonder, they will not turn the page. You must master plot, because no matter how profound or illuminating your vision of the world may be, you cannot convey it to those who do not read you.

When editors take the trouble to write a rejection letter to a young author (and they do so only when they think the author talented), the gist of the letter most frequently is: "This piece is sensitive (perceptive, vivid, original, brilliant, funny, moving), but it is not a *story*."

How do you know when you have written a story? And if you're not a natural-born wandering minstrel, can you go about learning to write one?

Sᴛʀᴜᴄᴛᴜʀᴇ ɪs ᴛʜᴇ ᴀʀᴛ ᴛʜᴀᴛ ᴄᴏɴᴄᴇᴀʟs ɪᴛsᴇʟꜰ—you only *see* the structure in a badly structured story, and call it formula.

STEPHEN FISCHER

It's interesting that we react with such different attitudes to the words "formula" and "form" as they apply to a story. A formula story is hackwork. To write one, you pick a sitcom plot line or a blockbuster hero, shuffle the characters and the situations around a little, and hope the trick works once more. By contrast, *form* is a term of the highest artistic approbation, even reverence, with overtones of *order, harmony, model, archetype*.

And "story" is a "form" of literature. Like a face, it has necessary features in a necessary harmony. We're aware of the infinite variety of human faces, aware of their unique individuality, which is so powerful that once you know a face you can recognize it twenty years after you last saw it, despite the changes it has undergone. We're aware that minute alterations in the features can express grief, anger, or joy. If you place side by side two photographs of, say, Anne Hathaway and Geronimo, you are instantly aware of the fundamental differences of age, race, sex, background, and century; yet these two faces are more like each other than either is like a foot or a fern, both of which have their own distinctive forms. Every face has two eyes, a nose between them, a mouth below, a forehead, two cheeks, two ears, and a jaw. If a face is missing one of these features, you may say, "I love this face in spite of its lacking a nose," but you must acknowledge the *in spite of*. You can't simply say, "This is a wonderful face."

The same is true of a story. You might say, "I love this piece even though there's no crisis action in it." You can't simply say, "This is a wonderful *story*."

Conflict, Crisis, and Resolution

One of the useful ways of describing the necessary features of story form is to speak of *conflict, crisis,* and *resolution.*

Conflict is a fundamental element of fiction. Playwright Elia Kazan describes it simply as "two dogs fighting over a bone"; William Faulkner reminds us that in addition to a conflict of wills, fiction also shows "the heart in conflict with itself," so that conflict seethes both within and between characters. In life, "conflict" often carries negative connotations, yet in fiction, be it comic or tragic, dramatic conflict is fundamental because in literature only trouble is interesting.

Only trouble is interesting. This is not so in life. Life offers periods of comfortable communication, peaceful pleasure, and productive work, all of which are extremely interesting to those involved. But passages about such times by themselves make for dull reading; they can be used as lulls in an otherwise tense situation, as a resolution, even as a hint that something awful is about to happen. They cannot be used as a whole plot.

ALMOST ALL GOOD STORIES ARE SAD because it is the human struggle that engages us readers and listeners the most. To watch characters confront their hardships and uncertainties makes us feel better about our own conflicts and confusions and fears. We have a sense of community, of sympathy, a cleansing sympathy, as Aristotle said, and relief that we are safe in our room only reading the story.

ROBERT MORGAN

Suppose, for example, you go on a picnic. You find a beautiful deserted meadow with a lake nearby. The weather is splendid and so is the company. The food's delicious, the water's fine, and the insects have taken the day off. Afterward, someone asks you how your picnic was. "Terrific," you reply, "really perfect." No story.

But suppose the next week you go back for a rerun. You set your picnic blanket on an anthill. You all race for the lake to get cold water on the bites, and one of your friends goes too far out on the plastic raft, which deflates. He can't swim and you have to save him. On the way in you gash your foot on a broken bottle. When you get back to the picnic, the ants have taken over the cake and a possum has demolished the chicken. Just then the sky opens up. When you gather your things to race for the car, you notice an irritated bull has broken through the fence. The others run for it, but because of your bleeding heel the best you can do is hobble. You have two choices: try to outrun him or stand perfectly still and hope he's interested only in a moving target. At this point, you don't know if your friends can be counted on for help, even the nerd whose life you saved. You don't know if it's true that a bull is attracted by the smell of blood.

A year later, assuming you're around to tell about it, you are still saying, "Let me *tell* you what happened last year." And your listeners are saying, "What a story!"

As Charles Baxter, in *Burning Down the House*, more vividly puts it:

Say what you will about it, Hell is story-friendly. If you want a compelling story, put your protagonist among the damned. The mechanisms of hell are nicely attuned to the mechanisms of narrative. Not so the pleasures of Paradise. Paradise is not a story. It's about what happens when the stories are over.

If it takes trouble to make a picnic into a story, this is equally true of the great themes of life: birth, love, sex, work, and death. Here is a very interesting love story to live: Jan and Jon meet in college. Both are beautiful, intelligent, talented, popular, and well adjusted. They're of the same race, class, religion, and political persuasion. They are sexually compatible. Their parents become fast friends. They marry on graduating, and both get rewarding work in the same city. They have three children, all of whom are healthy, happy, beautiful, intelligent, and popular; the children love and respect their parents to a degree that is the envy of everyone. All the children succeed in work and marriage. Jan and Jon die peacefully, of natural causes, at the same moment, at the age of eighty-two, and are buried in the same grave.

No doubt this love story is very interesting to Jan and Jon, but you can't make a novel of it. Great love stories involve intense passion and a monumental impediment to that passion's fulfillment. So: They love each other passionately, but their parents are sworn enemies (*Romeo and Juliet*). Or: They love each other passionately, but he's black and she's white, and he has an enemy who wants to punish him (*Othello*). Or: They love each other passionately, but she's married (*Anna Karenina*). Or: He loves her passionately, but she falls in love with him only when she has worn out his passion ("Frankly, my dear, I don't give a damn.")

In each of these plots, there is both intense desire and great danger to the achievement of that desire; generally speaking, this shape holds good for all plots. It can be called 3-D: *Drama* equals *desire* plus *danger*. One common fault of talented young writers is to create a main character who is essentially passive. This is an understandable fault; as a writer you are an observer of human nature and activity, and so you identify easily with a character who observes, reflects, and suffers. But such a character's passivity transmits itself to the page, and the story also becomes passive. Charles Baxter regrets that "In writing workshops, this kind of story is often the rule rather than the exception." He calls it:

> the fiction of finger-pointing.... In such fiction, people and events are often accused of turning the protagonist into the kind of person the protagonist is, usually an unhappy person. That's the whole story. When blame has been assigned, the story is over.

In such flawed stories, the central character (and by implication, the story's author) seems to take no responsibility for what that character wants to have happen. This is quite different from Aristotle's rather startling claim that a man *is* his desire.

FICTION IS THE ART FORM OF HUMAN YEARNING. That is absolutely essential to any work of fictional narrative art—a character who yearns. And that is not the same as a character who simply has problems.... The yearning is also the thing that generates what we call plot, because the elements of the plot come from thwarted or blocked or challenged attempts to fulfill that yearning.

ROBERT OLEN BUTLER

In fiction, in order to engage our attention and sympathy, the protagonist must *want*, and want intensely. The thing that the character wants need not be violent or spectacular; it is the intensity of the wanting that introduces an element of danger. A character may want, like the protagonist in David Madden's *The Suicide's Wife*, no more than to get her driver's license, but if so, she must feel that her identity and her future depend on her getting a driver's license, while a corrupt highway patrolman tries to manipulate her. A character may want, like Samuel Beckett's Murphy, only to tie himself to his rocking chair and rock, but if so, he will also want a woman who nags him to get up and get a job. A character may want, like the heroine of Margaret Atwood's *Bodily Harm*, only to get away from it all for a rest, but if so, she must need rest for her survival, while tourists and terrorists involve her in machinations that begin in discomfort and end in mortal danger.

It's important to realize that the great dangers in life and in literature are not necessarily the most spectacular. Another mistake frequently made by young writers is to think that they can best introduce drama into their stories by way of murderers, chase scenes, crashes, and vampires, the external stock dangers of pulp and TV. In fact, all of us know that the most profound impediments to our desire usually lie close to home, in our own bodies, personalities, friends, lovers, and families. Mostly, people have less cause to panic at the approach of a stranger with a gun than of Mama with the curling iron. More passion is destroyed at the breakfast table than in a time warp.

A frequently used critical tool divides possible conflicts into several basic categories: man against man, man against nature, man against society, man against machine, man against God, man against himself. Most stories fall into these categories, and in a literature class they can provide a useful way of discussing and comparing works. But the employment of categories can be misleading insofar as it suggests that literary conflicts take place in these abstract, cosmic dimensions. A writer needs a specific story to tell, and if you sit down to pit "man" against "nature," you will have less of a story than if you pit seventeen-year-old James Tucker of Weehawken, New Jersey, against a two-and-a-half-foot bigmouth bass in the backwoods of Toomsuba, Mississippi. (The value of specificity is a point to which we return again and again.)

Once conflict is established and developed in a story, the conflict must come to a crisis—the final turning point—and a resolution. Order is a major value that literature offers us, and order implies that the subject has been brought to closure. In life this never quite happens, but whether or not the lives of fictional characters end, the story does, and we are left with a satisfying sense of completion.

What I want to do now is to present several ways—they are all essentially metaphors—of seeing this pattern of *conflict-crisis-resolution* in order to make the shape and its variations clearer, and particularly to indicate what a crisis action is.

The Arc of the Story

Novelist John L'Heureux says that a story is about a single moment in a character's life that culminates in a defining choice after which nothing will be the same again. The editor and teacher Mel McKee states flatly that "a story is a war. It is sustained and immediate combat." He offers four imperatives for the writing of this "war" story: (1) get your fighters fighting; (2) make something—the stake—worth their fighting over; (3) have the fight dive into a series of battles, with the last battle in the series the biggest and most dangerous of all; (4) show a walking away from the fight. The stake over which wars are fought is usually a territory, and it's important that this "territory" in a story be as tangible and specific as the Gaza Strip.

Just as a minor "police action" may gradually escalate into a holocaust, story form follows its most natural order of "complications" when each battle is bigger than the last. It begins with a ground skirmish, which does not decide the war. Then one side brings in spies, and the other, guerrillas; these actions do not decide the war. So one side brings in the air force, and the other answers with antiaircraft. One side takes to missiles, and the other answers with rockets. One side has poison gas, and the other has a hand on the nuclear button. Metaphorically, this is what happens in a story. As long as one antagonist can recoup enough power to counterattack, the conflict goes on. But at some point in the story one of the antagonists will produce a weapon from which the other cannot recover. *The crisis action is the last battle and makes the outcome inevitable*; there can no longer be any doubt who wins the particular territory—though there can be much doubt about moral victory. When this has happened, the conflict ends with a significant and permanent *change*—which is the definition, in fiction, of a resolution.

Notice that although a plot involves a desire and a danger to that desire, it does not necessarily end happily if the desire is achieved, nor unhappily if it is not. The more morally complex the story, the less straightforward the idea of winning and losing becomes. In *Hamlet*, Hamlet's desire is to kill King Claudius, and he is prevented from doing so for most of the play by other characters, intrigues, and his own mental state. When he finally succeeds, it is at the cost of every significant life in the play, including his own. Although the hero "wins" his particular "territory," the play is a tragedy. In Margaret Atwood's *Bodily Harm*, on the other hand, the heroine ends up in a political prison. Yet the discovery of her own strength and commitment is such that we know she has achieved salvation. *What does my character win by losing his struggle, or lose by winning?* John L'Heureux suggests that the writer ask.

Patterns of Power

Novelist Michael Shaara described a story as a power struggle between equal forces. It is imperative, he argued, that each antagonist have sufficient power that the reader is left in doubt about the outcome. We may be wholly in sympathy with one character and even reasonably confident that she or he will triumph. But the antagonist must represent a real and potent danger, and the pattern of the story's complications will be achieved by *shifting the power back and forth from one antagonist to the other*. Finally, an action will occur that will shift the power irretrievably in one direction.

"Power" takes many forms—physical strength, charm, knowledge, moral power, wealth, ownership, rank, and so on. Most obvious is the power of brute force, as wielded by mobster Max Blue in Leslie Marmon Silko's epic novel *Almanac of the Dead*:

> ... Max thinks of himself as an executive producer of one-night-only performances, dramas played out in the warm California night breezes, in a phone booth in downtown Long Beach. All Max had done was dial a phone number and listen while the pigeon repeats, "Hello? Hello? Hello? Hello?" until .22-pistol shots snap *pop!pop!* and Max hangs up.

A character who blends several types of power—good looks, artistic talent, social privilege, and the self-assurance that stems from it—is Zavier Chalfant, son of a furniture factory owner in Donald Secreast's story "Summer Help." Zavier is seen through the eyes of Wanda, a longtime employee assigned the coveted job of painting designs on the most expensive pieces. As the plant supervisor introduces them:

> ...Zavier Chalfant was letting his gaze rest lightly on Wanda. Most boys— and that's what Zavier was, after all, a boy of about twenty-one—were very embarrassed their first day on the job. Zavier, in contrast, seemed more amused than embarrassed.... His thick blond hair covered the collar of his jacket but was clean and expertly cut so he looked more like a knight than a hippie.... [H]is face looked like a Viking's face; she'd always been partial to Vikings. Of course, Zavier was too thin to be a Viking all the way down, but he had the face of an adventurer. Of an artist.

Wanda's awe of Zavier's power is confirmed when he easily paints a design she must labor over.

> "Color is my specialty." Zavier deftly added the highlights to the woman's face and hands. "It's everything." He finished the flesh parts in a matter of minutes. He took another brush from Wanda and in six or seven strokes had filled in the woman's robe.

Yet if power is entirely one-sided, suspense will be lost, so it is important to identify a source of power for each character surrounding the story's conflict. Remember that "power" takes many forms, some of which have the external appearance of weakness. Anyone who has ever been tied to the demands of an invalid can understand this: Sickness can be great strength. Weakness, need, passivity, an ostensible desire not to be any trouble to anybody—all these can be used as manipulative tools to prevent the protagonist from achieving his or her desire. Martyrdom is immensely powerful, whether we sympathize with it or not; a dying man absorbs all our energies.

The power of weakness has generated the central conflict in many stories and in such plays as *Uncle Vanya* and *The Glass Menagerie*. Here is a passage in which it is swiftly and deftly sketched:

> This sepulchral atmosphere owed a lot to the presence of Mrs. Taylor herself. She was a tall, stooped woman with deep-set eyes. She sat in her living room all day long and chain-smoked cigarettes and stared out the picture window with an air of unutterable sadness, as if she knew things beyond mortal bearing. Sometimes she would call Taylor over and wrap her arms around him, then close her eyes and hoarsely whisper, "Terence, Terence!" Eyes still closed, she would turn her head and resolutely push him away.

Tobias Wolff, *This Boy's Life*

Connection and Disconnection

Some students, as well as critics, object to the description of narrative as a war or power struggle. Seeing the world in terms of conflict and crisis, of enemies and warring factions, not only constricts the possibilities of literature, they argue, but also promulgates an aggressive and antagonistic view of our own lives.

Speaking of the "gladiatorial view of fiction," Ursula Le Guin writes:

> People are cross-grained, aggressive, and full of trouble, the storytellers tell us; people fight themselves and one another, and their stories are full of their struggles. But to say that that *is* the story is to use one aspect of existence, conflict, to subsume all other aspects, many of which it does not include and does not comprehend.
>
> *Romeo and Juliet* is a story of the conflict between two families, and its plot involves the conflict of two individuals with those families. Is that all it involves? Isn't *Romeo and Juliet* about something else, and isn't it the something else that makes the otherwise trivial tale of a feud into a tragedy?

I'm indebted to dramatist Claudia Johnson for this further—and, it seems to me, crucial—insight about that "something else": Whereas the dynamic of the power struggle has long been acknowledged, narrative is also driven by a pattern of connection and disconnection between characters that is the main source of its emotional effect. Over the course of a story, and within the smaller scale of a scene, characters make and break emotional bonds of trust, love, understanding, or compassion with one another. A connection may be as obvious as a kiss or as subtle as a glimpse; a connection may be broken with an action as obvious as a slap or as subtle as an arched eyebrow.

In *Romeo and Juliet*, for example, the Montague and Capulet families are fiercely disconnected, but the young lovers manage to connect in spite of that. Throughout the play they meet and part, disconnect from their families in order to connect with each other, and finally part from life in order to be with each other eternally. Their ultimate departure in death reconnects the feuding families.

Johnson puts it this way:

> ... [u]nderlying any good story, fictitious or true—is a deeper pattern of change, a pattern of connection and disconnection. The conflict and the surface events are like waves, but underneath is an emotional tide, the ebb and flow of human connection....

Patterns of conflict and connection occur in every story, and sometimes they are evident in much smaller compass, as in this scene from the novel *Stoner* by John Williams. The protagonist of the novel, William Stoner, is an unhappily married English professor who is also a doting father. Prior to the excerpt below, Stoner had been struggling against his feelings for Katherine Driscoll, a graduate student. Katherine has recently failed to show up to teach her classes, and Stoner has overheard another teacher say that Katherine is ill. In this scene Stoner has come to Katherine's apartment with a book to lend her as an excuse to see her and speak with her.

"Perhaps you aren't feeling up to it," he said, "but I ran across something that might be helpful to you, and I thought—"

"I haven't seen you in nearly two weeks," she said and stubbed her cigarette out, twisting it fiercely in the ashtray.

He was taken aback; he said distractedly, "I've been rather busy—so many things—"

"It doesn't matter," she said. "Really, it doesn't. I shouldn't have . . ." She rubbed the palm of her hand across her forehead.

He looked at her with concern; he thought she must be feverish. "I'm sorry you're ill. If there's anything I can—"

"I am not ill," she said. And she added in a voice that was calm, speculative, and almost uninterested, "I am desperately, desperately unhappy."

And still he did not understand. The bare sharp utterance went into him like a blade; he turned a little away from her; he said confusedly, "I'm sorry. Could you tell me about it? If there's anything I can do . . ."

She lifted her head. Her features were stiff, but her eyes were brilliant in pools of tears. "I didn't intend to embarrass you. I'm sorry. You must think me very foolish."

"No," he said. He looked at her for a moment more, at the pale face that seemed held expressionless by an effort of will. Then he gazed at his large bony hands that were clasped together on one knee; the fingers were blunt and heavy, and the knuckles were like white knobs upon the brown flesh.

He said at last, heavily and slowly, "In many ways I am an ignorant man; it is I who am foolish, not you. I have not come to see you because I thought—I felt that I was becoming a nuisance. Maybe that was not true."

"No," she said. "No, it wasn't true."

Still not looking at her, he continued, "And I didn't want to cause you the discomfort of having to deal with—with my feelings for you, which, I knew, sooner or later, would become obvious if I kept seeing you."

She did not move; two tears welled over her lashes and ran down her cheeks; she did not brush them away.

"I was perhaps selfish. I felt that nothing could come of this except awkwardness for you and unhappiness for me. You know my—circumstances. It seemed to me impossible that you could—that you could feel for me anything but—"

"Shut up," she said softly, fiercely. "Oh, my dear, shut up and come over here."

In this short excerpt, both characters, naturally reticent and controlled people, are struggling to understand what is happening both to themselves and to their friendship. Only through a series of uncomfortable, unsuccessful attempts at communication does the truth become obvious to them both. Although they are finally able to declare their feeling for each other, the reader also sees that their painful awareness of their situation doesn't bode well for the future.

While the pattern of either conflict or connection may dominate in a given work, "stories are about *both* conflict and connection," says novelist and poet Robert Morgan.

A story which is only about conflict will be shallow. There must be some deepening of our understanding of the characters. Stories are rarely just about conflicts between good and bad. They are more often about conflicts of loyalty, one good versus another: does a man join up to serve his country, or stay home to help protect and raise his children? The writer strives to bring art to a level where a story is not so much a plot as about human connection, and not just about the conflict of good versus bad, but about the conflict of loyalty with loyalty.

Human wills clash; human belonging is necessary. In discussing human behavior, psychologists speak in terms of "tower" and "network" patterns, the need to climb (which implies conflict) and the need for community, the need to win out over others and the need to belong to others; and these two forces also drive fiction. Like conflict and its complications, connection and its complications can produce a pattern of change, and both inform the process of change recorded in scene and story.

Story Form as an Inverted Check Mark

The nineteenth-century German critic Gustav Freitag analyzed plot in terms of a pyramid of five actions: an exposition, followed by a complication (or *nouement,* "knotting up," of the situation), leading to a crisis, which is followed by a "falling action" or anticlimax, resulting in a resolution (or *dénouement,* "unknotting").

In the compact short-story form, the falling action is likely to be very brief or nonexistent, and often the crisis action itself implies the resolution, which is not necessarily stated but exists as an idea established in the reader's mind.

So for our purposes it is probably more useful to think of story shape not as a pyramid with sides of equal length but as an inverted check mark. If we take the familiar tale of Cinderella and diagram its power struggle using this model, we can see how the various elements reveal themselves even in this simple children's story.

At the opening of the tale we're given the basic conflict: Cinderella's mother has died, and her father has married a brutal woman with two waspish daughters. Cinderella is made to do all the dirtiest and most menial work, and

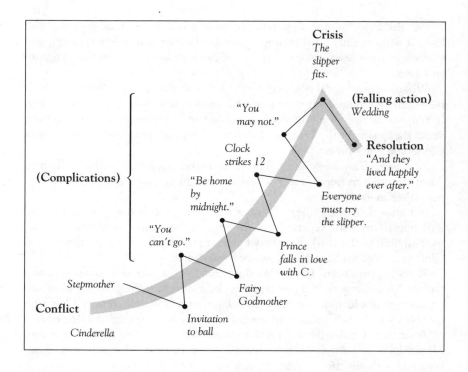

she weeps among the cinders. The Stepmother has on her side the strength of ugliness and evil (two very powerful qualities in literature, as in life). With her daughters she also has the strength of numbers, and she has parental authority. Cinderella has only beauty and goodness, but (in literature and life) these are also very powerful.

At the beginning of the struggle in "Cinderella," the power is very clearly on the Stepmother's side. But the first event (action, battle) of the story is that an invitation arrives from the Prince, which explicitly states that *all* the ladies of the land are invited to a ball. Notice that Cinderella's desire is not to triumph over her Stepmother (though she eventually will, much to our satisfaction); such a desire would diminish her goodness. She simply wants to be relieved of her mistreatment. She wants equality, so that the Prince's invitation, which specifically gives her a right equal to the Stepmother's and Stepsisters' rights, shifts the power to her.

The Stepmother takes the power back by blunt force: You may not go; you must get us ready to go. Cinderella does so, and the three leave for the ball.

Then what happens? The Fairy Godmother appears. It is *very* powerful to have magic on your side. The Fairy Godmother offers Cinderella a gown, glass slippers, and a coach with horses and footmen, giving her more force than she has yet had.

But the magic is not all-potent. It has a qualification that portends bad luck. It will last only until midnight (unlike the Stepmother's authority), and Cinderella must leave the ball before the clock strikes twelve or risk exposure and defeat.

What happens next? She goes to the ball and the Prince falls in love with her—and love is an even more powerful weapon than magic in a literary war. In some versions of the tale, the Stepmother and Stepsisters are made to marvel at the beauty of the Princess they don't recognize, pointing to the irony of Cinderella's new power.

And then? The magic quits. The clock strikes twelve, and Cinderella runs down the steps in her rags to her rats and pumpkin, losing a slipper, bereft of her power in every way.

But after that, the Prince sends out a messenger with the glass slipper and a dictum (a dramatic repetition of the original invitation in which all ladies were invited to the ball) that every female in the land is to try on the slipper. Cinderella is given her rights again by royal decree.

What happens then? In most good retellings of the tale, the Stepmother also repeats her assumption of brute authority by hiding Cinderella away, while our expectation of triumph is tantalizingly delayed with grotesque comedy: One sister cuts off a toe, the other a heel, trying to fit into the heroine's rightful slipper.

After that, Cinderella tries on the slipper and it fits. *This is the crisis action.* Magic, love, and royalty join to recognize the heroine's true self; evil, numbers, and authority are powerless against them. At this point, the power struggle has been decided; the outcome is inevitable. When the slipper fits, no further action can occur that will deprive Cinderella of her desire. Nothing will be the same again: The change in the lives of all concerned is significant and permanent.

The tale has a brief "falling action" or "walking away from the fight," when the Prince sweeps Cinderella up on his white horse and gallops away to their wedding. The story comes to closure with the classic resolution of all comedy: They lived happily ever after.

If we also look at "Cinderella" in terms of connection/disconnection, we see a pattern as clear as that represented by the power struggle. The first painful disconnection is that Cinderella's mother has died; her father has married (connected with) a woman who spurns (disconnects from) her; the Prince's invitation offers connection; the Stepmother's cruelty alienates again. The Fairy Godmother connects as a magical friend, but the disappearance of the coach and gown disconnect Cinderella temporarily from that grand and glorious fairy-tale union, marriage to the Prince. If we consult the emotions that this tale engenders—pity, anger, hope, fear, romance, anticipation, disappointment, triumph—we see that both the struggle between antagonist/protagonist and the pattern of alienation/connectedness is necessary to ensure not only that there is an action but also that we care about its outcome. The traditional happy ending, marriage, is the grand connection; the traditional tragic outcome, death, is the final disconnection.

Aʀᴛ ɪꜱ ᴘʟᴇᴀꜱɪɴɢ ʏᴏᴜʀꜱᴇʟꜰ.…But you can please yourself and it won't be art. Art is having the mastery to take your experience, whether it's visual or mental, and make meaningful shapes that convey a reality to others.

GAIL GODWIN

In the *Poetics*, the first work of Western literary criticism, Aristotle referred to the crisis action of a tragedy as a *peripeteia*, or reversal of the protagonist's fortunes. Critics and editors agree that a reversal of some sort is necessary to all story structure, comic as well as tragic. Although the protagonist need not lose power, land, or life, he or she must in some significant way be changed or moved by the action. Aristotle specified that this reversal came about because of *hamartia*, which has for centuries been translated as a "tragic flaw" in the protagonist's character, usually assumed to be, or defined as, pride. But more recent critics have defined and translated *hamartia* much more narrowly as a "mistake in identity," with the reversal coming about in a "recognition."

It is true that recognition scenes have played a disproportionately large role in the crisis actions of plots both comic and tragic, and that these scenes frequently stretch credibility. In real life, you are unlikely to mistake the face of your mother, son, uncle, or even friend, and yet such mistakes have provided the turning point of many traditional plots. If, however, the notion of "recognition" is extended to more abstract and subtle realms, it becomes a powerful metaphor for moments of "realization." In other words, the "recognition scene" in literature may stand for that moment in life when we "recognize" that the man we have considered good is evil, the event we have considered insignificant is crucial, the woman we have thought out of touch with reality is a genius, the object we have thought desirable is poison. There is in this symbolic way a recognition in "Cinderella." *We* knew that she was essentially a princess, but until the Prince recognizes her as one, our knowledge must be frustrated.

James Joyce developed a similar idea when he spoke of, and recorded both in his notebooks and in his stories, moments of what he called *epiphany*. As Joyce saw it, epiphany is a crisis action in the mind, a moment when a person, an event, or a thing is seen in a light so new that it is as if it has never been seen before. At this recognition, the mental landscape of the viewer is permanently changed.

In many of the finest modern short stories and novels, the true territory of struggle is the main character's mind, and so the real crisis action must occur there. Yet it is important to grasp that Joyce chose the word *epiphany* to represent this moment of reversal, and that the word means "a *manifestation* of a supernatural being"—specifically, in Christian doctrine, "the manifesta-tion of Christ to the gentiles." By extension, then, in a short story any mental reversal that takes place in the crisis of a story must be *manifested*; it must be triggered or shown by an action. The slipper must fit. It would not do if the Stepmother just happened to change her mind and give up the struggle; it would not do if the Prince just happened to notice that Cinderella looked like his love. The moment of recognition must be manifested in an action.

This point, that the crisis must be manifested or externalized in an action, is absolutely central, although sometimes difficult to grasp when the struggle of the story takes place in a character's mind. In a revenge story, it is easy to see how the conflict must come to crisis. The common revenge plot, from *Hamlet* to *Django Unchained*, takes this form: Someone important to the hero (family member, lover, friend) is killed, and for some reason the authorities who ought to be in charge of justice can't or won't avenge the death. The hero (or heroes) must do so, then, and the crisis action is manifested in the dagger, the sword, the pistol, the poison, or the explosion.

But suppose the story is about a struggle between two brothers on a fish-ing trip, and the change that takes place is that the protagonist, believing for most of the action that he holds his older brother in contempt, discovers at the end of the story that they are deeply bound by love and family history. Clearly this change is an epiphany, a mental reversal. A writer insufficiently aware of the nature of crisis action might signal the change in a paragraph that begins "Suddenly Larry remembered their father and realized that Jeff was very much like him." Well, unless that memory and that realization are manifested in an action, the reader is unable to share them, and therefore cannot be moved with the character.

> Jeff reached for the old net and neatly bagged the trout, swinging round to offer it with a triumphant "Got it! We got it, didn't we?" The trout flipped and struggled, giving off a smell of weed and water and fecund mud. Jeff's knuckles were lined with grime. The knuckles and the rich river smell filled him with a memory of their first fishing trip together, the sight of their father's hands on the same scarred net…

Here the epiphany, a memory leading to a realization, is triggered by an action and sensory details that the reader can share; the reader now has a good chance of also being able to share the epiphany. Less commonly, a story may offer readers an epiphany that the main character neglects to see, as in the short story "Everything That Rises Must Converge," which appears at the end of this chapter. Such characters are often on the verge of great change, yet lack the maturity or courage to take that difficult leap to recognition.

Much great fiction, and the preponderance of serious modern fiction, echoes life in its suggestion that there are no clear or permanent solutions, that the conflicts of character, relationship, and the cosmos cannot be permanently resolved. Most of the stories in this volume end, in Vladimir Nabokov's words, "with no definite full-stop, but with the natural motion of life." None could end "they lived happily ever after" or even "they lived unhappily ever after."

Yet the story form demands a resolution. Is there such a thing as a no-resolution resolution? Yes, and it has a very specific form. Go back to the metaphor that "a story is a war." After the skirmish, after the guerrillas, after the air strike, after the poison gas and the nuclear holocaust, imagine that the two surviving combatants, one on each side, emerge from their fallout shelters. They crawl, then stumble to the fence that marks the border. Each possessively grasps the barbed wire with a bloodied fist. The "resolution" of this battle is that neither side will ever give up and that no one will ever win; *there will never be a resolution*. This is a distinct reversal (the recognition takes place in the reader's mind) of the opening scene, in which it seemed eminently worthwhile to open a ground skirmish. In the statement of the conflict was an inherent possibility that one side or the other could win. Inherent in the resolution is a statement that no one can ever win. That is a distinct reversal and a powerful change.

Story and Plot

So far, I have used the words "story" and "plot" interchangeably. The equation of the two terms is so common that they are often comfortably understood as synonyms. When an editor says, "This is not a story," the implication is not that it lacks characters, theme, setting, or even incident, but that it has no plot.

Yet there is a distinction frequently drawn between the two terms, a distinction that although simple in itself gives rise to manifold subtleties in the craft of narrative and also represents a vital decision that you as a writer must make: Where should your narrative begin?

The distinction is easily made. A *story* is a series of events recorded in their chronological order. A *plot* is a series of events deliberately arranged so as to reveal their dramatic, thematic, and emotional significance. A story gives us only "what happened next," whereas plot's concern is "what, how, and why," with scenes ordered to highlight the workings of cause and effect.

Here, for example, is a fairly standard story: A sober, industrious, and rather dull young man meets the woman of his dreams. She is beautiful, brilliant, passionate, and compassionate; more wonderful still, she loves him. They plan to marry, and on the eve of their wedding his friends give him a stag party in the course of which they tease him, ply him with liquor, and drag him off to a whorehouse for a last fling. There he stumbles into a cubicle ... to find himself facing his bride-to-be.

Where does this story become interesting? Where does the *plot* begin?

You may start, if you like, with the young man's *Mayflower* ancestry. But if you do, it's going to be a very long story, and we're likely to close the book about the middle of the nineteenth century. You may begin with the first time he meets the extraordinary woman, but even then you must cover at least weeks, probably months, in a few pages. And that means you must summarize, skip, and generalize, and you'll have a hard time both maintaining your cred-ibility and holding our attention. Begin at the stag party? Better. If you do so, you will somehow have to let us know all that has gone before, either through dialogue or through the young man's memory, but you have only one evening of action to cover, and we'll get to the conflict quickly. Suppose you begin instead the next morning, when the man wakes with a hangover in bed in a brothel with his bride on his wedding day. Is that, perhaps, the best of all? An immediate conflict that must lead to a quick and striking crisis?

E. M. Forster distinguishes between plot and story by describing story as:

> the chopped off length of the tape worm of time ... a narrative of events arranged in their time sequence. A plot is also a narrative of events, the emphasis falling on causality. "The king died, and then the queen died," is a story. "The king died, and then the queen died of grief," is a plot. The time sequence is preserved, but the sense of causality overshadows it. Or again: "The queen died, no one knew why, until it was discovered that it was through grief at the death of the king." This is a plot with a mystery in it, a form capable of high development. It suspends the time sequence, it moves as far away from the story as its limitations will allow. Consider the death of the queen. If it is in a story we say, "and then?" If it is in a plot we ask, "why?"

The human desire to know *why* is as powerful as the desire to know what happened next, and it is a desire of a higher order. Once we have the facts, we inevitably look for the links between them, and only when we find such links are we satisfied that we "understand." Rote memorization in a science class bores almost everyone. Grasp and a sense of discovery begin only when we perceive *why* "a body in motion tends to remain in motion" and what an immense effect this actuality has on the phenomena of our lives.

A STORY HAS TO BE A GOOD DATE, because the reader can stop at any time....Remember, readers are selfish and have no compul-sion to be decent about anything.

KURT VONNEGUT

The same is true of the events of a story. Random incidents neither move nor illuminate; we want to know why one thing leads to another and to feel the inevitability of cause and effect.

Here is a series of uninteresting events chronologically arranged.

> Ariadne had a bad dream.
> She woke up tired and cross.
> She ate breakfast.
> She headed for class.
> She saw Leroy.
> She fell on the steps and broke her ankle.
> Leroy offered to take notes for her.
> She went to a hospital.

This series of events does not constitute a plot, and if you wish to fashion it into a plot, you can do so only by letting us know the meaningful relations among the events. We first assume that Ariadne woke in a temper because of her bad dream, and that Leroy offered to take notes for her because she broke her ankle. But why did she fall? Perhaps because she saw Leroy? Does that suggest that her bad dream was about him? Was she, then, thinking about his dream-rejection as she broke her egg irritably on the edge of the frying pan? What is the effect of his offer? Is it a triumph or just another polite form of rejection when, really, he could have missed class once to drive her to the X-ray lab? The emotional and dramatic significance of these ordinary events emerges in the relation of cause to effect, and where such relation can be shown, a possible plot comes into existence. Notice also that in this brief attempt to form the events into a plot, I have introduced both conflict and a pattern of connection/disconnection.

Ariadne's is a story you might very well choose to tell chronologically: It needs to cover only an hour or two, and that much can be handled in the compressed form of the short story. But such a choice of plot is not inevitable even in this short compass. Might it be more gripping to begin with the wince of pain as she stumbles? Leroy comes to help her up and the yolk yellow of his T-shirt fills her field of vision. In the shock of pain she is immediately back in her dream...

When "nothing happens" in a story, it is because we fail to sense the causal relationship between what happens first and what happens next. When something does "happen," it is because the resolution of a short story or a novel describes a change in the character's life, an effect of the events that have gone before. This is why Aristotle insisted with such apparent simplicity on "a beginning, a middle, and an end." A story is capable of many meanings, and it is first of all in the choice of structure—which portion of the story forms the plot—that you offer us the gratifying sense that we "understand."

The Short Story and the Novel

Many editors and writers insist that the short story and the novel are vastly different creatures. It is my belief, however, that, like the distinction between story and plot, the distinction between the two forms is very simple, and the many and profound possibilities of difference proceed from that simple source: A short story is short, and a novel is long.

Because of this, a short story can waste no words. It usually features the perspective of one or a very few characters. It may recount only one central action and one major change in the life of the central character or characters. It can afford no digression that does not directly affect the action. A short story strives to create what Edgar Allan Poe called "the single effect"—a single emotional impact that imparts a flash of understanding, though both impact and understanding may be complex. The virtue of a short story is its density, for it raises a single "what if" question, while a novel may raise many. If it is tight, sharp, economical, well knit, and charged, then it is a good short story because it has exploited a central attribute of the form—that it is short.

Occasionally in workshops, a new writer struggling to craft the shape of conflict-crisis-resolution may wonder if a story's lack of one of these elements means the work "must be a novel." Tempting as this hope may be, it only sidesteps the inevitable challenge of plotting, for not only must a novel have a large-scale plot structure, but individual chapters or episodes frequently are shaped around a pattern of conflict-crisis-incremental change that propels the novel onward.

Further, while no literary form is superior to another, few novelists achieve publication without first having crafted any number of short stories. The greater the limitation of space, the greater the necessity for pace, sharpness, and density. Short stories ask the writer to rise to the challenges of shaping, "showing," and making significance again and again, experiences that later may save that writer countless hours and pages when the time to tackle a novel comes along.

The form of the novel is an expanded story form. It asks for a conflict, a crisis, and a resolution, and no technique described in this book is irrelevant to its effectiveness.

Types of Fiction

While it's true that all stories need characters, a plot, a setting, and a particular point of view, it's also true that different types of fiction emphasize some of these elements more than others—and conceive of them in their own particular ways.

Readers of **genre fiction** have very specific expectations when it comes to plot, characters, setting, and theme, and each specific genre has its own conventions and rules. Genre fiction includes westerns, detective stories, spy stories, romance, science fiction, horror, and so on. Literary fiction differs from genre fiction fundamentally in the fact that the former is character-driven, the latter plot-driven. There is a strong tendency—though it is not a binding rule—of genre fiction to imply that life is fair and to let the hero or heroine, after great struggle, win out in the end; and of literary fiction to posit that life is not fair, that triumph is partial and happiness tentative, and that the heroine and hero are subject to mortality. Literary fiction also strives to reveal its meaning through the creation of unexpected or unusual characters, through patterns of action and turns of event that will surprise the reader. Genre fiction, on the other hand, tends to develop character stereotypes and set patterns of action that become part of the expectation, the demand, and the pleasure of the readers of that genre.

Readers of the **romance**, which has its roots in the fiction of the Bronte sisters, will expect a plucky-but-down-on-her-luck heroine, a handsome and mysterious hero with some dark secret (usually a dark-haired woman) in his background, a large house, some woods (through which the heroine will at some point flee in scanty clothing), and an eventual happy ending with the heroine in the hero's arms.

The **detective story** evolved simultaneously with widespread and intense interest in science, plus an optimistic expectation that violence and mystery could be rationally explained. The **western** dealt with the ambivalence felt by large numbers of westward-traveling Euro-Americans about the civilizing of the wilderness, the desire to rid the West of its brutality, the fear that "taming" it would also destroy its promise of solitude.

Science fiction, the most recently developed and still-developing genre, similarly deals with ambivalence—but about technology, the near-miraculous accomplishments of the human race through science, the dangers to human feeling, soul, and environment. The surge in popularity of **fantasy fiction** can probably be attributed to nostalgia for a time more free of technological accomplishment and threat, since fantasy employs a medieval setting and solves problems through magic. In contrast, science fiction is set in the future and solves problems through intelligence and technology. It is relevant that science fiction usually deals with some problem that can be seen to have a counterpart in contemporary culture (space travel, international or interplanetary intrigue, mechanical replacement of body parts, genetic manipulation), while the plots of fantasies tend to deal with obsolete or archaic traumas (wicked overlords, demon interlopers, and so forth).

Many teachers of fiction writing do not accept manuscripts in genre, believing that whereas writing literary fiction can teach you how to write good genre fiction, writing genre fiction does not teach you how to write good literary fiction—does not, in effect, teach you "how to write," by which I mean how to be original and meaningful in words.

Other teachers might take a slightly different stance, telling students that if they want to write stories featuring vampires or Vulcans, they may go ahead, but that they are not immune from reader expectations about what makes a good story—that is, character development, believable plot, vivid setting, nuanced use of theme, and so forth.

In any case, the tendency of recent literature is to move further away from rigid categories, toward a loosening or crossing of genres. Genre fiction is pressing at the bounds of literary fiction. Many writers are eager to experiment with pieces that blur the distinctions, approaching genre fiction with literary ambition and intent. Justin Cronin is writing a trilogy of literary vampire stories. Dan Chaon writes literary horror stories. Michael Chabon and Kate Atkinson have both written literary detective fiction. Ursula K. Le Guin, Margaret Atwood, and Doris Lessing have written literary science fiction, and Robert Coover and Angela Carter have published literary fairy tales.

Magic realism uses the techniques and devices of realism—verisimilitude, ordinary lives and settings, familiar psychology—and introduces events of impossible or fantastic nature, never leaving the tone and techniques of realism. Whereas fantasy will attempt to bedazzle its readers with the amazing quality of the magic, magic realism works in the opposite direction, to convince the reader that the extraordinary occurs in the context and the guise of the ordinary. For instance, in "St. Lucy's Home for Girls Raised by Wolves" (Chapter 5) young girls coming of age in a boarding school just happen to have had wolves for parents, and in "Mud" (this chapter) a man preparing to leave home for an important appointment is detained by the sudden appearance of his grandmother, his father, and his wife, all of whom happen to be dead.

David Lodge, in *The Art of Fiction*, interestingly points out that some of the practitioners of magic realism tend to have lived through some sort of historical upheaval—a political coup or terror, a literal war or gender war. Flight, he points out, is a central image in this fiction, because the defiance of gravity represents a persistent "human dream of the impossible." Colombian novelist Gabriel García Márquez is a foremost practitioner of magic realism, and his novel *One Hundred Years of Solitude* is the best-known example of the genre. Interested readers might also look for *Labyrinths* by Jorge Luis Borges, who is often considered the father of this experimental mode.

Experimental fiction is difficult to define, because by definition the experimental is the thing that nobody expects or predicts. There are, however, a number of kinds of experiments that have come to be recognized as subsets of literary fiction. For instance, **metafiction** takes as its subject matter the writing of fiction, calls attention to its own techniques, and insists that what is happening is that a story is being written and read. Often, the writing of the story is used as a metaphor for some other human struggle or endeavor.

Minimalism (also called miniaturism) refers to a flat, spare, and subdued style of writing, characterized by an accumulation of (sometimes apparently random) detail that gives an impression of benumbed emotion. The point of view tends to be objective or near-objective, the events accumulating toward a tense, disturbing—and inconclusive—conclusion.

The **short-short story**, or **sudden fiction**, is a fiction under 2,000 words. "Bullet in the Brain," "The Flowers," "Currents," "Mud," and "Reply All" are all examples of sudden fiction that appear in this book. **Microfiction** is a term sometimes used to distinguish stories under 250 words. Such pieces, according to Nancy Huddleston Packer, "push to the limit the basic elements of all short stories—compression, suggestion, and change. They combine the intensity and lyricism of a poem with the dramatic impact and movement of a short story— these stories are so compressed, they explode." In a short-short story, change is often subtle, taking form as a moment of surprise or a shift in perception.

Escapes

JOY WILLIAMS

When I was very small, my father said, "Lizzie, I want to tell you something about your grandfather. Just before he died, he was alive. Fifteen minutes before."

I had never known my grandfather. This was the most extraordinary thing I had ever heard about him.

Still, I said, No.

"No!" my father said. "What do you mean, 'No.'" He laughed.

I shook my head.

"All right," my father said, "it was one minute before. I thought you were too little to know such things, but I see you're not. It was even less than a minute. It was one *moment* before."

"Oh stop teasing her," my mother said to my father.

"He's just teasing you, Lizzie," my mother said.

In warm weather once we drove up into the mountains, my mother, my father and I, and stayed for several days at a resort lodge on a lake. In the afternoons, horse races took place in the lodge. The horses were blocks of wood with numbers painted on them, moved from one end of the room to the other by ladies in ball gowns. There was a long pier that led out into the lake and at the end of the pier was a nightclub that had a twenty-foot-tall champagne glass on the roof. At night, someone would pull a switch and neon bubbles would spring out from the lit glass into the black air. I very much wanted such a glass on the roof of our own house and I wanted to be the one who, every night, would turn on the switch. My mother always said about this, "We'll see."

I saw an odd thing once, there in the mountains. I saw my father, pretending to be lame. This was in the midst of strangers in the gift shop of the lodge. The shop sold hand-carved canes, among many other things, and when I came in to buy bubble gum in the shape of cigarettes, to which I was devoted, I saw my father, hobbling painfully down the aisle, leaning heavily on a dully gleaming yellow cane, his shoulders hunched, one leg turned out at a curious angle. My handsome, healthy father, his face drawn in dreams. He looked at me. And then he looked away as though he did not know me.

My mother was a drinker. Because my father left us, I assumed he was not a drinker, but this may not have been the case. My mother loved me and was always kind to me. We spent a great deal of time together, my mother and I. This was before I knew how to read. I suspected there was a trick to reading, but I did not know the trick. Written words were something between me and a place I could not go. My mother went back and forth to that place all the time, but couldn't explain to me exactly what it was like there, so I imagined it to be a different place.

As a very young child, my mother had seen the magician Houdini. Houdini had made an elephant disappear. He had also made an orange tree grow from a seed right on the stage. Bright oranges hung from the tree and he had picked them and thrown them out into the audience. People could eat the oranges or take them home, whatever they wanted.

How did he make the elephant disappear, I asked.

"He disappeared in a puff of smoke," my mother said. "Houdini said that even the elephant didn't know how it was done."

Was it a baby elephant, I asked.

My mother sipped her drink. She said that Houdini was more than a magician, he was an escape artist. She said that he could escape from handcuffs and chains and ropes.

"They put him in straitjackets and locked him in trunks and threw him in swimming pools and rivers and oceans and he escaped," my mother said. "He escaped from water-filled vaults. He escaped from coffins."

I said that I wanted to see Houdini.

"Oh, Houdini's dead, Lizzie," my mother said. "He died a long time ago. A man punched him in the stomach three times and he died."

Dead. I asked if he couldn't get out of being dead.

"He met his match there," my mother said.

She said that he turned a bowl of flowers into a pony who cantered around the stage.

"He sawed a lady in half too, Lizzie." Oh, how I wanted to be that lady, sawed in half and then made whole again!

My mother spoke happily, laughing. We sat at the kitchen table and my mother was drinking from a small glass which rested snugly in her hand. It was my favorite glass too but she never let me drink from it. There were all kinds of glasses in our cupboard but this was the one we both liked. This was in Maine. Outside, in the yard, was our car which was an old blue convertible.

Was there blood, I asked.

"No, Lizzie, no. He was a magician!"

Did she cry, that lady, I wanted to know.

"I don't think so," my mother said. "Maybe he hypnotized her first."

It was winter. My father had never ridden in the blue convertible which my mother had bought after he had gone. The car was old then, and was rusted here and there. Beneath the rubber mat on my side, the passenger side, part of the floor had rusted through completely. When we went anywhere in the car, I would sometimes lift up the mat so I could see the road rushing past beneath us and feel the cold round air as it came up through the hole. I would pretend that the coldness was trying to speak to me, in the same way that words written down tried to speak. The air wanted to tell me something, but I didn't care about it, that's what I thought. Outside, the car stood in the snow.

I had a dream about the car. My mother and I were alone together as we always were, linked in our hopeless and uncomprehending love of one another, and we were driving to a house. It seemed to be our destination but we only arrived to move on. We drove again, always returning to the house which we would circle and leave, only to arrive at it again. As we drove, the inside of the car grew hair. The hair was gray and it grew and grew. I never told my mother about this dream just as I had never told her about my father leaning on the cane. I was a secretive person. In that way, I was like my mother.

I wanted to know more about Houdini. Was Houdini in love, did Houdini love someone, I asked.

"Rosabelle," my mother said. "He loved his wife, Rosabelle."

I went and got a glass and poured some ginger ale in it and I sipped my ginger ale slowly in the way that I had seen my mother sip her drink many, many times. Even then, I had the gestures down. I sat opposite her, very still and quiet, pretending.

But then I wanted to know was there magic in the way he loved her. Could he make her disappear. Could he make both of them disappear was the way I put my question.

"Rosabelle," my mother said. "No one knew anything about Rosabelle except that Houdini loved her. He never turned their love into loneliness which would have been beneath him of course."

We ate our supper and after supper my mother would have another little bit to drink. Then she would read articles from the newspaper aloud to me.

"My goodness," she said, "what a strange story. A hunter shot a bear who was carrying a woman's pocketbook in its mouth."

Oh, oh, I cried. I looked at the newspaper and struck it with my fingers. My mother read on, a little oblivious to me. The woman had lost her purse years before on a camping trip. Everything was still inside it, her wallet and her compact and her keys.

Oh, I cried. I thought this was terrible. I was frightened, thinking of my mother's pocketbook, the way she carried it always, and the poor bear too.

Why did the bear want to carry a pocketbook, I asked.

My mother looked up from the words in the newspaper. It was as though she had come back into the room I was in.

"Why, Lizzie," she said.

The poor bear, I said.

"Oh, the bear is all right," my mother said. "The bear got away."

I did not believe this was the case. She herself said the bear had been shot.

"The bear escaped," my mother said. "It says so right here," and she ran her finger along a line of words. "It ran back into the woods to its home." She stood up and came around the table and kissed me. She smelled then like the glass that was always in the sink in the morning, and the smell reminds me still of daring and deception, hopes and little lies.

I shut my eyes and in that way I felt I could not hear my mother. I saw the bear holding the pocketbook, walking through the woods with it, feeling fine in a different way and pretty too, then stopping to find something in it, wanting something, moving its big paw through the pocketbook's small things.

"Lizzie," my mother called to me. My mother did not know where I was which alarmed me. I opened my eyes.

"Don't cry, Lizzie," my mother said. She looked as though she were about to cry too. This was the way it often was at night, late in the kitchen, with my mother.

My mother returned to the newspaper and began to turn the pages. She called my attention to the drawing of a man holding a hat with stars sprinkling out of it. It was an advertisement for a magician who would be performing not far away. We decided we would see him. My mother knew just the seats she wanted for us, good seats, on the aisle close to the stage. We might be called up on the stage, she said, to be part of the performance. Magicians often used people from the audience, particularly children. I might even be given a rabbit.

I wanted a rabbit.

I put my hands on the table and I could see the rabbit between them. He was solid white in the front and solid black in the back as though he were made up of two rabbits. There are rabbits like that. I saw him there, before me on the table, a nice rabbit.

My mother went to the phone and ordered two tickets, and not many days after that, we were in our car driving to Portland for the matinee performance. I very much liked the word matinee. Matinee, matinee, I said. There was a broad hump on the floor between our seats and it was here where my mother put her little glass, the glass often full, never, it seemed, more than half empty. We chatted together and I thought we must have appeared interesting to others as we passed by in our convertible in winter. My mother spoke about happiness. She told me that the happiness that comes out of nowhere, out of nothing, is the very best kind. We paid no attention to the coldness which was speaking in the way that it had, but enjoyed the sun which beat through the windshield upon our pale hands.

My mother said that Houdini had black eyes and that white doves flew from his fingertips. She said that he escaped from a block of ice.

Did he look like my father, Houdini, I asked. Did he have a mustache.

"Your father didn't have a mustache," my mother said, laughing. "Oh, I wish I could be more like you."

Later, she said, "Maybe he didn't escape from a block of ice, I'm not sure about that. Maybe he wanted to, but he never did."

We stopped for lunch somewhere, a dark little restaurant along the road. My mother had cocktails and I myself drank something cold and sweet. The restaurant was not very nice. It smelled of smoke and dampness as though once it had burned down, and it was so noisy that I could not hear my mother very well. My mother looked like a woman in a bar, pretty and disturbed, hunched forward saying, who do you think I look like, will you remember me? She was saying all matter of things. We lingered there, and then my mother asked the time of someone and seemed surprised. My mother was always surprised by time. Outside, there were woods of green fir trees whose lowest branches swept the ground, and as we were getting back into the car, I believed I saw something moving far back in the darkness of the woods beyond the slick, snowy square of the parking lot. It was the bear, I thought. Hurry, hurry, I thought. The hunter is playing with his children. He is making them something to play in as my father had once made a small playhouse for me. He is not the hunter yet. But in my heart I knew the bear was gone and the shape was just the shadow of something else in the afternoon.

My mother drove very fast but the performance had already begun when we arrived. My mother's face was damp and her good blouse had a spot on it. She went into the ladies' room and when she returned the spot was larger, but it was water now and not what it had been before. The usher assured us that we had not missed much. The usher said that the magician was not very good, that he talked and talked, he told a lot of jokes and then when you were bored and distracted, something would happen, something would have changed. The usher smiled at my mother. He seemed to like her, even know her in some way. He was a small man, like an old boy, balding. I did not care for him. He led us to our seats, but there were people sitting in them and there was a small disturbance as the strangers rearranged themselves. We were both expectant, my mother and I, and we watched the magician intently. My mother's lips were parted, and her eyes were bright. On the stage were a group of children about my age, each with a hand on a small cage the magician was holding. In the cage was a tiny bird. The magician would ask the children to jostle the cage occasionally and the bird would flutter against the bars so that everyone would see it was a real thing with bones and breath and feelings too. Each child announced that they had a firm grip on the bars. Then the magician put a cloth over the cage, gave a quick tug and cage and bird vanished. I was not surprised. It seemed just the kind of thing that was going to happen. I decided to withhold my applause when I saw that my mother's hands too were in her lap. There were several more tricks of the magician's invention, certainly nothing I would have asked him to do. Large constructions of many parts and colors were wheeled onto the stage. There were doors everywhere which the magician opened and slammed shut. Things came and went, all to the accompaniment of loud music. I was confused and grew hot. My mother too moved restlessly in the next seat. Then there was an intermission and we returned to the lobby.

"This man is a far, far cry from the great Houdini," my mother said.

What were his intentions exactly, I asked.

He had taken a watch from a man in the audience and smashed it for all to see with a hammer. Then the watch, unharmed, had reappeared behind the man's ear.

"A happy memory can be a very misleading thing," my mother said. "Would you like to go home?"

I did not want to leave really. I wanted to see it through. I held the glossy program in my hand and turned the pages. I stared hard at the print beneath the pictures and imagined all sorts of promises being made.

"Yes, we want to see how it's done, don't we, you and I," my mother said. "We want to get to the bottom of it."

I guessed we did.

"All right, Lizzie," my mother said, "but I have to get something out of the car. I'll be right back."

I waited for her in a corner of the lobby. Some children looked at me and I looked back. I had a package of gum cigarettes in my pocket and I extracted one carefully and placed the end in my mouth. I held the elbow of my right arm with my left hand and smoked the cigarette for a long time and then I folded it up in my mouth and I chewed it for a while. My mother had not yet returned when the performance began again. She was having a little drink, I knew, and she was where she went when she drank without me, somewhere in herself. It was not the place where words could take you but another place even. I stood alone in the lobby for a while, looking out into the street. On the sidewalk outside the theater, sand had been scattered and the sand ate through the ice in ugly holes. I saw no one like my mother who passed by. She was wearing a red coat. Once she had said to me, You've fallen out of love with me, haven't you, and I knew she was thinking I was someone else, but this had happened only once.

I heard the music from the stage and I finally returned to our seats. There were not as many people in the audience as before. On stage with the magician was a woman in a bathing suit and high-heeled shoes holding a chain saw. The magician demonstrated that the saw was real by cutting up several pieces of wood with it. There was the smell of torn wood for everyone to smell and sawdust on the floor for all to see. Then a table was wheeled out and the lady lay down on it in her bathing suit which was in two pieces. Her stomach was very white. The magician talked and waved the saw around. I suspected he was planning to cut the woman in half and I was eager to see this. I hadn't the slightest fear about this at all. I did wonder if he would be able to put her together again or if he would cut her in half only. The magician said that what was about to happen was too dreadful to be seen directly, that he did not want anyone to faint from the sight, so he brought out a small screen and placed it in front of the lady so that we could no longer see her white stomach, although everyone could still see her face and her shoes. The screen seemed unnecessary to me and I would have preferred to have been seated on the other side of it. Several people in the audience screamed. The lady who was about to be sawed in half began to chew on her lip and her face looked worried.

It was then that my mother appeared on the stage. She was crouched over a little, for she didn't have her balance back from having climbed up there. She looked large and strange in her red coat. The coat, which I knew very well, seemed the strangest thing. Someone screamed again, but more uncertainly. My mother moved toward the magician, smiling and speaking and gesturing with her hands, and the magician said, No, I can't of course, you should know better than this, this is a performance, you can't just appear like this, please sit down ...

My mother said, But you don't understand I'm willing, though I know the hazards and it's not that I believe you, no one would believe you for a moment but you can trust me, that's right, your faith in me would be perfectly placed because I'm not part of this, that's why I can be trusted because I don't know how it's done ...

Someone near me said, Is she kidding, that woman, what's her plan, she comes out of nowhere and wants to be cut in half ...

Lady ... the magician said, and I thought a dog might appear for I knew a dog named Lady who had a collection of colored balls.

My mother said, Most of us don't understand I know and it's just as well because the things we understand that's it for them, that's just the way we are ...

She probably thought she was still in that place in herself, but everything she said were the words coming from her mouth. Her lipstick was gone. Did she think she was in disguise, I wondered.

But why not, my mother said, to go and come back, that's what we want, that's why we're here and why can't we expect something to be done you can't expect us every day we get tired of showing up every day you can't get away with this forever then it was different but you should be thinking about the children ... She moved a little in a crooked fashion, speaking.

My God, said a voice, that woman's drunk. Sit down, please! someone said loudly.

My mother started to cry then and she stumbled and pushed her arms out before her as though she were pushing away someone who was trying to hold her, but no one was trying to hold her. The orchestra began to play and people began to clap. The usher ran out onto the stage and took my mother's hand. All this happened in an instant. He said something to her, he held her hand and she did not resist his holding it, then slowly the two of them moved down the few steps that led to the stage and up the aisle until they stopped beside me for the usher knew I was my mother's child. I followed them, of course, although in my mind I continued to sit in my seat. Everyone watched us leave. They did not notice that I remained there among them, watching too.

We went directly out of the theater and into the streets, my mother weeping on the little usher's arm. The shoulders of his jacket were of cardboard and there was gold braid looped around it. We were being taken away to be murdered which seemed reasonable to me. The usher's ears were large and he had a bump on his neck above the collar of his shirt. As we walked he said little soft things to my mother which gradually seemed to be comforting her. I hated him. It was not easy to walk together along the frozen sidewalks of the city. There was a belt on my mother's coat and I hung onto that as we moved unevenly along.

Look, I've pulled myself through, he said. You can pull yourself through. He was speaking to my mother.

We went into a coffee shop and sat down in a booth. You can collect yourself in here, he said. You can sit here as long as you want and drink coffee and no one will make you leave. He asked me if I wanted a donut. I would not speak to him. If he addressed me again, I thought, I would bite him. On the wall over the counter were pictures of sandwiches and pies. I did not want to be there and I did not take off either my mittens or my coat. The little usher went up to the counter and brought back coffee for my mother and a donut on a plate for me. Oh, my mother said, what have I done, and she swung her head from side to side.

I could tell right away about you, the usher said. You've got to pull yourself together. It took jumping off a bridge for me and breaking both legs before I got turned around. You don't want to let it go that far.

My mother looked at him. I can't imagine, my mother said.

Outside, a child passed by, walking with her sled. She looked behind her often and you could tell she was admiring the way the sled followed her so quickly on its runners.

You're a mother, the usher said to my mother, you've got to pull yourself through.

His kindness made me feel he had tied us up with rope. At last he left us and my mother laid her head down upon the table and fell asleep. I had never seen my mother sleeping and I watched her as she must once have watched me, the same way everyone watches a sleeping thing, not knowing how it would turn out or when. Then slowly I began to eat the donut with my mittened hands. The sour hair of the wool mingled with the tasteless crumbs and this utterly absorbed my attention. I pretended someone was feeding me.

As it happened, my mother was not able to pull herself through, but this was later. At the time, it was not so near the end and when my mother woke we found the car and left Portland, my mother saying my name. Lizzie, she said, Lizzie. I felt as though I must be with her somewhere and that she knew that too, but not in that old blue convertible traveling home in the dark, the soft, stained roof ballooning up in the way I knew it looked from the outside. I got out of it, but it took me years.

Mud

GEOFFREY FORSYTH

This morning I found my grandmother sitting at the kitchen table. She had been dead almost five years, but here she was now, sitting in my wife's old seat, covered in mud. I almost didn't recognize her because the mud had flattened her hair and darkened her normally pale skin. She said it wasn't easy digging her way out of the grave and that it took most of the night, and wasn't I going to at least offer her a glass of tomato juice?

"I don't get it," I said. "You're here?"

She said, "Am I going to have to ask twice for that juice?"

While alive, my grandmother's biggest pet peeve was having to ask twice for something she wanted. I poured her some juice.

"Grandma," I said. "I hate to say this, but today is not a good day. I have to be at the office early for a meeting, eight sharp. People are counting on me."

She stared at me, as if the tie I had on was all wrong.

"I have responsibilities and commitments that I can't get out of. It's a big day. They need me there today."

It was then that I heard the television in the living room.

"Who's watching the television?" I asked.

"Your father," she said.

"He's here, too?" I walked into the living room and found him sitting on the couch, mud all over his face and his arms and his hair.

"Dad?" I said. "What are you doing here?"

"Is that any way to greet your father?" he said. Turning to my grandmother, he said: "In seven years he hasn't seen me, and this is how he greets me?"

"You're getting mud on his remote, dear," said my grandmother.

He glared at his mother and rolled his eyes.

"Excuse me, Dad," I said, "but you're supposed to be dead."

He handed me my remote, mud all over the buttons. I held it away from my suit so I wouldn't get dirty.

"There's nothing on," he said.

When my father was alive, he loved watching television. He watched two hours of it before he went to his job at the phone company, then five more hours when he came home. His favorite show was All In The Family. He loved that show. Seeing him there in front of the television, hunched over with his hands resting flat on his stomach, injured me in the best possible way.

"I want to hug you," I said to my father. "But I have a meeting to get to. I can't afford to be late."

"You look sharp, kiddo," he said. The way he called me kiddo made me forget about work for a second. I had forgotten about kiddo. "Really, kiddo," he said. "You look like a million bucks."

"You think so?" I said.

Both of them nodded.

"I'd hug you guys, but I don't want to ruin my suit, you know?"

"Don't worry about it," said Grandma.

"I am worried about it," I said. "I never got to hug you goodbye, Grams."

"I was in Cleveland," she said.

"Still, I wish that I could've given you a proper goodbye."

"It's O.K."

"No it isn't," I said.

I spread my arms and walked towards her, but she backed away.

"Better not, kiddo," said my father. "You'll get dirty."

"I don't care," I said.

I turned to him and tried to throw my arms around his muddy neck, but he backed away from me as well.

"You've got a big day ahead of you," he said. "A really big day."

The phone rang. It was my boss, reminding me not to forget the reports. He sounded nervous. I asked him if I should bring anything besides the reports. He told me to bring my good sense and my sound judgment and the right frame of mind. Then he hung up.

While I was on the phone, my father and grandmother moved to the couch, tracking mud all over the carpet and the furniture. It tired me to look at it, gathering at their feet.

"I can't do this," I said. "Not now." I didn't know what exactly I couldn't do.

"Yes, you can," said my father. "You can do this."

He raised his arm, as if he meant to give me a high five, but then he remembered the mud, and folded his arms at his waist.

I gathered all the reports that were stacked on the dining room table and placed them neatly in my briefcase, then buckled it shut.

"I'm so sorry," I called to them. "I have to leave. I wish that I didn't, but I have to go now."

"We understand," said Grandma. "Don't you worry, darling."

"I can't help it," I said. "I always worry. Always. Always."

"Take a deep breath," came a new voice from the study.

It was my wife. Two years ago she died of cancer, but now I heard her voice from the study. I froze. Then I held my briefcase to my chest, wrapped my arms around it, and squeezed.

"Honey," I said. "Is that you?"

"You bet," she called back.

"I don't know how to tell you this," I said. "But I have to leave."

"I know," she said. "You've got a big day."

The next moment held a thoughtful silence.

"I'm not coming in there," I said finally.

"I know," she said.

My chest tightened. I wanted to run into the study and throw my arms around her and kiss her mouth and tell her how much I couldn't stand not having her around, but I knew if I went in there, she'd be covered in mud, too, and I had my life to think about, the life that was, any minute, going to start without me.

I went back into the living room and stood in front of my dead father and grandmother, briefcase still pressed to my chest. My briefcase had become like one of those square cushions that can also be used as a flotation device. Though I stood still, I felt like my legs were kicking.

"Show me the way out of here," I said.

My father got up and came within a few inches of me, making sure none of his mud touched the sleeves of my blazer. He leaned in, breath smelling like damp earth, and said: "I'm sorry we brought her here. She wasn't supposed to say anything. That was the deal. She was supposed to listen and not say a thing."

"It's O.K.," I said. "I'm glad she came. I just hate running out like this."

He nodded, then said, "Follow me."

I followed him to the front door, bow-legged over the wake of mud, so I wouldn't get dirty. Last night, after finishing my final report, I had used a half a tin of black Kiwi on my shoes. Buffed them until I thought I could see myself in the leather. I don't know why, but now the whole idea of rubbing black junk on my shoes to make them look better confounded me. It made me think: does anything really get clean?

My father opened the door. There must have been mica in the mud because his legs sparkled when sunlight entered the room. I thought for a moment that standing there, framed by the doorway, he meant to use his body to wall me in and keep me from going outside, where now I heard birds and passing cars and, every few seconds, the sound of a hammer, rapping in the hollow belly of someone's garage. But then he moved to the side, and I looked back towards the study, wondering if I should go in there, if it would be wise to go in there on the biggest day of my life. I listened for her, but all I heard was her silence. Her silence gave me a mother of a headache, like someone pounding a nail in the back of my head. If she'd spoken again, I'd have gone to her, but, lucky for me, I think, she didn't, and what I heard instead was my neighbor's hammer, calling me out.

Everything That Rises Must Converge

FLANNERY O'CONNOR

Her doctor had told Julian's mother that she must lose twenty pounds on account of her blood pressure, so on Wednesday nights Julian had to take her downtown on the bus for a reducing class at the Y. The reducing class was designed for working girls over fifty, who weighed from 165 to 200 pounds. His mother was one of the slimmer ones, but she said ladies did not tell their age or weight. She would not ride the buses by herself at night since they had been integrated, and because the reducing class was one of her few pleasures, necessary for her health, and *free*, she said Julian could at least put himself out to take her, considering all she did for him. Julian did not like to consider all she did for him, but every Wednesday night he braced himself and took her.

She was almost ready to go, standing before the hall mirror, putting on her hat, while he, his hands behind him, appeared pinned to the door frame, waiting like Saint Sebastian for the arrows to begin piercing him. The hat was new and had cost her seven dollars and a half. She kept saying, "Maybe I shouldn't have paid that for it. No, I shouldn't have. I'll take it off and return it tomorrow. I shouldn't have bought it."

Julian raised his eyes to heaven. "Yes, you should have bought it," he said. "Put it on and let's go." It was a hideous hat. A purple velvet flap came down on one side of it and stood up on the other; the rest of it was green and looked like a cushion with the stuffing out. He decided it was less comical than jaunty and pathetic. Everything that gave her pleasure was small and depressed him.

She lifted the hat one more time and set it down slowly on top of her head. Two wings of gray hair protruded on either side of her florid face, but her eyes, sky-blue, were as innocent and untouched by experience as they must have been when she was ten. Were it not that she was a widow who had struggled fiercely to feed and clothe and put him through school and who was supporting him still, "until he got on his feet," she might have been a little girl that he had to take to town.

"It's all right, it's all right," he said. "Let's go." He opened the door himself and started down the walk to get her going. The sky was a dying violet and the houses stood out darkly against it, bulbous liver-colored monstrosities of a uniform ugliness though no two were alike. Since this had been a fashionable neighborhood forty years ago, his mother persisted in thinking they did well to have an apartment in it. Each house had a narrow collar of dirt around it in which sat, usually, a grubby child. Julian walked with his hands in his pockets, his head down and thrust forward and his eyes glazed with the determination to make himself completely numb during the time he would be sacrificed to her pleasure.

The door closed and he turned to find the dumpy figure, surmounted by the atrocious hat, coming toward him. "Well," she said, "you only live once and paying a little more for it, I at least won't meet myself coming and going."

"Some day I'll start making money," Julian said gloomily—he knew he never would—"and you can have one of those jokes whenever you take the fit." But first they would move. He visualized a place where the nearest neighbors would be three miles away on either side.

"I think you're doing fine," she said, drawing on her gloves. "You've only been out of school a year. Rome wasn't built in a day."

She was one of the few members of the Y reducing class who arrived in hat and gloves and who had a son who had been to college. "It takes time," she said, "and the world is in such a mess. This hat looked better on me than any of the others, though when she brought it out I said, 'Take that thing back. I wouldn't have it on my head,' and she said, 'Now wait till you see it on,' and when she put it on me, I said, 'We-ull,' and she said, 'If you ask me, that hat does something for you and you do something for the hat, and besides,' she said, 'with that hat, you won't meet yourself coming and going.'"

Julian thought he could have stood his lot better if she had been selfish, if she had been an old hag who drank and screamed at him. He

walked along, saturated in depression, as if in the midst of his martyrdom he had lost his faith. Catching sight of his long, hopeless, irritated
face, she stopped suddenly with a grief-stricken look, and pulled back on
his arm. "Wait on me," she said. "I'm going back to the house and take
this thing off and tomorrow I'm going to return it, I was out of my head.
I can pay the gas bill with the seven-fifty."

He caught her arm in a vicious grip. "You are not going to take it
back," he said. "I like it."

"Well," she said, "I don't think I ought … "

"Shut up and enjoy it," he muttered, more depressed than ever.

"With the world in the mess it's in," she said, "it's a wonder we can
enjoy anything. I tell you, the bottom rail is on the top."

Julian sighed.

"Of course," she said, "if you know who you are, you can go anywhere." She said this every time he took her to the reducing class. "Most
of them in it are not our kind of people," she said, "but I can be gracious
to anybody. I know who I am."

"They don't give a damn for your graciousness," Julian said savagely.
"Knowing who you are is good for one generation only. You haven't the
foggiest idea where you stand now or who you are."

She stopped and allowed her eyes to flash at him. "I most certainly
do know who I am," she said, "and if you don't know who you are, I'm
ashamed of you."

"Oh hell," Julian said.

"Your great-grandfather was a former governor of this state," she
said. "Your grandfather was a prosperous landowner. Your grandmother
was a Godhigh."

"Will you look around you," he said tensely, "and see where you are
now?" and he swept his arm jerkily out to indicate the neighborhood,
which the growing darkness at least made less dingy.

"You remain what you are," she said, "Your great-grandfather had a
plantation and two hundred slaves."

"There are no more slaves," he said irritably.

"They were better off when they were," she said. He groaned to see
that she was off on that topic. She rolled onto it every few days like
a train on an open track. He knew every stop, every junction, every
swamp along the way, and knew the exact point at which her conclusion
would roll majestically into the station: "It's ridiculous. It's simply not
realistic. They should rise, yes, but on their own side of the fence."

"Let's skip it," Julian said.

"The ones I feel sorry for," she said, "are the ones that are half white.
They're tragic."

"Will you skip it?"

"Suppose we were half white. We would certainly have mixed feelings."

"I have mixed feelings now," he groaned.

"Well let's talk about something pleasant," she said. "I remember going to Grandpa's when I was a little girl. Then the house had double stairways that went up to what was really the second floor—all the cooking was done on the first. I used to like to stay down in the kitchen on account of the way the walls smelled. I would sit with my nose pressed against the plaster and take deep breaths. Actually the place belonged to the Godhighs but your grandfather Chestny paid the mortgage and saved it for them. They were in reduced circumstances," she said, "but reduced or not, they never forgot who they were."

"Doubtless that decayed mansion reminded them," Julian muttered. He never spoke of it without contempt or thought of it without longing. He had seen it once when he was a child before it had been sold. The double stairways had rotted and been torn down. Negroes were living in it. But it remained in his mind as his mother had known it. It appeared in his dreams regularly. He would stand on the wide porch, listening to the rustle of oak leaves, then wander through the high-ceilinged hall into the parlor that opened onto it and gaze at the worn rugs and faded draperies. It occurred to him that it was he, not she, who could have appreciated it. He preferred its threadbare elegance to anything he could name and it was because of it that all the neighborhoods they had lived in had been a torment to him—whereas she had hardly known the difference. She called her insensitivity "being adjustable."

"And I remember the old darky who was my nurse, Caroline. There was no better person in the world. I've always had a great respect for my colored friends," she said. "I'd do anything in the world for them and they'd … "

"Will you for God's sake get off that subject?" Julian said. When he got on a bus by himself, he made it a point to sit down beside a Negro, in reparation as it were for his mother's sins.

"You're mighty touchy tonight," she said. "Do you feel all right?"

"Yes I feel all right," he said. "Now lay off."

She pursed her lips. "Well, you certainly are in a vile humor," she observed. "I just won't speak to you at all."

They had reached the bus stop. There was no bus in sight and Julian, his hands still jammed in his pockets and his head thrust forward, scowled down the empty street. The frustration of having to wait on the bus as well as ride on it began to creep up his neck like a hot hand. The presence of his mother was borne in upon him as she gave a pained sigh. He looked at her bleakly. She was holding herself very erect under the preposterous hat, wearing it like a banner of her imaginary dignity. There was in him an evil urge to break her spirit. He suddenly unloosened his tie and pulled it off and put it in his pocket.

She stiffened. "Why must you look like *that* when you take me to town?" she said. "Why must you deliberately embarrass me?"

"If you'll never learn where you are," he said, "you can at least learn where I am."

"You look like a—thug," she said.

"Then I must be one," he murmured.

"I'll just go home," she said. "I will not bother you. If you can't do a little thing like that for me ... "

Rolling his eyes upward, he put his tie back on. "Restored to my class," he muttered. He thrust his face toward her and hissed, "True culture is in the mind, the *mind*," he said, and tapped his head, "the mind."

"It's in the heart," she said, "and in how you do things and how you do things is because of who you *are*."

"Nobody in the damn bus cares who you are."

"I care who I am," she said icily.

The lighted bus appeared on top of the next hill and as it approached, they moved out into the street to meet it. He put his hand under her elbow and hoisted her up on the creaking step. She entered with a little smile, as if she were going into a drawing room where everyone had been waiting for her. While he put in the tokens, she sat down on one of the broad front seats for three which faced the aisle. A thin woman with protruding teeth and long yellow hair was sitting on the end of it. His mother moved up beside her and left room for Julian beside herself. He sat down and looked at the floor across the aisle where a pair of thin feet in red and white canvas sandals were planted.

His mother immediately began a general conversation meant to attract anyone who felt like talking, "Can it get any hotter?" she said and removed from her purse a folding fan, black with a Japanese scene on it, which she began to flutter before her.

"I reckon it might could," the woman with the protruding teeth said, "but I know for a fact my apartment couldn't get no hotter."

"It must get the afternoon sun," his mother said. She sat forward and looked up and down the bus. It was half filled. Everybody was white. "I see we have the bus to ourselves," she said. Julian cringed.

"For a change," said the woman across the aisle, the owner of the red and white canvas sandals. "I come on one the other day and they were thick as fleas—up front and all through."

"The world is in a mess everywhere," his mother said. "I don't know how we've let it get in this fix."

"What gets my goat is all those boys from good families stealing automobile tires," the woman with the protruding teeth said. "I told my boy, I said you may not be rich but you been raised right and if I ever catch you in any such mess, they can send you on to the reformatory. Be exactly where you belong."

"Training tells," his mother said. "Is your boy in high school?"

"Ninth grade," the woman said.

"My son just finished college last year. He wants to write but he's selling typewriters until he gets started," his mother said.

The woman leaned forward and peered at Julian. He threw her such a malevolent look that she subsided against the seat. On the floor across the aisle there was an abandoned newspaper. He got up and got it and opened it out in front of him. His mother discreetly continued the conversation in a lower tone but the woman across the aisle said in a loud voice, "Well that's nice. Selling typewriters is close to writing. He can go right from one to the other."

"I tell him," his mother said, "that Rome wasn't built in a day."

Behind the newspaper Julian was withdrawing into the inner compartment of his mind where he spent most of his time. This was a kind of mental bubble in which he established himself when he could not bear to be a part of what was going on around him. From it he could see out and judge but in it he was safe from any kind of penetration from without. It was the only place where he felt free of the general idiocy of his fellows. His mother had never entered it but from it he could see her with absolute clarity.

The old lady was clever enough and he thought that if she had started from any of the right premises, more might have been expected of her. She lived according to the laws of her own fantasy world, outside of which he had never seen her set foot. The law of it was to sacrifice herself for him after she had first created the necessity to do so by making a mess of things. If he had permitted her sacrifices, it was only because her lack of foresight had made them necessary. All of her life had been a struggle to act like a Chestny without the Chestny goods, and to give him everything she thought a Chestny ought to have; but since, said she, it was fun to struggle, why complain? And when you had won, as she had won, what fun to look back on the hard times? He could not forgive her that she had enjoyed the struggle and that she thought *she* had won.

What she meant when she said she had won was that she had brought him up successfully and had sent him to college and that he had turned out so well—good looking (her teeth had gone unfilled so that his could be straightened), intelligent (he realized he was too intelligent to be a success), and with a future ahead of him (there was of course no future ahead of him). She excused his gloominess on the grounds that he was still growing up and his radical ideas on his lack of practical experience. She said he didn't yet know a thing about "life," that he hadn't even entered the real world—when already he was as disenchanted with it as a man of fifty.

The further irony of all this was that in spite of her, he had turned out so well. In spite of going to only a third-rate college, he had, on his own initiative, come out with a first-rate education; in spite of growing up dominated by a small mind, he had ended up with a large one; in spite of all her foolish views, he was free of prejudice and unafraid to face facts. Most miraculous of all, instead of being blinded by love for her as she was for him, he had cut himself emotionally free of her and could see her with complete objectivity. He was not dominated by his mother.

The bus stopped with a sudden jerk and shook him from his meditation. A woman from the back lurched forward with little steps and barely escaped falling in his newspaper as she righted herself. She got off and a large Negro got on. Julian kept his paper lowered to watch. It gave him a certain satisfaction to see injustice in daily operation. It confirmed his view that with a few exceptions there was no one worth knowing within a radius of three hundred miles. The Negro was well dressed and carried a briefcase. He looked around and then sat down on the other end of the seat where the woman with the red and white canvas sandals was sitting. He immediately unfolded a newspaper and obscured himself behind it. Julian's mother's elbow at once prodded insistently into his ribs. "Now you see why I won't ride on these buses by myself," she whispered.

The woman with the red and white canvas sandals had risen at the same time the Negro sat down and had gone further back in the bus and taken the seat of the woman who had got off. His mother leaned forward and cast her an approving look.

Julian rose, crossed the aisle, and sat down in the place of the woman with the canvas sandals. From this position, he looked serenely across at his mother. Her face had turned an angry red. He stared at her, making his eyes the eyes of a stranger. He felt his tension suddenly lift as if he had openly declared war on her.

He would have liked to get in conversation with the Negro and to talk with him about art or politics or any subject that would be above the comprehension of those around them, but the man remained entrenched behind his paper. He was either ignoring the change of seating or had never noticed it. There was no way for Julian to convey his sympathy.

His mother kept her eyes fixed reproachfully on his face. The woman with the protruding teeth was looking at him avidly as if he were a type of monster new to her.

"Do you have a light?" he asked the Negro.

Without looking away from his paper, the man reached in his pocket and handed him a packet of matches.

"Thanks," Julian said. For a moment he held the matches foolishly. A NO SMOKING sign looked down upon him from over the door. This alone would not have deterred him; he had no cigarettes. He had quit smoking some months before because he could not afford it. "Sorry," he muttered and handed back the matches. The Negro lowered the paper and gave him an annoyed look. He took the matches and raised the paper again.

His mother continued to gaze at him but she did not take advantage of his momentary discomfort. Her eyes retained their battered look. Her face seemed to be unnaturally red, as if her blood pressure had risen. Julian allowed no glimmer of sympathy to show on his face. Having got the advantage, he wanted desperately to keep it and carry it through. He would have liked to teach her a lesson that would last her a while, but there seemed no way to continue the point. The Negro refused to come out from behind his paper.

Julian folded his arms and looked stolidly before him, facing her but as if he did not see her, as if he had ceased to recognize her existence. He visualized a scene in which, the bus having reached their stop, he would remain in his seat and when she said, "Aren't you going to get off?" he would look at her as at a stranger who had rashly addressed him. The corner they got off on was usually deserted, but it was well lighted and it would not hurt her to walk by herself the four blocks to the Y. He decided to wait until the time came and then decide whether or not he would let her get off by herself. He would have to be at the Y at ten to bring her back, but he could leave her wondering if he was going to show up. There was no reason for her to think she could always depend on him.

He retired again into the high-ceilinged room sparsely settled with large pieces of antique furniture. His soul expanded momentarily but then he became aware of his mother across from him and the vision shriveled. He studied her coldly. Her feet in little pumps dangled like a child's and did not quite reach the floor. She was training on him an exaggerated look of reproach. He felt completely detached from her. At that moment he could with pleasure have slapped her as he would have slapped a particularly obnoxious child in his charge.

He began to imagine various unlikely ways by which he could teach her a lesson. He might make friends with some distinguished Negro professor or lawyer and bring him home to spend the evening. He would be entirely justified but her blood pressure would rise to 300. He could not push her to the extent of making her have a stroke, and moreover, he had never been successful at making any Negro friends. He had tried to strike up an acquaintance on the bus with some of the better types, with ones that looked like professors or ministers or lawyers. One morning he had sat down next to a distinguished-looking dark brown man who had answered his questions with a sonorous solemnity but who had turned out to be an undertaker. Another day he had sat down beside a cigar-smoking Negro with a diamond ring on his finger, but after a few stilted pleasantries, the Negro had rung the buzzer and risen, slipping two lottery tickets into Julian's hand as he climbed over him to leave.

He imagined his mother lying desperately ill and his being able to secure only a Negro doctor for her. He toyed with that idea for a few minutes and then dropped it for a momentary vision of himself participating as a sympathizer in a sit-in demonstration. This was possible but he did not linger with it. Instead, he approached the ultimate horror. He brought home a beautiful suspiciously Negroid woman. Prepare yourself, he said. There is nothing you can do about it. This is the woman I've chosen. She's intelligent, dignified, even good, and she's suffered and she hasn't thought it *fun*. Now persecute us, go ahead and persecute us. Drive her out of here, but remember, you're driving me too. His eyes were narrowed and through the indignation he had generated, he saw his mother across the aisle, purple-faced, shrunken to the dwarf-like proportions of her moral nature, sitting like a mummy beneath the ridiculous banner of her hat.

He was tilted out of his fantasy again as the bus stopped. The door opened with a sucking hiss and out of the dark a large, gaily dressed, sullen-looking colored woman got on with a little boy. The child, who might have been four, had on a short plaid suit and a Tyrolean hat with a blue feather in it. Julian hoped that he would sit down beside him and that the woman would push in beside his mother. He could think of no better arrangement.

As she waited for her tokens, the woman was surveying the seating possibilities—he hoped with the idea of sitting where she was least wanted. There was something familiar-looking about her but Julian could not place what it was. She was a giant of a woman. Her face was set not only to meet opposition but to seek it out. The downward tilt of her large lower lip was like a warning sign: DON'T TAMPER WITH ME. Her bulging figure was encased in a green crepe dress and her feet overflowed in red shoes. She had on a hideous hat. A purple velvet flap came down on one side of it and stood up on the other; the rest of it was green and looked like a cushion with the stuffing out. She carried a mammoth red pocketbook that bulged throughout as if it were stuffed with rocks.

To Julian's disappointment, the little boy climbed up on the empty seat beside his mother. His mother lumped all children, black and white, into the common category, "cute," and she thought little Negroes were on the whole cuter than little white children. She smiled at the little boy as he climbed on the seat.

Meanwhile the woman was bearing down upon the empty seat beside Julian. To his annoyance, she squeezed herself into it. He saw his mother's face change as the woman settled herself next to him and he realized with satisfaction that this was more objectionable to her than it was to him. Her face seemed almost gray and there was a look of dull recognition in her eyes, as if suddenly she had sickened at some awful confrontation. Julian saw that it was because she and the woman had, in a sense, swapped sons. Though his mother would not realize the symbolic significance of this, she would feel it. His amusement showed plainly on his face.

The woman next to him muttered something unintelligible to herself. He was conscious of a kind of bristling next to him, muted growling like that of an angry cat. He could not see anything but the red pocketbook upright on the bulging green thighs. He visualized the woman as she had stood waiting for her tokens—the ponderous figure, rising from the red shoes upward over the solid hips, the mammoth bosom, the haughty face, to the green and purple hat.

His eyes widened.

The vision of the two hats, identical, broke upon him with the radiance of a brilliant sunrise. His face was suddenly lit with joy. He could not believe that Fate had thrust upon his mother such a lesson. He gave a loud chuckle so that she would look at him and see that he saw. She turned her eyes on him slowly. The blue in them seemed to have turned a bruised purple. For a moment he had an uncomfortable sense of her innocence, but it lasted only a second before principle rescued him. Justice entitled him to laugh. His grin hardened until it said to her as plainly as if he were saying aloud: Your punishment exactly fits your pettiness. This should teach you a permanent lesson.

Her eyes shifted to the woman. She seemed unable to bear looking at him and to find the woman preferable. He became conscious again of the bristling presence at his side. The woman was rumbling like a volcano about to become active. His mother's mouth began to twitch slightly at one corner. With a sinking heart, he saw incipient signs of recovery on her face and realized that this was going to strike her suddenly as funny and was going to be no lesson at all. She kept her eyes on the woman and an amused smile came over her face as if the woman were a monkey that had stolen her hat. The little Negro was looking up at her with large fascinated eyes. He had been trying to attract her attention for some time.

"Carver!" the woman said suddenly. "Come heah!"

When he saw that the spotlight was on him at last, Carver drew his feet up and turned himself toward Julian's mother and giggled.

"Carver!" the woman said. "You heah me? Come heah!"

Carver slid down from the seat but remained squatting with his back against the base of it, his head turned slyly around toward Julian's mother, who was smiling at him. The woman reached a hand across the aisle and snatched him to her. He righted himself and hung backwards on her knees, grinning at Julian's mother. "Isn't he cute?" Julian's mother said to the woman with the protruding teeth.

"I reckon he is," the woman said without conviction.

The Negress yanked him upright but he eased out of her grip and shot across the aisle and scrambled, giggling wildly, onto the seat beside his love.

"I think he likes me," Julian's mother said, and smiled at the woman. It was the smile she used when she was being particularly gracious to an inferior. Julian saw everything lost. The lesson had rolled off her like rain on a roof.

The woman stood up and yanked the little boy off the seat as if she were snatching him from contagion. Julian could feel the rage in her at having no weapon like his mother's smile. She gave the child a sharp slap across his leg. He howled once and then thrust his head into her stomach and kicked his feet against her shins. "Behave," she said vehemently.

The bus stopped and the Negro who had been reading the newspaper got off. The woman moved over and set the little boy down with a thump between herself and Julian. She held him firmly by the knee. In a moment he put his hands in front of his face and peeped at Julian's mother through his fingers.

"I see yooooooo!" she said and put her hand in front of her face and peeped at him.

The woman slapped his hand down. "Quit yo' foolishness," she said, "before I knock the living Jesus out of you!"

Julian was thankful that the next stop was theirs. He reached up and pulled the cord. The woman reached up and pulled it at the same time. Oh my God, he thought. He had the terrible intuition that when they got off the bus together, his mother would open her purse and give the little boy a nickel. The gesture would be as natural to her as breathing. The bus stopped and the woman got up and lunged to the front, dragging the child, who wished to stay on, after her. Julian and his mother got up and followed. As they neared the door, Julian tried to relieve her of her pocketbook.

"No," she murmured, "I want to give the little boy a nickel."

"No!" Julian hissed. "No!"

She smiled down at the child and opened her bag. The bus door opened and the woman picked him up by the arm and descended with him, hanging at her hip. Once in the street she set him down and shook him.

Julian's mother had to close her purse while she got down the bus step but as soon as her feet were on the ground, she opened it again and began to rummage inside. "I can't find but a penny," she whispered, "but it looks like a new one."

"Don't do it!" Julian said fiercely between his teeth. There was a streetlight on the corner and she hurried to get under it so that she could better see into her pocketbook. The woman was heading off rapidly down the street with the child still hanging backward on her hand.

"Oh little boy!" Julian's mother called and took a few quick steps and caught up with them just beyond the lamppost. "Here's a bright new penny for you," and she held out the coin, which shone bronze in the dim light.

The huge woman turned and for a moment stood, her shoulders lifted and her face frozen with frustrated rage, and stared at Julian's mother.

Then all at once she seemed to explode like a piece of machinery that had been given one ounce of pressure too much. Julian saw the black fist swing out with the red pocketbook. He shut his eyes and cringed as he heard the woman shout, "He don't take nobody's pennies!" When he opened his eyes, the woman was disappearing down the street with the little boy staring wide-eyed over her shoulder. Julian's mother was sitting on the sidewalk.

"I told you not to do that," Julian said angrily. "I told you not to do that!"

He stood over her for a minute, gritting his teeth. Her legs were stretched out in front of her and her hat was on her lap. He squatted down and looked her in the face. It was totally expressionless. "You got exactly what you deserved," he said. "Now get up."

He picked up her pocketbook and put what had fallen out back in it. He picked the hat up off her lap. The penny caught his eye on the sidewalk and he picked that up and let it drop before her eyes into the purse. Then he stood up and leaned over and held his hands out to pull her up. She remained immobile. He sighed. Rising above them on either side were black apartment buildings, marked with irregular rectangles of light. At the end of the block a man came out of a door and walked off in the opposite direction. "All right," he said, "suppose somebody happens by and wants to know why you're sitting on the sidewalk?"

She took the hand and, breathing hard, pulled heavily up on it and then stood for a moment, swaying slightly as if the spots of light in the darkness were circling around her. Her eyes, shadowed and confused, finally settled on his face. He did not try to conceal his irritation. "I hope this teaches you a lesson," he said. She leaned forward and her eyes raked his face. She seemed trying to determine his identity. Then, as if she found nothing familiar about him, she started off with a headlong movement in the wrong direction.

"Aren't you going on to the Y?" he asked.

"Home," she muttered.

"Well, are we walking?"

For answer she kept going. Julian followed along, his hands behind him. He saw no reason to let the lesson she had had go without backing it up with an explanation of its meaning. She might as well be made to understand what had happened to her. "Don't think that was just an uppity Negro woman," he said. "That was the whole colored race which will no longer take your condescending pennies. That was your black double. She can wear the same hat as you, and to be sure," he added gratuitously (because he thought it was funny), "it looked better on her than it did on you. What all this means," he said, "is that the old world is gone. The old manners are obsolete and your graciousness is not worth a damn." He thought bitterly of the house that had been lost for him. "You aren't who you think you are," he said.

She continued to plow ahead, paying no attention to him. Her hair had come undone on one side. She dropped her pocketbook and took no notice. He stooped and picked it up and handed it to her but she did not take it.

"You needn't act as if the world had come to an end," he said, "because it hasn't. From now on you've got to live in a new world and face a few realities for a change. Buck up," he said, "it won't kill you."

She was breathing fast.

"Let's wait on the bus," he said.

"Home," she said thickly.

"I hate to see you behave like this," he said. "Just like a child. I should be able to expect more of you." He decided to stop where he was and make her stop and wait for a bus. "I'm not going any farther," he said, stopping. "We're going on the bus."

She continued to go on as if she had not heard him. He took a few steps and caught her arm and stopped her. He looked into her face and caught his breath. He was looking into a face he had never seen before. "Tell Grandpa to come get me," she said.

He stared, stricken.

"Tell Caroline to come get me," she said.

Stunned, he let her go and she lurched forward again, walking as if one leg were shorter than the other. A tide of darkness seemed to be sweeping her from him. "Mother!" he cried. "Darling, sweetheart, wait!" Crumpling, she fell to the pavement. He dashed forward and fell at her side, crying, "Mamma, Mamma!" He turned her over. Her face was fiercely distorted. One eye, large and staring, moved slightly to the left as if it had become unmoored. The other remained fixed on him, raked his face again, found nothing and closed.

"Wait here, wait here!" he cried and jumped up and began to run for help toward a cluster of lights he saw in the distance ahead of him. "Help, help!" he shouted, but his voice was thin, scarcely a thread of sound. The lights drifted farther away the faster he ran and his feet moved numbly as if they carried him nowhere. The tide of darkness seemed to sweep him back to her, postponing from moment to moment his entry into the world of guilt and sorrow.

Writing Exercises

1. Write a short story on a three-by-five card or the back of a postcard. Notice that if you're going to manage a conflict, crisis, and resolution in this small space, you'll have to introduce the conflict immediately.

2. For this exercise, you will create what Jerome Stern calls the "Bear at the Door" scene. In this scene, your character must have an external problem. ("Honey, there's a bear at the door.") The problem should be significant. ("Honey, it's huge.") The problem should be pressing. ("Honey, I think it's trying to get in.") And the problem should force your character to act. ("Honey, do something!") Your character should have an internal conflict that affects her/his ability to deal with this problem— the bear within him/herself.

   a. Come up with a list of external conflicts, avoiding the overly dramatic or overly mundane. Choose the most intriguing one.

   b. Write a scene that places a character in the middle of the external conflict. Complicate the situation with the character's internal needs and desires.

3. For each character in one of your stories-in-progress, list all the predictable actions each could take to keep the plot moving. Now try mixing up the characters and the actions and see if you come up with a more interesting and surprising plot.

4. Robert Olen Butler wrote a collection of short stories, *Tabloid Dreams*, that was inspired by headlines and articles in supermarket tabloids (e.g., "Jealous Husband Returns in Form of Parrot"). Buy a tabloid magazine of your own. Find the silliest story in it. Use it as the jumping-off point for a short, serious story.

5. Imagine an intriguing circumstance, or think of something puzzling you witnessed, heard, or read about in the newspaper. The circumstance should have no obvious explanation. (See page 11, "The Incongruity," about three women, one with a baby stroller, at a supermarket pay phone very late at night.)

   Write three very brief stories (200 words), each offering a different explanation for the same circumstance. Each story should have different characters and a different plot. Consider that within each story the same circumstance may function in different ways: In one story, it may be the opening scene; in another, it might appear at the end.

6. Imagine some deceit growing out of control. Your character "borrowed" something without asking, and now it's lost or broken. The babysitter was distracted on the phone, and now one of the kids is missing. A character told a lie that seemed harmless; the little lie is now big and has come back to haunt him.

   Now crank things up another notch: The lost item is irreplaceable; the missing child has a medical condition; etc. How might this trouble be related to the character's desire? She was desperate to impress others; he was fixated on getting into medical school. Take the situation and go with it.

8

CALL ME ISHMAEL
Point of View

- ♦ *Who Speaks?*

- ♦ *To Whom?*

- ♦ *In What Form?*

- ♦ *At What Distance?*

- ♦ *Consistency: A Caution*

Point of view is the most complex element of fiction. We can label and analyze it in a number of different ways, but however we describe it, point of view ultimately concerns the relationship among writer, characters, and reader.

The first thing to do is to set aside the common use of the phrase "point of view" as synonymous with "opinion," as in *It's my point of view that they all ought to be shot.* Rather than thinking of point of view as an opinion or belief, begin instead with the more literal synonym of "vantage point." *Who* is standing *where* to watch the scene?

Since we are dealing with words on a page, these questions might be better translated as: *Who speaks? To whom? In what form? At what distance from the action?*

Who Speaks?

The primary point-of-view decision that you as author must make before you can set down the first sentence of the story is *person*. This is the simplest and crudest subdivision that must be made in deciding who speaks. The story can be told

- *in the third person* (she walked out into the harsh sunlight),
- *in the second person* (you walked out into the harsh sunlight), or
- *in the first person* (I walked out into the harsh sunlight).

From the reader's perspective, third- and second-person stories are told by an author, first-person stories by the character acting as "I."

THIRD PERSON

Third-person point of view, in which the author is telling the story, can be sub-divided again according to the degree of knowledge the author assumes.

Omniscience.   The *omniscient author* has total knowledge and tells us directly what we are supposed to think. As omniscient author you are God. You can

1. objectively report the action of the story;
2. go into the mind of any character;
3. interpret for us that character's appearance, speech, actions, and thoughts, even if the character cannot do so;
4. move freely in time or space to give us a panoramic, telescopic, micro-scopic, or historical view and tell us what has happened elsewhere or in the past or what will happen in the future; and
5. provide general reflections, judgments, and truths.

In all these aspects, we will accept what the omniscient author tells us. If you tell us that Ruth is a good woman, that Jeremy doesn't really understand his own motives, that the moon is going to explode in four hours, and that everybody will be better off for it, we will believe you. Here is a paragraph that blatantly exhibits all five of these areas of knowledge.

(1) Joe glared at the screaming baby. (2) Frightened by his scowl, the baby gulped and screamed louder. I hate that thing, Joe thought. (3) But it was not really hatred that he felt. (4) Only two years ago he himself had screamed like that. (5) Children can't tell hatred from fear.

This illustration is awkwardly compressed, but authors well in control of their craft can move easily from one area of knowledge to another. In the first scene of *War and Peace*, Tolstoy describes Anna Scherer.

To be an enthusiast had become her social vocation, and sometimes even when she did not feel like it, she became enthusiastic in order not to disappoint the expectations of those who knew her. The subdued smile which, though it did not suit her faded features, always played around her lips, expressed as in a spoiled child, a continual consciousness of her charming defect, which she neither wished, nor could, nor considered it necessary to correct.

In two sentences Tolstoy tells us what is in Anna's mind, what the expectations of her acquaintances are, what she looks like, what suits her, what she can and cannot do; and he offers a general reflection on spoiled children.

The omniscient voice is the voice of the classical epic ("And Meleager, far-off, knew nothing of this, but felt his vitals burning with fever"), of the Bible ("And all the people departed, every man to his house; and David returned to bless his house"), and of most nineteenth-century novels ("Tito put out his hand to help him, and so strangely quick are men's souls that in this moment, when he began to feel that his atonement was accepted, he had a darting thought of the irksome efforts it entailed"). But it is one of the manifestations of modern literature's movement downward in class from heroic to common characters, from external action to the psychological action of the mind, that authors of realistic fiction have largely avoided the godlike stance of the omniscient author and have chosen to restrict themselves to fewer areas of knowledge.

Limited Omniscience.   The *limited omniscient* viewpoint is one in which the author may move with some, but not all, of the omniscient author's freedom. The most commonly used form of the limited omniscient point of view is one in which the author can see events objectively and also grants himself or herself access to the mind of one character, but *not* to the minds of the others, nor to any explicit powers of judgment. Limited omniscience is particularly useful for the short story because it very quickly establishes the point-of-view character or *means of perception*. The short story is so compressed a form that there is rarely time or space to develop more than one consciousness. Staying with external observation and one character's thoughts helps control the focus and avoid awkward point-of-view shifts. A further advantage of limited omniscience is that it mimics our individual experience of life—that is, our own inability to penetrate the minds and motivations of others—which can lead to the kinds of conflicts or struggles for connection that inspire much fiction.

Limited omniscience is also frequently used for the novel, as in Gail Godwin's *The Odd Woman*.

It was ten o'clock on the evening of the same day, and the permanent residents of the household on the mountain were restored to routines and sobriety. Jane, on the other hand, sat by herself in the kitchen, a glass of Scotch before her on the cleanly wiped table, going deeper and deeper into a mood she could recognize only as unfamiliar. She could not describe it; it was both frightening and satisfying. It was like letting go and being taken somewhere. She tried to trace it back. When, exactly, had it started?

It is clear here that the author has limited her omniscience. She is not going to tell us the ultimate truth about Jane's soul, nor is she going to define for us the unfamiliar mood that the character herself cannot define. The author has the facts at her disposal, and she has Jane's thoughts, and that is all.

The advantage of the limited omniscient voice is immediacy. Here, because we are not allowed to know more than Jane does about her own thoughts and feelings, we grope *with* her toward understanding. In the process, a contract has been made between the author and the reader, and this contract must not now be broken. If at this point the author should step in and answer Jane's question "When, exactly, had it started?" with "Jane was never to remember this, but in fact it had started one afternoon when she was two years old," we would feel it as an abrupt and uncalled-for *authorial intrusion*. As it is, however, within the limits the author has set herself there is fluidity and a range of possibilities.

The Objective Author. As an *objective author*, you restrict your knowledge to the external facts that might be observed by a human witness: to the senses of sight, sound, smell, taste, and touch. In the passage from "Hills Like White Elephants" quoted in Chapter 3, Ernest Hemingway reports what is said and done by the quarreling couple, both without any direct revelation of the characters' thoughts and without comment.

> The American and the girl with him sat at a table in the shade, outside the building. It was very hot and the express from Barcelona would come in forty minutes. It stopped at this junction for two minutes and went on to Madrid.
>
> "What should we drink?" the girl asked. She had taken off her hat and put it on the table.
>
> "It's pretty hot," the man said.
>
> "Let's drink beer."
>
> "Dos cervezas," the man said into the curtain.
>
> "Big ones?" a woman asked from the doorway.
>
> "Yes. Two big ones."
>
> The woman brought two glasses of beer and two felt pads. She put the felt pads and the beer glasses on the table and looked at the man and the girl. The girl was looking off at the line of hills. They were white in the sun and the country was brown and dry.

In the course of this story we learn, entirely by inference, that the girl is pregnant and that she feels herself coerced by the man into having an abortion. Neither pregnancy nor abortion is ever mentioned. The narrative remains clipped, austere, and external. What does Hemingway gain by this pretense of objective reporting? The reader is allowed to discover what is really happening. The characters avoid the subject, prevaricate, and pretend, but they betray their real meanings and feelings through gestures, repetitions, and slips of the tongue. The reader, focus directed by the author, learns by inference, as in life, so that we finally have the pleasure of knowing the characters better than they know themselves.

SECOND PERSON

First- and third-person points of view are most common in literature; the second person remains an idiosyncratic and experimental form, but it is worth mentioning because several contemporary authors have been attracted to its possibilities.

Lorrie Moore's story "How to Become a Writer" illustrates how a reader is made into a character through second person.

> First, try to be something, anything, else. A movie star/astronaut.
> A movie star/missionary. A movie star/kindergarten teacher. President
> of the World. Fail miserably. It is best if you fail at an early age—say,
> fourteen. Early, critical disillusionment is necessary so that at fifteen you
> can write long haiku sentences about thwarted desire. It is a pond, a cherry
> blossom, a wind brushing against sparrow wing leaving for mountain.
> Count the syllables. Show it to your mom.

Here the author assigns you, the reader, specific characteristics and reactions, and thereby—assuming that you go along with her characterization of you—pulls you deeper and more intimately into the story.

Some writers choose second person to depict trauma, as its slight sense of detachment mutes possible melodrama and mirrors the sense of shock; others may use it to make a highly individual experience feel more universal.

The second person is the basic mode of the story *only when a character* is referred to as *you*. When one character addresses "you" in letter or monologue, that narrative is still told by the "I" character. When an omniscient author addresses the reader as *you* (*You will remember that John Doderring was left dangling on the cliff at Dover*), this is called "direct address" and does not alter the basic third-person mode of the piece. Only when "you" becomes an actor in the drama, so designated by the author, is the story or novel written in second person.

Unlike third or first person, second person draws attention to itself, and it can also be difficult to maintain—it's easy to slip back into third or first person. Also, some readers may resist second person because they don't identify with the character they are supposed to be in the story. (*You go into a bar. You get very, very drunk.*) It is unlikely that the second person will ever become a major mode of narration as the first and third person are, but for precisely that reason you may find it an attractive experiment.

FIRST PERSON

A story is told in the first person when one of its characters relates the story's action and events. The term "narrator" is sometimes loosely used to refer to any teller of a tale, but strictly speaking a story has a narrator only when it is told in the first person by one of the characters. This character may be the protagonist, the *I* telling *my* story, in which case that character is a *central narrator* (as in "No One's a Mystery" at the end of this chapter); or the character may be telling a story about someone else, in which case he or she is a *peripheral narrator*.

In either case it's important to indicate early which kind of narrator we have so that we know who the story's protagonist is, as in the first paragraph of Alan Sillitoe's "The Loneliness of the Long-Distance Runner."

> As soon as I got to Borstal they made me a long-distance cross-country runner. I suppose they thought I was just the build for it because I was long and skinny for my age (and still am) and in any case I didn't mind it much, to tell you the truth, because running had always been made much of in our family, especially running away from the police.

The focus here is immediately thrown on the *I* of the story, and we expect that *I* to be the central character whose desires and decisions impel the action.

But from the opening lines of Amy Bloom's "Silver Water," it is the sister, Rose, who is brought alive through the description of her marvelous singing voice, while the narrator, Violet, is established as an observer and protector of her subject.

> My sister's voice was like mountain water in a silver pitcher; the clear, blue beauty of it cools you and lifts you up beyond your heat, beyond your body. After we went to see *La Traviata*, when she was fourteen and I was twelve, she elbowed me in the parking lot and said, "Check this out." And she opened her mouth unnaturally wide and her voice came out, so crystalline and bright, that all the departing operagoers stood frozen by their cars, unable to take out their keys or open their doors until she had finished and then they cheered like hell.
>
> That's what I like to remember and that's the story I told to all of her therapists. I wanted them to know her, to know that who they saw was not all there was to see.

The central narrator is always, as the term implies, at the center of the action. The peripheral narrator may be in virtually any position that is not the center; he or she may be the second most important character in the story (as in the Amy Bloom story above) or may appear to be a bystander for much of the story. It is even possible to make the first-person narrator plural, as William Faulkner does in "A Rose for Emily," which is told by a narrator identified only as one of "us," the people of the town in which the action has taken place.

That a narrator may be either central or peripheral, that a character may tell either his or her own story or someone else's, is both commonly assumed and obviously logical. But the author and editor Rust Hills, in his book *Writing in General and the Short Story in Particular*, takes interesting and persuasive exception to this idea. When point of view fails, Hills argues, it is always because the perception we are using for the course of the story is different from that of the character who is moved or changed by the action. Even when a narrator seems to be a peripheral observer and the story is "about" someone else, in fact it is the narrator who is changed, and must be, in order for us to be satisfied by our emotional identification with him or her.

> This, I believe, is what will always be the case in successful fiction: that either the character moved by the action will be the point-of-view character, or else the point-of-view character will *become* the character moved by the action. Call it Hills' Law.

Obviously, this view does not mean that we have to throw out the useful fictional device of the peripheral narrator. Hills uses the familiar example of *The Great Gatsby* to illustrate his meaning. Nick Carroway as a peripheral narrator observes and tells the story of Jay Gatsby, but by the end of the book it is Nick's life that has been changed by what he has observed.

Anton Chekhov (as paraphrased by Tobias Wolff) cautioned, "The narrator cannot escape the *consequences* of the story he is telling. If he does, it's not a story. It's an anecdote, a tale, or something else."

Central or peripheral, a first-person narrator is a character, so it's vital to remember that she or he has all the limitations of a human being and cannot be omniscient. The narrator is confined to reporting what she or he could realistically know. More than that, although the narrator may certainly interpret actions, deliver dictums, and predict the future, these remain the fallible opinions of a human being; we are not bound to accept them as we are bound to accept the interpretations, truths, and predictions of the omniscient author. You may want us to accept the narrator's word, and then the most difficult part of your task, and the touchstone of your story's success, will be to convince us to trust and believe the narrator. On the other hand, it may be an important part of your purpose that we should reject the narrator's opinions and form our own. If the answer to *Who speaks?* is *a child, a bigot, a jealous lover, an animal, a person suffering from schizophrenia, a murderer, a liar*, the implications may be that the narrator speaks with limitations we do not necessarily share. To the extent that the narrator displays and betrays such limitations, she or he is an *unreliable narrator*.

Here is a woman, imperious and sour, who tells her own story.

> I have always, always, tried to do right and help people. It's a part of my community duty and my duty to God. But I can tell you right now, you don't never gets no thanks for it! ...

Use to be a big ole fat sloppy woman live cross the street went to my church. She had a different man in her house with her every month! She got mad at me for tellin the minister on her about all them men! Now, I'm doin my duty and she got mad! I told her somebody had to be the pillar of the community and if it had to be me, so be it! She said I was the pill of the community and a lotta other things, but I told the minister that too and pretty soon she was movin away. Good! I like a clean community!

J. California Cooper, "The Watcher"

We mistrust every judgment this woman makes, but we are also aware of an author we do trust, manipulating the narrator's tone to expose her. The outburst is fraught with ironies, but because the narrator is unaware of them, they are directed against herself. We can hear that interference is being dressed up as duty. When she brags in cliché, we agree that she's more of a pill than a pillar. When she appropriates biblical language—"so be it!"—we suspect that even the minister might agree. Punctuation itself, the self-righteous overuse of the exclamation point, suggests her inappropriate intensity. It occurs to us that we'd probably like the look of that "big ole fat sloppy" neighbor; and we know for certain why that neighbor moved away.

In this case the narrator is wholly unreliable, and we're unlikely to accept any judgment she could make. But it is also possible for a narrator to be reliable in some areas of value and unreliable in others. Mark Twain's *Huckleberry Finn* is a famous case in point. Here Huck has decided to free his friend Jim, and he is astonished that Tom Sawyer is going along with the plan.

Here was a boy that was respectable, and well brung up; and had a character to lose; and folks at home that had characters; and he was bright and not leather-headed; and knowing and not ignorant; and not mean, but kind; and yet here he was, without any more pride, or rightness, or feeling, than to stoop to this business, and make himself a shame, and his family a shame, before everybody. I couldn't understand it, no way at all.

The extended irony in this excerpt is that slavery should be defended by the respectable, the bright, the knowing, the kind, and those of character. We reject Huck's assessment of Tom as well as the implied assessment of himself as worth so little that he has nothing to lose by freeing a slave. Huck's moral instincts are better than he himself can understand. (Notice, incidentally, how Huck's lack of education is communicated by word choice and syntax and how sparse the misspellings are.) So author and reader are in intellectual opposition to Huck the narrator, but morally identify with him. Similarly reliable "unreliable" narrators—whose distorted views reveal a strangely accurate portrait of the social institutions that confine them—include Chief Bromden, the narrator of Ken Kesey's *One Flew Over the Cuckoo's Nest*, and the "hysterical" wife and patient, forbidden to write, who relates Charlotte Perkins Gilman's 1892 story "The Yellow Wallpaper."

THE TRUTH IS NOT DISTORTED HERE, but rather a certain distortion is used to get at the truth.

FLANNERY O'CONNOR

The unreliable narrator—who has become one of the most popular characters in modern fiction—is far from a newcomer to literature and in fact predates fiction. Every drama contains characters who speak for themselves and present their own cases, and from whom we are partly or wholly distanced in one area of value or another. So we admire Oedipus's intellect but are exasperated by his lack of intuition; we identify with Othello's morality but mistrust his logic; we trust Mr. Spock's brain but not his heart; we count on Bridget Jones's wit, as revealed in her diary, but not her judgment. As these examples suggest, the unreliable narrator often presents us with an example of consistent inconsistency and always presents us with dramatic irony, because we always "know" more than he or she does about the characters, the events, and the significance of both.

THERE SHOULD BE THE ILLUSION that it's the character's point of view, when in fact it isn't; it's really the narrator who is there but who doesn't make herself...known in that role....What I really want is that intimacy in which the reader is under the impression that he isn't really reading this; that he is participating in it as he goes along.

TONI MORRISON

To Whom?

In choosing a point of view, the author implies an identity not only for the teller of the tale but also for the intended audience. To whom is the story being told?

THE READER

Most fiction is addressed to a literary convention, "the reader." When we open a book, we tacitly accept our role as a member of this unspecified audience. After all, the most common assumption of the tale-teller, whether omniscient author or narrating character, is that the reader is an open and amenable Everyman, and that the telling needs no justification.

ANOTHER CHARACTER

More specifically, the story may be told to *another character*, or *characters*, in which case we as readers "overhear" it; the teller of the tale does not acknowledge us even by implication.

In the *epistolary* novel or story, the narrative consists entirely of letters written from one character to another, or between characters. The recipient of the letter may be a stranger or a close friend or relative, like the near-annual readers of *The Christmas Letters*, by Lee Smith.

> First, my apologies for not writing a Christmas letter last year (for not returning calls, for not returning letters, etc.). The fact is, for a long time I couldn't do anything. Not a damn thing. Nothing. I was shell-shocked, immobilized. This was followed by a period when I did *too many things*. Marybeth, who has been through it, wrote to me about this time, saying, "Don't make any big decisions"—very good advice, and I wish I'd followed it. Instead, I agreed to a separation agreement, then to a quick no-fault divorce, then to Sandy's plan of selling the house P.D.Q. I just wanted everything *over with*—the way you feel that sudden irresistible urge to clean out your closet sometimes.

Or the convention of the story may be that of a monologue, spoken aloud by one character to another.

> May I, *monsieur*, offer my services without running the risk of intruding? I fear you may not be able to make yourself understood by the worthy ape who presides over the fate of this establishment. In fact, he speaks nothing but Dutch. Unless you authorize me to plead your case, he will not guess that you want gin.
>
> Albert Camus, *The Fall*

Again, the possible variations are infinite: The narrator may speak in intimate confessional to a friend or lover, or may present his case to a jury or a mob; she may be writing a highly technical report of the welfare situation, designed to hide her emotions; he may be pouring out his heart in a love letter he knows (and we know) he will never send.

In any of these cases, the convention employed is the opposite of that employed in a story told to "the reader." The listener as well as the teller is involved in the action; the assumption is not that we readers are there but that we are not. We are eavesdroppers, with all the ambiguous intimacy that position implies.

THE SELF

An even greater intimacy is implied if the character's story is as secret as a diary or as private as a mind, addressed to *the self* and not intended to be heard by anyone inside or outside the action.

In a *diary* or *journal*, the convention is that the thoughts are written but not expected to be read by anyone except the writer.

> Tuesday 3 January
> 9 A.M. Ugh. Cannot face thought of going to work. Only thing which makes it tolerable is thought of seeing Daniel again, but even that is inadvisable since I am fat, have spot on chin, and desire only to sit on cushion eating chocolate and watching Xmas specials. It seems wrong and unfair that Christmas, with its stressful and unmanageable financial and emotional challenges, should first be forced upon one wholly against one's will, then rudely snatched away just when one is starting to get into it.
>
> Helen Fielding, *Bridget Jones's Diary*

The protagonist here is clearly using her diary to vent her feelings and does not intend it to be read by anyone else. Still, she has deliberately externalized her secret thoughts in a journal.

INTERIOR MONOLOGUE

Because the author has the power to enter a character's mind, the reader also has the power to eavesdrop on that character's thoughts. Overheard thoughts are generally of two kinds, of which the more common is *interior monologue*, the convention being that we follow that character's thoughts in their sequence.

> I must organize myself. I must, as they say, pull myself together, dump this cat from my lap, stir—yes, resolve, move, do. But do what? My will is like the rosy dustlike light in this room: soft, diffuse, and gently comforting. It lets me do ... anything ... nothing. My ears hear what they happen to; I eat what's put before me; my eyes see what blunders into them; my thoughts are not thoughts, they are dreams. I'm empty or I'm full ... depending; and I cannot choose. I sink my claws in Tick's fur and scratch the bones of his back until his rear rises amorously. Mr. Tick, I murmur, I must organize myself, I must pull myself together. And Mr. Tick rolls over on his belly, all ooze.
>
> William H. Gass, "In the Heart of the Heart of the Country"

This interior monologue ranges, as human thoughts do, from sense impression to self-admonishment, from cat to light to eyes and ears, from specific to general and back again. But the logical connections between these things are all provided; the mind "thinks" logically and grammatically as if the character were trying to express himself.

STREAM OF CONSCIOUSNESS

Stream of consciousness acknowledges the fact that the human mind does not operate with the order and clarity of the monologue just quoted. Even what little we know of its operations makes clear that it skips, elides, makes and breaks images, leaps faster and further than any mere sentence can suggest. Any mind at any moment is simultaneously accomplishing dozens of tasks that cannot be conveyed simultaneously. As you read this sentence, part of your mind is following the sense of it; part of your mind is directing your hand to hold the book open; part of it is twisting your spine into a more comfortable position; part of it is still lingering on the last interesting image of this text, Mr. Tick rolling over on his belly, which reminds you of a cat you had once that was also *all ooze*, which reminds you that you're nearly out of milk and have to finish this chapter before the store closes; and so forth.

In *Ulysses*, James Joyce tried to catch the speed and multiplicity of the mind with the technique that has come to be known as stream of consciousness. The device is difficult and in many ways thankless: Since the speed of thought is so much faster than that of writing or speaking, and stream of consciousness tries to suggest the process as well as the content of the mind, *it requires a much more—not less—rigorous selection and arrangement* than ordinary grammar requires. But Joyce and a very few other writers have handled stream of consciousness as an ebullient and exciting way of capturing the mind.

> Yes because he never did a thing like that before as ask to get his breakfast in bed with a couple of eggs since the City Arms hotel when he used to be pretending to be laid up with a sick voice doing his highness to make himself interesting to that old faggot Mrs. Riordan that he thought he had a great leg of and she never left us a farthing all for masses for herself ...

The preceding two examples, of interior monologue and stream of consciousness, respectively, are written in the first person, so that we overhear the minds of narrator characters. We may also overhear the thoughts of the characters through the third-person omniscient and limited omniscient authors, as in John Edgar Wideman's *tour de force* story "The Tambourine Lady." Here, Wideman succeeds in the challenging fusion of third-person narrative and stream of consciousness, so that although the answer to the question "who speaks?" is technically "the author," nevertheless we are aware of the point-of-view character speaking to herself in rapid-fire associative thought:

> ...She thinks about how long it takes to get to the end of your prayers, how the world might be over and gone while you are still saying the words to yourself. Words her mama taught her, words her mama said her mother had taught her so somebody would always be saying them world without end amen. So God would not forget his children...

In What Form?

The form of the story also contributes to the overall point of view. That form may announce itself as a generalized *story*, either *written* or *spoken*; or it may suggest *reportage, confessional, interior monologue*, or *stream of consciousness*; or it may be overtly identified as *monologue, oratory, journal*, or *diary*. This list is not exhaustive; you can tell your story in the form of a catalog, a television commercial, or an e-mail exhange, as long as you can also contrive to give it the form of a story.

Form is important to point of view because the form in which a story is told indicates the degree of self-consciousness on the part of the teller. This will in turn affect the language chosen, the intimacy of the relationship, and the honesty of the telling. An account that purports to be a character's thought will imply more spontaneity than a spoken one, which in turn will seem more spontaneous than one deliberately written down. A narrator writing a letter to his grandmother may be less honest than he is when he tells the same facts aloud to his friend.

Certain relationships established by the narrative between teller and audience make certain forms more likely than others, but almost any combination of answers is possible to the questions *Who speaks? To whom? In what form?* If you are speaking as an omniscient author to the literary convention of "the reader," we may assume that you are using the convention of "written story" as your form. But you might say:

> Wait, step over here a minute. What's this in the corner, stuffed down between the bedpost and the wall?

If you do this, you slip at least momentarily into the different convention of the spoken word—the effect is that we are drawn more immediately into the scene—and the point of view of the whole is slightly altered. A central narrator might be thinking, and therefore "talking to herself," while actually angrily addressing her thoughts to another character. Conversely, one character might be writing a letter to another but letting the conscious act of writing deteriorate into a betrayal of his own secret thoughts. Any complexities such as these will alter and inform the overall point of view.

At What Distance?

As with the chemist at her microscope and the lookout in his tower, fictional point of view always involves the *distance*, close or far, of the perceiver from the thing perceived. *Authorial distance*, sometimes called *psychic distance*, is the degree to which we as readers feel on the one hand intimacy and identification with, or on the other hand detachment and alienation from, the characters.

When desired, a sense of distance may be increased through the use of abstract nouns, summary, typicality, and apparent objectivity. Such techniques, which in other contexts might be seen as writing flaws, are employed in the following passage purposely to detach readers from characters.

> It started in the backyards. At first the men concentrated on heat and smoke, and on dangerous thrusts with long forks. Their wives gave them aprons in railroad stripes, with slogans on the front—*Hot Stuff, The Boss*—to spur them on. Then it began to get mixed up who should do the dishes, and you can't fall back on paper plates forever, and around that time the wives got tired of making butterscotch brownies and jello salads with grated carrots in them and wanted to make money instead, and one thing led to another.

> Margaret Atwood, "Simmering"

Conversely, you can achieve closeness and sympathy with concrete detail, scene, a character's thoughts, and so forth.

> She dreams she does not already have three children. A squeeze around the flowers in her hands chokes off three and four and five years of breath. Instantly she is ashamed and frightened in her superstition. She looks for the first time at the preacher, forces humility into her eyes, as if she believes he is, in fact, a man of God. She can imagine God, a small black boy, timidly pulling the preacher's coattail.

> Alice Walker, "Roselily"

Or a combination of techniques may make us feel simultaneously sympathetic and detached—a frequent effect of comedy—as in this example:

> I'm a dishwasher in a restaurant. I'm not trying to impress anybody. I'm not bragging. It's just what I do. It's not the glamorous job people make it out to be. Sure, you make a lot of dough and everybody looks up to you and respects you, but then again there's a lot of responsibility. It weighs on you. It wears on you. Everybody wants to be a dishwasher these days, I guess, but they've got an idealistic view of it.

> Robert McBrearty, "The Dishwasher"

As author you may ask us to identify completely with one character and totally condemn another. One character may judge another harshly, while you as author suggest that we should qualify that judgment. If there is also a narrator, that narrator may think himself morally superior, while behind his back you make sure that we will think him morally deficient.

The one relationship in which there must not be any distance, however, is between author and reader.

It is a frustrating experience for many beginning (and established) authors to find that although they meant the protagonist to appear sensitive, their readers find him self-pitying; although the author meant her to be witty, the readers find her vulgar. When this happens there is a failure of authorial or psychic distance: The author did not have sufficient perspective on the character to convince us to share his or her judgment. I recall one class in which a student author had written, with excellent use of image and scene, the story of a young man who fell in love with an exceptionally beautiful young woman, and whose feelings turned to revulsion when he found out she had had a mastectomy. The most vocal feminist in the class loved this story, which she described as "the exposé of a skuzzwort." This was not, from the author's point of view, a successful reading of his story. He had meant for the young man to be seen as a sympathetic character.

WHEN WRITERS ARE SELF-CONSCIOUS about themselves as writers they often keep a great distance from their characters, sounding as if they were writing encyclopedia entries instead of stories. Their hesitancy about physical and psychological intimacy can be a barrier to vital fiction.

Conversely, a narration that makes readers hear the characters' heavy breathing and smell their emotional anguish diminishes distance. Readers feel so close to the characters that, for those magical moments, they *become* those characters.

JEROME STERN

A writer may also create either distance or closeness through the use of time, space, tone, and irony. A story that happened long ago in a far away land, told by a detached narrator, won't feel the same as one happening in present tense, told by one of the characters. A story's tone and use of irony are also indications of how the reader should view the characters and their situations.

Point of View

WHO SPEAKS?

The Author	*The Author*	*A Character*
In: Third Person	In: Second Person	In: First Person
Editorial Omniscient	"You" as Character	Central Narrator
Limited Omniscient	"You" as Reader-	Peripheral Narrator
Objective	Turned-Character	

To Whom?

The Reader	Another Character or Characters	The Self

In What Form?

Story, Monologue, Letter, Journal, Interior Monologue, Stream of Consciousness, etc.

At What Distance?

Complete Identification		Complete Opposition

Choosing and *controlling* the psychic distance that best suits a given story is one of the most elusive challenges a writer faces. The good news for novice writers feeling overwhelmed by all these considerations is that point-of-view choices, like plot and theme, are seldom calculated and preplanned. Rather, point of view tends to evolve organically as a story develops, and you can usually trust intuition to guide you through several drafts. It is when a story is well underway that analysis of its specific point-of-view issues becomes most useful, and the feedback of other workshop members may be of particular value. If you are having trouble accessing the mind or heart of your character, it may be that a change in point of view will allow you to get closer and gain understanding. This can be accomplished by switching from first person to third or vice versa. After experimenting with a new point of view, you'll probably know within a paragraph or two if the switch will improve the story.

Consistency: A Caution

In establishing the story's point of view, you make your own rules, but having made them, you must stick to them. Your position as a writer is analogous to that of a poet who may choose whether to write free verse or a ballad stanza. If the poet chooses the stanza, then he or she is obliged to rhyme. Beginning writers of prose fiction are often tempted to shift viewpoint when it is both unnecessary and disruptive for readers.

> Leo's neck flushed against the prickly weave of his uniform collar. He concentrated on his buttons and tried not to look into the face of the bandmaster, who, however, was more amused than angry.

This is an awkward point-of-view shift because, having felt Leo's embarrassment with him, we are suddenly asked to leap into the bandmaster's feelings. The shift can be corrected by moving instead from Leo's mind to an observation that he might make.

> Leo's neck flushed against the prickly weave of his uniform collar. He concentrated on his buttons and tried not to look into the face of the bandmaster, who, however, was astonishingly smiling.

The rewrite is easier to follow because we remain with Leo's mind as he observes that the bandmaster is not angry. It further serves the purpose of implying that Leo fails to concentrate on his buttons, and so intensifies his confusion.

Apart from the use of significant detail, there is no more important skill for a writer of fiction to grasp than this: the control of point of view. Sometimes it may be hard simply to recognize that your narrative has leapt from one point of view to another. Often, in workshop, students are troubled by a point-of-view shift in someone else's story but can't spot one in their own. In other cases there's a healthy desire to explore every possibility in a scene, and a mistaken sense that this can't be done without changing point of view. Indeed, no writing rule is so frequently broken to such original and inventive effect as *consistency in point of view*, as several stories in this volume attest. Yet the general rule of consistency holds, and a writer shows his amateurism in the failure to stick to a single point of view. Once established, point of view constitutes a contract between author and reader, and it will be difficult to break the contract gracefully. If you have restricted yourself to the mind of James Lordly for five pages, as he observes the actions of Mrs. Grumms and her cats, you will violate the contract by suddenly dipping into Mrs. Grumms's mind to let us know what she thinks of James Lordly. We are likely to feel misused, and likely to cancel the contract altogether, if you then suddenly give us the thoughts of the cats.

◈

Victory Lap

GEORGE SAUNDERS

Three days shy of her fifteenth birthday, Alison Pope paused at the top of the stairs.

Say the staircase was marble. Say she descended and all heads turned. Where was {special one}? Approaching now, bowing slightly, he exclaimed, How can so much grace be contained in one small package? Oops. Had he said *small package*? And just stood there? Broad prince-like face totally bland of expression? Poor thing! Sorry, no way, down he went, he was definitely not {special one}.

What about this guy, behind Mr. Small Package, standing near the home entertainment center? With a thick neck of farmer integrity yet tender ample lips, who, placing one hand on the small of her back, whispered, Dreadfully sorry you had to endure that bit about the small package just now. Let us go stand on the moon. Or, uh, in the moon. In the moonlight.

Had he said, *Let us go stand on the moon*? If so, she would have to be like, {eyebrows up}. And if no wry acknowledgment was forthcoming, be like, Uh, I am not exactly dressed for standing on the moon, which, as I understand it, is super-cold?

Come on, guys, she couldn't keep treading gracefully on this marble stairwell in her mind forever! That dear old white-hair in the tiara was getting all like, *Why are those supposed princes making that darling girl march in place ad nausea?* Plus she had a recital tonight and had to go fetch her tights from the dryer.

Egads! One found oneself still standing at the top of the stairs.

Do the thing where, facing upstairs, hand on railing, you hop down the stairs one at a time, which was getting a lot harder lately, due to, someone's feet were getting longer every day, seemed like.

Pas de chat, pas de chat.

Changement, changement.

Hop over thin metal thingie separating hallway tile from living-room rug.

Curtsy to self in entryway mirror.

Come on, Mom, get here. We do not wish to be castrigated by Ms. Callow again in the wings.

Although actually she loved Ms. C. So strict! Also loved the other girls in class. And the girls from school. *Loved* them. Everyone was so nice. Plus the boys at her school. Plus the teachers at her school. All of them were doing their best. Actually, she loved her whole town. That adorable grocer, spraying his lettuce! Pastor Carol, with her large comfortable butt! The chubby postman, gesticulating with his padded envelopes! It had once been a mill town. Wasn't that crazy? What did that even mean?

Also she loved her house. Across the creek was the Russian church. So ethnic! That onion dome had loomed in her window since her Pooh footie days. Also loved Gladsong Drive. Every house on Gladsong was a Corona del Mar. That was amazing! If you had a friend on Gladsong, you already knew where everything was in his or her home.

Jeté, jeté, rond de jambe.

Pas de bourrée.

On a happy whim, do front roll, hop to your feet, kiss the picture of Mom and Dad taken at Penney's back in the Stone Ages, when you were that little cutie right there {kiss} with a hair bow bigger than all outdoors.

Sometimes, feeling happy like this, she imagined a baby deer trembling in the woods.

Where's your mama, little guy?

I don't know, the deer said in the voice of Heather's little sister Becca.

Are you afraid? she asked it. Are you hungry? Do you want me to hold you?

Okay, the baby deer said.

Here came the hunter now, dragging the deer's mother by the antlers. Her guts were completely splayed. Jeez, that was nice! She covered the baby's eyes and was like, Don't you have anything better to do, dank hunter, than kill this baby's mom? You seem like a nice enough guy.

Is my mom killed? the baby said in Becca's voice.

No, no, she said. This gentleman was just leaving.

The hunter, captivated by her beauty, toffed or doffed his cap, and, going down on one knee, said, If I could will life back into this fawn, I would do so, in hopes you might defer one tender kiss upon our elderly forehead.

Go, she said. Only, for your task of penance do not eat her. Lay her out in a field of clover, with roses strewn about her. And bestow a choir, to softly sing of her foul end.

Lay who out? the baby deer said.

No one, she said. Never mind. Stop asking so many questions.

Pas de chat, pas de chat

Changement, changement.

She felt hopeful that {special one} would hail from far away. The local boys possessed a certain *je ne sais quoi*, which, tell the truth, she was not *tres* crazy about, such as: actually named their own nuts. She had overheard that! And aspired to work for County Power because the work shirts were awesome and you got them free.

So ixnay on the local boys. A special ixnay on Matt Drey, owner of the largest mouth in the land.

Kissing him last night at the pep rally had been like kissing an underpass. Scary! Kissing Matt was like suddenly this cow in a sweater is bearing down on you, who will not take no for an answer, and his huge cow head is being flooded by chemicals that are drowning out what little powers of reason Matt actually did have.

What she liked was being in charge of her. Her body, her mind. Her thoughts, her career, her future.

That was what she liked.

So be it.

We might have a slight snack.

Un petit repas.

Was she special? Did she consider herself special? Oh, gosh, she didn't know. In the history of the world many had been more special than her. Helen Keller had been awesome; Mother Teresa was amazing Mrs. Roosevelt was quite chipper in spite of her husband, who was handicapped, which, in addition, she had been gay, with those big old teeth, long before such time as being gay and First Lady was even conceptual. She, Alison, could not hope to compete in the category of those ladies. Not yet, anyway!

There was so much she didn't know! Like how to change the oil. Or even check the oil. How to open the hood. How to bake brownies. That was embarrassing actually, being a girl and all. And what was a mortgage? Did it come with the house? When you breast-fed, did you have to push the milk out?

Egads. Who was this wan figure, visible through the living-room window, trotting up Gladsong Drive? Kyle Boot, palest kid in all the land? Still dressed in his weird cross-country-running toggles?

Poor thing. He looked like a skeleton with a mullet. Were those cross-country shorts from the like *Charlie's Angels* days or *quoi*? How could he run so well when he seemed to have literally no muscles? Every day he ran home like this, shirtless with his backpack on, then hit the remote from down by the Fungs' and scooted into his garage without breaking stride.

You almost had to admire the poor goof.

They'd grown up together, been little beaners in that mutual sandbox down by the creek. Hadn't they bathed together when wee or some such crud? She hoped that never got out. Because in terms of friends, Kyle was basically down to Feddy Slavko, who walked leaning way backward and was always retrieving things from between his teeth, announcing the name of the retrieved thing in Greek, then re-eating it. Kyle's mom and dad didn't let him do squat. He had to call home if the movie in World Culture might show bare boobs. Each of the items in his lunch box was clearly labeled.

Pas de bourrée.

And curtsy.

Pour quantity of Cheez Doodles into compartmentalized old-school Tupperware dealie.

Thanks, Mom, thanks, Dad. Your kitchen *rocks.*

Shake Tupperware dealie back and forth like panning for gold, then offer to some imaginary poor gathered round.

Please enjoy. Is there anything else I can do for you folks?

You have already done enough, Alison, by even deigning to speak to us.

That is so not true! Don't you understand, all people deserve respect? Each of us is a rainbow.

Uh, really? Look at this big open sore on my poor shriveled flank.

Allow me to fetch you some Vaseline.

That would be much appreciated. This thing kills.

But as far as that rainbow idea? She believed that. People were amazing. Mom was awesome, Dad was awesome, her teachers worked so hard and had kids of their own, and some were even getting divorced, such as Mrs. Dees, but still always took time for their students. What she found especially inspiring about Mrs. Dees was that, even though Mr. Dees was cheating on Mrs. Dees with the lady who ran the bowling alley, Mrs. Dees was still teaching the best course ever in Ethics, posing such questions as: Can goodness win? Or do good people always get shafted, evil being more reckless? That last bit seemed to be Mrs. Dees taking a shot at the bowling-alley gal. But seriously! Is life fun or scary? Are people good or bad? On the one hand, that clip of those gauntish pale bodies being steamrolled while fat German ladies looked on chomping gum. On the other hand, sometimes rural folks, even if their particular farms were on hills, stayed up late filling sandbags.

In their straw poll she had voted for people being good and life being fun, with Mrs. Dees giving her a pitying glance as she stated her views: To do good, you just have to decide to do good. You have to be brave. You have to stand up for what's right. At that last, Mrs. Dees had made this kind of groan. Which was fine. Mrs. Dees had a lot of pain in her life, yet, interestingly? Still obviously found something fun about life and good about people, because otherwise why sometimes stay up so late grading you come in next day all exhausted, blouse on backward, having messed it up in the early-morning dark, you dear discombobulated thing?

Here came a knock on the door. Back door. In-ter-est-ing. Who could it be? Father Dmitri from across the way? UPS? FedEx? With *un petit* check *pour Papa?*

Jeté, jeté, rond de jambe.

Pas de bourrée.

Open door, and—

Here was a man she did not know. Quite huge fellow, in one of those meter-reader vests.

Something told her to step back in, slam the door. But that seemed rude.

Instead she froze, smiled, did {eyebrow raise} to indicate: May I help you?

Kyle Boot dashed through the garage, into the living area, where the big clocklike wooden indicator was set at All Out. Other choices included: Mom & Dad Out; Mom Out; Dad Out; Kyle Out; Mom & Kyle Out; Dad & Kyle Out; and All In.

Why did they even need All In? Wouldn't they know it when they were All In? Would he like to ask Dad that? Who, in his excellent totally silent downstairs woodshop, had designed and built the Family Status Indicator?

Ha.

Ha ha.

On the kitchen island was a Work Notice.

Scout: New geode on deck. Place in yard per included drawing. No goofing. Rake areas first, put down plastic as I have shown you. Then lay in white rock. THIS GEODE EXPENSIVE. Pls take seriously. No reason this should not be done by time I get home. This = five (5) Work Points.

Gar, Dad, do you honestly feel it fair that I should have to slave in the yard until dark after a rigorous cross-country practice that included sixteen 440s, eight 880s, a mile-for-time, a kajillion Drake sprints, and a five-mile Indian relay?

Shoes off, mister.

Yoinks, too late. He was already at the TV. And had left an incriminating trail of microclods. Way verboten. Could the microclods be hand-plucked? Although, problem: if he went back to hand-pluck the microclods, he'd leave an incriminating new trail of microclods.

He took off his shoes and stood mentally rehearsing a little show he liked to call WHAT IF ... RIGHT NOW?

WHAT IF they came home RIGHT NOW?

It's a funny story, Dad! I came in thoughtlessly! Then realized what I'd done! I guess, when I think about it, what I'm happy about? Is how quickly I self-corrected! The reason I came in so thoughtlessly was, I wanted to get right to work, Dad, per your note!

He raced in his socks to the garage, threw his shoes into the garage, ran for the vacuum, vacuumed up the microclods, then realized, holy golly, he had thrown his shoes into the garage rather than placing them on the Shoe Sheet as required, toes facing away from the door for ease of donnage later.

He stepped into the garage, placed his shoes on the Shoe Sheet, stepped back inside.

Scout, Dad said in his head, has anyone ever told you that even the most neatly maintained garage is going to have some oil on its floor, which is now on your socks, being tracked all over the tan Berber?

Oh gar, his ass was grass.

But no—*celebrate good times, come on*—no oil stain on rug.

He tore off his socks. It was absolutely verboten for him to be in the main living area barefoot. Mom and Dad coming home to find him

Tarzaning around like some sort of white trasher would not be the least fucking bit—

Swearing in your head? Dad said in his head. Step up, Scout, be a man. If you want to swear, swear aloud.

I don't want to swear aloud.

Then don't swear in your head.

Mom and Dad would be heartsick if they could hear the swearing he sometimes did in his head, such as crap-cunt shit-turd dick-in-the-ear butt-creamery. Why couldn't he stop doing that? They thought so highly of him, sending weekly braggy emails to both sets of grandparents, such as: Kyle's been super-busy keeping up his grades while running varsity cross-country though still a sophomore, while setting aside a little time each day to manufacture such humdingers as cunt-swoggle rear-fuck—

What was wrong with him? Why couldn't he be grateful for all that Mom and Dad did for him, instead of—

Cornhole the ear-cunt.

Flake-fuck the pale vestige with a proddering dick-knee.

You could always clear the mind with a hard pinch on your own minimal love handle.

Ouch.

Hey, today was Tuesday, a Major Treat day. The five (5) new Work Points for placing the geode, plus his existing two (2) Work Points, totaled seven (7) Work Points, which, added to his eight (8) accrued Usual Chore Points, made fifteen (15) Total Treat Points, which could garner him a Major Treat (for example, two handfuls of yogurt-covered raisins) plus twenty free-choice TV minutes, although the particular show would have to be negotiated with Dad at time of cash-in.

One thing you will not be watching, Scout, is *America's Most Outspoken Dirt Bikers.*

Whatever.

Whatever, Dad.

Really, Scout? "Whatever"? Will it be "whatever" when I take away all your Treat Points and force you to quit cross-country, as I have several times threatened to do if a little more cheerful obedience wasn't forthcoming?

No, no, no. I don't want to quit, Dad. Please. I'm good at it. You'll see, first meet. Even Matt Drey said—

Who is Matt Drey? Some ape on the football team?

Yes.

Is his word law?

No.

What did he say?

Little shit can run.

Nice talk, Scout. Ape talk. Anyway, you may not make it to the first meet. Your ego seems to be overflowing its banks. And why? Because you can jog? Anyone can jog. Beasts of the field can jog.

I'm not quitting! Anal-cock shit-bird rectum-fritz! Please, I'm begging
you, it's the only thing I'm decent at! Mom, if he makes me quit I swear
to God I'll—

Drama doesn't suit you, Beloved Only.

If you want the privilege of competing in a team sport, Scout, show
us that you can live within our perfectly reasonable system of directives
designed to benefit you.

Hello.

A van had just pulled up in the St. Mikhail's parking lot.

Kyle walked in a controlled, gentlemanly manner to the kitchen
counter. On the counter was Kyle's Traffic Log, which served the dual
purpose of (1) buttressing Dad's argument that Father Dmitri should
build a soundproof retaining wall and (2) constituting a data set
for a possible Science Fair project for him, Kyle, entitled, by Dad,
"Correlation of Church Parking Lot Volume vs. Day of Week, with
Ancillary Investigation of Sunday Volume Throughout Year."

Smiling agreeably as if he enjoyed filling out the Log, Kyle very leg-
ibly filled out the Log:

Vehicle: VAN.
Color: GRAY.
Make: CHEVY.
Year: UNKNOWN.

A guy got out of the van. One of the usual Rooskies. "Rooskie" was
an allowed slang. Also "dang it." Also "holy golly." Also "crapper." The
Rooskie was wearing a jean jacket over a hoodie, which, in Kyle's experience, was not unusual church-wear for the Rooskies, who sometimes
came directly over from Jiffy Lube still wearing coveralls.

Under "Vehicle Driver" he wrote, PROBABLE PARISHIONER.

That sucked. Stank, rather. The guy being a stranger, he, Kyle, now had
to stay inside until the stranger left the neighborhood. Which totally futzed
up his geode placing. He'd be out there until midnight. What a detriment!

The guy put on a Day Glo-vest. Ah, dude was a meter reader.

The meter reader looked left, then right, leaped across the creek,
entered the Pope backyard, passed between the soccer-ball rebounder
and the in-ground pool, then knocked on the Pope door.

Good leap there, Boris.

The door swung open.

Alison.

Kyle's heart was singing. He'd always thought that was just a
phrase. Alison was like a national treasure. In the dictionary under
"beauty" there should be a picture of her in that jean skort. Although
lately she didn't seem to like him all that much.

Now she stepped across her deck so the meter reader could show her
something. Something electrical wrong on the roof? The guy seemed eager
to show her. Actually, he had her by the wrist. And was like tugging.

That was weird. Wasn't it? Something had never been weird around here before. So probably it was fine. Probably the guy was just a really new meter reader?

Somehow Kyle felt like stepping out onto the deck. He stepped out. The guy froze. Alison's eyes were scared-horse eyes. The guy cleared his throat, turned slightly to let Kyle see something.

A knife.

The meter reader had a knife.

Here's what you're doing, the guy said. Standing right there until we leave. Move a muscle, I knife her in the heart. Swear to God. Got it?

Kyle's mouth was so spitless all he could do was make his mouth do the shape it normally did when saying Yes.

Now they were crossing the yard. Alison threw herself to the ground. The guy hauled her up. She threw herself down. He hauled her up. It was odd seeing Alison tossed like a rag doll in the sanctuary of the perfect yard her dad had made for her. She threw herself down.

The guy hissed something and she rose, suddenly docile.

In his chest Kyle felt the many directives, Major and Minor, he was right now violating. He was on the deck shoeless, on the deck shirtless, was outside when a stranger was near, had engaged with that stranger.

Last week Sean Ball had brought a wig to school to more effectively mimic the way Bev Mirren chewed her hair when nervous. Kyle had briefly considered intervening. At Evening Meeting, Mom had said that she considered Kyle's decision not to intervene judicious. Dad had said, That was none of your business. You could have been badly hurt. Mom had said, Think of all the resources we've invested in you, Beloved Only. Dad had said, I know we sometimes strike you as strict but you are literally all we have.

They were at the soccer-ball rebounder now, Alison's arm up behind her back. She was making a low repetitive sound of denial, like she was trying to invent a noise that would adequately communicate her feelings about what she'd just this instant realized was going to happen to her.

He was just a kid. There was nothing he could do. In his chest he felt the lush release of pressure that always resulted when he submitted to a directive. There at his feet was the geode. He should just look at that until they left. It was a great one. Maybe the greatest one ever. The crystals at the cutaway glistened in the sun. It would look nice in the yard. Once he placed it. He'd place it once they were gone. Dad would be impressed that even after what had occurred he'd remembered to place the geode.

That's the ticket, Scout.

We are well pleased, Beloved Only.

Super job, Scout.

Holy crap. It was happening. She was marching along all meek like the trouper he'd known she'd be. He'd had her in mind since the baptism of what's-his-name. Sergei's kid. At the Russian church. She'd been standing in her yard, her dad or some such taking her picture.

He'd been like, Hello, Betty.

Kenny had been like, Little young, bro.

He'd been like, For you, grandpa.

When you studied history, the history of cultures, you saw your own individual time as hidebound. There were various theories of acquiescence. In Bible days a king might ride through a field and go: That one. And she would be brought unto him. And they would duly be betrothed and if she gave birth unto a son, super, bring out the streamers, she was a keeper. Was she, that first night, digging it? Probably not. Was she shaking like a leaf? Didn't matter. What mattered was offspring and the furtherance of the lineage. Plus the exaltation of the king, which resulted in righteous kingly power.

Here was the creek.

He marched her through.

The following bullet points remained in the decision matrix: take to side van door, shove in, follow in, tape wrists/mouth, hook to chain, make speech. He had the speech down cold. Had practiced it both in his head and on the recorder: *Calm your heart, darling, I know you're scared because you don't know me yet and didn't expect this today but give me a chance and you will see we will fly high. See I am putting the knife right over here and I don't expect I'll have to use it, right?*

If she wouldn't get in the van, punch hard in gut. Then pick up, carry to side van door, throw in, tape wrists/mouth, hook to chain, make speech, etc., etc.

Stop, pause, he said.

Gal stopped.

Fucksake. Side door of the van was locked. How undisciplined was that. Ensuring that the door was unlocked was clearly indicated on the pre-mission matrix. Melvin appeared in his mind. On Melvin's face was the look of hot disappointment that had always preceded an ass whooping, which had always preceded the other thing. Put up your hands, Melvin said, defend yourself.

True, true. Little error there. Should have double-checked the pre-mission matrix.

No biggie.

Joy not fear.

Melvin was dead fifteen years. Mom dead twelve.

Little bitch was turned around now, looking back at the house. That willfulness wouldn't stand. That was going to get nipped in the bud. He'd have to remember to hurt her early, establish a baseline.

Turn the fuck around, he said.

She turned around.

He unlocked the door, swung it open. Moment of truth. If she got in, let him use the tape, they were home free. He'd picked out a place in Sackett, big-ass cornfield, dirt road leading in. If fuckwise it went good they'd pick up the freeway from there. Basically steal the van. It was Kenny's van. He'd borrowed it for the day. Screw Kenny. Kenny had once called him stupid. Too bad, Kenny, that remark just cost you one van. If fuckwise it went bad, she didn't properly arouse him, he'd abort the activity, truncate the subject, heave the thing out, clean van as necessary, go buy corn, return van to Kenny, say, Hey, bro, here's a shitload of corn, thanks for the van, I never could've bought a suitable quantity of corn in my car. Then lay low, watch the papers like he'd done with the nonarousing redhead out in—

Gal gave him an imploring look, like, Please don't.

Was this a good time? To give her one in the gut, knock the wind out of her sails?

It was.

He did.

The geode was beautiful. What a beautiful geode. What made it beautiful? What were the principal characteristics of a beautiful geode? Come on, think. Come on, concentrate.

She'll recover in time, Beloved Only.

None of our affair, Scout.

We're amazed by your good judgment, Beloved Only.

Dimly he noted that Alison had been punched. Eyes on the geode, he heard the little *oof.*

His heart dropped at the thought of what he was letting happen. They'd used goldfish snacks as coins. They'd made bridges out of rocks. Down by the creek. Back in the day. Oh God. He should've never stepped outside. Once they were gone he'd just go back inside, pretend he'd never stepped out, make the model-railroad town, still be making it when Mom and Dad got home. When eventually someone told him about it? He'd make a certain face. Already on his face he could feel the face he would make, like, What? Alison? Raped? Killed? Oh God. Raped and killed while I innocently made my railroad town, sitting cross-legged and unaware on the floor like a tiny little—

No. No, no, no. They'd be gone soon. Then he could go inside. Call 911. Although then everyone would know he'd done nothing. All his future life would be bad. Forever he'd be the guy who'd done nothing. Besides, calling wouldn't do any good. They'd be long gone. The parkway was just across Featherstone, with like a million arteries and cloverleafs or whatever spouting out of it. So that was that. In he'd go. As soon as they left. Leave, leave, leave, he thought, so I can go inside, forget this ever—

Then he was running. Across the lawn. Oh God! What was he doing, what was he doing? Jesus, shit, the directives he was violating! Running in the yard (bad for the sod); transporting a geode without its protective wrapping; hopping the fence, which stressed the fence, which had cost a pretty penny; leaving the yard; leaving the yard barefoot; entering the Secondary Area without permission; entering the creek barefoot (broken glass, dangerous microorganisms), and, not only that, oh God, suddenly he saw what this giddy part of himself intended, which was to violate a directive so Major and absolute that it wasn't even a directive, since you didn't need a directive to know how totally verboten it was to—

He burst out of the creek, the guy still not turning, and let the geode fly into his head, which seemed to emit a weird edge-seep of blood even before the skull visibly indented and the guy sat right on his ass.

Yes! Score! It was fun! Fun dominating a grown-up! Fun using the most dazzling gazelle-like leg speed ever seen in the history of mankind to dash soundlessly across space and master this huge galoot, who otherwise, right now, would be—

What if he hadn't?

God, what if he hadn't?

He imagined the guy bending Alison in two like a pale garment bag while pulling her hair and thrusting bluntly, as he, Kyle, sat cowed and obedient, tiny railroad viaduct grasped in his pathetic babyish—

Jesus! He skipped over and hurled the geode through the windshield of the van, which imploded, producing an inward rain of glass shards that made the sound of thousands of tiny bamboo wind chimes.

He scrambled up the hood of the van, retrieved the geode.

Really? Really? You were going to ruin her life, ruin my life, you cunt-probe dick-munch ass-gashing Animal? Who's bossing who now? Gash-ass, jizz-lips, turd-munch—

He'd never felt so strong/angry/wild. Who's the man? Who's your daddy? What else must he do? To ensure that Animal did no further harm? You still moving, freak? Got a plan, stroke-dick? Want a skull gash on top of your existing skull gash, big man? You think I won't? You think I—

Easy, Scout, you're out of control.

Slow your motor down, Beloved Only.

Quiet. I'm the boss of me.

FUCK!

What the hell? What was he doing on the ground? Had he tripped? Did someone wonk him? Did a branch fall? God damn. He touched his head. His hand came away bloody.

The beanpole kid was bending. To pick something up. A rock. Why was that kid off the porch? Where was the knife?

Where was the gal?

Crab-crawling toward the creek.

Flying across her yard.

Going into her house.

Fuck it, everything was fucked. Better hit the road. With what, his good looks? He had like eight bucks total.

Ah Christ! The kid had smashed the windshield! With the rock! Kenny was not going to like that one bit.

He tried to stand but couldn't. The blood was just pouring out. He was not going to jail again. No way. He'd slit his wrists. Where was the knife? He'd stab himself in the chest. That had nobility. Then the people would know his name. Which of them had the balls to samurai themselves with a knife in the chest?

None.

Nobody.

Go ahead, pussy. Do it.

No. The king does not take his own life. The superior man silently accepts the mindless rebuke of the rabble. Waits to rise and fight anew. Plus he had no idea where the knife was. Well, he didn't need it. He'd crawl into the woods, kill something with his bare hands. Or make a trap from some grass. Ugh. Was he going to barf? There, he had. Right on his lap.

Figures you'd blow the simplest thing, Melvin said.

Melvin, God, can't you see my head is bleeding so bad?

A kid did it to you. You're a joke. You got fucked by a kid.

Oh, sirens, perfect.

Well, it was a sad day for the cops. He'd fight them hand to hand. He'd sit until the last moment, watching them draw near, doing a silent death mantra that would centralize all his life power in his fists.

He sat thinking about his fists. They were huge granite boulders. They were a pit bull each. He tried to get up. Somehow his legs weren't working. He hoped the cops would get here soon. His head really hurt. When he touched up there, things moved. It was like he was wearing a gore cap. He was going to need a bunch of stitches. He hoped it wouldn't hurt too much. Probably it would, though.

Where was that beanpole kid?

Oh, here he was.

Looming over him, blocking out the sun, rock held high, yelling something, but he couldn't tell what, because of the ringing in his ears.

Then he saw that the kid was going to bring the rock down. He closed his eyes and waited and was not at peace at all but instead felt the beginnings of a terrible dread welling up inside him, and if that dread kept growing at the current rate, he realized in a flash of insight, there was a name for the place he would be then, and it was Hell.

Alison stood at the kitchen window. She'd peed herself. Which was fine. People did that. When super-scared. She'd noticed it while making the call. Her hands had been shaking so bad. They still were. One leg was doing that Thumper thing. God, the stuff he'd said to her. He'd punched her. He'd pinched her. There was a big blue mark on her arm.

How could Kyle still be out there? But there he was, in those comical shorts, so confident he was goofing around, hands clenched over his head like a boxer from some cute alt universe where a kid that skinny could actually win a fight against a guy with a knife.

Wait.

His hands weren't clenched. He was holding the rock, shouting something down at the guy, who was on his knees, like the blindfolded prisoner in that video they'd seen in History, about to get sword-killed by a formal dude in a helmet.

Kyle, don't, she whispered.

For months afterward she had nightmares in which Kyle brought the rock down. She was on the deck trying to scream his name but nothing was coming out. Down came the rock. Then the guy had no head. The blow just literally dissolved his head. Then his body tumped over and Kyle turned to her with this heartbroken look of, My life is over. I killed a guy.

Why was it, she sometimes wondered, that in dreams we can't do the simplest things? Like a crying puppy is standing on some broken glass and you want to pick it up and brush the shards off its pads but you can't because you're balancing a ball on your head. Or you're driving and there's this old guy on crutches, and you go, to Mr. Feder, your Driver's Ed teacher, Should I swerve? And he's like, Uh, probably. But then you hear this big clunk and Feder makes a negative mark in his book.

Sometimes she'd wake up crying from the dream about Kyle. The last time, Mom and Dad were already there, going, That's not how it was. Remember, Allie? How did it happen? Say it. Say it out loud. Allie, can you tell Mommy and Daddy how it really happened?

I ran outside, she said. I shouted.

That's right, Dad said. You shouted. Shouted like a champ.

And what did Kyle do? Mom said.

Put down the rock, she said.

A bad thing happened to you kids, Dad said. But it could have been worse.

So much worse, Mom said.

But because of you kids, Dad said, it wasn't.

You did so good, Mom said.

Did beautiful, Dad said.

◈

No One's a Mystery

ELIZABETH TALLENT

For my eighteenth birthday Jack gave me a five-year diary with a latch and a little key, light as a dime. I was sitting beside him scratching at the lock, which didn't seem to want to work, when he thought he saw his wife's Cadillac in the distance, coming toward us. He pushed me down onto the dirty floor of the pickup and kept one hand on my head while I inhaled the musk of his cigarettes in the dashboard ashtray and sang along with Rosanne Cash on the tape deck. We'd been drinking tequila and the bottle was between his legs, resting up against his crotch, where the seam of his Levi's was bleached linen-white, though the Levi's were nearly new. I don't know why his Levi's always bleached like that, along the seams and at the knees. In a curve of cloth his zipper glinted, gold.

"It's her," he said. "She keeps the lights on in the daytime. I can't think of a single habit in a woman that irritates me more than that." When he saw that I was going to stay still he took his hand from my head and ran it through his own dark hair.

"Why does she?" I said.

"She thinks it's safer. Why does she need to be safer? She's driving exactly fifty-five miles an hour. She believes in those signs: 'Speed Monitored by Aircraft.' It doesn't matter that you can look up and see that the sky is empty."

"She'll see your lips move, Jack. She'll know you're talking to someone."

"She'll think I'm singing along with the radio."

He didn't lift his hand, just raised the fingers in salute while the pressure of his palm steadied the wheel, and I heard the Cadillac honk twice, musically; he was driving easily eighty miles an hour. I studied his boots. The elk heads stitched into the leather were bearded with frayed thread, the toes were scuffed, and there was a compact wedge of muddy manure between the heel and the sole—the same boots he'd been wearing for the two years I'd known him. On the tape deck Rosanne Cash sang, "Nobody's into me, no one's a mystery."

"Do you think she's getting famous because of who her daddy is or for herself?" Jack said.

"There are about a hundred pop tops on the floor, did you know that? Some little kid could cut a bare foot on one of these, Jack."

"No little kids get into this truck except for you."

"How come you let it get so dirty?"

"'How come,'" he mocked. "You even sound like a kid. You can get back into the seat now, if you want. She's not going to look over her shoulder and see you."

"How do you know?"

"I just know," he said. "Like I know I'm going to get meat loaf for supper. It's in the air. Like I know what you'll be writing in that diary."

"What will I be writing?" I knelt on my side of the seat and craned around to look at the butterfly of dust printed on my jeans. Outside the window Wyoming was dazzling in the heat. The wheat was fawn and yellow and parted smoothly by the thin dirt road. I could smell the water in the irrigation ditches hidden in the wheat.

"Tonight you'll write, 'I love Jack. This is my birthday present from him. I can't imagine anybody loving anybody more than I love Jack.'"

"I can't."

"In a year you'll write, 'I wonder what I ever really saw in Jack. I wonder why I spent so many days just riding around in his pickup. It's true he taught me something about sex. It's true there wasn't ever much else to do in Cheyenne.'"

"I won't write that."

"In two years you'll write, 'I wonder what that old guy's name was, the one with the curly hair and the filthy dirty pickup truck and time on his hands.'"

"I won't write that."

"No?"

"Tonight I'll write, 'I love Jack. This is my birthday present from him. I can't imagine anybody loving anybody more than I love Jack.'"

"No, you can't," he said. "You can't imagine it."

"In a year I'll write, 'Jack should be home any minute now. The table's set—my grandmother's linen and her old silver and the yellow candles left over from the wedding—but I don't know if I can wait until after the trout a la Navarra to make love to him.'"

"It must have been a fast divorce."

"In two years I'll write, 'Jack should be home by now. Little Jack is hungry for his supper. He said his first word today besides "Mama" and "Papa." He said "kaka."'"

Jack laughed. "He was probably trying to finger-paint with kaka on the bathroom wall when you heard him say it."

"In three years I'll write, 'My nipples are a little sore from nursing Eliza Rosamund.'"

"Rosamund. Every little girl should have a middle name she hates."

"'Her breath smells like vanilla and her eyes are just Jack's color of blue.'"

"That's nice." Jack said.

"So, which one do you like?"

"I like yours," he said. "But I believe mine."

"It doesn't matter. I believe mine."

"Not in your heart of hearts, you don't."

"You're wrong."

"I'm not wrong," he said. "And her breath would smell like your milk, and it's kind of a bittersweet smell, if you want to know the truth."

Reply All

ROBIN HEMLEY

To: Poetry Association of the Western Suburbs Listserve
From: Lisa Drago-Harse
Subject: Next Meeting
Date: July 17th

Hi all,

I wanted to confirm that our next meeting will be held in the Sir Francis Drake Room at the Bensonville Hampton Inn on August 3rd. Minutes from our last meeting and an agenda for the next meeting will follow shortly.

Peace and Poetry,
Lisa Drago-Harse
Secretary/PAWS

To: Poetry Association of the Western Suburbs Listserve
From: Michael Stroud
Re: Re: Next Meeting
Date: July 17th

Dearest Lisa,

First of all, I LOVE your mole and don't find it unsightly in the least! There is absolutely no reason for you to be ashamed of it (though it might be a good idea to have it checked out). But please don't remove it! Heaven forbid, my darling! As I recall, I gave you considerable pleasure when I sucked and licked it like a nipple. A nipple it is in size and shape, if not placement. That no one else knows your mole's position on your body (other than your benighted husband, poor limp Richard, that Son(net) of a Bitch as you call him) is more the pity (if Marvell had known such a mole, he undoubtedly would have added an extra stanza to his poem). But my coy mistress is not SO terribly coy as all that, if I remember correctly (and how could I forget!) You were not at all what I had expected in bed—not that I had any expectations at all. When you started massaging my crotch with your foot underneath the table in the Sir Francis Drake Room, I was at first shocked. For a moment, I thought perhaps the unseen massager was none other than our esteemed president, the redoubtable Darcy McFee, (makeup and wardrobe courtesy of Yoda). Is that terrible of me? I have nothing personal against her, really, except for her execrable taste in poetry, and the fact that you should be president, not she. And her breath. And that habit of pulling her nose when she speaks and that absolutely horrific expression of hers, Twee. As in, "I find his poetry just so twee." What does twee mean and why does she keep inflicting it upon us! So imagine my horror when I felt this foot in my crotch and I stared across the table at the two of you—she twitching like a slug that's had salt poured on it and you immobile except for your Mont Blanc pen taking down the minutes. Ah, to think that the taking down of minutes could be such an erotic activity, but in your capable hands, it is. To think that mere hours later, it would be my Mont Blanc you'd grasp so firmly, guiding me into the lyrical book of your body. But initially, I thought the worst, that it was Darcy, not you. My only consolation was the idea that at least I had her on a sexual harassment suit, her being my boss after all at Roosevelt. Another reason, I thought it was her and not you was because I know you're married and she isn't and I knew that Richard is a member of our esteemed organization, too (and he was in the room, seated beside you no less!). It was only that sly smile in your eyes that tipped me off. I, too, love the danger that illicit public sex brings, as long as it's kept under the table, so to speak. And yes, maybe someday we can make love on that very same table in the Sir Francis Drake Room, my darling. But I must ask you, sweetheart, where did you learn that amazing trick. I have seen people wiggle their ears before, but never that! What amazing talent and such a pity that this is not something you bring out at parties or poetry readings to awe the dumb masses! Would Darcy find that too twee? I think not! Thinking of you now makes me so hot. I want to nibble you. I want to live in your panties. I want to write a series of odes to you equal in number to every lucky taste bud on my tongue, every nerve ending (no, not endings but beginnings!) on my body that live in rapture of your every pore. No, not poor, but rich. I am rich. I make metaphors of your muscles, of your thighs, of the fecund wetness bursting with your being and effulgence. I must swallow now. I must breathe. I must take my leave, my darling, and go now to relieve myself of my private thoughts of you and you alone.

With undying love and erotic daydreams,
Mikey

P.S. Do you think you could get away for an evening next week? Could you be called away from Richard for an emergency meeting of the Public Relations Committee?

To: PAWS Listserve
From: Darcy McFee
Re: Re: Re: Next Meeting
Date: July 17th

I am traveling now and will not be answering e-mails until I return on July 21st.

Thanks!
Darcy

To: PAWS Listserve
From: Sam Fulgram, Jr.
Re: Re: Re: Re: Next Meeting
Date: July 17th

Whoa boy! Do you realize you just sent out your love note to the entire Poetry Association of the Western Suburbs listserve?

Cheers,
Sam

P.S. That mole? You've got my imagination running wild. As long as the entire organization knows about it now, would you mind divulging its location? I'd sleep better at night knowing it.

To: PAWS Listserve
From: Betsy Midchester
Re: Re: Re: Re: Re: Next Meeting
Date July 17th

Hi all,

Well! That last message from "Mikey" Stroud certainly made my day. I thought at first the message was addressed to me. As I had no memory of placing my foot in Mike's crotch, I naturally assumed that I needed an adjustment of my medication so that I wouldn't forget such episodes in the future. Now I see it's simply Michael ("Down Boy") Stroud and our esteemed Secretary of the Galloping Mont Blaaaaanc who need the medication adjustments. Thanks, in any case, for a much needed lift in an otherwise humdrum day.

Betsy Midchester
Treasurer/PAWS

To: PAWS Listserve
From: Lisa Drago-Harse
Re: Re: Re: Re: Re: Re: Next Meeting
Date: July 17th

This is a nightmare. I'm not quite sure what to say except that life is unpredictable and often irreversible. While I do not wish to go into details or make excuses for the above e-mail from Michael Stroud, I would like to clarify one thing: that was not my foot in your crotch Michael. But your belief that it was my foot in your crotch explains a few things concerning your subsequent behavior toward me that were, up until this moment, a mystery.

LDH

To: PAWS Listserve
From: Michael Stroud
Re: Re: Re: Re: Re: Re: Re: Next Meeting
Date: July 17th

I'm

To: PAWS Listserve
From: Michael Stroud
Re: Re: Re: Re: Re: Re: Re: Re: Next Meeting
Date: July 17th

I hit the send button by mistake before I was ready. This isn't my day, to say the least! I'm sorry!!!! I'd like to apologize to the entire PAWS community, and also to Lisa's husband Richard and to Darcy. And to you, Lisa. I don't mean to make excuses for myself, but I would like to say that I've been under a tremendous amount of pressure of late, at school, at home, and I am nothing if not vulnerable and flawed.

All I can say is that in poetry I find some solace for the petty actions of others and the sometimes monstrous actions of which I'm all too capable. As déclassé as Truth and Beauty are these days, it is in such expressions as those of Matthew Arnold, Keats, Byron, and Shelly to whom I look for my meager draught of the Divine. And sometimes, I must admit, I seek in the affection of my fellow poetry lovers, the divinity which I myself lack. I ask you all to blame me, not Lisa, for what has happened.

But if not your foot, Lisa, then whose?
Michael Stroud

To: PAWS Listserve
From: Greg Rudolfsky
Re: Re: Re: Re: Re: Re: Re: Re: Re: RESPECT
Date: July 17th

Just a little bit, Just a little bit.
Sock it to me, sock it to me, sock it to me, sock it to me, sock it to me, sock it to me, sock it to me, sock it to me, RESPECT, Just a little bit, just a little bit...

To: PAWS Listserve
From: Samantha M. Poulsen, RN
Subject: Fecund Poets
Date: July 17th

I do not care whose foot is in whose crotch, but I think it's insulting and idiotic that so-called educated people would use such phrases as, "the fecund wetness bursting with your being and effulgence." And officers of the PAWS at that!

To: PAWS Listserve
From: Richard Harse
Re: Fecund Poets
Date: July 17th

I would like to tender my resignation in the Poets of the Western Suburbs, as I will be tendering my resignation in several other areas of my life. I only belonged to PAWS in any case because of my wife's interest in poetry. I wanted to share her interests, but clearly not all of them.

To: PAWS
From: Darcy McFee
Re: Fecund Poets
Date: July 22nd

Well, it seems that our little organization has been busy in my absence. I have over 300 new messages in my e-mail account, all, it seems from my fellow poetry lovers! I haven't yet had a chance to read your exchanges, but I will soon. In the meantime, I wanted to convey some exciting news. This weekend, while attending a workshop at Wright State in Dayton, I ran into the former Poet Laureate, Billy Collins, who has agreed to be our special guest at our annual Poetry Bash in Oak Park. He said he's heard quite a lot about our organization in recent days and that our board had achieved near legendary status in the poetry community. I knew this would make you as proud as it makes me.

To: PAWS Listserve
From: Darcy McFee
Subject: Twee
Date: July 24th

So this is how it is. Upon reading the 300 e-mails that collected in my inbox over the weekend, my mind is a riot of emotions. I have not slept for nearly 48 hours. Never before have I been so insulted. Yet, I also know that I am, at least in part, to blame. Had I not stuck my foot in Michael Stroud's crotch, none of this would have happened. Twitching like a slug that's had salt poured on it? That hurts, Michael. It really does. I didn't realize you were so shallow. But in reading your collective e-mails, I see that at least half our membership has a decidedly sadistic bent. In any case, it was not your crotch, I aimed for, Michael, but the crotch of our Vice-President, Amir Bathshiri, with whom I have long been intimately acquainted, both of us having lost our spouses several years ago. If the seating arrangements in the Sir Francis Drake Room were any less cramped, none of these misunderstandings would have occurred. Of course, I never would have tried to fondle you, Michael. In the first place, you are the most boring, tedious person I have met in my life, and believe me, as Chair of the English Dept. at Roosevelt, I have met my share of boring, tedious people. You recite poetry with all the grace of a highway sign that cautions one to beware of falling rocks. In fact, I would rather make love to a falling rock. But enough! I know that it is my errant foot to blame. Amir and I have talked this over and have decided to withdraw from PAWS as well as from academia. Early retirement calls, Michael and Lisa, and I will give neither of you a thought as I walk along the beach hand in hand with Amir in the months and years to come, listening to the mermaids singing each to each.

Yes, Michael, I find you and your crotch and your paramour the very essence of Twee.

To: PAWS Listserve
From: Betsy Midchester/Treasurer
Subject: New Elections
Date: July 30th

Please note that the agenda for our next meeting has changed. We will spend most of the meeting on new elections to be held for the positions of President, Vice-President and Secretary of our organization. Note, too, that we will no longer be meeting in the Sir Francis Drake Room of the Bensonville Hampton Inn. Instead, we will be meeting in the cafeteria of Enchanted Gardens Residence for Seniors in Glen Ellyn. The change in venue was planned well in advance of recent events, so members should not read anything into this (though if any organization's members are skilled at reading between the lines, it should be ours). Please think about whom you would like to nominate for these important positions in our organization. And in the meantime, please remember to always be conscious and considerate of your audience.

Peace and poetry,
Betsy Midchester
Treasurer and Acting President/PAWS

Writing Exercises

1. Part 1: In the first-person or third-person limited omniscient, write a scene where your character hears the sound of someone trying to break into the house. Your character is home alone (although it may not be her house), vulnerable in some way (in the bath, or in bed, or trapped in a windowless room). The scene should begin with the first hint of danger, and it should end the moment before your narrator actually sees the intruder. Your goal here is to imagine in a convincing way your narrator's emotions and perceptions, and to create as much suspense as possible.

   Part 2: Write the same scene from the perspective of the intruder. This might be a random break-in by a common burglar, or maybe the intruder's story is more complex. Consider your intruder's expectations: Does he expect the home to be empty? If not, who does he think might be there? Consider whether or not your intruder knows (or thinks he

knows) the occupant of the house. In this scene, the reader should identify with the intruder, and again, your goal is to create suspense.

2. Write five openings to a story, each from a different authorial distance.
   The first version should be written from a great distance. With each version you should lessen the authorial distance, so that by the fifth version
   we immediately feel close to the character. It may help to use filmmaking
   as an analogy: Your first version should be like a panoramic establishing
   shot, and your fifth version an extreme close-up. For instance:
   a. It was the blizzard of 1972, the worst storm Boston had experienced in
      a decade. A young woman, holding her coat closed over her pregnant
      stomach, struggled down Broad Street.
   b. Jennifer Meyers clutched her coat and prayed she wouldn't slip on a
      patch of ice.
   c. Jenny waddled down the snowy sidewalk and imagined how silly she
      must look: a pregnant woman staggering around in a blizzard.
   d. How Jenny wished she were back inside her little apartment, at one with her
      futon couch, an afghan pulled up to her chin, watching *Days of Our Lives*.
   e. What was she thinking? Trudging through a blinding storm to the
      Circle K just for a pint of Chunky Monkey? Pregnancy cravings were
      one thing, but this was ridiculous.

   Now write the opening paragraph of your story. Start at a great distance, but
   steadily reduce the psychic distance with each sentence, so that by the final
   sentence of the paragraph the reader feels extremely close to the character.

3. Choose a significant incident from a child's life (your own or invented). First,
   write a scene from the point of view of the child in first-person present tense.
   Try to capture a child's perceptions, vocabulary, and syntax. Now rewrite the
   scene in first-person past tense from the perspective of the same character
   as an adult. In this version, your character will not only possess an adult's
   perception of the event but will also be able to recall his own childish reaction to it. Try to convey how your character feels about his child-self through
   his tone (affectionate, amused, nostalgic, embarrassed, mocking, ironic and
   detached, etc.). What do you gain/lose with the two different points of view?

4. Write a gossipy letter from the point of view of one family member
   who passes scathing judgments on another, but let readers know that
   the speaker really loves or envies the other (an unreliable narrator).
   Alternatively, have the speaker loudly praise the other family member,
   but let readers hear harsh criticism implied.

5. Write down a false statement about yourself, such as "I have a pet snake."
   Keep going, elaborating on the false statement, allowing the "I" character
   to develop. You are beginning to create a narrator who is not like you,
   which will give you more imaginative freedom than you might feel when
   writing about yourself as the "I" narrator.

9

PLAY IT AGAIN, SAM
Revision

"Talent is a long patience," Anton Chekhov remarked, an acknowledgment that the creative process is not all inventive and extends far beyond the first heated rush. Partly corrective, critical, nutritive, and fostering, revision is a matter of rendering a story the best that it can be. William C. Knott, in *The Craft of Fiction*, cogently observes that "anyone can write—and almost everyone you meet these days is writing. However, only the writers know how to rewrite. It is this ability alone that turns the amateur into a pro."

While the focus of this chapter is the overall revision of stories and the best use of readers' feedback, the methods of shaping, enriching, and enlivening stories discussed throughout this book implicitly concern the revision of fiction, element by element. We have already visited the process of revision through the discussion of the story workshop in Chapter 1 (a discussion that will continue here); in the Chapter 4 review "Character: A Summary"; and in the Chapter 6 section "Revising Summary and Scene."

Re-Vision

Revising is a process more dreaded than dreadful. The resistance to rewriting is, if anything, greater than the resistance to beginning in the first place. Yet chances are that once you have committed yourself to a first draft, you'll be unable to leave it in an unfinished and unsatisfying state. You'll be *unhappy* until it's right. Making it right will involve a second commitment, to seeing the story fresh and creating it again with the advantage of this "re-vision." Alice Munro, in the introduction to her *Selected Stories*, describes the risk, the readiness, and the reward.

> ... The story, in the first draft, has put on rough but adequate clothes, it is "finished" and might be thought to need no more than a lot of technical adjustments, some tightening here and expanding there, and the slipping in of some telling dialogue and chopping away of flabby modifiers. It's then, in fact, that the story is in the greatest danger of losing its life, of appearing so hopelessly misbegotten that my only relief comes from abandoning it. It doesn't do enough. It does what I intended, but it turns out that my intention was all wrong.... I go around glum and preoccupied, trying to think of ways to fix the problem. Usually the right way pops up in the middle of this.
>
> A big relief. Renewed energy. Resurrection.
>
> Except that it isn't the right way. Maybe a way *to* the right way. Now I write pages and pages I'll have to discard. New angles are introduced, minor characters brought center stage, lively and satisfying scenes are written, and it's all a mistake. Out they go. But by this time I'm on the track, there's no backing out. I know so much more than I did, I know what I want to happen and where I want to end up and I just have to keep trying till I find the best way of getting there.

To find the best way of getting there, you may have to "see again" more than once. The process of revision involves external and internal insight. You'll need your conscious critic, your creative instinct, and readers you trust. You may need each of them several times, not necessarily in that order. A story gets better not just by polishing and refurbishing, not by improving a word choice here and an image there, but by taking risks with the structure, reenvisioning, being open to new meaning itself. "In the first draft is the talent," said French poet Paul Valery, "in the second is the art."

Worry It and Walk Away

To write your first draft, you banished the internal critic. Now make the critic welcome. Revision is work, but the strange thing is that you may find you can concentrate on the work for much longer than you could play at freedrafting. It has occurred to me that writing a first draft is very like tennis or softball—I have to be psyched for it. Energy level up, alert, on my toes. A few hours is all I can manage, and at the end of it I'm wiped out. Revision is like careful carpentry, and if I'm under a deadline or just determined to get this thing crafted and polished, I can be good for twelve hours of it.

The first round of rewrites is probably a matter of letting your misgivings surface. Focus for a while on what seems awkward, overlong, undeveloped, flat, or flowery. Tinker. Tighten. Sharpen. More important at this stage than finishing any given page or phrase is that you're getting to know your story in order to open it to new possibilities. You will also get tired of it; you may feel stuck.

Then put it away. Don't look at it for a matter of days or weeks, until you feel fresh on the project. In addition to getting some distance on your story, you're mailing it to your unconscious—not consciously working out the flaws but temporarily letting them go. Rollo May, in *The Courage to Create*, describes what frequently happens next:

> Everyone uses from time to time such expressions as, "a thought pops up," an idea comes "from the blue" or "dawns" or "comes as though out of a dream," or "it suddenly hit me." These are various ways of describing a common experience: the breakthrough of ideas from some depth below the level of awareness.

It is my experience that such realizations occur over and over again in the course of writing a short story or novel. Often I will believe that because I know who my characters are and what happens to them, I know what my story is about—and often I find I'm wrong, or that my understanding is shallow or incomplete.

In the first draft of one novel, for instance, I opened with the sentence "It took a hundred and twelve bottles of champagne to see the young Poindexters off to Arizona." A page later one character whispered to another that the young Mr. Poindexter in question had "consumption." I worked on this book for a year (taking my characters off to Arizona, where they dealt with the desert heat, lack of water, alcoholism, loss of religion, and the development of mining interests and the building trade) before I saw the connection between "consumption" and "champagne." When I understood that simple link, I understood the overarching theme—surely latent in the idea from the moment it had taken hold of me—shared by tuberculosis, spiritual thirst, consumerism, and addiction, all issues of "consumption."

"... THE FIRST IMPULSE IN WRITING IS TO FLOOD IT OUT, let as much run freely as you possibly can. Then to take a walk or go to the bank ... and come back in a day or six months later. To read it with a cold eye and say, "This is good. This is not. That sentence works. This is magical. This is crummy." You have to maintain your critical sensibility and not just assume, because it was an extraordinary dream for you, that it will be a dream for other people. Because people need maps to your dreams.

ALLAN GURGANUS

It might seem dismaying that you should see what your story is about only after you have written it. Try it; you'll like it. Nothing is more exhilarating than the discovery that a complex pattern has lain in your mind ready to unfold.

Note that in the early stages of revision both the worrying and the walking away are necessary. Perhaps it is bafflement itself that plunges us to the unconscious space where the answer lies.

Criticism and the Story Workshop

Once you have thought your story through, drafted it, and worked on it to the best of your ability, someone else's eyes can help to refresh the vision of your own. Wise professionals rely on the help of an agent or editor at this juncture (although even the wisest still smart at censure); anyone can rely on the help of friends, family, or classmates in a story workshop. The trick to making good use of criticism is to be utterly selfish about it. Be greedy for it. Take it all in. Ultimately you are the laborer, the arbiter, and the boss in any dispute about your story, so you can afford to consider any problem and any solution. Most of us feel not only committed to what we have put on the page, but also defensive on its behalf—wanting, really, to be told only that it is a work of genius or, failing that, to find out that we have gotten away with it. Therefore, the first exigency of revision is that you learn to hear, absorb, and accept criticism.

"Revising is like cutting your own hair," says novelist Robert Stone, for while you may sense the need for improvement, it's hard to get right what you can never entirely see for yourself. This is the major advantage of a workshop: Your fellow writers may not be able to tell you how to style the material in the way that best suits the story, but they can at least hold up the mirror and see from a more distanced perspective. (If you are just beginning the practice of group critiques, you may wish to look back at the description of common workshop procedures in Chapter 1.)

How can you assimilate so many opinions, let alone choose what is useful? First, give special consideration to the comments of those two or three workshop members with whose responses you have generally agreed before. However, the best—or at any rate the most useful—criticism, John L'Heureux suggests, simply points out what you had already sensed for yourself but had hoped to get away with. Or as Flannery O'Connor put it, with typical bluntness, in fiction "you can do anything you can get away with, but nobody has ever gotten away with much."

It used to be popular to speak of "constructive criticism" and "destructive criticism," but these are misleading terms suggesting that positive suggestions are useful and negative criticism useless. In practice the opposite is usually the case. You're likely to find that the most constructive thing a reader can do is say *I don't believe this, I don't like this, I don't understand this*, pointing to precisely the passages that made you uneasy. This kind of laying-the-finger-on-the-trouble-spot produces an inward groan, but it's also satisfying; you know just where to go to work. Often the most destructive thing a reader can do is offer you a positive suggestion—*Why don't you have him crash the car?*—that is irrelevant to your vision of the story. Be suspicious of praise that is too extravagant, of blame that is too general. If your impulse is to defend the story or yourself, still the impulse. Behave as if bad advice were good advice, and give it serious consideration. You can reject it after you have explored it for anything of use it may offer.

> ... **T**HE WRITING WORKSHOP FINALLY IS THE ONE PLACE where you can be sure you and your work are taken seriously, where your writing intentions are honored, where even in a mean-spirited comment you can divine—if you wish—the truth about your writing, its strengths and its weaknesses. It is a place where you are surrounded by people whose chief interest is also yours, where the talk is never anything but writing and writing well and writing better....It is where you somehow pick up the notion that what you're doing is a good and noble thing, and though you may not write as well as you'd like, it is enough and will suffice.
>
> JOHN L'HEUREUX

Workshop members often voice sharply divided responses to a manuscript, a situation that may confuse and frustrate the author. Editor Duncan Murrell of Algonquin Books of Chapel Hill advises workshop writers to pay close attention to the parts of their work that make readers stumble, but to disregard most of the solutions those readers suggest. Give a flawed story to ten good readers and they'll accurately find the flawed passages before offering ten wildly varying explanations and a handful of contradictory solutions. Good readers have a gut level understanding that something's wrong in a story, but they're often unclear about what it is, or what to do about it. Yet once pointed to the weak sections, authors almost always come up with better solutions than anything a reader or an editor can offer; they know the story and the characters better. The trick is to bite your lip when readers tell you how to fix your story, while noting the passages that need repair.

Indeed, while the author may or may not benefit from peer suggestions, everyone else in the workshop does because the practice of thinking through and articulating responses to a story's challenges eventually makes all participants more objective critics of their own work. You will notice that the more specific the criticism you offer—or receive—the more useful it proves and the less it stings; similarly, the more specific the praise of "what works," the more likely it is to reinforce good habits—and to be believed. After a semester's experience of workshopping, you'll find that you can critique a story within your own imagination, knowing who would say what, with whom you would agree, and telling yourself what you already know to be true.

Within a day or two of the workshop, novelist, playwright, and teacher Michelle Carter advises that the author try to "re-hear criticism"; that is, assess what it is readers are responding to, which may not be apparent from the suggested "fix." For example, if a number of readers suggest changing the story's point of view from third person to first, Carter might reinterpret that to mean that the narrator seems overly remote from the characters—not that first-person narration is literally a better choice, but that readers want a more immediate experience of the main character's emotional dilemma.

A second example would be wanting "to know more about Character X." This doesn't necessarily mean sprinkling on some facts and history, but rather that the reader may want a greater understanding of the character's motivations or a closer rendering of crucial moments.

Additionally, Carter cautions, be tough with yourself, even when you realize that criticism is based on a misreading. Rarely is misinterpretation solely the mistake of the reader: Ask what awkwardness of writing or false emphasis might have led to that skewed reading. Novelist Wally Lamb reinforces this point: "Often I think we let the writer get away with too much. If the writing is unclear, we'll read it a second time and make it clear to ourselves and then let the writer off the hook, when, in fact, the writing has to stand for itself.... You want to work on the writing until it is good enough that the writer doesn't have to be in the room explaining and interpreting."

322 PLAY IT AGAIN, SAM

Kenneth Atchity, in *A Writer's Time*, advises compulsory "vacations" at crucial points in the revising process, in order to let the criticism cook until you feel ready, impatient, to get back to writing. So once again, walk away, and when you feel that you have acquired enough distance from the story to see it anew, go back to work. Make notes of your plans, large and small. Talk to yourself in your journal about what you want to accomplish and where you think you have failed. Let your imagination play with new images or passages of dialogue. Always keep a copy (and/or an electronic document) of the story as it is so that you can go back to the original, and then be ruthless with another copy. Eudora Welty advised cutting sections apart and pinning them back together so that they can be easily rearranged. I like to use the whole surface of the kitchen table as a cut-and-paste board. Some people can keep the story in their heads and do their rearranging directly onto the computer screen—which in any case has made the putting-back-together process less tedious than retyping.

Asking the Big Question: What Have I Written?

In a piece of literary criticism, your goal is to say as clearly and directly as possible what you mean. In fiction, your goal is to make people and make them do things and, ideally, never to "say what you mean" at all. Theoretically, an outline can never harm a paper for a literature class: This is what I have to say, and I'll say it through points A, B, and C. But if a writer sets out to write a story to illustrate an idea, the fiction will almost inevitably be thin. Even if you begin with an outline, as many writers do, it will be an outline of the action and not of your "points." You may not know the meaning of the story until the characters begin to tell you what it is. You'll begin with an image of a person or a situation that seems vaguely to embody something important, and you'll learn as you go what that something is. Likewise, what you mean will emerge in the reading experience and take place in the reader's mind—"not," as the narrator says of Marlow's tales in *Heart of Darkness*, "inside like a kernel but outside, enveloping the tale which brought it out."

Early on in the revision process, you may find yourself impelled by, under pressure of, or interested primarily in your theme. It will seem that you have set yourself this lonely, austere, and tortuous task because you do have something to say. Therefore, attempting to articulate the theme of your story is something you'll want to do when you're preparing to revise, so as to direct your revision work toward exploring your understanding of the theme.

At this point you will, and you should, begin to let the sorting-comparing-cataloging neocortex of your brain go to work on the stuff of your story. Rather than "putting in a theme," you'll be looking back to see what you've already, mostly subconsciously, been doing all along. John Gardner describes the process in *The Art of Fiction*.

Theme, it should be noticed, is not imposed on the story but evoked from within it—initially an intuitive but finally an intellectual act on the part of the writer. The writer muses on the story idea to determine what it is in it that has attracted him, why it seems to him worth telling. Having determined...what interests him—and what chiefly concerns the major character...he toys with various ways of telling his story, thinks about what has been said before about [his theme], broods on every image that occurs to him, turning it over and over, puzzling it, hunting for connections, trying to figure out—before he writes, while he writes, and in the process of repeated revisions—what it is he really thinks....Only when he thinks about a story in this way does he achieve not just an alternative reality or, loosely, an imitation of nature, but true, firm art—fiction as serious thought.

So, theme is what your story is about. But that is not enough, because a story may be "about" a dying Samurai or a quarreling couple or two kids on a trampoline, and those would not be the themes of those stories. A story is also "about" an abstraction, and if the story is significant, that abstraction may be very large; yet thousands of stories are about love, other thousands about death, and still other thousands about both love and death, and to say this is to say little about the theme of any of them.

We might better understand theme if we ask questions such as these: What does the story have to say about the idea or abstraction that seems to be contained in it? What attitudes or judgments does it imply? Above all, how do the elements of fiction contribute to our experience of those ideas and attitudes in the story?

How Fictional Elements Contribute to Theme

Whatever the idea and attitudes that underlie the theme of a story, that story will bring them into the realm of experience through its particular and unique pattern. Theme involves emotion, logic, and judgment—all three. But the pattern that forms the particular experience of that theme is made up of every element of fiction this book has discussed: the arrangement, shape, and flow of the action, as performed by the characters, realized in their details, seen in their atmosphere, from a unique point of view, through the imagery and the rhythm of the language.

This book, for example, contains at least six stories that may be said to have what used to be called "the generation gap" as a major theme: "Everything That Rises Must Converge," "A Visit of Charity," "Fiesta, 1980," "St. Lucy's Home for Girls Raised by Wolves," "The Fun House," "Binocular Vision," and "Following the Notes." All of these happen to be written from the point of view of a member of the younger generation, but there are other stories about this subject written from the point of view of a member of the older generation—Toni Cade Bambara's "My Man Bovanne," for instance. In some, conflict is resolved by bridging the gap; in others, it is not. The characters are variously poor, middle-class, rural, urban, male, female, adolescent, middle-aged, old, Latino, Native American, white. The imagery variously evokes food, landscape, institutions, religion, music, cars, dancing, sex, and death. It is in the different uses of the elements of fiction that each story makes unique what it has to say about, and what attitude it takes toward, the idea of "the generation gap."

The process of discovering the theme of your story—worrying it until its theme reveals itself, connections occur, images recur, a pattern emerges—is more conscious than readers know, beginning writers want to accept, or established writers are willing to admit. It has become a popular—cliché—stance for writers to claim that they haven't the faintest idea what they meant in their writing. *Don't ask me; read the book. If I knew what it meant, I wouldn't have written it. It means what it says.* When an author makes such a response, it is well to remember that an author is a professional liar. What he or she means is not that there are no themes, ideas, or meanings in the work but that these are not separable from the pattern of fictional experience in which they are embodied. It also means that, having done the difficult writerly job, the writer is now unwilling also to do the critic's work. But beginning critics also resist. Students irritated by the analysis of literature often ask, "How do you know she did that on purpose? How do you know it didn't just happen to come out that way?" The answer is that you don't. But what is on the page is on the page. An author no less than a reader or critic can see an emerging pattern, and the author has both the possibility and the obligation of manipulating it. When you have put something on the page, you have two possibilities, and only two: You may cut it or you are committed to it. Gail Godwin asks:

> But what about the other truths you lost by telling it that way?
>
> Ah, my friend, this is my question too. The choice is always a killing one. One option must die so that another may live. I do little murders in my workroom every day.

In the unified pattern of a fiction there is something to which the name of "magic" may be given, where one empty word is placed upon another and tapped with a third, and a flaming scarf or a long-eared hope is pulled out of the tall black heart. The most magical thing about this magic is that once the trick is explained, it is not explained, and the better you understand how it works, the better it will work again.

Finally, through revision, through deciding what to cut and what to commit to, you will, or at least might, arrive at a story that is of a piece, a story that is organic, a story that cannot be reduced to theme, but that embodies one.

Revision Questions

As you plan the revision and as you rewrite, you will know (and your critics will tell you) what problems are unique to your story. There are also general, almost universal, pitfalls that you can avoid if you ask yourself the following questions.

Is there unnecessary summary? Remember that it is a common impulse to try to cover too much ground. Tell your story in the fewest possible scenes; cut down on summary and unnecessary flashback. These dissipate energy and lead you to tell rather than show.

Why should the reader turn from the first page to the second? Is the language fresh? Are the characters alive? Does the first sentence, paragraph, page introduce real tension? If it doesn't, you have probably begun at the wrong place. If you are unable to find a way to introduce tension on the first page, you may have to question whether you have a story after all.

Is it original? Almost every writer thinks first, in some way or other, of the familiar, the usual, the given. This character is a stereotype, that emotion is too easy, that phrase is a cliché. First-draft laziness is inevitable, but it is also a way of being dishonest. A good writer will comb the work for clichés and labor to find the exact, the honest, and the fresh.

Is it clear? Although ambiguity and mystery provide some of our most profound pleasures in literature, beginning writers are often unable to distinguish between mystery and muddle, ambiguity and sloppiness. You may want your character to be rich with contradiction, but we still want to know whether that character is male or female, black or white, old or young. We need to be oriented on the simplest level of reality before we can share your imaginative world. Where are we? When are we? Who are they? How do things look? What time of day or night is it? What's the weather? What's happening?

Is it self-conscious? Probably the most famous piece of advice to the rewriter is William Faulkner's "kill all your darlings." When you are carried away with the purple of your prose, the music of your alliteration, the hilarity of your wit, the profundity of your insights, then chances are you are having a better time writing than the reader will have reading. No reader will forgive you, and no reader should. Just tell the story. The style will follow of itself if you just tell the story.

Where is it too long? Most of us, and even the best of us, write too long. We are so anxious to explain every nuance, cover every possible aspect of character, action, and setting that we forget the necessity of stringent selection. In fiction, and especially in the short story, we want sharpness, economy, and vivid, telling detail. More than necessary is too much. I have been helped in my own tendency to tell all by a friend who went through a copy of one of my novels, drawing a line through the last sentence of about every third paragraph. Then in the margin he wrote, again and again, "Hit it, and get out." That's good advice for anyone.

Where is it undeveloped in character, action, imagery, theme? In any first, second, or third draft of a manuscript there are likely to be necessary passages sketched, skipped, or skeletal. What information is missing, what actions are incomplete, what motives obscure, what images inexact? Where does the action occur too abruptly so that it loses its emotional force? Is the crisis presented as a scene?

Where is it too general? Originality, economy, and clarity can all be achieved through the judicious use of significant detail. Learn to spot general, vague, and fuzzy terms. Be suspicious of yourself anytime you see nouns such as *someone* and *everything*, adjectives such as *huge* and *handsome*, adverbs such as *very* and *really*. Seek instead a particular thing, a particular size, an exact degree.

Although the dread of "starting over" is a real and understandable one, chances are that the rewards of revising will startlingly outweigh the pains. Sometimes a character who is dead on the page will come to life through the addition of a few sentences or significant details. Sometimes a turgid or tedious paragraph can become sharp with a few judicious cuts. Sometimes dropping page one and putting page seven where page three used to be can provide the skeleton of an otherwise limp story. And sometimes, often, perhaps always, the difference between an amateur rough cut and a publishable story is in the struggle at the rewriting stage.

Further Suggestions for Revision

- If you have been writing your story on a computer, retype at least one full draft, making both planned and spontaneous changes as you go. The computer's abilities can tempt us to a "fix-it" approach to revision, but jumping in and out of the text to correct problems can result in a revision that reads like patchwork. Rather, the effect of even small changes should ripple through the story, and this is more likely to happen if the writer reenters the story as a whole by literally rewriting it from start to finish.

- Screenwriter Stephen Fisher emphasizes that "writing is not a monolithic process, just as cooking is not a monolithic process. You don't just go in the kitchen and cook—you do a number of very specific things that you focus on one at a time—you peel garlic, you dice garlic, you saute onions—these are separate processes. You don't go into a kitchen and flap your arms and just cook—and in the same way, you don't 'just write.'"

  To put this analogy into practice, write two or three revisions of a story draft, focusing on a different issue each time. For example, you might zero in on the motivations of a character whose behavior and dialogue don't yet ring true; or you might simply focus on using setting to reflect emotion or threading physical activity through dialogue scenes. Focusing on a single goal lets you concentrate your efforts, yet other developments will naturally occur in response to the single-focus changes.

- In an interview in *Conversations on Writing Fiction*, novelist and teacher Jane Smiley says she asks her student writers to confront their own sets of "evasions," the counterproductive "rituals which don't actually allow them to spend time with or become engaged with their chosen themes or characters." For example, many people find conflict hard to handle in real life and therefore avoid it, often for good reason. Yet many of us sidestep conflict in our fiction too, even knowing its necessity in driving a character toward a defining crisis. If this sounds like an evasion you've experienced, take a look back at places in the story where explosive scenes *should* happen—places where characters ought to confront or defend. Are these, in fact, all-out scenes? Or do your characters neatly sidestep the conflict and retreat to their private thoughts? Does another character too conveniently knock at the door?

Taking refuge in the making of metaphors, however vivid, rather than clearly depicting what *is*, may be another form of evasion, perhaps reflecting a writer's lack of confidence in the interest of his or her material.

Spiraling off into the weird and random may reflect a similar lack of confidence, or indecision; overly clever, bantering dialogue that strains to entertain may reflect a desire to dazzle, while avoiding the harder search for dialogue that is both realistic and revealing.

Evasions may be easier to observe in others' work at first, so you might want to ask a trusted workshop friend to help you recognize the evasions in your own stories. As you revise and encounter points of resistance—those places where you hesitate to probe further or describe more specifically—ask yourself, Is this right for the story or is it simply my comfortable habit?

... YOU GENERALLY START OUT WITH SOME OVERALL IDEA that you can see fairly clearly, as if you were standing on a dock and looking at a ship on the ocean. At first you can see the entire ship, but then as you begin work you're in the boiler room and you can't see the ship anymore.... What you really want in an editor is someone who's still on the dock, who can say, Hi, I'm looking at your ship, and it's missing a bow, the front mast is crooked, and it looks to me as if your propellers are going to have to be fixed.

MICHAEL CRICHTON

Examples of the Revision Process

When reading a polished, published story, it can be difficult to imagine that it once was any other way, difficult to realize that the author made both choices and unplanned connections, difficult to envision the story's history. After all, by the point of publication, the writer has likely heeded Annie Dillard's admonition: "Process is nothing; erase your tracks. The path is not the work."

Yet a glimpse of these earlier "tracks" may reveal the paths writers forged to final versions of their stories, and this may in turn inspire you to a more thorough reenvisioning of your own work. What follows are authors' accounts of the revision process.

In her book-length essay *The Writing Life*, Annie Dillard uses the metaphor of knocking out "a bearing wall" for the revising writer's sacrifice of the very aspect of the story that inspired its writing. Strange as it sounds, this is an experience familiar to many accomplished writers: "The part you must jettison," says Dillard, "is not only the best-written part; it is also, oddly, that part which was to have been the very point. It is the original key passage, the passage on which the rest was to hang, and from which you yourself drew the courage to begin."

Joyce Carol Oates describes this phenomenon—and more—in her essay "Smooth Talk: Short Story Into Film." Readers of "Where Are You Going, Where Have You Been?" one of the most famous American stories of the late twentieth century, may be surprised to learn that the author's initial impulse to write the story disappeared in the drafting process. Recounts Oates:

Some years ago in the American Southwest, there surfaced a tabloid psychopath known as "The Pied Piper of Tucson." I have forgotten his name, but his specialty was the seduction and occasional murder of teen-aged girls. He may or may not have had actual accomplices, but his bizarre activities were known among a circle of teenagers in the Tucson area; for some reason they kept his secret, deliberately did not inform parents or police. It was this fact, not the fact of the mass murderer himself, that struck me at the time. And this was a pre-Manson time, early or mid-1960s.

The Pied Piper mimicked teenagers in their talk, dress, and behavior, but he was not a teenager—he was a man in his early thirties. Rather short, he stuffed rags in his leather boots to give himself height. (And sometimes walked unsteadily as a consequence: did none among his admiring constituency notice?) He charmed his victims as charismatic psychopaths have always charmed their victims, to the bewilderment of others who fancy themselves free of all lunatic attractions. The Pied Piper of Tucson: a trashy dream, a tabloid archetype, sheer artifice, comedy, cartoon—surrounded, however improbably, and finally tragically, by real people. You think that, if you look twice, he won't be there. But there he is.

I don't remember any longer where I first read about this Pied Piper— very likely in *Life* Magazine. I do recall deliberately not reading the full article because I didn't want to be distracted by too much detail. It was not after all the mass murderer himself who intrigued me, but the disturbing fact that a number of teenagers—from "good" families—aided and abetted his crimes. This is the sort of thing authorities and responsible citizens invariably call "inexplicable" because they can't find explanations for it. *They* would not have fallen under this maniac's spell, after all.

An early draft of my short story, "Where Are You Going, Where Have You Been?" —from which the film *Smooth Talk* was adapted by Joyce Chopra and Tom Cole—had the rather too explicit title "Death and the Maiden."

It was cast in a mode of fiction to which I am still partial—indeed, every third or fourth story of mine is probably in this mode— "realistic allegory," it might be called. It is Hawthornean, romantic, shading into parable. Like the medieval German engraving from which my title was taken, the story was minutely detailed yet clearly an allegory of the fatal attractions of death (or the devil). An innocent young girl is seduced by way of her own vanity; she mistakes death for erotic romance of a particularly American/trashy sort.

In subsequent drafts the story changed its tone, its focus, its language, its title. It became "Where Are You Going, Where Have You Been?" Written at a time when the author was intrigued by the music of Bob Dylan, particularly the hauntingly elegiac song "It's All Over Now, Baby Blue," it was dedicated to Bob Dylan. The charismatic mass murderer drops into the background and his innocent victim, a fifteen-year-old, moves into the foreground. She becomes the true protagonist of the tale, courting and being courted by her fate, a self-styled 1950s pop figure, alternately absurd and winning. There is no suggestion in the published story that "Arnold Friend" has seduced and murdered other young girls, or even that he necessarily intends to murder Connie. Is his interest "merely" sexual? (Nor is there anything about the complicity of other teenagers. I saved that yet more provocative note for a current story, "Testimony.") Connie is shallow, vain, silly, hopeful, doomed—but capable nonetheless of an unexpected gesture of heroism at the story's end.

Annie Dillard concludes the section of her essay "The Writing Life" by suggesting that a writer may save the abandoned idea for another story: "So it is that a writer writes many books. In each book, he intended several urgent and vivid points, many of which he sacrificed as the book's form hardened.... The writer returns to these materials, these passionate subjects, as to unfinished business, for they are his life's work."

Following are two examples of the revision process. The first one consists of an early version of Pia Erhardt's story "Following the Notes," a short description of her revision process, and the story as it appeared in its final, published version. The second example comes from Janet Burroway's novel *Indian Dancer* and shows her grappling with voice, point-of-view, language and verisimilitude in order to get the opening scene just right.

Revising "Following the Notes"

"Following the Notes" was first called "Battery," and then, for awhile, "His Hand Restless on My Leg." The piece started off of a five-word prompt, one word of which, I remember, was the word "battery." The first draft was about 600 words, curt bordering on rude, mostly dialogue, and heavy on the Electra complex. In later drafts, I added scenes to slow the tension down and open the story up to the father's character, and to the narrator's relationship with Sherman. The spirit of the first draft is in the final lines, with ten pounds more tenderness. The story was included in the *Norton Anthology, Sudden Fiction: Short-Short Stories from America and Beyond,* and the editors recommended the title the story has today, because they felt that the "Hand" title skewed the story in a different way, and I agreed, and I still thank them.

Battery

PIA Z. EHRHARDT

My father came to the mall parking lot to give me a jump. He dug for the cables in his trunk, pissed that he'd been called away from what he was doing at home.

"You left the headlights on?" he said.

"The passenger light," I said, pointing at the back seat. "Door wasn't shut all the way."

"Who was in the back?" he said. "I thought you were driving to work and home, only."

My daily comings and goings were charted in the kitchen, reviewed when I got home in the evening. I had the use of a Buick Century as long as I kept it filled with gas, washed it once a week in our driveway, and didn't joy ride with my friends.

"Sorry for the inconvenience," I said

"Don't be smart." He clipped the cables on the battery, and told me to get in the car and rev the engine.

The parking lot was dark. Some of my co-workers stood outside under the lamp, smoking. I waited tables at The Cannery, a seafood restaurant at Cloverleaf Mall.

My boyfriend Jimmy's sweatshirt lay on the back seat, where he'd stripped it off. We'd fucked there before my shift, at the far edge of the parking lot, then switched T-shirts for the day. He had on my Sacred Heart tee, small for him but it showed the muscles he was sculpting for me. I wore his faded Ninja turtles tee, too big, but I'd stuffed it into my jeans and loved the smooth feel of it against my skin. It'd been washed a thousand times and smelled like Downy. I zipped my jacket to my neck so my father wouldn't see.

"This isn't working," he said. "There's no juice."

I drove home with him, a kid riding shot gun, and listened to him whistle the music he'd been writing when I called for help. We caught every red light. I smelled like cigarette smoke and sex with a busy top layer of peppermint Tic Tac. Half a box in my mouth.

"You didn't leave the house in that shirt," my father said.

"Grease stain," I mumbled. "I borrowed someone's."

Bugs flew toward our headlights and hit the windshield like rain.

"Is Mom feeling better?" I said. She'd been in bed when I'd left for work, said she had a cold, but I knew it was a hangover. I'd rinsed out her mug in the morning and it smelled like scotch.

"She's okay," he said. He pressed the washer button but nothing came out.

"I showed you how to fill this," he said. The wipers squeaked across the dry windshield, smudging the spots into a mess. "Goddammit, Liddie," he said. "I can't see."

I knew what to do to make him forget my screw-ups. I could place him right there in the palm of my hand. "What were you working on before I so rudely interrupted?"

He told me too much, like he'd been waiting all day for someone to ask. "A choral piece—SATB—with organ. I'm setting a John Ashbery text. "

Didn't he know I was kissing his butt? His readiness made me sad. The boys I liked used just a few words to explain what they meant, left the rest mysterious, but my father answered anything I asked like he had one chance left on earth.

He leaned forward, squinting through the streaks, and asked me to be another set of eyes and help get us home safely.

"Why don't we pull into a gas station, Dad? I'll get out and clean."

That night, after dinner, my mother said she was going up to watch TV. He was still in love with me, and asked if I'd go in his study and turn pages for him so he could play what he'd written that day.

Following the Notes

PIA Z. EHRHARDT

In high school I had a job as the hostess at The Trawler, a seafood restaurant at Esplanade Mall. My battery went dead and my father had to come to the mall parking lot to give me a jump. He dug for the cables in his trunk, pissed that he'd been called away from the new piece of music he was writing at home. It was Father's Day and what he'd asked for was for a quiet house and lemon pie for dessert.

"You left the headlights on?" he said.

"The passenger light," I said, pointing at the back seat. "Door wasn't shut all the way."

"Who was in the back?" he said. "I thought you were driving to work and home, only."

My daily comings and goings were charted in the kitchen, reviewed when I got back in the evening. I had the use of a Buick Century as long as I kept it filled with gas, washed it once a week in our driveway with mild detergent, and didn't joy ride with my friends.

"Sorry for the inconvenience," I said

"Don't be a smart-ass." He clipped the cables on the battery. "Get in and rev the engine when I tell you."

The parking lot was dark. Some of my co-workers stood outside under the street lamp, smoking. Bugs were flying in from everywhere to swarm in the light.

My father raised his arm for me to step on the gas.

Sherman's sweatshirt lay on the back seat, where he'd stripped it off. We'd had sex there before my shift, at the far edge of the parking lot, then switched shirts for the day. He wanted my Sacred Heart tee so he could show off the muscles he was sculpting for me. That's what he'd said. I wore his faded Ninja Turtles tee, had it stuffed into my jeans. Washed a thousand times, so smooth against my skin. I zipped my jacket to my neck so my father wouldn't see.

"This isn't working," he said. "There's no juice."

I drove home with him in his old green Mercedes. Sometimes he let me drive this car. Last week I'd taken Sherman for an evening drive out in Richburg Hills to look at the twinkling lights of the power plant. Oz. The front seat was a bench and Sherman scooted next to me, his hand restless on my leg.

My father whistled what he'd been working on when I called for help. We caught every red light. I smelled like cigarette smoke and sex with a busy top layer of peppermint Tic Tac. Half a box in my mouth.

"You didn't leave the house in that shirt," he said.

"Grease stain," I mumbled. "I borrowed someone's."

Bugs out of nowhere dove into the windshield. "Is Mom feeling better?" I said. She'd been in bed when I'd left that morning, said she had a cold, but I knew it was a hangover. I'd rinsed out her mug and it smelled like scotch.

"She's okay," he said. He pressed the washer button but nothing came out.

"I showed you how to fill this." The wipers squeaked across the dry windshield, smudging the spots into a mess. "Goddammit, Liddie," he said. "I can't see."

I knew what to do to make him forget my screw-ups. I simply placed him right there in the palm of my hand. "What were you working on before I interrupted?"

He told me too much, like he'd been waiting all day for someone to ask. "A choral piece—SATB—with woodwinds. I'm setting a John Ashbery poem. *The Grapevine.*" He falsettoed the soprano part because it carried the melody.

"Lyrical," I said.

My father's readiness made me sad. The guys I liked used just a few words to explain what they meant, left the rest mysterious, but my father answered anything I asked like he had one chance left on earth.

He leaned forward, squinting through the streaks, and asked me to be another set of eyes and help get us home safely.

"Why don't we pull into a gas station, Dad? I'll get out and clean."

I called Sherman when I got home to tell him about my dead battery, but he didn't have time to talk. I heard a giggle in the background and he said it was his sister, but I knew.

For dinner we had my father's favorite meal—chicken cacciatore with a warm loaf of Italian bread for dunking. My mother was quiet and excused herself during dessert to go upstairs to watch TV. My father looked sad, dumped, and I pushed the rest of my lemon pie at him. "I'm full," I said, and wanted back the one who would always be true, so I asked if he'd play for me what he'd written that day. We sat on the piano bench. I followed the notes and turned the page when he nodded.

The Opening of Indian Dancer: A Revision Narrative

JANET BURROWAY

As I write this, I am still in the process of revising a novel, *Indian Dancer*. The novel tells the story of a girl born in Belgium in 1930 who escapes to England during World War II and later emigrates to America. Most of the novel deals with her adolescent and adult life, but after I had written many of the later scenes, it seemed to me that the novel should begin with an image of that childhood escape, which affects everything she later does. I felt "inspired" when I woke up one morning and tapped out this:

Always,

she retained one image from the boat, too fleeting for a memory but too substantial for a dream, like a few frames clipped from a kinetoscope. She was standing in the stern, embraced from behind by a woman who was wrapping her in rough blanket stuff. Her shoes and the hem of her coat above her knees were wet. She knew that the woman was kind, but the smell of anxiety and too many nights' sweat filled her with dark judgment. There was no moon at all, which was the point, but all the same she could watch the wake of the boat widening behind them. She also knew, in a cold, numbed way, that her father was bleeding on the shore, but what presented itself as monstrous was the wake, dark and glutinous, ever spreading toward the land, as if she herself were a speck being washed from a wound. *I will never go back. I will never.* This was experienced as grief, not yet a vow.

After a day or so I felt this was melodramatic—that "dark judgment," her father "bleeding on the shore," the "monstrous" and "glutinous" sea. I noticed that "kinetoscope" stuck out like a piece of show-off research. I thought there should be more sense of the woman trying to help her, and of the others on the boat. The past tense also troubled me. If she "always retained," then wouldn't the memory be in the present?

Always,

also, she is standing in the stern, embraced from behind by a woman who swaddles her in coarse blanket stuff. Her shoes and the hem of her coat above her knees are wet. There is no moon—which is the point—but all the same she can see the wake widening in the Channel, and close beside her on the deck the boy who broke his shin, the bone stub moving under the flesh like a tongue in a cheek. The man—his father?—still has the boy's mouth stuffed with a forearm of loden coat to keep him from crying out, although they are far enough from shore that the oars have been shipped and the motor roped into life. It sputters like a heart. Behind her the people huddle—you can't tell heroes from refugees—over flasks of tea and Calvados whose fireapple smell flings up on the smell of sea. She will never see any of these people again. The woman's armpit cups her chin, old wet wool and fear. She knows unflinchingly that her father has been left behind. What presents itself as monstrous is the wake—dark, glutinous—which seems to be driving them from the land on its slubbed point as if the boat is a clot being washed from a wound.

I will never go back. I will never. This is experienced as grief, not yet a vow.

I fiddled with this a lot, still dissatisfied with its tone, which seemed to set the book on a loftier course than I intended, but it was several months before it struck me that *the woman should tell this scene.* I think it was the image of the boy's broken bone "like a tongue in a cheek" that gave me the first hint of the woman's voice. She was a British woman; I imagined her as working class, one of the accidental heroes of the Resistance, a practical, solid sort. This revelation must have occurred to me on an airplane (the disembodied feeling of airplanes *always* sets me writing) because I scribbled on a page of a yellow pad:

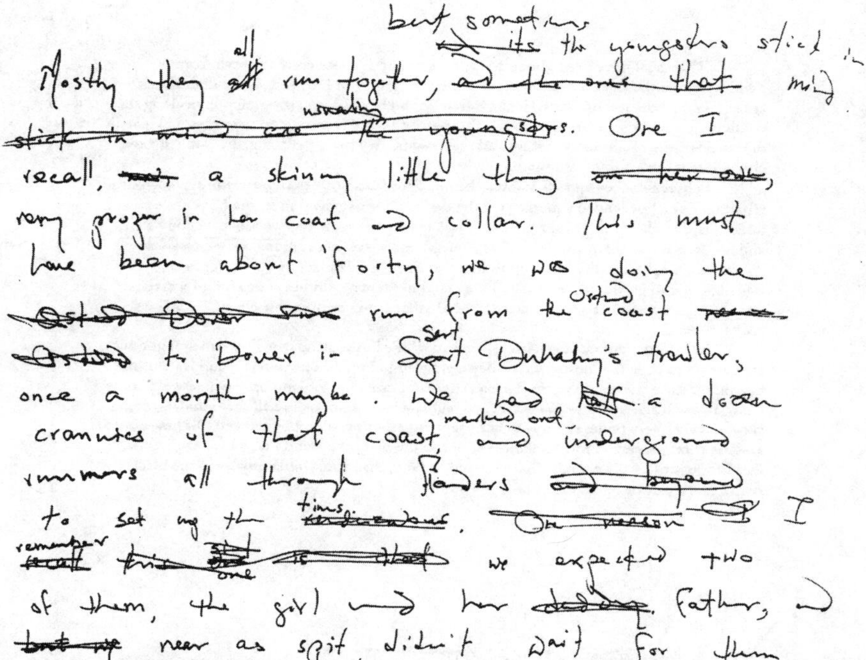

[handwritten draft with many crossings-out]

Mostly they ~~all run together, and the ones that~~ but sometimes its the youngsters stick ~~in mind~~ mind. One I recall, ~~~~ a skinny little thing ~~on her own~~, very proper in her coat and collar. This must have been about 'forty, we ~~was~~ doing the ~~Ostend Dover run~~ run from the coast ~~~~ to Dover in Spit Dunahy's trawler, once a month maybe. We ~~had, half~~ a dozen cranuies of that coast marked out and underground rumours all through Flanders ~~and beyond~~ to set up the times. ~~~~ I remember ~~this one is that~~ we expected two of them, the girl and her ~~daddy~~ father, and ~~but we~~ near as spit didn't wait for them. ~~Well because the other~~ there was a ~~boy~~ jumped ~~eatvcorns~~ squee jam off the dock and broke a leg landing in the ~~biu~~ One of the men gave him a mouthful of loden coat to keep him quiet, but it scared us, and Dunahy cast off. Then I ~~saw~~ her running down the ~~time~~, like, when she could have run straight to us if she chose and I went to coax her into running straight at us up to her

---

Now I started over, putting the scene back in chronological order but always chasing the woman's voice, also reading up on the period and the events of the war, checking out British expressions with my son who lives in London:

This must have been about 'forty, the Vicar and I were coming down from Teddington maybe once a month to make the crossing from Dover to Ostend and back again. We had the use of Duck Henley's trawler and half a dozen meeting points along the coast, underground runners all through that part of Flanders setting up the times. ~~Usually they came on foot, talk about misery and scared, and~~ they mostly run together, only it's the children that stick out in your mind.

~~Sometimes they were that dumb brave. There were babies never made a peep, and~~ I remember one boy landed squeejaw off the dock and broke his shin so the bone rolled under his skin like a tongue in a cheek. It was maybe the same trip we was expecting a girl and her father and nearly pushed off without when we saw her running ~~all by herself~~ down the rocks, straight into the water up to her coat hem. O'Hannaughy swung his arm signalling her to go round the dock and lowered her down with her shoes full of water. I wrapped her up and she says po-faced, "My Father sends me to come ahead." She says, "My fah-zer."

What I remember ~~about her~~ is, we had a little bunsen and usually when you got out far enough to rope the motors alive, they were glad to hunker down over a cuppa. But this one didn't leave the stern six, maybe eight hours of crossing, looking back where we'd come from. ~~It was black dark--we always picked nights with no moon--but all the same you could see the wake~~. Very polite she was in her soggy shoes, but couldn't be budged. ~~I knew not to ask about her father~~. And I remember I tucked the blanket around her, which she let me, and I thought the way we must have looked to God, that greasy little trawler in the black ~~water~~, like a clot being washed ~~out of~~ a wound.

They came in all sorts, talk about misery & scared, and I never saw a one of them again. / were / them / or maybe another / all / rough / from / wake, / in the ~~black~~ dark ~~with no moon~~. / arrives not. He ~~keeps back but~~ / is ~~not able~~ to

Over the course of several months I kept coming back to this scene, trying to imagine it more fully, to heighten the sense of danger as the little boat flees the mines and U-boats, but to keep it in the chatty, down-to-earth voice of the woman who was (when? I asked myself suddenly; why?) telling this story (to whom?). At some point, having spent perhaps a couple of full-time work weeks on this tiny but crucial scene, it came to me that the woman was being interviewed on television, for one of those anniversary documentaries of the war. At once, though I do not describe the scene of the interview, I could see and hear her more clearly.

The book now begins this way:

Transit: Ostend–Dover

All that spring and summer we brought back boatloads of the refugees. The Vicar organized us. They didn't mind I was a woman because I was able-bodied. We traveled down from Teddington once a month to make the crossing, and we had the use of Duck Henley's trawler and half a dozen meeting points along the Flemish coast. Underground runners all through Belgium setting up the rendezvous.

It's a wonder what you remember. Great swollen blanks, and then some daft thing bobs up like flotsam. Such as, I'd never worn a pair of trousers, and what I couldn't get used to was the twill going swish between my thighs. Is that camera running? Don't show me saying *thighs*, will you? Anyway, that and the smells. Tar, old fish in the wet boards. Seasick, of course. And off your own skin a bit of metal smell, with a sourness like fireworks. When they say "sweating bullets" I expect that's what they mean.

The ones we ferried came in every sort—rich man, poor man, tinker, tailor. I never saw a one of them again. Now and then I cross via Newhaven over to Normandy for the shopping, and I look around and think: they're not so different, take away their pocket books and their sunburn. What struck me, in Teddington everybody got raw noses from the cold and spider veins from the fire, but those ones were always drained-looking like they hadn't been out of doors, although most had been living rough or walking nights. You probably think I misremember it from a newsreel—not that we ever made it into the Movietone—but I said it at the time: every one of them gray, and eyes like drain holes that the color washed right down.

It's the children stick in your mind—a wee tiddler with its eyes wide open and its mouth tight shut. I remember one boy landed crooked off the dock and broke his shin, so the bone stub rolled under the skin like a tongue in a cheek. Somebody gave him a mouthful of coat sleeve to keep him quiet.

It was that same trip we were expecting a father and daughter that didn't show up, and we about pushed off without them. We'd heard dogs, and you never knew the meaning of dogs—it could be the patrols, or just somebody's mutt in a furore. One thing I've never understood, you pick a night with no moon and a piece of shore without a light—a disused lighthouse this was, great dark lump in the dark—and you can't see a whit, *can not see*. And then there's a click, like, in the back of your eyes, and you can. Sandiford was pressing off the piling, and the Vicar said, *no, steady on*. Duck was reluctant—you couldn't know when the boy would yell out—and then he felt it too and had them put up the oars. The waves were thick as black custard, and the black shore, and now, click! there's this girl, maybe ten or twelve, gawky little tyke, slogging straight into the water up to her coat hem. Sandiford swung his arm signaling her to go round the dock and fetched her down with her shoes full of water. She's got one hand done up in a fist against her collar bone. I wrapped her up, and she says po-faced, "My father arrives not. I arrive alone." She says, "My fah-zer." I knew better than to ask.

From there across—you understand, nobody said U-boats. Nobody said *mines*. Mostly you didn't keep an eye out, except for Duck and Sandiford whose job it was, because you were superstitious you would call them up. All the same that's what was in everybody's mind. You just hoped the kiddies didn't know the odds. What I remember is, we had a little paraffin stove, and usually when you got out far enough to rope the motors into life, they were all glad to settle down over a cuppa. But this one didn't leave the stern maybe eight hours of rough crossing, looking back where we'd come from in the dark. She held that one hand tight as lockjaw, and I thought she had some money in there, maybe, or a bit of jewelry, something she'd been told to keep from harm. You'd think you wouldn't be curious under the circumstances, but eight hours is a long time to be standing, your mind must be doing something. I remember I tucked the blanket tighter around her and held it there, which she let me, and for most of the way we just stood till it was lightening a little down by the horizon. She dozed, I thought. She sagged against me and bit by bit her hand relaxed over the top of the blanket. There was nothing in it. Not a thing. I cupped it in my own and chafed it back to life a little. And I thought the way we must have looked to God, that greasy little trawler in the black wake, like a clot being washed from a wound.

My folder of drafts of this passage now runs to forty pages, excessive and obsessive perhaps, but it is after all the beginning of the book and must be right. I have noticed over the years that my digging at, fiddling with, scratching away at a scene will often turn up something much more fundamental than a new image or a livelier verb. In this case, I gradually realized that the reason the scene must be in somebody else's voice is that *the heroine does not remember it.* Traumatized by her flight, she cannot recall witnessing her father's death until she is nearly fifty years old. When I realized that, I understood much better what story I was telling and how the plot could be shaped and resolved. I had the delicious chance to let my heroine see the television documentary in the 1980s—in a twenty-year-old rerun—and let that chunk of interview, which contained the reader's first view of her, finally jog her memory.

Writing Exercises

1. Do a word count of one of your stories. Suppose that it has been accepted for publication, but the magazine has one condition: You must cut it by twenty-five percent. Figure out your word-count goal and edit toward it. Be both aggressive and picky. Cut any expendable scenes or paragraphs, but also wring out every extraneous word and phrase. Cut beyond the twenty-five percent if it feels right to do so.

2. For his novel *A Farewell to Arms*, Ernest Hemingway wrote thirty-nine endings before finding the one he decided was best. For one of your stories, write three different endings, each one showing, in some way, how your main character has been changed by the action in the story. Think about what is resolved and what is left unresolved with each ending. Then ask yourself what really needs to happen, emotionally, to your character by the end. In each ending, have the main character's emotional needs truly been addressed, or have you simply tied up some loose ends the reader doesn't care about?

3. Write three new openings to one of your stories. Each one should be at least a few paragraphs long. In each opening, start from a different moment in the story—maybe even at the very end. (Richard Ford's story "Great Falls" opens with these two sentences: "This is not a happy story. I warn you.") What possibilities are created by these new openings?

4. Select one of your stories that is causing you trouble. Print out a hard copy and cut it into scenes, summary, and flashbacks. Number each piece in the order in which it appears. Then lay these pieces out on a table or floor and see what you've got. How many scenes are there? Is every scene necessary? Can some be combined, deleted, or summarized? Are important scenes buried in sections of summary? Are there missing scenes? Is the material from the past in the right places? Try rearranging the sequence of events. Experiment. Move beyond fiddling with sentences to this kind of reenvisioning and rearranging.

5. Choose one of your stories that seems low in tension and try to pump up every conflict you find and add new ones. Don't be afraid to be ridiculous; you can always back off later. Throw more and bigger obstacles in your character's way. Let this revision sit for a day or two; then go back and see how much of what you've added does in fact work.

6. Take one of your stories that isn't quite working yet and explore the main character by writing from that character's point of view. You might have her write out a diary entry, an e-mail, a dream, a letter, or even a short autobiography. Don't worry about whether or not what you write will

actually fit into the story. It might, but it might not. In either case, you'll probably learn something important about your character and her story.

7. Each year in the back of *The Best American Short Stories* and *Pen/O. Henry Prize Stories*, the winning authors write a paragraph or two in which they discuss the genesis of their stories. Take a look at some of these, and then try it yourself. After your story has been workshopped, but before you've started the next draft, write a "contributor's note" similar to those in the back of *Best American* or *O. Henry*. How did the story first occur to you? What intrigued you about it? How did the story evolve? Which of your plans changed, and why? What do you hope that readers will think the story is "about"? Read these contributors' notes aloud in class. Do they help you and your classmates articulate the dramatic and thematic elements you wish to address in the revision process? Does your note illuminate the story, or is it merely an explanation of what should be in the story but hasn't yet made it there?

APPENDIX

WHAT NEXT? PROFESSIONALISM AND LITERARY CITIZENSHIP

What Good Is It?

See if this scene sounds familiar. You're home from school for Thanksgiving or some other holiday. The last bowl game is over, all the dishes have been washed, and you and Aunt Mildred are having a late-night piece of pie at the kitchen table. She's your favorite aunt, the one you can talk to. In the course of the conversation, you tell her you're taking a fiction-writing course or maybe that you've decided to major in Creative Writing. Instinctively but with real concern she asks, "What are you going to do with that?"

What do you say?

You could be defensive, and if you were, you'd hardly be the first. Some people do ask the question thoughtlessly, sarcastically, and dismissively, but not Aunt Mildred. She's taking you seriously and so should you. Why have you decided to major in writing? Why do we need writers? Why do writers do what they do? Why is writing important? What does it mean to want to become a writer, or an author (i.e., someone who is not just writing but has written and published)? And what *are* you going to do with it?

In his famous essay "Of Studies" (1625), Sir Francis Bacon wrote, "Reading maketh a full man; conference a ready man; and writing an exact man." This classic statement of Renaissance humanism may not satisfy Aunt Mildred (let alone your parents who are paying tuition), but it's true and it's a start.

Your relatives aren't the only one's worried about your future. Legislatures and others are asking colleges and universities to move away from the Liberal Arts toward job training and practical, marketable skills. One might argue that this leads to a retreat from the big questions that the Liberal Arts have always asked and a consequent dumbing down of higher education, but on the other hand, we do need to eat. Works of art from Puccini's *La bohème* to Patti Smith's *Just Kids* have advanced a romanticized notion of the artist starving in a garret, but there is nothing romantic about starvation.

Usually those who emphasize practicality and argue that universities should focus on job training also push for a return to "the basics," often forgetting that Creative Writing is the home of two of the three Rs. Reading closely, writing well, and thinking critically *are* practical and important skills, but they aren't always seen that way—even sometimes by those of us who have devoted our lives to them. If you have majored in Creative Writing just so you can wear a beret and pose as an *artiste*, you're going to have a hard time convincing Aunt Mildred.

Some of you may become published authors—some of you may even become famous and fabulously wealthy published authors—while others of you may not publish a word. But whether you become a published author or not, you can still be a writer. You can still be one who writes and writes well. Keeping a journal, writing a family history, or composing your neighborhood association's newsletter—these too are important writing projects. Reality is sly, life takes unexpected turns, and accomplishment comes in many forms. Doctor Benjamin Spock was a famous pediatrician, an Olympic Gold medalist in rowing, and a peace activist who ran for president on the People's Party ticket in 1972. He was also an English major. His book *Baby and Child Care* sold more copies than any book except the Bible during its first fifty years in print. Even if you never publish a novel, a story, an essay, or a poem, being an English major and learning to write well can help you be successful in life, whatever you do.

Being an Accounting or Computer Science major is not the only road to success. Creative Writing majors can make a living too. They become actors, screenwriters, magazine editors, teachers, arts administrators, lawyers, and even pediatricians. But in the end, Aunt Mildred's question still holds: What are you going to do with it?

Getting Serious and Submitting Your Work to Magazines

The first thing you need to do with your Creative Writing major is to take it seriously. This means many things: turning in drafts on time for workshop, responding generously and specifically to the drafts of others, reading widely and closely the work of published writers, and working hard at your own writing.

One path you might consider is going on to graduate school to earn a Master of Fine Arts or even a PhD in Creative Writing. It's not the only way to begin a writing career, but it has become an increasingly common route in recent years. Graduate school provides you with a community of writers, time to write, deadlines for getting that writing done, and often the opportunity to teach writing and work on the staff of a national literary magazine. Getting into a graduate program in Creative Writing, however, requires preparation. For a start, you can put together a portfolio of your work, submit your work for publication, and research what program might be best for you.

Your portfolio is an accessible, neatly organized collection of everything that you currently consider done. In order to assemble a portfolio, you need to be organized and keep good files. In our electronic age, this means backing up your files on an external drive or the Cloud, but it also means keeping hard copies of at least some revisions. There are many reasons to keep copies of your work and to organize them carefully. You don't want to lose any of your work and the time you've invested in it. But you also want to keep early drafts because, as you continue to write and become more prolific, you'll have multiple projects going on at once, some of which will need to sit for a while—certainly weeks or months, but perhaps even years. Well-organized files make it possible for you to find an early draft when you're ready to take another look at it or when a mentor needs to see that story you wrote in her class in order to write you a good, specific letter of recommendation. Your portfolio will need updating often, or at least when you apply for an internship, a job, or graduate school.

If you haven't already, soon you may want to submit work for publication. At first, you'll likely submit to the publications at your own school. Some professors may ask their writing workshops to work in small groups or together as a class to develop a magazine featuring work the class produced that semester. That is a good exercise, as it gives you a feel for how the selection process works. You might also want to work on your school's literary magazine, where you can get a feel for how hard it is to read through the slush pile (i.e., all the material that comes in unsolicited), find out what a story must do in the first few pages to catch an editor's attention, and see how hard it is for an editorial board to make its final decisions.

Whether you work on your school's literary magazine or not, that magazine may still be the first place you submit your work. Then, you may want to look for other venues. Most fiction writers, even if they feel they have the ambition and wherewithal to begin working on a novel, begin their publishing careers by publishing short stories in literary quarterlies and other "little magazines." If you don't feel your stories are quite ready to send out, you might go ahead and submit some other work that you're not as heavily invested in, such as book reviews or interviews with authors, both of which are easier to place and can help you break into the ranks of the published and build your résumé.

There are several ways to go about deciding which magazines you want to submit to first. Classmates and teachers who are already submitting work and publishing may be willing to help, but there are other resources you can consult on your own. *Writer's Market* is an annual index of magazines (as well as agents and book publishers) edited by Robert Bowker and published by Writer's Digest Books. It includes short descriptions of magazines—their circulations, submissions guidelines, writers they've published, the URL to their website, a paragraph about the kind of work they publish, and whether or not they accept multiple submissions (i.e., whether they allow you to submit to other magazines at the same time you're submitting a story to them). The

Writer's Market listings are also available in digital form at www.writersmarket. com. Other sources that can help introduce you to the world of little magazines include *Poets & Writers*, *The Writer's Chronicle*, and *Writers Digest*. These magazines also offer listings and articles about grants, contests, retreats, and conferences. Another excellent online listing of little magazines is NewPages. com. Before you send out your work, make sure you read several issues of the magazine to which you plan to submit to make sure that it publishes the kind of story you write.

A weeklong writing conference (such as the Iowa Summer Writing Festival) or a stay at a writers' retreat (such as Yaddo in Saratoga Springs, New York) can be an excellent way to jumpstart your writing and meet other writers.

Each year two important anthologies of the previous year's best short stories appear. Anchor Books (a Random House imprint) publishes the *PEN/O. Henry Prize Stories*, which has been edited since 2003 by Laura Furman; Mariner Books (a division of Houghton Mifflin Harcourt) publishes *The Best American Short Stories*, of which Heidi Pitlor is series editor. Not only will these two anthologies introduce you to some of today's best writers, but they also tell you where the winning and short-listed stories were published and give you contact information for those magazines.

Many magazines now have their own online systems for submitting work. You'll need to check each magazine's submissions guidelines, usually available at their website. Many magazines, however, still want to receive work through the mail. The websites and publications mentioned above offer advice on how to write a one-page cover letter to accompany your submission. This letter is short, but you should take your time with it and make sure it is clear and says only what it needs to say. Include your credentials in a sentence or two, and provide the title of the story you're submitting. Make sure you address a specific editor by name—probably the fiction editor, but perhaps the editor in chief or the managing editor, depending on what the submissions guidelines specify.

Not All Rejection Is the Same—Some of It Isn't Even Rejection

A word about rejection: You will get rejected. I repeat: You will get rejected. In fact, you'll be rejected time and time again. Many people write, editors have particular tastes, and magazine space is limited, all of which means you shouldn't take rejection personally though it's almost impossible not to. Cheryl Strayed, whose memoir *Wild: From Lost to Found on the Pacific Crest Trail* spent months and months on the *New York Times* best seller list, offers this advice:

> "Going through a drawer I found the submissions/applications log I've kept off and on over the years. Just in case you think it's all been roses I'd like to report that Yaddo rejected me (as recently as 2011). McDowell rejected me. Hedgebrook rejected me twice. *The Georgia Review* rejected me and

Ploughshares rejected me and *Tin House* rejected me, as did about twenty other journals and magazines. Both *The Sun* and *The Missouri Review* rejected me before I appeared in their pages. Literary Arts declined to give me a fellowship three times before I won one. I've applied for an NEA [National Endowment of the Arts] five times and it's always been a no. *Harper's* magazine never even bothered to reply. I say it all the time but I'll say it again: keep on writing. Never give up. Rejection is part of a writer's life. Then, now, always."

As Strayed's mention of her submissions log suggests, it's important to keep a good record of where you send your work. You need to do this, because if you sent a piece out to more than one place and it is accepted, you will want to notify *immediately* those you haven't heard from yet. Another reason a submissions log is important is that, to paraphrase George Orwell in *Animal Farm*, not all rejections are equal, and you should keep track of what kind of rejection you received. A form letter, an unsigned rejection slip, or an e-mail from "The Editors" is one thing, and while it certainly isn't encouraging it probably doesn't say, "NEVER try us again." A signed note, even if it is just written in the margin of a form letter and especially if it is legible, is a good sign; if you have another story ready, send it to them right away. A full letter or e-mail from an editor that addresses the perceived strengths and weaknesses of the story, that indicates the decision to reject was a difficult one, or that specifically asks you to try the magazine again, should be read as encouragement. And if an editor suggests some revisions and says she'd be willing to take a second look at the story if you are amenable to the suggestions, you probably want to dance around the house and then begin revising the story.

Graduate Programs in Creative Writing

In 1922, Carl Seashore, dean of the Graduate College at the University of Iowa, announced that Iowa would accept creative work as the thesis for advanced degrees. This was a new model for graduate work in the United States. Fourteen years later, in 1936, Iowa went further and established the first creative writing degree program in the country. For the next few decades, the Iowa Writers Workshop held a near monopoly among graduate creative writing programs. For twenty-four of those years, the noted poet, novelist, translator, and critic Paul Engle directed the Workshop. While Iowa remains one of the best such programs—its graduates have won a total of seventeen Pulitzer Prizes—there are now many other fine programs.

In 1967, fifteen writers representing thirteen writing programs founded the Associated Writing Programs, or AWP (later to be called the Association of Writers & Writing Programs). The organization now provides support and resources to approximately 50,000 individual writers, 500 college or university writing programs, and 150 writers' conferences and centers. The first

AWP annual conference in 1972, held in Washington, D.C., at the Library of Congress, consisted of just six events featuring sixteen presenters. Now, over 10,000 people attend the annual AWP Conference & Bookfair, which features nearly a thousand presenters at 550 panel discussions, readings, and lectures. Six hundred bookfair exhibitors sponsor book signings, receptions, and other events.

Many graduate students attend the conference, but you don't have to attend to make use of many of the services of AWP. You may want to subscribe, for instance, to the aforementioned *Writer's Chronicle*, which goes out six times a year to 40,000 readers and contains interviews and articles about writers, writing, and the writing life as well as postings about conferences, workshops, retreats, and contests. If you are thinking about applying to a graduate program in creative writing, the AWP website is a good place to start. The website offers advice on selecting a program and a listing where you can search hundreds of programs by location, genre, and type of degree programs offered. Graduate programs can lead to a Masters (MA), Master of Fine Arts (MFA), or doctorate (PhD), though the MFA is the most popular. Some programs are studio programs, which means that they emphasize writing courses; others may require research or theory courses as well. The number of course hours required also varies. Some MFA programs specify two years in residence, others three. In recent years, many good low-residency programs have also appeared, in which students are required to be on campus only a few weeks each year and most discussion of manuscripts takes place online. This flexibility makes them a good fit for students with families or a full-time job. Like residential programs, most low-residency programs expect a student to complete a book-length thesis as a degree requirement. The AWP site also provides information about each program's size, faculty, financial aid packages, teaching opportunities, literary magazine, and reading series. *Poets & Writers* offers a similar listing—the MFA Programs Database.

Current and prospective graduate students in creative writing have also established several blogs and listservs where they share tips, set up online writing groups, and discuss their experiences in different writing programs. Among these are the Creative Writing MFA Blog, the Creative Writing PhD Blog, the MFA Chronicles, and a group for students and applicants on Facebook called the MFA Draft Group. *Writers Digest* sponsors the MFA Confidential Blog. *Poets & Writers* publishes a controversial but influential ranking of graduate programs each year. Individual authors have also taken it upon themselves to publish information about graduate programs and how to pick one. The best book on the subject is Tom Kealey's *Creative Writing MFA Handbook: A Guide for Prospective Graduate Students* (Bloomsbury, 2008). Writer and blogger Erika Dreifus maintains a useful website at www.erikadreifus.com.

If you do decide to apply to a graduate program, you'll need to take the Graduate Record Exam, pay application fees, and fill out online forms, but two other tasks stand out. You must submit a writing sample and request some letters of recommendation. Deadlines vary, but most applications are due in

December or January, and you'll want to start on these two key tasks well in advance of your due dates.

Your writing sample is far and away the most important part of your application. Spend time on it, revise it, show it to others, revise it, read it aloud, and revise it again. Like magazine editors, the members of admissions committees have to read a lot of manuscripts in a short time, so you'll want yours to grip them from page one and never let go. And it goes without saying that the writing must be free of errors—grammatical, mechanical, or spelling. Different programs require writing samples of different lengths, but twenty to thirty pages, double-spaced (or somewhere between 5,000 and 8,000 words), is most common. Again, you'll need to check the specific requirements of the programs to which you are applying, but your sample can probably consist of one to three short stories or an excerpt (probably the opening) of a novel.

Your letters of recommendation are the second most important part of your application. Many people feel they need to ask for a letter from that famous writer they met once at a conference, reception, or book signing, but you are much better off asking people who know you and your work well. Ask your teachers, but ask them well in advance of the application deadline—early in the fall is best. Most teachers receive a lot of requests for letters, but if you did well in their course and especially if you took more than one course with them, they'll probably be happy to write a supportive letter. Because they have a lot of letters to write, they probably will ask you for some basic information. So be ready to give it to them as soon as they have agreed. This information will likely include a list of the programs to which you are applying and their application deadlines, whether those programs use an online submission service or expect a hard copy of the letter in a sealed envelope, what courses you took with that professor and when you took them, and a reminder about what you wrote in that class. They may even want to see a copy of that work or of your writing sample. If your résumé includes information that may be especially relevant (i.e., publications, fellowships, internships, work on student publications, volunteering at your school's reading-writing center, etc.), send a copy of that as well. All this information helps the teacher write a strong, specific letter that will help your application stand out.

Writing in the Cold

Again, graduate school is not the only way to begin a writing career, and even if you choose to pursue a graduate degree, you may not want to do it right away. There is much to be said for taking some time off from school in order to travel, teach English as a second language in China, earn some money to pay down your student loans, or otherwise experience life outside the academy. Any of these experiences can bring rich, new material to your writing, but if you are a writer, you will need to keep writing. Once you are out in the working world, you will need to provide yourself with your own deadlines and discipline, establish your own daily writing schedule, and find your own support community. In the working world, being a writer is no longer a matter of signing up for a creative writing class or declaring your major. In all likelihood, no one will ask you to write, though Aunt Mildred will continue to ask why you are doing this at all, and you will need to keep providing her and yourself with answers.

In 1985, the writer and editor Ted Solotaroff published a now-legendary essay titled "Writing in the Cold: The First Ten Years," which later appeared in his collection A Few Good Voices in My Head: Occasional Pieces on Writing, Editing, and Reading My Contemporaries (Harper & Row, 1987). Solotaroff's essay was uncompromising but borne of much experience. Of writing success (by which he meant not so much big money and prestigious awards as having produced good and important work), he wrote,

> It doesn't appear to be a matter of the talent itself—some of the most natural writers, the ones who seemed to shake their prose or poetry out of their sleeves, are among the disappeared. As far as I can tell, the decisive factor is durability. For the gifted writer, durability seems to be directly connected to how one deals with uncertainty, rejection, and disappointment, from within as well as from without, and how effectively one incorporates them into the creative process itself, particularly in the prolonged first stages of a career.

What does it mean to incorporate uncertainty, rejection, and disappointment into one's creative process? Well, according to Solotaroff, it means writing anyway, writing no matter what, letting rejection spur you on, and learning from everything, even the stuff that gets you down. Here are the last lines of Solotaroff's essay:

> Writing itself, if not misunderstood and abused, becomes a way of empowering the writing self. It converts anger and disappointment into deliberate and durable aggression, the writer's main source of energy. It converts sorrow and self-pity into empathy, the writer's main means of relating to otherness. Similarly, his wounded innocence turns into irony, his silliness into wit, his guilt into judgment, his oddness into originality, his perverseness into his stinger.

The emphasis on aggression, as well as the choice of pronouns, may show the passage as distinctly male, but the larger point, I think, is that writing out in the cold requires strength and resolve, wherever you find it.

Literary Community and Literary Citizenship

It also requires community. Don't try to go it alone. You can start now by finding, building, and maintaining a writing community of your own. Who was that person who offered the fullest and most insightful critiques in workshop last semester? Why not ask her if she wants to have coffee and exchange manuscripts? Which of your friends might want to go to that poetry reading next week? How can you play a leadership role on your school literary magazine? Is there a local small press or little magazine that offers internships or needs volunteers?

Other writers and readers need your help and you need theirs. See if you can organize a writing group that gets together once a month. There are lots of ways to organize such a group. Three, four, or five people can be enough; ten might be too many. Meet at a local bar, bookstore, or coffee shop, or rotate among the members' houses and apartments. Potluck, desserts, or a glass of wine can help foster conviviality. Exchange manuscripts by e-mail in advance so that you have at least two or three pieces to talk about at each meeting. The monthly deadlines help you get things done. You can also help each other polish up query letters, grant or book proposals, even blog posts. Not everyone in the group has to be a writer. It's fine to work a reader or would-be editor into the mix. Their comments will be helpful, and their very presence helps maintain the critical mass. Nor does everyone need to be working in the same genre. Poets have helpful things to say about the work of fiction writers, and vice versa.

With your writing group as a start, you can begin to think about writing and community in larger ways as well. Maybe your group can attend a reading together or even organize one of your own. Are there journals you can subscribe to individually or as a group, or books you can buy at your local bookstore and then share with each other, thereby giving yourselves stories, poems, essays, reviews, and novels to talk about? Circulating publications in that way is a win-win situation for everyone, including the independent bookstores and literary journals. Maybe one of the members of your group has a writing project in mind that requires funding, wants to launch a magazine, or plans to stage a benefit reading. The rest of you can pitch in and help by taking tickets, donating refreshments, cleaning up after, or publicizing the Kickstarter or Indiegogo campaign. The work of your group needn't be all civic good and sacrifice. If someone in your group places a story in a magazine or, better yet, lands a book deal, celebrate. Have a party.

Building Literary Community in the Digital Age

These days, people build communities online, and so can you. At first you might just start reading, bookmarking, and submitting comments to book blogs and online magazines, or looking for Facebook groups that seem to contain interesting discussions. But after a bit, if you have an idea for a new approach, you might want to start your own blog. Plan ahead, have some posts already written, and make a schedule of posts to follow those. Maybe your blog will include celebrations of your favorite authors, or reviews of recent novels, or advice on how to land a magazine internship, or discussions of issues writers face, or interviews with writers or ... it's up to you. It should be something that interests you enough that you'll to be able to sustain it over time. Coming up with an idea for a blog is the first step, but then you need to learn how to pick a blog platform, write short and quick, embed video, use hyperlinks, and develop an eye for design. You can do it. Most universities offer courses on writing in the digital age and some offer majors in the field. The writer and teacher Cathy Day maintains a helpful blog—which she calls Literary Citizenship—that explores these issues.

Literary citizenship, building a career, becoming a writer, or whatever you want to call it—this is the life you've decided to pursue. Aunt Mildred expects nothing less of you.

Credits

Edith Pearlman. "Self-Reliance" from *Binocular Vision: New and Selected Stories* by Edith Pearlman, Introduction by Ann Patchett. Copyright © 2011 by Edith Pearlman. Reprinted by permission of Lookout Books. All rights reserved.

Yehuda Amichai. From "We Did It" from *Songs of Jerusalem and Myself* by Yehuda Amichai and translated by Harold Schimmel. Copyright © 1973 by Yehuda Amichai, English Translation copyright © 1973 by Harold Schimmel. Reprinted by permission of HarperCollins Publishers and Deborah Harris Agency.

Stacey Richter. "Goal 666" from *My Date with Satan* by Stacey Richter. Copyright © 1999. Reprinted by permission of Scribner Book Company.

Stuart Dybek. "We Didn't" from *I Sailed with Magellan* by Stuart Dybek. Copyright © 2003 by Stuart Dybek. Reprinted by permission of Farrar, Straus and Giroux, LLC and International Creative Management.

ZZ Packer. "Every Tongue Shall Confess" from *Drinking Coffee Elsewhere* by ZZ Packer. First published in Great Britain by Canongate Books Ltd, 14 High Street, Edinburgh, EH1 1TE. Copyright © 2003 by ZZ Packer. Used by permission of Riverhead Books, an imprint of Penguin Group (USA) Inc. and Canongate Books, Ltd.

Junot Diaz. "Fiesta 1980" from *Drown* by Junot Diaz. Copyright © 1996 by Junot Diaz. Used by permission of Penguin Group (USA) and Faber and Faber (UK) Inc.

Denis Johnson. "Emergency" from *Jesus' Son* by Denis Johnson. Copyright © 1992 by Denis Johnson. Reprinted by permission of Farrar, Straus and Giroux, LLC and Robert Cornfield Literary Agency. All rights reserved.

Richard Bausch. "Tandolfo the Great" from *The Stories of Richard Bausch* by Richard Bausch. Copyright © 1992 by Richard Bausch. Reprinted by permission of HarperCollins Publishers.

Tobias Wolff. "Bullet in the Brain" from *The Night in Question* by Tobias Wolff. Copyright © 1996 by Tobias Wolff. Reprinted by permission of Alfred A. Knopf, a division of Random House, Inc. and International Creative Management, Inc.

Joyce Carol Oates. From "Where Are You Going, Where Have You Been?: Smooth Talk: Short Story Into Film" from *(Woman*

Writer: Occasions and Opportunities by Joyce Carol Oates. Copyright © 1988 by *The Ontario Review*. Used by permission of Dutton, a division of Penguin Group (USA) Inc. and John Hawkins Associates, Inc.

Sandra Cisneros. "Eleven" From *Woman Hollering Creek* by Sandra Cisneros. Copyright © 1991 by Sandra Cisneros. Published by Vintage Books, a division of Random House, Inc., and originally in hardcover by Random House Inc. By permission of Susan Bergholz Literary Services, New York, NY and Lamy, NM. and Bloomsbury Plc. All rights reserved.

Karen Russell. "St. Lucy's Home for Girls Raised by Wolves" from *St. Lucy's Home for Girls Raised by Wolves* by Karen Russell. Copyright © 2006 by Karen Russell. Reprinted by permission of Alfred A. Knopf, a division of Random House, Inc. All rights reserved.

Alice Walker. "The Flowers" from *In Love & Trouble: Stories of Black Women*, copyright © 1973 by Alice Walker, reprinted by permission of Houghton Mifflin Harcourt Publishing Company and Joy Harris Literary Agency, Inc. All rights reserved.

Eudora Welty. "A Visit of Charity" from *A Curtain of Green and Other Stories* by Eudora Welty. Copyright © 1941 and renewed 1969 and 1983 by Eudora Welty. Reprinted by permission of Houghton Mifflin Harcourt Publishing Company and Russel & Volkening as agents for the author.

Lorrie Moore. "You're Ugly, Too" from *Like Life: Stories* by Lorrie Moore. Copyright © 1988, 1989, 1990 by Lorrie Moore. Reprinted by permission.

Sherman Alexie. "The Fun House" from *The Lone Ranger and Tonto Fistfight in Heaven* by Sherman Alexi. Copyright © 1993 by Sherman Alexie. Used by permission of Grove/Atlantic, Inc.

Hannah Bottomy. "Crosscurrents" from *Flash Fiction Forward: 80 Very Short Stories* edited by James Thomas and Robert Shapard. Published 2006 by W. W. Norton & Company. Reprinted by permission of the author.

Geoffrey Forsyth. "Mud" from *In the Land of the Free*. Brookline: Rose Metal Press. Copyright © 2008. pgs 28–33. Used by permission of Rose Metal Press.

Flannery O'Connor. "Everything That Rises Must Converge" from *The Complete Stories* by

Flannery O'Connor. Copyright © 1971 by the Estate of Mary Flannery O'Connor. Reprinted by permission of Farrar, Straus and Giroux, LLC.

Flannery O'Connor. Copyright © 1956, 1957, 1958, 1960, 1961 and 1962 by Flannery O'Connor. Copyright renewed 1993 by Regina Cline O'Connor. Reprinted by permission of Mary Flannery O'Connor Charitable Trust via Harold Matson Company, Inc.

Joy Williams. "Escapes" from *Escapes: Stories* by Joy Williams. Copyright © 1990 by Joy Williams. Used by permission of The Atlantic Monthly Press.

Robin Hemley. "Reply All" from *Sudden Fiction* by Robin Hemley. Copyright © 2007 by Robin Hemley. Reprinted by permission of International Creative Management, Inc.

George Saunders. "Victory Lap" from *The Tenth of December* by George Saunders. Copyright © 2013 by George Saunders. Reprinted by permission of Random House, Inc.

Pia Z. Erhardt. "Following the Notes" by Pia Z. Erhardt. Reprinted by permission of the author.

Rosellen Brown. "Before and After" by Rosellen Brown from *So, Is It Done?* Copyright © 1992 by Rosellen Brown. Used by permission of the author. Copyright Elephant Rock Production.

John L'Heureux. Quote by John L'Heureux. Reproduced by the permission of the author.

Octavia E. Butler. Quote by Octavia E. Butler. Copyright © Octavia E. Butler. Used by permission of the author.

Joan Wickersham. From "Commuter Marriage" by Joan Wickersham.*The Hudson Review*, Vol. 42, No. 1 (Spring, 1989), pp. 77–91.

Ernest Hemingway. From "Hills Like White Elephants" reprinted with the permission of Scribner, a Division of Simon & Schuster, Inc., from *The Short Stories of Ernest Hemingway* by Ernest Hemingway. Copyright © 1927 by Charles Scribner's Sons. Copyright renewed © 1955 by Ernest Hemingway. All rights reserved.

Masuji Ibuse. From "Tajinko Village" from *Lieutenant Lookeast and Other Stories* by Masuji Ibuse. Published by Kodansha International, 1971. Used by permission.

Zora Neale Hurston. From "The Gilded Six-Bit" by Zora Neale Hurston.

Eudora Welty. *The Collected Stories of Eudora Welty*, Harcourt, Brace and Company, 1982.

Robert Olen Butler. *From Where You Dream*. New York: Grove Press, 2005. Used by permission of the author.

Hemingway, Ernest. From "Hills Like White Elephants" reprinted with the permission of Scribner, a Division of Simon & Schuster, Inc., from *The Short Stories of Ernest Hemingway* by Ernest Hemingway. Copyright © 1927 by Charles Scribner's Sons. Copyright renewed © 1955 by Ernest Hemingway. All rights reserved.

Amy Bloom. From "Silver Water" in *Come to Me* by Amy Bloom. Copyright © 1993 by Amy Bloom. Reprinted by permission of HarperCollins Publishers and Macmillan Publishers Ltd.

California Cooper. From *Homemade Love* © 1986 by California Cooper. Reprinted by permission of St. Martin's Press. All rights reserved.

John Edgar Wideman. "The Tamborine Lady" in *Fever: Twelve Stories* by John Edgar Wideman. Copyright © 1989 by John Edgar Wideman. Reprinted by permission of Henry Holt and Company.

Margaret Atwood. "Simmering" from *Good Bones and Simple Murders* by Margaret Atwood, copyright © 1983, 1992, 1994, by O.W. Toad Ltd. A Nan A. Talese Book. Used by permission of Doubleday, a division of Random House, Inc.

Alice Walker. "Roselilly" from *In Love & Trouble: Stories of Black Women* by Alice Walker. Copyright © 1973 by Alice Walker. Reprinted by permission of Houghton Mifflin Harcourt Publishing Company and Joy Harris Literary Agency, Inc. All Rights reserved.

Robert Garner McBrearty. From *Let the Birds Drink in Peace* by Robert Garner McBrearty, copyright © 2011 by Robert Garner McBrearty. Used by permission of Conundrum Press, a division of Samizdat Publishing Group, LLC (http://conundrum-press.com).

Alice Munro. From Introduction in *Selected Stories* by Alice Munro. Copyright © 1996, 1997 by Alice Munro. Used by permission of Vintage Books, a division of Random House, Inc.

John L'Heureux. Quote by John L'Heureux. Reproduced by permission of the author.

Elizabeth Tallent. "No One's A Mystery" from *Time with Children* by Elizabeth Tallent. Copyright © 1986, 1987 by Elizabeth Tallent. Reprinted by permission of Alfred A. Knopf Inc., 1987, a division of Random House, Inc.

Index